Contested Architectural Pasts and Futures of a Regional City, Geelong, Australia

Contested Architectural Pasts and Futures of a Regional City, Geelong, Australia

Edited by

Mirjana Lozanovska and Ursula de Jong

Cambridge
Scholars
Publishing

Contested Architectural Pasts and Futures of a Regional City, Geelong, Australia

Edited by Mirjana Lozanovska and Ursula de Jong

This book first published 2024

Cambridge Scholars Publishing

Lady Stephenson Library, Newcastle upon Tyne, NE6 2PA, UK

British Library Cataloguing in Publication Data
A catalogue record for this book is available from the British Library

ISBN (10): 1-0364-0617-2
ISBN (13): 978-1-0364-0617-2

TABLE OF CONTENTS

Part 3
Propositional Geelong

List of Figures

ACKNOWLEDGEMENTS

We are grateful to Wadawurrung Elder Deanne Gilson for her evocative words and imaginative artwork. The voice and words are the first story of a deep past revealed in the present. Gilson's artwork, *Karringalabil Bundjil Murrup, Manna Gum Tree (The Creation Tree of Knowledge)*, 2020, inspires a connectiveness to Country and to the place of Djilang, envisioning new iterations of enduring significant knowledges.

We respectfully acknowledge the Traditional Owners and Custodians of the lands across Australia discussed in this book and pay our respects to their Elders, past and present. They include the Wadawurrung of the Kulin nation. We extend this to others noted in the chapters of this book, as well as First Nations peoples in other parts of the world. In our chapters, we have followed the recommendations of the Australian Institute of Aboriginal and Torres Strait Islander Studies ethical publishing guidelines; we use the terms "Aboriginal", "Torres Strait Islander" and names of individual groups, such as Wadawurrung, to describe Traditional Owner/custodian groups or individuals when an identity is known, and "Aboriginal and Torres Strait Islander peoples" when it is not. However, we remain mindful of the recent changes to these descriptors both in academia and in politics. Concurrent practices of identification include – First Nations' peoples, First Peoples and Indigenous Australians. We have striven to be consistent across all the chapters, as well as allowing for the use of appropriate identification in those chapters where collaboration directly with the Wadawurrung has occurred.

We are grateful for the financial support from the School of Architecture and Built Environment, Deakin University, Geelong. The idea for this book evolved from the VacantGeelong project, with Mirjana Lozanovska leading a team of academics in Arts and Architecture at Deakin University, to collaboratively examine industrial architecture at a pivotal point in the history of deindustrialisation. Artists, professionals and the immigrant communities of past workers contributed to this research and practice agenda. Funded by Creative Victoria and the City of Greater Geelong, VacantGeelong delivered a series of works in 2017 – site-activation at the Open Studio, the exhibition Iconic Industry (with the National Wool Museum), a film, *Industry Tracks*, and the catalogue, Lozanovska et al., *Iconic Industry: Exploring the Industrial Built Fabric of Geelong*. These works generated what is called in Australia, non-traditional research – research that is not easily measurable by metrics or academic papers, but rather promotes artistic practice, and with partners, engages the community.

From this basis Mirjana Lozanovska conceptualised and proposed a book on Geelong as an exemplary study of regional cities undergoing significant transformation(s). With appreciation for the research undertaken by colleagues, the book's broad, sometimes contradictory approach, now presents as a compelling set of chapters. Over the three years since 2021, Mirjana has worked closely with Ursula de Jong towards the development of a book for publication – it has been a wonderful collaboration as colleagues, friends and editors.

We offer our deep and sincere gratitude to Chayakan Siamphukdee whose research assistance and scholarship provided a strong knowledge on other cities as second cities, and the process of deindustrialisation. We thank him for his readiness to assist in many and varied tasks – digital and organisational – to bring this book to realisation. Chay's drawings are simply beautiful.

We thank all the authors for their commitment to testing their scholarship and developing stronger arguments in the process of researching and writing their chapters. We also thank authors who accepted invitations at a late stage to fill gaps, on landscape (Josh Zeunert) and on architectural practice (Joel McGuinness); we thank readers of chapters, Louise Johnson and Steven Cooke. We thank Geelong Gallery and Deakin Gallery for expediting the reproduction of works in their collections. Our sincere gratefulness to Andrew Strachan and the administration staff at Deakin for their willingness to assist, and often save the day. We cannot overstate our appreciation for the comprehensive, timely and attentive work of our copy editor Alison Munnery – we are indebted to her expertise and preparedness to do extensive work to form all the content into a coherent manuscript package.

Mirjana Lozanovska and Ursula de Jong,
Editors

Welcome to Country

Deanne Gilson

Kimbarne – welcome in Wadawurrung language

My name is Dr Deanne Gilson, I am a proud Wadawurrung woman, mother, sister, Aunty, cultural educator and award winning multidisciplinary visual artist and Blak designer.

As this book is situated on my ancestral Country, Wadawurrung Dja, I would like to pay my respects to my ancestors, old people and family past and present. We practice Bunjil's lore, that states we must care for Country, each other and our children.

I acknowledge the strength and resilience of all Traditional Custodians including Aboriginal and Torres Strait Islander Peoples of this land. I pay my respects to all Elders, past and present, along with their families and acknowledge our continued relationship to the Land, Sky Country, Waterways, Under Country and Mountains in which we live and grow.

The notion of *terra nullius* assumed that this land was not occupied before settlement, discounting the 65,000 years of First Peoples' knowledge and caring for this land.

By contributing my Creation Story, I am overriding *terra nullius* to show we were here first and how art can draw upon traditional practices of Wadawurrung women, oral story-telling, history, culture and identity, placing our knowledge back to pre-settlement.

I acknowledge that Sovereignty has never been ceded and this is and always will be Aboriginal land.

With respect to the editors of this book, Mirjana Lozanovska and Ursula de Jong, for allowing me to include our story first.

Kolingwada-ngal – let's all walk together in friendship, love and peace.

Nyatne, gobata, thank you and goodbye.

Aunty Deanne Gilson, Wadawurrung Elder

WADAWARRUNG CREATION STORY

DEANNE GILSON

Deanne Gilson, *Karringalabil Bundjil Murrup, Manna Gum Tree (The Creation Tree of Knowledge)* 2020, ochre, acrylic on linen, Purchase 2021, Deakin University Art Collection, image © and courtesy of the artist.

At the beginning of time on Wadawurrung Country, the people of the Kulin nation were created by a powerful being called Karringalabil. Karringalabil was once a man who had magical powers. He called upon all the spirits residing in the great manna gum tree to assist in the creation of all things. He turned the spirits into all the birds we see today. Waa the crow was his first helper, breathing life into the people in which Karringalabil formed from bark of the manna gum and clay from the river. Karringalabil created Parrwang the magpie, who lifted the sky from darkness to light, giving us the first sunrise. Once the sun came up, he could see his creation of the endless mountains, waterways, plants, birds, animals and people. He created a lore to always protect Country and its people.

After which he turned himself into a wedge-tailed eagle we call Bunjil and flew high up into the night sky with his two wives Kunuwarra the black swan sisters. Once in the sky, Bunjil then turned himself and his wives into the brightest stars in the night sky. He is said to watch over us all today as an eagle in the day and a star in the night.

PART 1

CONTEXTS:
MULTIPLE OTHERS WHO BUILT GEELONG

CHAPTER 1

CONSERVATION AND TRANSFORMATION:
CONTESTED PASTS AND RADICAL FUTURES OF GEELONG

MIRJANA LOZANOVSKA AND URSULA DE JONG

Transition of a regional town

Geelong is a regional city in Victoria, Australia, and is the second largest city after the state's capital city, Melbourne (see Figure 1.1). It is a city currently metamorphosing. Seismic economic, cultural and social shifts due to deindustrialisation have generated the emergence of a new service economy. Present debates around Geelong's identity are building a critical mass towards a very different future to its dominant industrial past. Current urban strategies seek to reimagine the city's future by transforming its architectural and urban character. These changes are not only the result of the city's recently designated status as UNESCO City of Design. Daryl Le Grew [then Dean of Design and Technology] spearheaded Deakin University's establishment on Geelong's waterfront, in the Dalgety Woolstores in 1996 with a vision for a university town.[1] Since 1998, the redevelopment of Geelong's waterfront by highly awarded landscape architects, Taylor Cullity Lethlean, has invited new recreational and cultural uses, and their distinctive landscape has created a new urban image.[2] Adjacent to the waterfront, the Transport Accident Commission (TAC) headquarters was established in the central business district (CBD) in 2009, relocating from Melbourne. In the nearby "cultural precinct", Ashton Raggatt McDougall's (ARM) Geelong Library and Heritage Centre, completed in 2015, and their Geelong Arts Centre, opened in 2023, present bold theatrical architectural statements. However, recent high-rise apartment buildings standing substantially above the existing urban fabric at the edges of the CBD (since 2019) herald a more controversial approach. Observing how new architecture and urbanism are shaping the physical and spatial order of a future-focused Geelong, this book positions architecture as central to the transformation of regional cities. Illustrating the impact beyond major capital cities, the in-depth study of the regional city of Geelong provides theoretical frameworks and detail to inform debates in the often too rapid transformation of cities pre-empted by deindustrialisation.

Intersected by colonising histories, migrant labour histories and current initiatives to embark on decolonising urbanisms, as well as new design and cultural economies, the spatial focus, multi-disciplinary thinking and collaboration embedded in these chapters expands into interdisciplinary fields, informing heritage, urban renewal, historiography, community engagement and place-making more generally.

Both the pasts and the futures of Geelong are contested territories. Rather than considering the past as a stable foundation from which to develop future visions or narratives, the voices of those who have been dispossessed, exploited, overlooked and forgotten must rupture the evolutionary processes of strategic development. First Nations people speak. Their collective memories and individual agency intervene in the perpetuation of neo-colonial narratives of history. It is important to note at the outset that these are not alternative or plural perspectives but rather direct and opposing, differential realities. Under British colonising strategies, the Wadawurrung, the Traditional Owners of the area now occupied by the city of Geelong, like other Aboriginal and Torres Strait Islander peoples in Victoria and Australia, suffered unfathomable loss. Indigenous spiritual, cultural and ecological approaches to land management were brutally replaced by colonial settler strategies of ownership and land claims, supported by colonial industriousness. British colonial settler industries implemented extractive and exploitative methods that in a short time razed and scarred the land, decimated the flora and fauna, and destroyed the livelihoods of Aboriginal and Torres Strait Islander peoples. Civilisations clashed and by the 1860s Wadawurrung populations around Djilang had plummeted (see Figure 1.3).

Heritage plays a major role in defining which narratives of the past inform the new image of a city, accentuated by the current forces of change – cultural and heritage tourism, narrower nationalising histories, expanded deindustrialisation in developing economies, and accelerated urbanisation affecting the finer grain of the built fabric. Yet this becomes limited when, as Stefan Berger argues, heritage aligns its focus with the cleaning up momentum of 'dirty industrial sites' and an agenda aligned with gentrification.[3] Cultural theorist Stuart Hall states that 'in a culture, meaning often depends on larger units of analysis – narratives, statements, groups of images, whole discourses which

---

[1] Daryl Le Grew, Professor of Architecture and Dean, Faculty of Design and Technology at Deakin University, proposed a Deakin Geelong CBD campus, alongside the Deakin Waurn Ponds campus that was established in 1974. The adaptive reuse of the waterfront, designed by McGlashan Everist architects was awarded an AIA architecture award for heritage and conservation (see Chapter 9).

[2] In the years following, Taylor Cullity Lethlean (TCL) gained numerous national awards for their distinctive designs. https://tcl.net.au/projects/geelong-waterfront, accessed January 2024.

[3] Stefan Berger (ed), *Constructing Industrial Pasts: Heritage, Historical Culture and Identity in Regions Undergoing Structural Economic Transformation* (Berghahn Books, 2020).

Figure 1.1 Location map of the regional city of Geelong, Victoria, Australia.

operate across a variety of texts, areas of knowledge about a subject which have acquired widespread authority'.[4] Hall then outlines how hierarchy and power operate across authorial discourses as a collective rather than as individual professions or disciplines. In this book we are interested in an alignment between heritage and urban renewal strategies,

---

[4] Stuart Hall (ed), *Representation: Cultural Representations and Signifying Practices*, (London: Sage Publications, 1997), 42.

and how these pursue environmental agendas. Rather than interpreting this alignment as progressive, we question how various discourses operating together determine, govern and implement a unified and complicit vision of the future. Alignment between discourses that were considered opposing or conflictual – heritage on the one hand, "smart city" on the other – squeeze potential debates or criticisms out of the picture. Strategies for urban change have shown an excess of activity – workshops, consultation, stakeholder meetings, community engagement, conferences, committees – without necessarily producing effective agendas.[5]

An approach examining contested and marginalised narratives of the past brings into focus diverse and difficult histories that have made the place we now call Geelong. An awareness of difficult histories and an interest in correcting the "dispossession" histories of colonisation may be presented as a beginning, but conservation heritage confronts its own problematic paradigm when asked to conceptualise the multiple and multicultural makers of the built environment. Architectural theorist Asra Akcan proposes that historians have a significant role to play, arguing that because history writing risks producing an ignorance that brings about conflicts and disaster, an accountability is required of historians.[6] Akcan therefore proposes the idea of "open architecture" for an inclusive history that invites historians to step out of their specific expertise to perceive how history is intertwined and to pay attention to the multiple makers of history.[7] This book – its concept and content – extends this invitation to heritage practitioners, planners, urban designers, architects, artists, academics, architectural historians, educators, and local and state urban strategists.

To avoid the continuity of dominating narratives of history and their assumed choices and selection of heritage conservation practices, it invites experts to engage with power structures, hierarchies and inequalities of history, and to acknowledge the many communities who have made Geelong.[8] The coining of the term "Authorial Heritage Discourse" (AHD), relating particularly to Western paradigms of archaeological practice, generated a substantial wave of criticism of heritage, arguing that its policy and practices were dominated by the conservation of monuments and this reinforced hierarchical nationalist narratives.[9] However, Laurajane Smith argues that:

> It is important to stress that the AHD, despite its dominance, is contested and challenged. In Australia, for instance, the archaeological discourses of heritage, and the Australian AHD more generally, has been publicly challenged by Aboriginal communities and activists.[10]

The authorial institutions of heritage have also responded by including social value and intangible and tangible heritage, ensuring that heritage is understood more broadly and deeply than through materiality alone. While steps have been taken, heritage policies and practices have not yet come to terms with "dark histories of place". The heritage frameworks in Australia are three tiered – at federal national level, state level and local municipal level. Pertinent to our discussion here are the two separate legislative acts that govern heritage in the State of Victoria: the *Heritage Act 2017* and the *Aboriginal Heritage Act 2006*.[11] The three tiers and different legislative frameworks have hitherto thwarted a holistic approach to policies and to works on the ground.

VacantGeelong

The VacantGeelong project began at Deakin University in 2015 as a response to vacant industrial architecture in Geelong which was at the risk of demolition. Major industries including Ford (vehicles), Alcoa (aluminium), timber sawmills,

---

[5] Owen Kelly, "She'll Be Right: The Post-Industrial City of Newcastle in New South Wales is Currently Undergoing Rapid Gentrification. But is the City's Laid-Back Attitude Denying its Potential?", *Landscape Architecture Australia* 147 (August 1, 2015): 29–32; Louise C. Johnson, Sally Weller and Tom Barnes, "(Extra) Ordinary Geelong: State-Led Urban Regeneration and Economic Revival" in John R. Bryson, Ronald V. Kalafsky and Vida Vanchan (eds), *Ordinary Cities, Extraordinary Geographies*, [Cities Series] (Cheltenham, UK; Massachusetts, USA: Edward Elgar Publishing, 2021), 85–107; Carl Grodach, J. O'Connor and C. Gibson, "Manufacturing and Cultural Production: Towards a Progressive Policy Agenda for the Cultural Economy", *City, Culture and Society*, 1, 10 (2017): 17–25.

[6] Asra Akcan, *Open Architecture: Migration, Citizenship and the Urban Renewal of Berlin-Kreuzberg by IBA 1984–87* (Basel: Birkhauser, 2018).

[7] Akcan, *Open Architecture.*

[8] Christian Wicke et al. (eds), *Industrial Heritage and Regional Identities* (Taylor & Francis Group, 2018); Linde Egberts, *Chosen Legacies: Heritage in Regional Identity* (Routledge, Taylor & Francis Group, 2017).

[9] Laurajane Smith, *Archaeological Theory and the Politics of Cultural Heritage* (London: Routledge, 2004); Laurajane Smith, *Uses of Heritage* (London: Routledge, 2006); Laurajane Smith and Emma Waterton, *Heritage, Communities and Archaeology* (London: Duckworth, 2009).

[10] Laurajane Smith, "Discourses of heritage: implications for archaeological community practice", accessed December 11, 2023, https://journals.openedition.org/nuevomundo/64148.

[11] The purpose of the *Heritage Act 2017* is to provide for the protection and conservation of the cultural heritage of Victoria. The Act creates a framework to identify the most important non-Aboriginal heritage in Victoria and regulates changes to those places. The Act also creates offences and other enforcement measures to protect and conserve heritage. Parliament passed the *Heritage Amendment Bill 2023*. The bill will come into effect on 1 February 2024. Refer to https://www.heritage.vic.gov.au/about-us/legislation-and-regulations (accessed January 2024). The main purpose of the *Aboriginal Heritage Act 2017* is to provide for the protection of Aboriginal cultural heritage in Victoria. *Aboriginal Heritage Amendment Act 2016* (Vic) improved reporting requirements in relation to Aboriginal cultural heritage, to introduce provisions regarding Aboriginal intangible heritage, and to establish an Aboriginal Cultural Heritage Fund. Refer to https://aiatsis.gov.au/ntpd-resource/566 (accessed January 2024).

wool mills, Pilkington Glass, cement works, and the oil refinery once defined the city's industrial landscape, transforming the architectural and cultural terrain. The decline and closure of many industries herald another metamorphosis. Despite the cycles of transformation and erasure, and to counter a progressive and chronological approach to change, the VacantGeelong project set out to explore the paradox of vacancy of industrial operations on the one hand and the continued presence of industrial architecture on the other. Through inscriptions – artworks, design projects, creative research, installations, texts – it addressed material realities that lingered on, the industrial structures – silos, ducts, chimneys, warehouses – that give Geelong its continuing industrial character (see Figure 1.2).[12] In that process it sought to engage with an often-overlooked community – immigrant industrial workers. This book has grown out of the continuing research and practice of VacantGeelong.

The pasts and the futures in the title of this introduction bring attention to the task of writing history as intertwined and contingent. Even when smoothed out and covered over, the multiple makers and realities of history re-emerge, sometimes with arresting vigour. This book comprises chapters by authors who develop their scholarly, pedagogical and critical positions as individuals and /or as teams. Its proposition is situationalist – intersecting the space and place of Geelong are a myriad of pathways, approaches, interests, agendas and politics. Together they present debates on Geelong's transition, and represent debates from sometimes opposing positions, and provide a 'messy' critical historiography of the past and imagined futures of Geelong. This informative collection of essays open onto a platform for inclusivity in the city's architectural policies and urban strategies. And yet, neither the author positions, nor the critical approach of the chapters comprising this anthology, are intended to be aligned with one another, to reinforce similar theoretical framings or present a unified agenda. As editors, we have been keen to collate the various studies, research and work on Geelong at a pivotal time in the city's urban transformation. This book does not mask conflict and contestation, but rather foregrounds a proposition for intellectual and creative investigation, and invites engagement with work that identifies, oversees, and ruptures sites of sustained practices, as well as collaboration.

The book's three-part structure enables a focus on diverse approaches. The chapters in "Contexts: Multiple others who built Geelong", consider the multiple makers of the city as place, recognising the conflicting pasts of Geelong's history; they probe which of these are integral to the urban strategies or debates determining Geelong's future. In "Entwined histories", the research identifies and investigates the nature of Geelong's transition and transformation, considering key aspects of the aims as opposed to the realities, and what and who have been overlooked. Discussions focus on why this is a matter of concern for the socio-cultural as well as environmental futures of Geelong. In "Propositional Geelong", the chapters bring the projective role of architectural imagination to the foreground through works exploring the future of Geelong. These chapters critique the very idea of future-oriented agendas, arguing that too often futures are construed by fantasy narratives that are disconnected from the embodied spaces and realities of Geelong.

Contexts: Multiple others who built Geelong

In 1995 Australian historian Henry Reynolds wrote the foreword to a book that pioneered an understanding of the impact of colonisation on the traditional owners of the land in western Victoria, including the Wadawurrung:

> Ian Clark's book *Scars in the Landscape: A Register of Massacre Sites in Western Victoria, 1803-1859* takes us forward into a new phase of frontier historiography. For the first time we have a detailed, meticulously researched study of massacre in one Australian region. It bears out and bolsters much of the generalist historiography. It provides a powerful riposte to those who doubt the intensity and ubiquity of frontier conflict as well as standing alone as a fine piece of detailed scholarship. It provides a model for what now needs to be done all over Australia.[13]

Heather Threadgold's Chapter 2 on "Colonial Recollections of Aboriginal Cultural Landscapes in Djilang" examines early encounters on the land of "Djilang" in Wadawurrung Country. Its focus on envisioning a place as it was perceived at the time, intensifies a historical landmark that is often overlooked. While this was early in the colonial history of Djilang, and spanned a short period from the 1830s to the 1880s, the places explored emerge as verging on natural destruction from an ecological perspective and cultural collapse from an Aboriginal livelihood perspective. Threadgold uses travel documents of colonial settlers and the fieldwork of mid-twentieth century anthropologists and historians to reconstruct representations of these transforming and conflicted cultural landscapes. In Chapter 10, Paul Sanders, Mirjana Lozanovska and Yolanda Esteban, conclude that colonial survey maps are a valuable source for evidencing the form and location of important sites of lost landscape features that may be remembered, arguing that these may have implications for realising a more meaningful reconciliation of cultural heritage and identity.

From a central place of Wadawurrung histories in and around Geelong, an open architecture and an inclusive historiography expands to a significantly broader cultural diversity related to the present. The 2021 census reveals that

---

[12] Mirjana Lozanovska and Akari Nakai Kidd, "'Vacant Geelong' and its lingering industrial architecture", *Arq: Architectural Research Quarterly* 24, no. 4 (2020): 353–68, DOI:10.1017/S1359135520000421.

[13] Henry Reynolds, "Foreword" in *Ian D. Clark, Scars in the Landscape: A register of Massacre Sites in Western Victoria, 1803–1859* (Canberra: Aboriginal Studies Press for the Australian Institute of Aboriginal and Torres Strait Islander Studies, 1995), 169–75, http://nationalunitygovernment.org/pdf/2014/IanDClark-Scars_in_the_landscape.pdf.pdf.

Figure 1.2 Poster for VacantGeelong *Iconic Industry* exhibition, 2017, VacantGeelong, Mirjana Lozanovska, David Beynon, Cameron Bishop and Anne Scott Wilson (eds).

50% of the population in Australia are linked either ethnically or racially to other parts of the world.[14] This highlights Australia's multiculturalism. After the Second World War, mass immigration and immigrants' backbreaking labour was key to Australia's nation-building agenda.[15] A central strategy of industrial decentralisation brought thousands of culturally diverse immigrants to the northern suburbs of Geelong – Polish, Croatian, Dutch, Macedonian, Greek and Italian – and was pivotal to the transformation of the urban cultures of Geelong. Deindustrialisation has affected these communities. As Peter Malatt has observed:

> … we face the very real prospect of cities without industry. Paradoxically, at the same time, the millennial generation is showing great interest in pre-industrial manufacturing such as organic farming and foods, crafts such as ceramics and craft production such as alcohol and coffee roasting. Which is a bit like going back to the nineteenth century, except without the tuberculosis. What then, is an industrial city such as Geelong to do with all of this stuff it has used to make things?[16]

Listening to past Ford workers from the Macedonian community in Geelong was central to exploring the role of immigrants in the shaping and making of Geelong. In "Dialogues Between Space and Time" (Chapter 3), Lozanovska, Beynon and Fullaondo explore industrial architecture in a deindustrialised context, generating a discussion on embodied memory and emotional heritage. Can vacant industrial buildings stir the collective memory of Geelong's industrial era? Drawing on the works of the VacantGeelong project and the local community, Chapter 3 explores how an art-architecture collaborative practice can create a pause in the acceleration of urban (re)development and provide a means to rethink the value of those buildings that remain, even though the original function has ceased.

Much research related to migrant heritage and to industrial heritage, however, illustrates that good intentions have not filtered through to practices of assessment.[17] Southern European migrants who settled in the inner suburbs in Melbourne and Sydney in the post-war period provided 'a practical demonstration of the possibilities of urban renewal, and arguably caused the majority Anglo-Celtic population to rethink their pejorative attitude towards these areas', argues architectural historian David Beynon.[18] Beynon adds, there has been a 'disavowal of the seminal role of immigrant communities' in bringing attention to the inner suburbs and the heritage value of their interventions. The "heritage" industry still disproportionately protects the "British" heritage of Australia. Large settlements of immigrants saw the transformation of streets such as Pakington Street in West Geelong, where many post-war immigrants settled, with an emerging new urban culture of cafes, espresso bars, bakeries, patisseries and delicatessen stores.[19] Immigration scholars illustrate that this urban renewal was pivotal to a new (and more cosmopolitan) Australian urbanism, but this does not necessarily filter through into Australian urban/architectural history, or to heritage practitioners. Urban visions and strategies for Geelong have not yet investigated or referenced immigrant urban making as a precedent.

In Chapter 4, Tuba Kocaturk and Russell Kennedy end this first section on the contexts of Geelong by examining Geelong's current identity as UNESCO City of Design. They argue that an evolving landscape of design innovation within the city is instrumental to Geelong's transformation and conduct a comparative analysis with other cities of similar scale and industrial heritage. Integral to this capacity to envision itself as a city of design is the work of Deakin University's DesignMind laboratory, which has generated the expansion of a design ecosystem through collaborative ventures with a diverse spectrum of stakeholders. A series of case studies detail this shift. The chapter concludes by looking to the future, exploring design-driven urban and economic transformation(s).

Entwined histories

In this introduction we set out the theoretical framings around historiography, heritage and conservation within an urban futures agenda. We argue that, in contrast to separation and often opposition between these discursive practices in the past, a neoliberal global economic agenda has brought them in closer alignment. Decarbonisation and a moral environmental imperative deemed a forward-looking, future-oriented agenda, could impose an imperative for speediness for change and transformation. This is highlighted in the diverse chapters in this part of the book and demonstrated through some of the unintended outcomes of ongoing urban renewal in Geelong.

---

[14] Tom McCilroy, "Census 2021: Australia Becomes a Majority Migrant Nation", *Financial Review*, June 28, 2022, https://www.afr.com/politics/federal/census-2021-australia-becomes-a-majority-migrant-nation-20220627-p5awto.

[15] See forthcoming book: Anoma Pieris, Mirjana Lozanovska, Alexandra Dellios, David Beynon and Andrew Saniga, *Immigrant Industry: Building Postwar Australia* (New York: Berghahn, August 2024) (ISBN 978-1-80539-456-3 DP190101531).

[16] Peter Malatt, "Panel Discussion" (Vacancy and Preservation: The Architecture of the Post-Industrial City Symposium, National Wool Museum, Geelong, 2017).

[17] See the essays in the anthology Stefan Berger (ed), *Constructing Industrial Pasts,* (Berghahn Books, 2020); Denis Byrne, "Heritage Corridors: Transnational Flows and the Built Environment of Migration", *Journal of Ethnic and Migration Studies*, 42, no. 14 (2016): 2360–78. See also Alexandra Dellios, "Commemorating Migrant Camps: Vernacular Memories in Official Spaces", *Journal of Australian Studies* 39, no. 2 (2015): 252–71; Alexandra Dellios, "Migration Parks and Monuments to Multiculturalism: Finding the challenge to Australian Heritage Discourse through Community Public History Practice", *The Public Historian* 42, no. 2 (2020): 7–32.

[18] David Beynon, "Architecture, Multiculturalism and Cultural Sustainability in Australian Cities", *The International Journal of Environmental, Cultural, Economic and Social Sustainability* 5, no. 2 (2009): 43–57.

[19] David Rowe, *About Corayo: A Thematic History of Greater Geelong* (City of Greater Geelong, 2021).

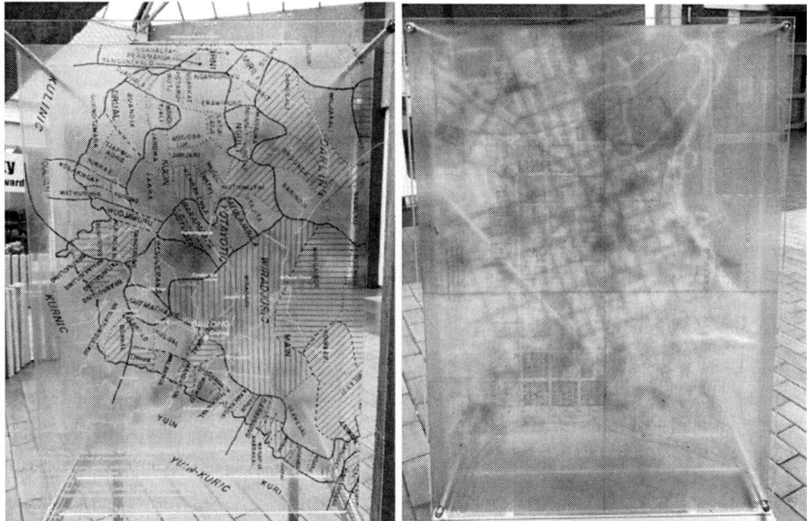

Figure 1.3 Mapping and counter-mapping become tools for decolonising practices. This installation comprises layering a series of maps referring to Djilang/Geelong–Wadawurrung clan and language groups, landscape sketches and Hoddle's grid. Its play on visibility/invisibility explores the (lack of) truth in evidence and documentation. Mirjana Lozanovska (with assistance from Julie Pham and Beverlea Low), *Psycho-geography: Map of Geelong,* 2020, created as part of *VACANTCitY 1000 years BackForward* project (Mirjana Lozanovska, Cameron Bishop and Anne Wilson), Centrepoint Arcade, Geelong (first installation) (City of Greater Geelong Arts Industry Commission).

Mizanur Rashid, Sanja Rodeš and Chin Koi Khoo in Chapter 5, "Tracing the Transformation of Little Malop Street: Visualising Geelong's Past through Digital Media", highlight legitimate concerns regarding the preservation of both the tangible and intangible aspects of the city's industrial history. While much of Geelong's central business district is being revitalised and reshaped from former industrial uses to more contemporary offices, institutions and shopping areas, certain areas remain underutilised voids, including the eastern half of Little Malop Street, which borders Market Square Mall. The chapter considers how new technologies – digital media such as Matterport VR scanning, time-lapse video, and virtual modelling – might help in documenting history and heritage, to collate the fragmented information available to us to better understand the lost buildings and recreate a past urbanscape. The authors suggest that this project serves as a potential model for preserving the legacy and cultural heritage of industrial cities in Australia and around the world.

In Chapter 6, "Reimagining Geelong via Systems Thinking", Richard Tucker and Louise Johnson reflect on the impacts, accumulated knowledge, achievements, limitations and future possibilities of three research projects that all seek to reimagine Geelong by improving the lives of groups facing accessibility and social inclusion obstacles. These three projects addressed the needs of different groups: Geelong Microvillage considered low-income earners excluded from the housing market; Accessible & Inclusive Geelong Feasibility Study informed a collective plan of action to include people living with mental ill-health or disability; and Vital Communities provided recommendations for those living in three Geelong suburbs evidenced as amongst the most disadvantaged in Victoria. The chapter firstly outlines the approach of how to reimagine Geelong in each of these instances before detailing how each was constituted to deliver a small reimagining: a set of modular housing units for the homeless, an accessibility centre for central Geelong, and a revitalised neighbourhood shopping centre in one of Geelong's most disadvantaged areas.

One important aspect to imagining different Geelongs in these projects was the process by which outcomes were generated. Key to all three projects was the combination of community-based participatory research with a systems thinking framework to better understand the complex inter-relatedness of what shaped the issues in each. From the systems thinking workshops there also emerged a range of feasible and impactful actions that could then be realised on the ground. This approach allowed researchers and participants together to visualise the complex and dynamic characteristics of obstacles faced by those affected by disadvantage and identify intervention points to inform collective plans of action. These plans linked actions as interdependent regional interventions, connecting urban planning policy to health, liveability, housing provision, co-design of public buildings, community infrastructure, neighbourhood renewal, and inclusive employment practices.

Joshua Zuenert's visual essay "Agriculture's Shadow Connections: Tracing Heavy Industries to Food Landscapes" (Chapter 7) situates the landscape of the Geelong region into a new era of landscape research investigation linking industrial developments and agricultural (or food-producing) landscapes. The chapter explores four industrial–agricultural sites of Geelong – fertiliser production, grains and oilseeds, food additives, and crude-oil by-products – to highlight the networked and interconnectedness of often assumed disparate parts of a place. Further, Zeunert's discussion of an underpinning extractive industry reinforces an argument that exploitation is both exploitation of the land and of the people. Zeunert's method of "field research aerial photography" juxtaposes the usual abstract interpretation of such distant views with the evidential analysis of the economies that produced it.

In Chapter 8, "Mapping Industrial Vacancy", Igor Martek, Chayakan Siamphukdee and Diego Fullaondo reconsider Geelong's industrial legacy, which has long been thought of as an eyesore, an embarrassment and, to city planners, an unsavoury handicap to future development. In contrast, this chapter contends that the legacy of Geelong's vacant industrial buildings present a unique opportunity for the establishment of a world-class showcase urban redevelopment. The focuse is on Geelong's North Shore, an area that has so far been largely ignored. It compares the developments in North Shore with those elsewhere in the Geelong region and acknowledges part of the problem is that Geelong's urban regeneration initiatives remain state-led and focused, like many of its international counterparts, on waterfront renewal. With that, ignorance persists as to the character and significance of Geelong's North Shore. This chapter argues that the successful regeneration of Geelong's industrial North Shore area must acknowledge and accommodate its historic, cultural and asset-rich legacy.

"The Place of Heritage in a Reimagined Geelong" is considered by Ursula de Jong and Chayakan Siamphukdee in Chapter 9. They acknowledge that heritage is complex and deeply connected to history, identity and politics, and review our understandings of heritage – tangible and intangible – and its place in Geelong through selected case studies of historically significant industrial buildings and structures. What is revealed is a complex relationship that Geelong city has with its heritage. In its self-reinvention or reimagination, Geelong has witnessed major losses as well as sensitive interventions. However, no holistic approach to dealing with the city's heritage has been implemented. This chapter uses the Burra Charter, a national charter that establishes principles for the management and conservation of cultural sites in Australia, as a reference point for its critical analysis of the place of heritage in a reimagined Geelong. It argues that in 2024 heritage is about much more than "appreciating old buildings". Cultural values, economics, and ecological sustainable development, among other approaches, inform a multitude of aspects that embrace the significant role heritage can and should play in reimagining Geelong.

The Western Gully, noted in Heather Threadgold's Chapter 2, becomes the subject of Paul Sanders, Mirjana Lozanovska and Yolanda Esteban's Chapter 10, "Lost Landscape Features of Country: The Western Gully in Geelong". This chapter contributes to a historiography that critically examines "settlement drawings" and investigates the tools of representation – maps, charts and surveys – especially as these are the central tools in the spatial disciplines of urban history, urban design, architecture, and planning. Drawing on Michel de Certeau's theory of maps as instruments of power, the Western Gully is first problematised by charting its "existence" or emergence through maps, and then charting its disappearance – it was literally submerged within an enclosed canal. By looking at colonial paintings that can illustrate the landscape at moments of European "encounter", the chapter unfolds a narrative about the loss of pre-colonial landscapes, rather than a colonial narrative about the beginning of the colonial shaping of Djilang.

Propositional Geelong

In the third and final part of this book, radical pedagogies and practices frame an agenda and a way of considering approaches to the future by creatively and critically engaging with Geelong's built and landscape environments.

Two chapters, Chapter 11 and Chapter 12, present work at the interface of research and teaching, and examine two aspects of this interface to further progress a creative response to the city.

In Chapter 11, "Radical Pedagogies: Intimacies of Observation", Akari Nakai Kidd and Mirjana Lozanovska draw on the projects of students in the final research thesis subject of the Master of Architecture at Deakin University. These students were part of the collaborative teaching model that evolved from the VacantGeelong project and contributed to a direct teaching–research nexus as a core creative research stream in the curriculum. The chapter discusses two student projects: the first addresses the methods of recording observation of architecture, centred on the Alcoa manufacturing plant on Point Henry, a thin peninsula that extends into the sea east of Geelong. The second focuses on the layered historical vacancy of Geelong's CBD through careful and experimental ways of mapping. These creative labours have evolved in what the authors have called "Intimacies of distant observation" and "Intimacy of layered observation", respectively, and it is these that are examined in this chapter. By focusing on the realm of representation, the chapter proposes a novel lens for research into Geelong's built environment.

Chapter 12, "The A+B Studio: Contributing Drivers for Change with the City of Greater Geelong 2000–2021", by Yolanda Esteban, John Rollo and James Doerfler argues that the space of the architecture and building studio at Deakin University's School of Architecture and Built Environment, both as a large open warehouse space for all year architecture students, and its relocation at the waterfront edge of the CBD of Geelong in 1996, were critical to a refocus of studio programs. A series of studios collectively examining Urbanheart extended the architectural program to the urban scale, many exploring Geelong in collaboration with the local municipality and industry partners. Prefab 21 is a design-build studio and is linked to a project discussed in Chapter 6 (Richard Tucker and Louise Johnston). *VITAL SIGNS – Alternative Futures* explores Geelong through four time periods: 2019, 2026, 2050 and 2100. Chapter 12 pleads for the recognition of the fresh thinking of students and the application of their imaginations to real problems facing a regional city like Geelong.

The most provocative chapter in this part of the book is a challenge to the "smart city" agenda that has taken hold of many cities around the globe. Perhaps most vulnerable to this agenda are cities that are undergoing a transition. By boldly staking a position for the human relations that industry engendered in Geelong in the twentieth century, Cameron Bishop and Anne Wilson in Chapter 13, "*VACANTCitY*: Community and Connection in a Clever and Creative Geelong", develop an anti-thesis to the smart city phenomenon, and by extension a critique of urban strategies and policies that increasingly invest in various digital visions. Through analysis and interpretation of the projects emerging from the art-architecture collaboration of VacantGeelong, Bishop and Wilson argue that the projects privileged the human and human relations by devising ways to engage with technology's losses and gains through artist residencies, research and social contact, to learn about Geelong from a human and creative perspective. This chapter reclaims the vital role artists have played in reflecting on and responding to vacant sites, community groups and histories in Geelong during the project's lifespan. This is an important claim, set against the supposition that the city's support for artists, as well as culture and art, could also align more emphatically with the digital visions of the smart city.

Our book ends with Chapter 14 on the co-design practice for the remaking of the Geelong Arts Centre. Joel McGuiness, as CEO and Creative Director of the Geelong Arts Centre at the time, writes of the ways the Wadawurrung Traditional Owners Aboriginal Corporation and the wider First Nations community – working collaboratively with the architects Ashton Raggatt McDougall (ARM) Architecture – have woven traditional stories of the land, language, water and sky, and the colours and textures of Moonah trees, ochre, and granite stone throughout the layers of the building. This project begins to construct a platform and a stage for Wadawurrung subjectivity to enter the cultural and institutional field as makers of Geelong's futures. The experimental nature of the processes of collaboration, engagement and creative-making exemplify the effort, learning and labour, and commitment required. At the same time, it raises questions about the risk of not undertaking such deeper approaches to making cultural institutions and designing architecture that shapes our cities.

This book in embracing the possibility of an "open architecture" demonstrates that architecture – its processes of making, the images presented, and histories drawn upon – are a critical medium in the transformation of the city. Its proposition is that architecture is instrumental to the making (and shaping) of society and local communities. Such architecture not only represents the multiple realities of its inhabitants (or users) but builds a platform, a stage, to allow diverse actors with a new sense as makers of Geelong to enter. In doing so, the architecture as well as the program become a reflexive interface along which entwined, contested and difficult histories are the narratives through which futures can be imagined.

CHAPTER 2

COLONIAL RECOLLECTIONS OF ABORIGINAL CULTURAL LANDSCAPES IN DJILANG, WADAWURRUNG COUNTRY

HEATHER THREADGOLD

Cultural landscapes and living spaces

Wadawurrung people are the Traditional Owners of Geelong (from now on referred to in their language as "Djilang"). The boundaries of Wadawurrung Country, in south-western Victoria, Australia (see Figure 1.1) extend from the Werribee River, east to the Bellarine Peninsula, south to Painkalac Creek and north-west to Beaufort. This chapter reflects upon natural and cultural landscapes from the colonial historical perspective and does not impinge upon Wadawurrung narrative or Traditional Owner cultural knowledge. It draws on terms and concepts including "cultural landscapes," "living spaces," and "living stations" to explore connections within land and landscapes.

"Cultural landscapes" is a term recognised in the field of heritage and defined by the International Council on Monuments and Sites (ICOMOS) as:

Cultural landscapes are cultural properties and represent the "combined works of nature and of man" designated in Article 1 of the Convention. They are illustrative of the evolution of human society and settlement over time, under the influence of the physical constraints and/or opportunities presented by their natural environment and of successive social, economic and cultural forces, both external and internal.[1]

However, the term "cultural landscapes" is also recognised by Traditional Owners across Australia as a layering of tangible and intangible knowledge, cultural heritage, and holistic connection to Country.[2] For Traditional Owners, Caring for Country is crucial for natural resource management, with low-impact industry associated with social and cultural organisation. Doolan explains that, apart from a spiritual connection to land and as part of creation stories:

these same sites have a continuing economic relevance to their owners in terms of traditional food resources and materials (such as ochre, raw materials for weapons and implement manufacture), that were left at the sites by mythological beings.[3]

This chapter acknowledges the cultural landscapes in Djilang that draw upon natural landscapes to highlight diverse landforms and waterways and complex associations, so as to identify cultural connections, which extend to the contemporary.

"Living spaces" is a term devised by the author to explain a holistic approach to understanding permanent living, as well as industrious and cultural uses of Aboriginal manipulated landscapes.[4] The definition of living spaces draws upon theoretical and tangible evidence of Aboriginal sites and links with the uses of pre-colonisation Aboriginal landscapes. The term stems from the work of former archaeologist and anthropologist Louis Lane, her research of Aboriginal stone arrangements and twenty years of fieldwork and research interpreting Wadawurrung landscapes. The term also expands upon Porter's description of "lived" spaces and Lane's "living-stations".[5] Planner and urban geographer Libby Porter's definition indicates a space in the past, with the term "lived" promoting Aboriginal connection to Country as pre-colonial but taking away the contemporary connection that exists and survives today.[6] Lane explains how living-stations incorporate a purposeful residential space positioned within natural landforms, near to water and diverse natural

---

[1] "ICOMOS Glossary", International Council on Monuments and Sites, January 1, 2023, https://www.icomos.org/en.

[2] "Budj Bim Cultural Landscape", Budj Bim Cultural Landscape, Gunditj Mirring Traditional Owners Aboriginal Corporation, January 1, 2023. https://www.budjbim.com.au/.

[3] James Doolan, "Aboriginal Concept of Boundary", *Oceania* 49, no. 3 (1979): 162.

[4] Heather Threadgold, "Aboriginal Stone Sites and Living Spaces along the Victorian Volcanic Plains: A Modelling System of Incorporated Natural Resources and 'Living Spaces' Determining Non-Nomadic Settlements" (10th Issue of Excavations, Surveys and Heritage Management conference; presentation, Victorian Archaeology Colloquium, held online, 1–4 February, 2021), https://doi.org/10.26181/61970dd72e60c; Heather Threadgold, "What the Stones Tell Us: Gulidjan Country Stone Sites and Living Spaces" (PhD thesis, Deakin University, 2020).

[5] Libby Porter, *Planning in Indigenous Australia* (London: Francis & Taylor, 2018); Louis Lane, "The Sheltered Cup" (unpublished manuscript, 1984).

[6] Porter, *Planning in Indigenous Australia.*

resources, over a long period of time.[7] Lane identifies two main contributors for living-stations: '1. Aliment i.e., food and water, and 2. Warmth i.e., the temperature of the immediate environment must be tolerable for the organism concerned'.[8] Further to this, Lane reflects upon the fact that:

> Coutts teaches us that Living-stations were usually situated in places which afforded a variety of bio-communities so that a broad range of edible and materials resources were within easy travelling-distance of the inhabitants. Hunters would lope up to fifteen (15) kilometres to find fast game like marsupials.[9]

The land is a resource for living; 'life came from and through the land, and was manifested in the land', with waterways providing crucial support systems.[10] Layer upon layer of settlement tell us this and enable us to reimagine and recognise existing Aboriginal landscapes. Defining a singular aspect of Aboriginal settlement is unworkable without considering the incorporation of practical and industrial use as biocultural knowledge, and intangible aspects of natural resources as living spaces. Most importantly:

> Access is the key, accessibility to permanent fresh water, strategically allocated and reliable shelter, and practical and valuable resources utilised for industry for not just everyday use, long term availability and productivity of quality long lasting materials, for storing foodstuff, and trading goods.[11]

Alongside waterways, for instance, aquaculture activities such as stone eel traps are entwined with the agricultural harvesting of water reeds used for baskets as part of a trap system, with sapling boughs as fencing holding the nets in place between the stone structures. While tending to the aquaculture system for months on end, food must be sourced and supplied, and housing structures maintained. Short-finned eel is smoked by the natural method, utilising trees for smoking meat, and sun-dried methods for long-term use and trade. Trade routes, ritualised as objects, were traded only between one tribe and the next, never from one tribe to a third tribe through a second tribe's territory.[12] Complexities on, and within, borders and boundaries are strictly adhered to, and protect and define living spaces and allocated resources.

More detail about the concept and working knowledge of the living space model is developed within the argument of this chapter, which takes the reader on a journey with early colonial travellers throughout the Djilang region between the You Yangs to the north, Lake Modewarre to the west, Lake Connewarre to the south and the Bellarine Peninsula to the east. Wadawurrung places, including indicators of living spaces, are mentioned within the travellers' diaries. Along with knowledge from anthropologists and historians, and their fieldwork (which is key to industry practice prior to the era of armchair anthropology), this chapter reflects a colonial perspective for a basis of cultural mapping. This is not to undermine the vital component of Traditional Owner knowledge and input that must take place during the detailed process of cultural mapping. Base mapping crucially requires an understanding of the natural landscape (see Figure 2.1 in colour plate section).

Cultural mapping is an emerging concept for depicting Aboriginal Australian cultural heritage. The focus is mostly on archaeological methodology to determine topological consistencies and to incorporate tangible and intangible aspects of Country with Traditional Owner-based projects. However, there is a deep connection to Country that connects to a responsibility to keep knowledge and law/lore intact and within family groups. Aboriginal Australia sits subtly within the environment, with accountability to ensure that very little impact is a successful way of living for thousands of generations but is now overshadowed by vast changes in the landscape over the past 250 years. Anthropologists Lyn Russell and Ian McNiven explain that Aboriginal people know place and that oral history and "walking on the land" help retain that knowledge, and further that Western thinking and perceptions of the land must shy away from the imagined and imaginary, which create misinterpretations.[13]

Working with Russell and McNiven's concept that the on-ground presence helps to present a visible perspective of Aboriginal connection to place, research is essentially undertaken with Aboriginal people.[14] Robyn Heckenberg, a Wiradjuri Traditional Owner discusses the "Wagirra Trail" in the Albury region of the Murray River in New South Wales (NSW).[15] Heckenberg explains that:

---

[7] Lane, "The Sheltered Cup".

[8] Lane, "The Sheltered Cup", 1.

[9] Louis Lane, "Jerringot Living Station: Wathaurong Territory No23." (unpublished manuscript: 1991), 1–2.

[10] Ronald M. Berndt, *Aboriginal Sites, Right and Resource Development* (Perth: University of Western Australian Press, 1981), 2.

[11] Fred Cahir et al., *Aboriginal Biocultural Knowledge in South-East Australia: Perspectives of Early Colonialists* (Clayton South: CSIRO Publishing, 2018); Heather Threadgold and David Jones "What the Stones Tell Us" (Urban History, Urban Planning conference, RMIT, 2018), 5.

[12] Ken James, *Aborigines in the Werribee District* (Werribee: Werribee District Historical Society, 1978), 71.

[13] Lyn Russell and Ian McNiven, "Monumental Colonialism: Megaliths and the Appropriation of Australia's Aboriginal Past", *Journal of Material Culture* 3, no. 3 (1998): 283–99.

[14] Russell and McNiven, "Monumental Colonialism: Megaliths and the Appropriation of Australia's Aboriginal Past" .

[15] Robyn Heckenberg (ed.), "Learning in Place, Cultural Mapping and Sustainable Values on the Millawa Billa (Murray River)", *Australian Journal of Indigenous Education* 45, no. 1 (2016).

the trail is rich with story and environmental lessons, the mapping of "peoples" histories and the river's story being imbided [sic] into the narrative of place and that this is somewhat shared with the broader community.[16]

The development of the Wagirra Trail came out of the documentation of the dialogue with community pertaining to the 'history of the river, a history of the people, and an accompanying natural history of the region'.[17] It was important for elders to be the overseers of the project. Heckenberg explains that the trail 'represents a living cultural mapping that nourishes the spirit and informs through cultural expression and affiliations to totems through story-making' and representation of sense of both place and relationship to nature.[18] Geopiety is a term that describes this connection to both place and nature. The geographer Yi-Fu Tuan explains that the relationship between humans and land requires a reciprocal approach in taking and giving, and a reverent approach to appeasing layers of place and people and spirits.[19] Justin Butler, a Kalkadoon and Bandjin man of north-western Queensland, speaks about the concept of Aboriginal mapping as 'an act of survival' and that it can 'provide a fundamental step in decolonising the ways we tell our stories.'[20] Remembering stories, sharing stories and asking questions is crucial to reflecting this narrative back to place.

Another aspect to the notion of cultural mapping is the ability to ensure that the initial recording of significant sites incorporated in the archaeological mapping must occur without disturbing the site itself. Scholar Heather Richards-Rissetto reports that satellite imagery such as geographic information systems (GIS) began to be used by archaeologists in the 1980s and 1990s.[21] Other techniques such as:

> remotely sensed digital elevation models (DEMs) and digital surface models (DSMs) are useful datasets for investigating the distribution of archaeological sites in a broad landscape context, giving researchers the ability to classify and model terrains with greater accuracy and less subjectivity than traditional field methods.[22]

GIS methodology was utilised in the Packsaddle Valley in Murujuga Country of the Pilbara of Western Australia (WA) in recoding stone arrangements to determine whether sites are more likely to occur typologically on higher ground.[23] The techniques for defining the age and use of stone arrangements are relatively new (300 years according to Boone Law et al.)[24] Similar technology is used in remote sensing of habitat environments for native wildlife. However, it is not only the importance of dating sites – and in turn understanding the natural landscape settings – but also the human approach to anthropology and change in landscape, as suggested by Fanning et al.[25] A chronology of landscape change is equally as important as artefact analysis and dating in interpreting the archaeological record of past hunter-gatherer activity.

Richards-Rissetto argues that '2D imagery techniques require the introduction of 3D dimensions for landscape archaeology'.[26] She explains that GIS mapping does not critically record human socialisation, does not ask the question, how does the organisation of the landscape influence where people go, who interacts with who, and how does this shape their experiences? Richards-Rissetto's method of modelling land use with the experimental use of 2D and 3D imagery and mention of further immersive interaction of place is combined with the use of Oculus Rift (a tool from virtual reality).[27]

Advanced technology is no doubt advantageous for creating precise and analytical understandings of Aboriginal sites and landscapes. However, the author does not promote the quest for improvement or enforcement of a Western concept of interpretation or the use of Russell's term "reimagining".[28] Instead, the author is promoting a formula of cultural mapping that deliberately underestimates the complexities of significant sites, and, at the same time, explores the prospect of visually enhancing the natural landscapes and localised and regional aspects of living spaces (see Figure 2.2). This allows for a partial understanding of the extent of Aboriginal landscapes without attempting to interpret them or, rather, respectively acknowledging that most aspects of cultural sites and living spaces will only be held with Aboriginal knowledge.

---

[16] Heckenberg, "Learning in Place, Cultural Mapping and Sustainable Values on the Millawa Billa (Murray River)", 2.

[17] Heckenberg, "Learning in Place, Cultural Mapping and Sustainable Values on the Millawa Billa (Murray River)", 2.

[18] Heckenberg, "Learning in Place, Cultural Mapping and Sustainable Values on the Millawa Billa (Murray River)", 8.

[19] Yi-Fu Tuan, "'Geopiety", in David Lowenthal and Martyn Bowden (eds), *Geographies of the Mind* (1976): 11–39.

[20] Justin Butler 2017 "Who's Your Mob?: Aboriginal mapping, beginning with the strong story", *The International Journal of Narrative Therapy and Community Work* No.3, (22-26): 23 (Dulwich Centre Publications).

[21] Heather Richards-Rissetto, "What Can GIS + 3D Mean for Landscape Archaeology?", *Journal of Archaeological Science*, 84 (2017): 10–21.

[22] W. Boone Law et al., "Digital Terrain Analysis Reveals New Insights into the Topographic Context of Australian Aboriginal Stone Arrangements", *Archaeological Prospection*, 24 (2017): 169–79.

[23] Boone Law et al., "Digital Terrain Analysis Reveals New Insights into the Topographic Context of Australian Aboriginal Stone Arrangements".

[24] Boone Law et al., "Digital Terrain Analysis Reveals New Insights into the Topographic Context of Australian Aboriginal Stone Arrangements", 27.

[25] Patricia Fanning, Simon Holdaway and Ed Rhodes, "A New Geoarchaeology of Aboriginal Artefact Deposits in Western NSW, Australia: Establishing Spatial and Temporal Geomorphic Controls on the Surface Archaeological Record", *Geomorphology* 101 (2018): 524–32.

[26] Richards-Rissetto, "What Can GIS + 3D Mean for Landscape Archaeology?", 12.

[27] Richards-Rissetto, "What Can GIS + 3D Mean for Landscape Archaeology?".

[28] Russell and McNiven, "Monumental Colonialism: Megaliths and the Appropriation of Australia's Aboriginal Past".

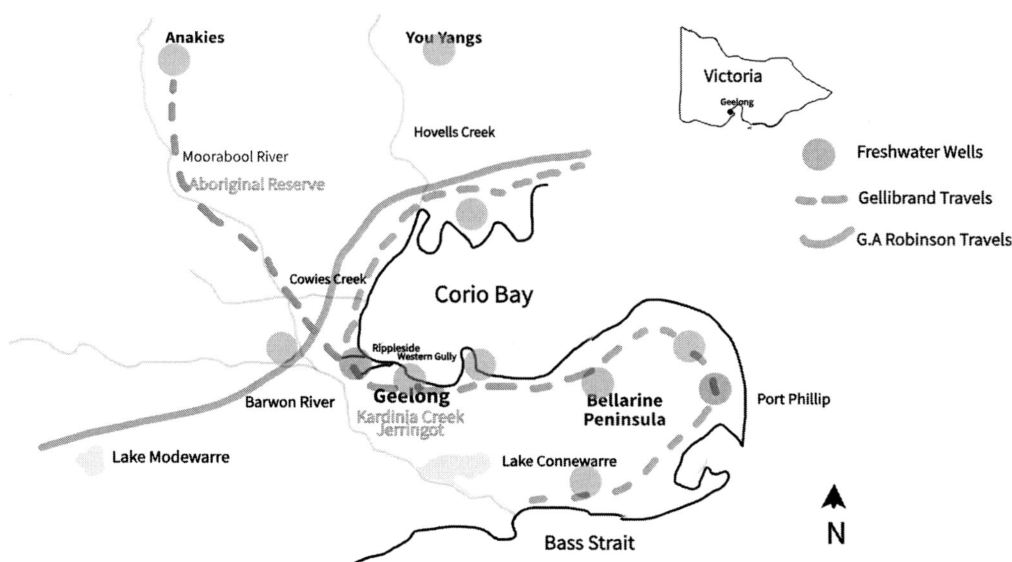

Figure 2.2 Exploration sites by early colonialists and key freshwater wells in Djilang mentioned in this chapter.

Freshwater wells

Joseph Tice Gellibrand (1786–1837) is a well-known historical figure due to his disappearance in the Western District of Victoria along with George B. L. Hesse when they failed to take directions by locals in 1837.[29] Gellibrand took part in John Batman's Port Phillip Association scheme to utilise pre-settlement regulations allowing the take up of large tracts of land in the Port Phillip District for sheep production – similar to those made available in Van Diemen's Land (Tasmania). On his visit from Melbourne to Geelong and the Bellarine Peninsula in the summer of 1836, Gellibrand recorded in his journal the landscapes and waterways of the Western Grasslands and, most particularly, places of fresh water. These key freshwater places or wells are described in Gellibrand's diary as "Native Wells". Freshwater wells held water all year round and they still exist today, in places such as the granite You Yang ranges. Anthropologist, Aldo Massola states that:

> In granite country, waterholes were veritable underground reservoirs containing many hundreds of gallons, which seldom ran dry. The "mouth", as the natives [sic] called it, of these underground basins was generally a natural hole in a rock slab. The natives [sic] kept these rock holes covered with a flat stone to prevent dirt being blown into them: consequently, unless the exact spot were known, "the mouth" was very difficult to locate.[30]

The inability to find these wells hindered Mathew Flinders' travels in 1802. Flinders complained of the lack of fresh water in the You Yangs region. After climbing Station Peak (the highest point of the You Yangs, now named Flinders Peak), he remarked that he was 'much fatigued, having walked 20 miles without finding a drop of water'.[31] Other typologies of wells are soaks and permanent waterholes located throughout the Western Plains District. These include chains of ponds (a term described by early visitors such as William Westgarth in 1840 and John Batman in 1835) and areas between Werribee and Colac and other volcanic regions.[32] Gellibrand also describes some "Native Wells" near the point of Geelong Harbour and calls them "Geewar".[33] Gellibrand encountered further wells on the banks of Corio Bay on his way to the Bellarine Hills.[34] These places of water sources are a clear indication of related living spaces.[35] Massola notes that coastal camps existed around Corio Bay and Point Henry.[36] Old residents of Djilang remember middens along the Corio Bay foreshore near Rippleside, and noted that the 'shells, cockles or oysters, were larger than those we know'.[37]

---

[29] Thomas Francis Bride (ed), *Letters from Victorian Pioneers* (Adelaide: The Griffin Press, 1898; published 1969).

[30] Aldo Massola, *Bibliography of the Victorian Aborigines* (Melbourne: Hawthorn Press, 1971) 118–119.

[31] C. P. Billot, *The Life of our Years: In and around Geelong* (Melbourne: Lothian Publishing Co Pty Ltd, 1969), 3.

[32] William Westgarth (1815–1889) and Sir Archibald Michie, *Personal Recollections of Early Melbourne & Victoria* (George Robertson and Co., Alfred Deakin Library, 1888); Philip L. Brown (ed), *The Todd journal 1835* (Geelong: Geelong Historical Society, 1989); Bruce Pascoe, *Dark Emu Black Seeds (Broome,* Magabala Books Aboriginal Corporation, 2014), 40–41.

[33] Bride (ed), *Letters from Victorian Pioneers*, 18 (Massola calls the You Yang wells "gnamma"); Massola, *Bibliography of the Victorian Aborigines,* 118.

[34] Bride, *Letters from Victorian Pioneers,* 19.

[35] Threadgold, "Aboriginal Stone Sites and Living Spaces along the Victorian Volcanic Plains: A Modelling System of Incorporated Natural Resources and 'Living Spaces' Determining Non-Nomadic Settlements".

[36] Aldo Massola, *Journey to Aboriginal Victoria* (Adelaide: Rigby, 1969), 41.

[37] Middens are remnant piles of shell and charcoal that indicate cooking places over long periods of time by Aboriginal people. Middens are found along coastlines and nearby fresh waterways; Gladys Seaton, *The Ashby Story: A History of Geelong West* (Geelong: Geelong West City Council, 1978), 13.

Aboriginal people were seen nearby some of these wells and it was the first-hand knowledge of guide William Buckley that led Gellibrand's party to freshwater wells.[38] A further set of wells were located on the Bellarine Peninsula, where Massola reveals that the whole area between Portarlington and Indented Head appears to have been a huge campsite, extending to the vicinity of Barwon Heads.[39] The wells and freshwater points highlight the myriad of waterways within the Djilang region (see Figure 2.3).

The volcanic landscapes of the Victorian Volcanic Plains (VVP) provide for the waterways and landscapes we see today. The VVP are reliant on the freshwater systems spread throughout the region. Nineteenth century geologist Reginald Augustus Frederick Murray explains that:

> the Werribee [River] rises in the Main Divide and enters Port Phillip midway between Melbourne and Geelong. The Barwon River enters the sea through Lake Connewarre, a little to the west of Port Phillip Heads, and takes its rise at Mount Sabine, the culminating part of the Otway Ranges.[40]

The Anakie hills located 30 km northwest of Djilang are extinct volcanic eruption points and are ingrained in Wadawurrung creation stories. Gellibrand described the rich landscape of the Anakie hills and viewpoints.[41] When he and his party found some 'waterholes at the foot of the Annikie and the herbage for miles round and even to the top the Annikie of the finest description'. The naming of this herbage, or "Eurt", according to Lane, stood for the 'ground cover, or under-story greenery, the herbs, and the lower shrubs'.[42] Adaptation to significant changes in an ecological environment is part of Aboriginal peoples' ethos and their responsibility to the land. The advantages of the VVP region for Aboriginal habitation were created by environmental factors. These include higher rainfall levels; continuous access to fresh water via lake and river systems, aquifers and wetlands providing access to clean drinking water for people, animals and birds; rich fertile soils affording a rich biodiversity of flora and fauna to harvest; hunting grounds; shade; and pathways to and from family group borders. The availability of basalt rock in the Western District contributed to effective long-term structures, homes and engineering projects. When colonial settlement occurred, these ideal conditions soon came under threat. Victorian Government Geologist Alfred Selwyn described the grassy plains in the Murdeduke/Mount Hesse region in 1858 most unfavourably:

> the formation of the plains is limestone, though usually this is concealed beneath the basalt rocks. The soil is not good for agriculture w[ith much] of it … regarded as too poor for pastoral purposes; but the feed has greatly improved of late years. Exposure to cold winds unbroken by hills or hedges, renders cultivation up on the plains anything but profitable ... lack of trees … Stations have occasionally to send thirty or even forty miles [48–64 km] for firewood and suffer much from want of running water.[43]

Dahlhaus et al., in the 2003 *Victorian Volcanic Plains Scoping Study (Final Report)* describes current threats, noting that:

> the grasslands are in dire threat, that the grassland was formerly widespread across the plain but is now reduced to mostly small and degraded fragments with less than five per cent of the grassland remaining and that it continues to be threatened by clearing, inappropriate management, and weeds, threatening habitats for many threatened species, such as the small golden moths orchid, and the striped legless lizard.[44]

The geological significance of the Anakies incorporates a volcanic crater system, part of the Rowsley Fault, granite outcrops and variations of Pleistocene and the Newer Volcanics landforms within the Brisbane Ranges and along the nearby Moorabool River. In 1862 geologist Reginald A. T. Murray recorded that 'our geological survey party prospected all the gullies of the Brisbane ranges emptying on the plain from Little River up to Long Gully'.[45] Murray presented geological maps and reports of the area covering Sutherlands Creek, Anakie Creek and the Moorabool River detailing quartz for mining and mentioning greenstone.[46] Greenstone was a valuable resource for axe heads and a high value trade commodity for the Wadawurrung throughout other parts of the Kulin Nation and beyond.[47]

Surveyor Alezander J. Skene describes geological landscapes between Anakie and Little River:

---

[38] William Buckley escaped his convict holdings in Sorrento in 1802 and found his way around to Wadawurrung Country where he lived for 33 years until he made contact with John Batman in 1835.

[39] Massola, *Journey to Aboriginal Victoria*, 14.

[40] Reginald Augustus Frederick Murray, *Victoria: Geology and Physical Geography* (Melbourne: Government Printer, 1887), 10.

[41] Bride, *Letters from Victorian Pioneers*, 22.

[42] Louis Lane, "The Eurt-Eaters of the Great Basalt Plain" (unpublished manuscript, 1996), 4.

[43] James Bonwick, *Western Victoria* (Geelong: Thomas Brown, 1858), 6.

[44] Dahlhaus et al., *Victorian Volcanic Plains Scoping Study (Final Report). Client Report for Corangamite Catchment Management Authority.* (Canberra, ACT: CSIRO Land and Water, 2003), 11.

[45] Reginald A.T Murray, F.R.G.S., "Geological Report", *Bacchus Marsh Express* (Vic.: 1866–1918), December 11, 1909.

[46] Murray, "Geological Report"

[47] Massola, *Journey to Aboriginal Victoria.*

… as open forest country timbered with Gum and She-oak, the soil generally light and loamy increasing in richness towards the banks of the Creek and River.[48]

Between the You Yangs and Staughton Vale, an ancient swamp and campsite described by Massola as 'a sandy patch, or "blow" and that at the western sides of the blow there is a stretch of low-lying land which has all the appearances of once having been a swamp'.[49] This campsite later became an Aboriginal reserve. John Charles von Stieglitz reported in the 1849 *Report from the Select Committee on Aborigines (British Settlements)* that:

the 'tribe frequenting this neighbourhood is fast decreasing, and there are no children, therefore the idea of schools here would be completely useless'. A Reserve for Aborigines [sic] was designated at Staughton Vale an example of being placed where Aboriginal people frequented. [50]

Researcher Blake explains the reserve:

With the abolition of the Aboriginal Protectorate in 1849, there followed a decade of relative government neglect of the Wathawurrung and other Victorian people. In 1859 the Steiglitz Reserve of 640 acres [259 ha] was set aside on the Little River at Anakie. The reserve was maintained until 1901.[51]

The site of the reserve depicts a natural living space as it is located near a freshwater spring – a scarred tree nearby marking the spring site and associated cultural boundaries. The Brisbane Ranges provided for plants and animals and several waterways deliver birdlife, fish and short-finned eel. Lane describes how the menus would vary depending on where they were encamped and during periods of drought:

their hunting and foraging strategies were changed to address the problems of a reduced quantity of food, both protein and carbohydrate … leaves, shoots, stems, buds, flowers; rhizomes, roots, bulbs, corms; berries and other fruits; nectars and gums were all for the taking.[52]

The combination of key water sources, ideal natural landscapes and resources in the region of Djilang witnessed and recorded in a natural presence confirms working living spaces.

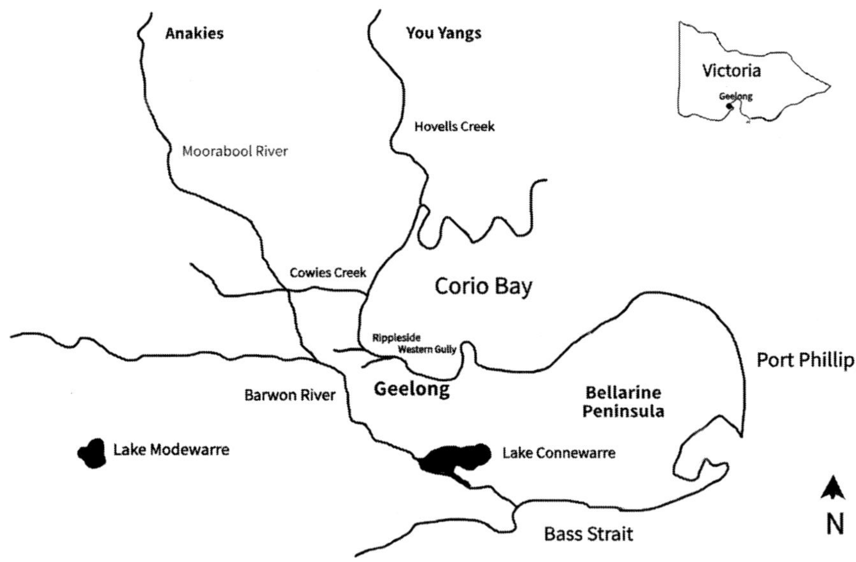

Figure 2.3 Djilang waterways.

Western Gully, the Bay, rivers and lake systems

The waterways of Djilang have been both modified and exploited. This began with the building of the Breakwater on the Barwon River by convicts in 1840 to separate freshwater from the incoming tidal saltwater. Early townspeople relied

---

[48] Maurice Weston, Assistant Surveyor, Parish of Anakie, County of Grant [Cartographic Material], August 28, 1855; Surveyor General's Office, September 19, 1855; J. B. Philp. Lith., Melbourne: Surveyor General's Office, 1855.

[49] Massola, *Journey to Aboriginal Victoria.*

[50] Report from the Select Committee on Aborigines (British Settlements), *Aborigines and Protectorate.* (Sydney: The Government Printing Office, Sydney 1849), 35.

[51] Barry J. Blake (ed), *Wathawurrung and the Colac Language of Southern Victoria* (Canberra: Pacific Linguistics, The Australian National University, 1998) 63.

[52] Lane, "The Eurt-Eaters of the Great Basalt Plain", 2.

on this freshwater system. Water was even drawn from the Barwon to the town centre to 'the Tank' in Market Square.[53] During construction of the straightening of the head of the Barwon River in 1929 for rowing, an Aboriginal shield was found, said to be eighty or ninety years old, and it was stated in *The Herald* that 'years ago the spot was the scene of camps and corroboree'.[54]

A waterway, unrecognisable today, known as the Western Gully was a key attribute of the western edge of Geelong city, separating the bush from the Bay (see Chapter 10, "Lost Landscape Features of Country: The Western Gully in Geelong"). The Western Gully:

> was a real creek bed, an ever-present fact of life. To provide easy access to town for wheeled and foot traffic, La Trobe had ordered, in February 1848, the building of a dam.[55]

The dam was otherwise known as the "ornamental lake" and became a modified city feature along with a parkland that became Johnston's Park in the city centre. However, the stoppage of the natural watercourse from the Western Gully to Corio Bay led to a stagnant pool and the dam became a dumping ground with sanitary issues.[56] The Western Gully in its natural state was well timbered and wild and 'as late as 1849 the aborigines [sic] were reputed to have a camping ground in Ashby'.[57] The natural Western Gully system and extension to a swamp in Market Square was an important meeting place for Wadawurrung and a well-known birthplace of Wadawurrung people.[58]

Further north from the Western Gully, another waterway at Rippleside once existed with a trickling creek running through its yellow clay.[59] Cowies Creek is another waterway and is named after John Anthony Cowie, an early colonial-settler who took up land with David Stead in 1836 stretching from the:

> Moorabool River to Corio Bay, including what is now Bell Post Hill. This is said to take its name from a bell hung on a tree by the partners and used to warn settlers - particularly shepherds - of impending Aboriginal attacks.[60]

Fresh fish and, most significantly, oysters were found at Cowies Creek and Duck Ponds (Lara from Hovells Creek) due to the natural combination of freshwater and saltwater flows.[61] Exploitation of these conditions led to depletion and 'in 1875 fishing were scarce and dear in Geelong'.[62] Various early settler fishing techniques mimicked Aboriginal technologies, including fish netting, traps and spearing. However, some methodologies exemplified the symbiotic relationship between nature and people. This is illustrated by police magistrate Foster Fyans' observation of Aboriginal people fishing at Geelong in partnership with dolphins who drove the fish in to the shore.[63]

Two key lake systems of the Djilang area are Lake Connewarre and Lake Modewarre. Lake Connewarre is attached to salt and fresh water with the merging of the Barwon River system and the estuary system, leading into the Bass Strait at Barwon Heads. The unique ecosystems created by this merging now include Ramsar wetlands and mangroves. Lake Connewarre provides habitats for birdlife (including the black swan), shellfish, fish and reptiles, as well as being an unexpected refuge for whales. A female whale and calf were sighted in Lake Connewarre in 1861 and a whale, described as a fin-backed species, and her calf in 1911.[64] Lake Connewarre is part of a Wadawurrung songline story that connects across the Djilang region and beyond.[65]

Lake Modewarre lies approximately 30 km south-west of Geelong and was formed as part of the Mount Moriac volcanic system. Aboriginal Protectorate G.A Robinson described Lake Modewarre on his travels in 1841:

> Lake Mourdewarrer [sic], its clear water and broad white sandy margin had an interesting and pleasing effect as it lay at our feet, embedded as it were in forest. Cape Barren geese and ducks and swans were on the water and on the sands on the shore.[66]

---

[53] Billot, *The Life of our Years: In and around Geelong,* 29.

[54] "Aborigine Shield Found in River", *The Herald* (Melbourne), April 26, 1929, http://nla.gov.au/nla.news-article244450978.

[55] Seaton, *The Ashby Story: A History of Geelong West,* 28.

[56] "Ashby Association", *Geelong Advertiser*, May 29, 1863, 3, https://trove.nla.gov.au/newspaper/article/150409038.

[57] Brownhill, 1849 quoted in Seaton, *The Ashby Story: A History of Geelong West,* 13.

[58] "Geelong", *Geelong Advertiser* (Geelong), December 19, 1879, http://nla.gov.au/nla.news-article150170441; "King Billy", Torquay Museum without Walls, 2023, https://www.torquayhistory.com/brief-history-of-torquay/first-austsralians/wathaurong/king-billy/.

[59] Seaton, *The Ashby Story: A History of Geelong West,* 208.

[60] Billot, *The Life of our Years: In and around Geelong*, 20.

[61] "Geelong", *Sydney Morning Herald*, July 10, 1855, http://nla.gov.au/nla.news-article12971511.

[62] G.A, 1875, quoted in Seaton, *The Ashby Story: A History of Geelong West,* 65.

[63] Pascoe, *Dark Emu Black Seeds*, 54.

[64] "Memories of Old Geelong", *Geelong Advertiser*, October 22, 1904, http://nla.gov.au/nla.news-article148219887; "Whale in Lake Connewarre", *Geelong Advertiser*, May 6, 1911. http://nla.gov.au/nla.news-article149207048.

[65] Heather Threadgold, "The case of Dooliebeal and Wurdi Youang on Wadawurrung Country: Threats to, and spatial awareness of Aboriginal cultural heritage and landscapes within urban growth" (10th Issue of Excavations, Surveys and Heritage Management conference; presentation, Victorian Archaeology Colloquium, held online, 1–4 February, 2021), https://DOI 10.26181/619701f1bb3f2.

[66] Gary Presland, *Journals of George Augustus Robinson March–May 1841* (Records of the Victorian Archaeological Survey, 1977), 3.

Leading from Lake Modewarre, east through the Barrabool Hills, Robinson described:

the base [of the hills] of which is washed by the Moorabool. For several miles our route lay through open forest of the she oak and this is the prevailing timber. They are like most of the trees in the country, of a dwarf species … and the ground as a plain… .[67]

Robinson heard the roar of water (Buckley Falls), and descended the hill to the river, to Fyans' ford. Here he observed some old native huts, opposite Fyans' property.[68] This is the location of the confluence of the Moorabool and Barwon Rivers.

The river systems are key resources for fishing and other industrial uses of natural resources. Methodologies used were spearing, trapping and netting. Anthropologist Jane Balme states that historic and ethnographic accounts cite two main technologies used by Aboriginal people to capture large numbers of animals: traps and nets.[69] Traps were used to capture large numbers of fish and, in some places, eels. Nets were used to capture a wide variety of animals including mammals, bats, birds and fish. This also describes the organisation of labour for gatherings and large events. The most intact examples of Aboriginal industrial activity around Djilang are in the context of waterways represented by the aquaculture of fish, eels and shellfish. Evidence of a vast aquaculture industry includes Budj Bim/Lake Condah (Tae'rak), where it stretches for over 30 km.[70] Archaeologist Heather Builth explains that:

The Gunditjmara reveal … the physical manifestation of a highly developed socioeconomic and political organisation … the formation of wetlands within the varying pattern of wood and grassland has provided a highly biologically productive environment with a correspondingly high potential for human resource exploitation.[71]

Pascoe, Steffensen, Hallam and Gammage discuss landscape modification using fire and the manipulation of flora storey growth and plantations to enhance hunting grounds, industrial activities and living spaces.[72]

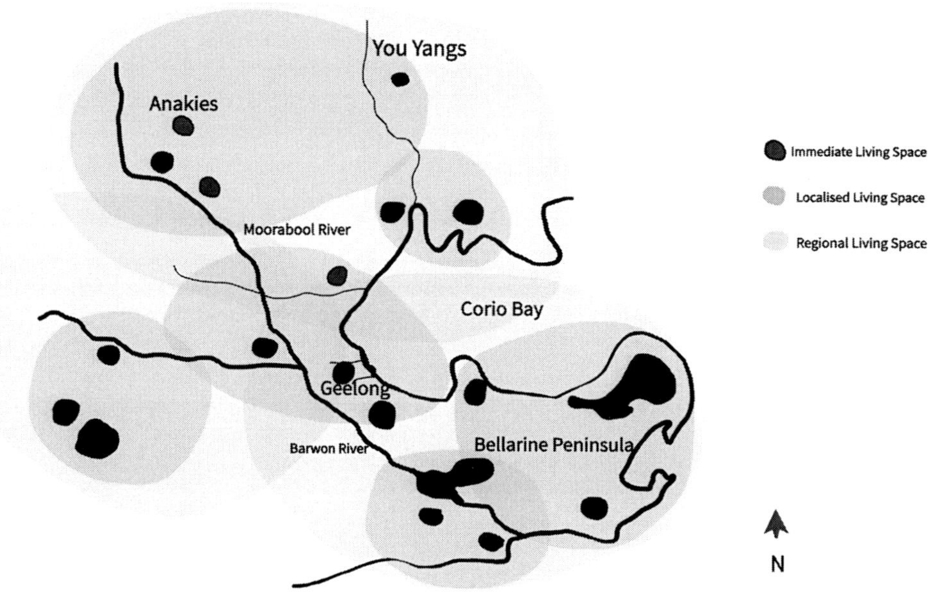

Figure 2.4 Djilang living spaces in the location area.

---

[67] Presland, *Journals of George Augustus Robinson March–May 1841,* 153.

[68] Presland, *Journals of George Augustus Robinson March–May 1841,* 153.

[69] Jane Balme, "Communal hunting by Aboriginal Australians: Archaeological and ethnographic evidence", in Kristen A. Carlson and Leland C. Bement (eds), *The Archaeology of Large-Scale Manipulation of Prey,* 1st edn (Louisville, Colorado: University Press of Colorado, 2018), 42–62.

[70] Heather Builth, "Gunditjmara Environmental Management: The Development of a Fisher Gatherer-Hunter Society in Temperate Australia", *Jstor* (2006), accessed August 14, 2018; Refer also to "Budj Bim Cultural Landscape", UNESCO, 2023, https://whc.unesco.org/en/list/1577.

[71] Builth, 'Gunditjmara Environmental Management: The Development of a Fisher Gatherer-Hunter Society in Temperate Australia', 4–5.

[72] Pascoe, *Dark Emu Black Seeds;* Victor Stefferson, *Fire Country* (Melbourne: Hardie Grant Publishing, 2020); Sylvia Joy Hallam, *Fire and hearth: a study of Aboriginal usage and European usurpation in south-western Australia* (Canberra: Australian Institute of Aboriginal Studies,1975); Bill Gammage, *The Biggest Estate on Earth* (Crows Nest: Allen & Unwin, 2011).

The living spaces of Jerringot and Kardinia Creek

I have developed a simplified method and model to describe living spaces as housing, the associated natural resources and industry, along with knowledge sharing and cultural places.[73] The focus is on relaying the definition of living spaces as a practical understanding of people and space and the notion of semi-permanency and permanency. The model is based on the combination of collective categories of immediate stone sites and layering of natural and manipulated landforms with the incorporation of flora and fauna, stone sites, scarred trees, waterways and housing. The living space model outlines "immediate" known sites. This is extended by the factor of one or two landforms, waterways and/or landscapes associated with the "localised" aspect of the "immediate" site. A regional extension of the localised aspect extends the living space, incorporating more layers of landforms, waterways and/or landscapes that may incorporate more stone sites and/or living spaces. See Figure 2.4 for a mapping of living spaces within the Djilang region.

Living spaces measure the extent of living in association with landscapes and waterways throughout the VVP via evidence of stone sites, recollections, knowledge and archaeological evidence.[74] Lane's recordings of what she called 'Living-stations' present two examples within Wadawurrung Country situated along the Barwon River in Djilang, Victoria.[75] The first is named by Lane as "Kardinia Creek" (the "Sheltered Cup") and the second is named "Jeringot" (now known as "Jerringot").[76] Both spaces are strategically placed on the south side of the Barwon River on river bends with attached extensions to other tributaries. This is a prime position for permanent living, incorporating key element indicators that Lane describes as essential:

> near fresh water, a camping-station must be, in a position sheltered by land-formations which would deflect the weather-winds [where able] to obtain sufficient food-stuffs … as well as sufficient materials[77]

The two main elements – the terrain and waterway – are demonstrated at Kardinia Creek and Jerringot: flanked by high terrain on the west side and sheltered from westerly winds, showing floodplain zones, permanent wetland and a creek tributary.

The living space at Kardinia Creek is a 'living-place where the [people] camped on for considerable periods of time'.[78] The name "Sheltered Cup" defines the location of the space sheltered from the winter winds and weather and protected from the Barrabool Hills and Mounts Moriac and Pollock situated further away. Lane describes the site as 'previously a billabong surrounded by wattles and casuarinas [she oak] [that] stand … knee deep in tussock grass. It was fringed with reeds and rushes and was frequented by waterbirds, frogs and snakes [and utilised in the] winter months'.[79] Lane further describes the diversity of resources that supported the living-station site, ranging from short-finned eel and blackfish, to yabbies, tortoise, bandicoot and a long list of birds, and also notes multiple uses of Wadawurrung plants.[80] In 1982, the living space was uncovered after a dry period, unveiling over 250 artefacts recorded by Lane. Water pipes closed off Kardinia Creek in 1984 for housing, with infrastructure development disturbing the site; today, the area, known as Yollinko Park, is partly protected by tree planting.

The Jerringot site, also sheltered by hills rising directly to the west, was adjacent to fresh water and had direct access to an abundance of natural resources. Lane outlines how living-stations were reused and revisited and that:

> when returning to the Living-station after an absence, [the people] cleared the whole area of vegetation and the remains of old shelters; then spread a layer of new sand, like a carpet. Jerringot is one such site re-used over many generations.[81]

Many artefacts were recorded within the Jerringot space including shell remnants, tools such as axe heads and scrapers, grinding stones, etc. The site recorded by Lane is a distinct non-natural-shaped dome above a natural mound curved above the wetland flood plain of the Barwon River where it enters into the Lake Connewarre system.[82] Jerringot still exists on the prominent corner of a busy tourist road intersection, under a modern car yard and showroom, and overlooking a golf course. The wetlands still exist and the overflow from the Barwon River creates an extension to the wetlands during wet seasons.

Further regional aspects of the two sites incorporate Lake Connewarre to the south-east, Moorabool River to the north-west, Corio Bay to the north-east and the Barrabool Hills to the west. Lane's collected body of work on Wadawurrung living-stations, combined with interpretations of language and resource use, inspires the term 'living spaces' to present a realistic version of Victorian Aboriginal settlement where Aboriginal people did not need to wander

---

[73] Threadgold, "Aboriginal Stone Sites and Living Spaces along the Victorian Volcanic Plains: A Modelling System of Incorporated Natural Resources and 'Living Spaces' Determining Non–Nomadic Settlements".

[74] Threadgold, "Aboriginal Stone Sites and Living Spaces along the Victorian Volcanic Plains: A Modelling System of Incorporated Natural Resources and 'Living Spaces' Determining Non–Nomadic Settlements".

[75] Lane, "The Sheltered Cup".

[76] Lane, "The Sheltered Cup"; Lane, "Jerringot Living Station: Wathaurong Territory No23.".

[77] Lane, "The Sheltered Cup".

[78] Lane, "The Sheltered Cup", 4.

[79] Lane, "The Sheltered Cup", 1–2.

[80] Lane, "The Sheltered Cup".

[81] Lane, "Jerringot Living Station: Wathaurong Territory No23.", 1.

[82] Lane, "Jerringot Living Station: Wathaurong Territory No23."

the district in search of food.[83] The immediate sites of Kardinia Creek and Jerringot were successful long-term living spaces, and the surrounding landscapes and regional environments were integral contributing factors.

At times archaeologists and heritage advisors, as recorders of Aboriginal sites in Victoria, only recognised limited aspects of a living space, mostly associated with tangible objects or a site, such as an artefact or stone arrangement, object or place. However, the broader perspective of a living space must be acknowledged and as I have proposed, be inclusive of the following:

- natural geological landforms, waterways, landscapes and resources
- aboriginal modification of natural resources for utilisation as living spaces
- housing, food and water sources, aquacultural and agricultural infrastructure and industry, cultural participation, and ceremonial and meeting grounds.

The notion of living spaces contributes to an analytical contemporary view that Victorian Aboriginal people were living on the land in a settlement situation, whether transient, semi-permanent or permanent. It is important not to confuse transient with nomadic, as nomadic presents movement of people in a somewhat sporadic or unplanned manner and this was not the case in Victoria.[84] Settlement typology varies throughout Victoria from the coast to mountains, valleys, the Mallee, major river systems such as the Murray River, lagoons and volcanic landscapes. Housing is naturally adapted to sheltered spaces, formed by dips and ridges shaped within the landscape. Fresh water is essential, and the proximity of game or water life and plant resources provide family groups with reliable and diverse food sources. Riverbeds, lake foreshores and lunettes provide for ovens. Close vantage points allow for protection with the ability to watch for approaching friends or foes. Living spaces extend well beyond basic supplies to survive; these are complex and intrinsic layered spaces.

Mapping Traditional Owner knowledge and information from colonial settler histories produces knowledge and understandings of cultural landscapes that contain separate and distinct inscriptions that nonetheless are integral to a place-specific historiography. Traditional Owner living spaces co-existed as parallel places, practices, realities and histories, and continued to be maintained during British colonial settler settlement construction, especially in the period 1832–80s. Developing a framework that examines the parallel existence of Aboriginal and colonial settler practices sets the scene for developing a perspective of cultural connection between the land and people. It gives rise to the recognition of spatial living histories, and people and place and Country connection that continue to shape Djilang.

---

[83] Lane, "The Sheltered Cup".
[84] Doolan, "Aboriginal Concept of Boundary".

CHAPTER 3

DIALOGUES BETWEEN SPACE AND TIME:
VACANTGEELONG'S WORK ON INDUSTRIAL VACANCY

MIRJANA LOZANOVSKA, DAVID BEYNON AND DIEGO FULLAONDO

Industrial buildings, workers and heritage

The global phenomenon of deindustrialisation has been characterised by declining regional economies, vacant buildings and increasing unemployment in manufacturing sectors.[1] In Australia, major cities accommodate the rapid growth of urban populations within an escalating expansion of outer suburbs and increasing density of inner city areas.[2] However, regional cities and towns often find themselves dealing with a parallel and simultaneous population depletion and shrinkage, needing to adjust to less stable futures, and questioning their identities, particularly where such identities have been based on manufacturing industries.[3] In the face of declining regional economies, ageing demographics, a rise in derelict and inactivated buildings, increasing unemployment in manufacturing and the need for a reassessment of skills, trades and cultural perceptions, many regional cities and towns are in the position of needing to revitalise and reinvent their identities to remain viable.[4]

More particularly, industrial buildings worldwide are coming under ever increasing pressure from urban growth, new order economics and environmental concerns. In the case of Geelong, much of its northern industrial zone lies on prime waterfront real estate. With such forces bearing implicitly or explicitly upon them, architectural debates and responses to this situation (when drawn away from demolition and new construction) have centred on approaches and processes of adaptive reuse of existing buildings based on a developing sense of the value of built heritage as an element of cultural heritage. The built environment is an integral part of a spatially constructed community, making the history of buildings also a history of places and cultural identity. David Howard argues that 'On the one hand, buildings exist as stand-alone artifacts, and on the other, they are artifacts that express the deep meanings, aspirations, and social order of a culture.'[5]

This chapter rethinks the value of industrial buildings at the point of the departure of their functional purpose – characterised through vacancy – by examining the conceptual framing and works of the VacantGeelong project developed since its beginning in 2015.[6]

The view from the fourth floor of the School of Architecture and Built Environment at Geelong's Deakin University Waterfront campus, a red brick wool store adapted for a new tertiary institution (see Chapter 9, "The Place of Heritage in a Reimagined Geelong"), looks over Corio Bay to the northern suburbs of Norlane, Corio and North Geelong, home to vast industrial landscapes interfacing with the coastal edge of Corio Bay, including the Ford Motor Company complex, the gigantic grain silos and the moonscape of the oil refinery.

The habitual observation of this view shifted from an appreciation of the picturesque silhouette to a more active "looking again", as Kaja Silverman has argued, as a way of looking that sees industry's vast scale and its siting at the northern waterfront of Geelong.[7] Knowing of the imminent final stages of deindustrialisation, looking again was also a

---

[1] Carl Grodach and Renia Ehrenfeucht, *Urban Revitalization. Remaking Cities in a Changing World* (Basingstoke: Taylor & Francis Group, 2016).

[2] Seamus O'Hanlon (ed), *City Life: The New Urban Australia* (Sydney: NewSouth Publishing, 2018).

[3] Erik Eklund, *Steel Town: The Making and Breaking of Port Kembla* (Melbourne: Melbourne University Press, 2003).

[4] Julianne Schultz, *Steel City Blues* (Ringwood, Vic: Penguin Books, 1985).

[5] David Howard, *The Culture of Building* (New York: Oxford University Press, 2006), 95.

[6] Deakin University VacantGeelong research team: 2016 Mirjana Lozanovska, David Beynon, Cameron Bishop, Diego Fullaondo; 2017 +Anne Scott Wilson; 2018 + Ciro Márquez, Akari Nakai Kidd. Ciro Márquez also developed a studio brief for the reuse of industrial architecture focusing on cross-programming. VacantGeelong artists: Bindi Cole Chocka, Sarah Duyshart, Alexander Hamilton, Merinda Kelly, Robert Mihajlovski, Amanda Shone. Deakin University VacantGeelong thesis supervision team and students (2016–2017): Mirjana Lozanovska, David Beynon, Cameron Bishop, Diego Fullaondo, Anne Wilson, Cristina Garduño Freeman, Robert Fuller, Angela Kreutz, Akari Nakai Kidd, Ciro Márquez, Chayakan Siamphukdee, Colin Van den Brandt, Aditya Godbole, Hazirah Hanisah Harun, Jonathan Tan Ern Wei, Arshadl Ibad Mohd Faudzi, Angelina Chan Yee Ching, Megan Jones, Michael Faulks, Evelyn Jing Pan, Daniel Out, Lucas Sánchez Arlt, Mark McKinlay, Bronte French, Katsuto Ikeda.

[7] Kaja Silverman, *The Threshold of the Visible World* (New York: Routledge, 1996).

call to note its presence; an existential call that opens onto alternative perceptions of what is seen and what is unseen.[8] Such a *looking again* speaks directly to architecture's methods of observation and to interdisciplinary dialogues.[9] Retrospective histories can smooth things over into an order that does not acknowledge the undecidedness and incidental nature of how projects evolve. A meeting with the effervescent, formidable Kaz Paton – Manager of the Arts & Culture Department of the City of Greater Geelong – was followed by meetings between individual Deakin academics, who were to become researchers and creative participants in the VacantGeelong project, culminating in the submission of a successful grant application to local government which provided the basis to develop collaborative work.[10]

Figure 3.1 Panoramic photograph of industrial landscape taken from the abandoned Powerhouse building in Geelong. Top: view to Corio Bay and CBD, Geelong. Bottom: view northwards to industry and surrounding suburbs. VacantGeelong team with Victorian State Minister for the Arts, 2017.

Intensive experimentation and development of creative research methods rather than strategic alignment influenced and sustained VacantGeelong's longer program of architectural teaching practices, local community engagement, creative works with commissioned artists, and participation in Geelong's core cultural events. This included ethnographic research with past Ford workers from the Macedonian community in Geelong, many of whom arrived as part of Australia's nation-building campaign. VacantGeelong's agenda has been to confront the difficult histories of industry. Through interviews, we were able to obtain oral histories by participants who are hard to get to and are therefore avoided in many studies.[12] The trans-national realities of immigrant worker communities brought a societal gravitas to creative briefs. A series of works were consequently developed – including film and video, artworks, installations, exhibitions, workshops/seminars/symposia, student theses, architectural design and site activation, as well as publications – drawing on the capacity of art to drive alternative visions of ex-industrial architecture and sites, beyond their usual pragmatic utilisation and the negative perceptions commonly ascribed to them.

This body of work provides the basis from which this chapter explores the concepts and meanings of vacancy. Two emergent theories are developed around *embodied memory* and *emotional heritage*. Further, the chapter is grounded in exploring the role of non-monumental architecture, and how looking at buildings with these aspects in mind can alter perceptions of them as "eyesores" once they have outlasted their functional purpose. Core to the concept of embodied memory is the idea that architecture – its walls, spatial order, aesthetic, scale, light, sensory textures, sounds and colour – is inscribed and traced through the memory, histories and narrations of inhabitation, engaging with the ancient tension of the architectural canon about whether architecture is a thing or a story about a thing.[13] The idea of embodied memory in this context can be compared with embodied energy which is understood as a means of evaluating the environmental cost of a building. We propose that buildings have an equivalent embeddedness of socio-spatial histories and practices within their architectural materiality. The concept of emotional heritage draws on the proposition by architects Flores and Prats at their installation at the 2023 Venice Architecture Biennale, where they proposed that people are not the only

---

[8] Ciro Márquez developed a design studio brief for the reuse of industrial architecture focusing on cross-programming (2017–2019). Mirjana Lozanovska generated studios around hybrid programmes, housing, community facilities (kindergartens) and soap factories at the American University of Beirut (1995–1998).

[9] Mirjana Lozanovska, *Migrant Housing: Architecture, Dwelling, Migration* (London: Routledge, 2019); Suzanne Hall, *The Migrant's Paradox: Street Livelihoods and Marginal Citizenship in Britain* (Minneapolis: University of Minnesota Press, 2021).

[10] Mirjana Lozanovska, *Vacant Geelong: Rethink, Reinterpret and Revision the Way we Inhabit the City* (Community Arts grant, City of Greater Geelong, 2015).

[12] Ian Burnley, *The Impact of Immigration on Australia: A Demographic Approach* (Melbourne: Oxford University Press, 2001).

[13] Gülsüm Baydar, "The Cultural Burden of Architecture," *Journal of Architectural Education* 57, no. 4 (May, 2004): 19–27.

holders of memory, and that buildings and architecture are imbued with the memories of a place.[14] Flores and Prats proposed that architects are the readers of the memories held in buildings. To this proposal, we add the memories of people about buildings.[15] This definition of "emotional heritage" is distinct from Laurajane Smith's focus on the emotional experience and engagement of visitors with museums and heritage sites.[16] Smith's approach emerges from the discipline of heritage, but we ask whether an architectural approach can bring another dimension to heritage, not as experienced in a museum but as the experience of heritage in ex- and post-industrial landscapes.

Vacancy – a space-time concept and its architectural positioning

Figure 3.2 shows a 1925 photograph of the newly assembled Ford Motor Company manufacturing complex in Geelong in an empty field. In the following decades, Geelong would evolve around this Ford complex as it had previously done around the shipping industry, the wool mills, paper mills and timber sawmills. While the area of greater Geelong remained supported by agricultural industries throughout the twentieth century, it was manufacturing industries that shaped Geelong as a city, and the departure of these industries between 2008 and 2017 mark a significant phase in Geelong's evolving history.

Figure 3.2 Aerial photograph of the Ford site in Geelong prior to its construction, 1925.

The closures of the Ford factory and other industries have variously resulted in deteriorating sites, the demolition of vacant buildings, and often the expedient replacement of industrial buildings with new developments that are unresponsive to the communities that live and operate in proximity to industrial sites. Reacting to Geelong's decline in key manufacturing sectors over the past twenty to thirty years, there have been numerous attempts to redirect the city towards different economic, social and cultural bases (see Chapter 1). Beyond incremental change, there have also been desires for a major catalyst to turn the city's fortunes around, including attempts to secure or imitate a Guggenheim in

---

[14] Ricardo Flores and Eva Prats, *Emotional Heritage*, 2023 (installation, *18th International Architecture Exhibition – La Biennale di Venezia*, in Section, Dangerous Liaisons, Corderie, Arsenale, Venice, 2023, visited August 2023); See also Ricardo Flores and Eva Prats, "Emotional Heritage", Designboom, https://www.designboom.com/architecture/flores-prats-emotional-heritage-installation-arsenale-venice-architecture-biennale-05-25-2023/ May 2023.
[15] VacantGeelong undertook an ethnographic study of past Ford workers of the Macedonian community in Geelong.
[16] Laurajane Smith, *Emotional Heritage: Visitor Engagement at Museums and Heritage Sites* (Abingdon, Oxon; New York, NY: Routledge, 2021).

Geelong.[17] An approach to harnessing Geelong's cultural economy briefly turned its attention to the ex-industrial buildings. However, except for the revitalisation of the port and passenger terminal to serve the *Spirit of Tasmania*, the urban strategies of Geelong UNESCO City of Design have not yet adequately addressed the city's industrial zones (see Chapter 4), or the issue that Geelong's working communities negatively perceive the departure of industry.

The VacantGeelong project has called for a pause in the expedient development or demolition of ex-industrial space to bring to the fore artistic processes on the reactivation of memory and erasure. Such a pause can be understood as a space-time gap between deindustrialisation and the vision of a post-industrial city, between the negativity linked to an economic crisis and unemployment, and a bright new future. The post-industrial city, taken up by strategic planning and urban design professions, presents a future-oriented rather than backward looking time, and hence creates visions that use existing industrial infrastructure as a picturesque backdrop, if at all. If the city has been long dependent on industry, new urban strategies and policies quickly and actively seek to move towards a new city with a new identity.

Reflecting on the space-time realities of change, this chapter takes a different position. Rather than holding onto the past too nostalgically or speculating on the new too expediently, the VacantGeelong works explore what it means to be vacant, to have vacancy, to be vacated, and what vacancy as idea, as positioning and as poetics may offer in the present moments of change. The focus of VacantGeelong is not whether cities have transitioned towards a cultural rather than a manufacturing or industrial base, although this is part of the context. Instead, the project takes its cue from uncoupling the binary of deindustrialisation and the post-industrial city, moving from a reactive and compressive space-time to a philosophical pause, or a "non-time" to counter the familiar and excessive subdivision of time into minutes, seconds and milliseconds.[18] This space-time interval or gap is not only temporary or in-between, but an actual existential presence. The pause is not passive in terms of "waiting" but latent with hidden activity.[19] The pause VacantGeelong has called for invites observation, followed by intellectual and creative practices of reflection on the physical presence of industrial architecture and the role it plays in a city and community.

Researchers in non-architectural (as well as architectural) disciplines too easily forget, overlook or marginalise the physical remainders and reminders of industrial pasts.[20] These are concrete manifestations, empirical objects, structures, artefacts, that – unlike industries – do not depart, do not go "off-shore", do not withdraw into the interiors of houses (like many of the workers) or dissolve into the soil (like contaminants).[21] The binary approach bracketed by the crisis of deindustrialisation and the aspirational momentum towards sparkling new post-industrial futures, squeeze the reality of the architecture and landscapes of industry out of the picture. Meanwhile, past workers and their communities are forgotten or worse, relegated to a difficult history of industrial labour that is avoided in urban visions and heritage agendas, while industrial structures are transformed beyond recognition or meet their unfortunate destiny of demolition.[22]

In the 1925 photograph (see Figure 3.2), "vacancy" appears as an empty landscape surrounding the Ford factory building site. Ford, an American international car manufacturing company, negotiated that a very long jetty be built for this facility and the "building" which arrived by ship in prefabricated components was installed and assembled on the site.[23] The Ford plant served to reinforce a manufacturing industrial future.[24] Being built on lands which had been irreversibly altered, the emptiness of the landscape in the photograph masks British colonialisation and British colonial settler strategies, including – as Jessie Mitchell puts it – how 'Aboriginal people had to be there, in order to vanish, in order to prove the legitimacy of colonial Victoria'.[25] By 1880 colonial settler practices had destroyed the lands that the Wadawurrung people inhabited, cared for and maintained for tens of thousands of years (see Chapters 2 and 10). Emerging global theories on climate colonialism examine those very areas located within cities undergoing

---

[17] "Geelong still Hoping for Bilbao Effect", *The Age*, September 15, https://www.theage.com.au/entertainment/art-and-design/geelong-still-hoping-for-bilbao-effect-20020915-gdul7g.html.

[18] Bernard Stiegler, *Acting out*, trans. D. Barison, D. Ross and P. Crogan (California: Stanford University Press, 2009).

[19] Julia Kristeva, "Women's Time", trans. Alice Jardine and Harry Blake, *Signs* 7 no. 1 (The University of Chicago Press, Autumn 1981): 13–35.

[20] Anoma Pieris and Mirjana Lozanovska (eds), "Industry + Architecture", *Fabrications: Journal of the Society of Architectural Historians, Australia and New Zealand*, Special Issue 2 no. 29 (Routledge, June 2019).

[21] Stefan Berger, "Pre-conditions for the Making of an Industrial Past: Comparative Perspectives," in Stefan Berger (ed), *Constructing Industrial Pasts: Heritage, Historical Culture and Identity in Regions Undergoing Structural Economic Transformation* (Oxford, UK: Berghan Books, 2020), 1–26.

[22] Two projects exploring industrial or vacant architecture at the Venice Architecture Biennale 2010 were influential in the conceptualisation of the VacantGeelong project (including the title). "Factory Russia" (town of Vishny Volochok with a film exploring time lapse between memories and realities of two past workers), Russian Pavilion, *Venice Architecture Biennale 2010*, visited June 2010, https://www.dezeen.com/2010/09/01/the-russia-factory-by-sergei-tchoban-pavel-khoroshilov-and-grigory-revzin/ (visited September 2016). "Vacant NL" (Model and Atlas documentation of 10,000 vacant buildings), Dutch Pavilion, RAAAF, *Venice Architecture Biennale* 2010, visited June 2010.

[23] "Ford Motor Works: Geelong Site Chosen: Factory for Body Building: Two Companies to be formed", *The Argus*, 1925.

[24] Steven Tolliday and Jonathan Zeitlin, *Between Fordism and Flexibility: The Automobile Industry and Its Workers* (Oxford: Berg 1986); Norm Darwin, *The History of Ford in Australia*, (Newstead, Vic.: Eddie Ford Publications 1986), 42.

[25] Jessie Mitchell, "The Galling Yoke of Slavery: Race and Separation in Colonial Port Phillip", *Journal of Australian Studies* 33, no. 2 (2009): 125–37; 135.

deindustrialisation, decline and devaluation, and populated by marginalised, minority and low-income communities.[26] Analysis from the United States illustrates that defining sites as "waste", brownfield, or "underutilised" invites exploitation by developers that 'reap the rewards of reusing inexpensive, urban contaminated waste landscapes and enjoy limited liability and high resale value'.[27] Geographer Shiloh Krupar has argued that contaminated land mapping (using GIS) often 'catalyses a violent feedback loop of land *re*possession as dispossession', extending historical understanding of land as wilderness or in the Australian case as *terra nullius*.[28]

An important aspect of Australia's post-war manufacturing modernisation was that it was contingent on non-Anglophone immigration, and this is critical to understanding the spatial and cultural character of Geelong. In the 1960s, at the height of Geelong's manufacturing era, thousands of non-Anglophone immigrants were directed to labour in its major industries – Ford was a major focus for this development, as were Alcoa Aluminium, Pilkington Glass, cement works, shipping industry facilities, an oil refinery and seven woollen mills, along with numerous carpet manufacturing and biscuit factories.[29] The focus on the Ford factory in Geelong by the VacantGeelong team drew on ethnographic work of past Ford workers from Geelong's Macedonian community with the aim of building a picture of the multiple makers of history and the multiple realities of histories.[30] By the 1960s the plant was honing its methods in what has been described as a post-Fordist manner (moving from mass production to specialisation, and from constancy of production to flexibility in response to the changing demands of consumerism).[31] However, the post-war era was also the time when new immigrants and refugees became critical resources for this new assembly process. This mechanisation broadened the supplies of labour, allowing the factory to conduct non-stop manufacturing, but it also broadened the culture of the community of factory workers. In Geelong, this meant the arrival and settlement of large numbers of new migrants and their families, many specifically to take up employment at the Ford plant. The presence of Geelong's Macedonian community is almost entirely due to the employment offered by Ford.

However, the present situation is that Ford and other industries have disappeared or have been severely reduced in size as employers in Geelong, aligning with statistics that have shown the steep decline in employment in the industrial sector in Australia from over 25% in the mid 1960s to only 8% in 2015. VacantGeelong projects have explored each of these aspects of Geelong's industrial legacy as represented by sites of former or extant factories, warehouses and other infrastructures through both analytical and creative means. First, a series of VacantGeelong projects mapped the extent of vacant industrial buildings in Geelong.[32] Mapping vacancy comprised dividing Geelong into four sections to provide coherent and manageable zones in which the research could be undertaken. These four sections were based on topography, infrastructure, zoning and the identified concentrations of commercial and industrial buildings. A variety of research methods were used to "quantify" the vacancies, including exploring existing archives, reviewing information from the City of Greater Geelong Council, utilities and real estate agents, and – most importantly – site visits and systematic direct observation. This systematic observation proved to be the most reliable method from which to construct a comprehensive database (see also Chapter 8).

Key indicators were used to detect vacant buildings and ensure consistent data:

- Building physical attributes: presence of signage such as an advertisement for lease/rent, broken windows or other signs of forced entry, barricades across openings, condition of walls and structure (chipped/discoloured/graffiti/posters), overgrown vegetation, poor paving and/or driveway condition, presence of rubbish or dumping in vicinity, and general lack of maintenance.
- Building activity: human presence or not during normal operating hours, vehicles present (parked or mobile), lights in use, extractors, fans or appliances active, possible noise, rolling electricity meters.

From these complex and nuanced methods, their vacancy "status" evolved using the following definitions:

- Vacant: indicating an entirely empty building

---

[26] Shiloh Krupar, "Brownfields as Climate Colonialism: Land Reuse and Development Divides" in N. Bobic and F. Haghighi (eds), *The Routledge Handbook of Architecture, Urban Space and Politics, Volume 1: Violence, Spectacle and Data*, (Routledge: New York, 2023), 446–62.

[27] Allen Berger, *Drosscape: Wasting Land in Urban America* (New York: Princeton Architectural Press, 2006), 74 (quoted in Krupar, 449).

[28] Krupar, "Brownfields as Climate Colonialism: Land Reuse and Development Divides", 447; See also *VACANTCitY 1000 yearsBackForward*, 2020, installation at Centre Point Arcade, Geelong. VacantGeelong team: Mirjana Lozanovska, Cameron Bishop, Anne Wilson (with assistance Beverlea Low and Julie Pham), https://architecturevacancylab.deakin.edu.au/vacantcity-1000-years-backforward-exhibition/.

[29] Cecil P. Billot, "Geelong: A Bibliography of Victoria's Second City" (Thesis submitted for Fellowship of the Library Association, 1968).

[30] Esra Akcan, *Open Architecture: Migration, Citizenship and Urban Renewal in Berlin Kreuzberg by IBA 1984–87* (Basel: Birkhauser, 2018).

[31] Bernard, Mitchell, "Post-Fordism and Global Restructuring", in Richard Stubbs and Geoffrey R. D. Underhill (eds), *Political Economy and the Changing Global Order* (Canada: Oxford University Press, 2000).

[32] Diego Fullaondo and Robert Fuller, "Mapping the Traces of De-industrialisation in the Built Fabric of a Regional City of Australia" (unpublished paper, based on 2016 and 2017 research developed by a team of students and supervisors, led by Fullaondo, 2017).

- Part vacant: indicating a semi-vacant building that may have separate units, on one floor or several floors, that were partially vacant
- Refurbishing: indicating a building currently undergoing construction/renovation work
- Reused: indicating a building of historical or industrial significance currently being reused for a program/use other than its original industrial activity

Figure 3.3 Lucas Sancehz Arlt, "Industrial Typologies in Geelong". Unpublished Master of Architecture thesis, Deakin University, 2017, supervisor Diego Fullaondo. First presented at *Iconic Industry* exhibition, National Wool Museum, Geelong, 2017.

The aim of this research was to identify and catalogue the vacant industrial building stock in Geelong's CBD and adjacent industrial areas as a quantifiable body of evidence (see also Chapter 8, "Mapping Industrial Vacancy").[33]

One iteration of the collaboration between art and architecture was site-specific activation. Sites were activated through workshops, film screening and exhibition. Conscious that these activities occur somewhere, the VacantGeelong team foregrounded the role of architecture in staging and setting the scene, and to bring attention to industrial architecture and landscape.[34] VacantGeelong's Open Studio, located in a small warehouse building close to the North Geelong train station amongst warehouses and industries, generated a direct and immersive interface with the industrial zone of Geelong, and provided a space and the means to focus artistic processes on the reactivation of memory and erasure. In the winter of 2017, VacantGeelong artist Robert Mihajlovski spent three months working at the studio site, combining daily walks with observation and sketching. Mihajlovski's flickering colourful light on metal paintings or the darker nostalgia in the black and white woodcut prints speak of the present as past (see Figure 3.4 in the colour plate section). VacantGeelong artist Amanda Shone's installation using building materials – sisalation (silvery shiny on one side, blue on the other) – was hung in radial fashion from the ceiling (see Chapter 13, "*VACANTCitY*"), inspired by the exuberant interior of the Macedonian Orthodox Community Centre. Many past Ford workers of the Macedonian community participated at the Open Studio, as did Deakin final year architecture students. Vacant buildings in the industrial zone stirred a flurry of memories. Past Ford workers were interviewed by journalist Abby Durham for the nation-wide SBS television news at the Open Studio (see Figure 3.5).[35] The Open Studio discussions provided the local creative community with an opportunity to reflect on artworks-in-process – videos, drawings, sounds, objects, prints and

---

[33] Fullaondo and Fuller, "Mapping the Traces of De-industrialisation in the Built Fabric of a Regional City of Australia".

[34] Eliza Sum, "Ford Thinking on our Historic Plant", *Geelong Advertiser*, July 27, 2016. A media photographic session with the Minister of Arts (Victoria) took place on the roof of the magnificent Powerhouse, a large, abandoned building that commands panoramic views over Corio Bay and towards to the CBD of Geelong.

[35] Abby Dinham, "After the Factory: Ford's Long-Serving Macedonian Workers Honoured in Geelong Art Project", *SBS World News*, published May 28 2017, https://www.sbs.com.au/news/article/after-the-factory-fords-long-serving-macedonian-workers-honoured-in-geelong-art-project/1ynnirrz6.

installation. These sessions also drew in local media production, the Telematic Café group, led by Marita Batna, who interviewed participants, researchers and students and disseminated a programme onto a digital media platform.[36]

A more direct architectural design site-activation was implemented at the galleries of the National Wool Museum (NWM), where the exhibition *Iconic Industry* was shown.[37] Existing gallery spaces comprised educational and informative systems of installed panels with green pin-up fabric. The VacantGeelong architectural team members considered that the panel system, while at times showcasing the machinery of wool manufacturing, covered and concealed the former materiality of the industrial building – of the wool museum - especially of the perimeter walls and its fenestration. Architectural design researchers Fullaondo, Lozanovska and Beynon proposed to strip the interior and reveal the industrial character and developed a new model for the gallery space, both revealing the existing wool mill – a bluestone building which had been a wool store since the late nineteenth century – and expanding the spatial scope by replacing the panel system with a new system of exhibition and lighting. This integrated approach of "content" and "architecture" forged a stronger design force and made the gallery space a more active industrial setting for the works of artists and student.

Figure 3.5 Past Ford workers from the Macedonian community of Geelong participating at the Open Studio in North Geelong. Interview by SBS Television on 28 May 2017.

Within the exhibition, the VacantGeelong artists then developed the results of their immersive experiences in the industrial environments of North Geelong and participation in the project's workshops and events. Extraordinary visions of futures, pasts and parallel present worlds were inscribed onto ordinary industrial sites in the work of Alexander Hamilton. The flickering light on the metal surfaces of industrial architecture was explored by Robert Mihajlovski's joyful choreographies in paint, an optimism of ducts and engineering nonetheless burdened with the title, *The Last Industrial Museum II*. Aboriginal artist Bindi Cole Chocka experimented with an estranged vacancy as a digital boomerang play of the Australian flag on the Ford factory complex and its barbed wire fencing. Seen with the 1925 photograph, these works present an uncanny relationship between the arrival and departure of industry in Geelong.[38]

First presented at the Geelong After Dark festival in May 2017, *Industry Tracks* is a film, an aural–visual composition, developed by the VacantGeelong team, which sought to frame the past, present and possible future of deindustrialisation as soundscape or – to be more specific to its geo-cultural context – an aural trainscape, as industry still provides the gateway to Geelong when travelling from Melbourne by rail.[39] *Industry Tracks* provides an aural–visual experience that evokes the atmosphere, memories and experiences of the rail traveller's journey, its soundbed being the engine noise of a passenger train on its journey to and from Lara on the edge of the City of Greater Geelong, through the industrial northern suburbs of Geelong, to central Geelong Railway Station. This journey, including stops at intermediate stations, takes fourteen minutes and the soundbed unfolds in real time. The visuals (filmed directly through the windows on each side of the train) are first split horizontally in two (the train leaving Lara/Geelong stations) and then further split as the journey proceeds and intensifies before re-merging at its conclusion(s) (see Figure 3.6). Sounds are directly related to the train's physical journey (announcements and whistles as the train leaves its first station) and elements in the passing landscape (the whooshing of gas as the train passes an oil refinery, the squawking of seagulls as Corio Bay is glimpsed). Other sounds evoke the past in both generalised and culturally specific ways. The sounds of actual industries past and present (lathes, drills, etc.) intervene directly as buildings and other infrastructure come into view. For instance, the revving of a Ford car engine can be heard as the train passes the Ford engine plant. More evocatively, excerpts of music and narration from a short film, *Life in Australia: Geelong*, are overlaid at intervals.[40] Lending a more recent cultural specificity to the project are looped segments of Macedonian folk music, aurally connecting the viewed sites to Geelong's Macedonian community – a large part of which is connected to the Ford plant and other industries along the train's route. The film was projected onto a screen from the civility of the urban space of

---

[36] Robert Mihajlovski and David Beynon, "Labour of Making", interview by Marita Batna, *Telematics* (Open Studio, VacantGeelong, 2017).

[37] See catalogue Mirjana Lozanovska, David Beynon, Cameron Bishop, Diego Fullaondo and Ann Scott Wilson (eds), *Iconic Industry*: *Vacant Geelong*, National Wool Museum (Geelong: Deakin University, 2017), https://architecturevacancylab.deakin.edu.au/. Catalogue of exhibition.

[38] Lozanovska et al. (eds), *Iconic Industry*: *Vacant Geelong.*

[39] David Beynon, Mirjana Lozanovska, Diego Fullaondo, Cameron Bishop, and Ann Scott Wilson (eds), *Industry Tracks,* 2017, first presented at Geelong After Dark, Beavers Lane, Geelong, *https://www.youtube.com/watch?v=0jzUfHFEN6A&t=11s.*

[40] *Life in Australia: Geelong*, directed by Antonio Colacino (1966: The Commonwealth Film Unit, Department of Immigration).

Geelong's CBD towards the real image of distant industrial structures on the edge of north Geelong, producing a viewing device between filmic representation and reality. In this contextualisation, the screening evoked an ambitious public performance, and the aural power of place, time and industry of the *Symphony of Sirens* by the composer Arseny Avraamov [*Arseny Mikhaylovich Krasnokutsky*].[41] Beyond the direct resonances between industrial contexts across time and space, constructivist conceptualisations of the importance of sound to architectonic space also triggered resonances between the industrial architectural landscape represented in the film and the "real" industrial landscape on the northern edge of Corio Bay.

Figure 3.6 *Industry Tracks*, 2017, audio-visual production by VacantGeelong team: David Beynon, Mirjana Lozanovska, Diego Fullaondo and Anne Wilson. First presented at *Geelong After Dark 2017*, Brearley Lane, Waterfront Campus, Deakin University, Geelong.

Embodied memory and emotional heritage

No space is ever vacant – it's whether or not it is recognised as such. Or whether the people or animals occupying that space are recognised. Once it is labelled as vacant it is legitimised for capitalism.[42]

These works demonstrate the ways in which vacancy can mask multiple and contested histories and continue exploitative land practices that accelerate dispossession and inequality. They also illustrate how artistic works, installations and projections in various media, can extend time or create a pause that can reactivate memory and bring attention to industrial architecture and those difficult histories on which industrial cities have been founded. When buildings are vacated, abandoned, or allowed to deteriorate, the sensory properties of their built forms, shapes, structures and materials induce a mnemonic quality. While most obvious in the visual dimension, the smell of a building, the touch of its surfaces and the acoustic properties of its spaces all contribute to memory. For instance, the sound of revving a Ford car engine heard in north Geelong may have a general resonance for casual passers-by, but for ex-workers at the Ford factory (or Ford aficionados) its precise roar could be identified as that of a Falcon XR8, the type last manufactured at the plant. Memory always exists in relation to the temporal and the spatial, both of which are anchored in place. Philosopher Jeff Malpas has noted that when spatial content is removed, memory becomes disconnected, and part of its meaning is lost.[43] In contrast the space that is framed by a building provides a fixed point in space and a reference point for times around which memories can gather.

---

41 Arseny Avraamov, *Symphony of Sirens* (in Russian "Sinfoniya Gudkov", first performed in Baku, 1922.
42 Susan Ballard, "Panel discussion" (Vacancy and Preservation: The Architecture of the Post-Industrial City Symposium, National Wool Museum, Geelong, 2017).
43 Jeff Malpas, "Putting Space in Place: Relational Geography and Philosophical Topography", *Planning and Environment D: Space and Society* 30 (2012): 226–42.

Figure 3.7 Ford building, interior of production zone prior to closure, April 2016.

The Ford building's architecture contains direct references to its former use, and the remnants of the manufacturing process within its walls also present a critical part of its embodied memory.[44] The central role of immigrant labour is signified by a mural at the reception entry of the Ford factory, illustrating at least forty-eight origin countries of the workers at Ford (see Figure 3.8). The former Ford workers verbally acknowledge their pride in having worked at Ford and mention how they still love passing the building.[45] However, many are now elderly - so is this relationship between physical and spatial qualities and these former workers ephemeral or enduring? If they built a culture around their work at Ford and other industries in Geelong, what happens now those industries are no longer there? Apart from the reality that not all will be able to find alternative employment, there is also the question of how their identity up until the closure of the plant was so closely identified with their work. Probed further to describe and detail their work, the embodied *and* emotional memories of former Ford workers are evident.[46] On her first day of employment at Ford, Nada Božinska was given the "hardest job", and all the participants cringe knowingly about what this might mean, but as it was in the past, they laugh. Božinska talked about the *smell* and was able to describe an inventory of oil odours – anti-rust oil, black oil, spot welding burnt oil and smoking oil, and the machine shop smell of petroleum. All the participants remembered the early days of difficult manual labour, strenuous conditions and no training, no induction and no safety protection. Many recall the noise was loud and constant. A particularly piercing noise was heard in the engine section. The physical strain was amplified if the first person on the conveyor belt was super quick because it meant everyone had to keep pace. In the early days all the workers caught the bus. Once enough funds were saved, for instance, and Ilo Najdovski became the proud owner of a 1975 V8 Mustang from America and a V8 Ford Falcon, carpooling workers to the site became a possibility.[47]

---

[44] Mirjana Lozanovska and Akari Nakai Kidd, "'Vacant Geelong' and its lingering industrial architecture", *Architecture Research Quarterly (ARQ)* 24, no. 4 (2020): 353–68.

[45] VacantGeelong, "Past Ford Workers Geelong", ethnographic project with Macedonian community participants, the Macedonian Cultural Centre, Geelong, 2017. Participants were supported by the Macedonian Pensioners Club, Geelong.

[46] Participants spoke in English and Macedonian.

[47] VacantGeelong, "Past Ford Workers Geelong".

Figure 3.8 Wall mural "flags" of worker origins, reception area of Ford building, April 2016.

A broader question is how is memory, as well as history, embodied in buildings? Related to this is the question of how such memories are affected by changes to buildings, especially when they have outlived their original purpose. Built heritage can be considered to comprise two inseparable dimensions or components: the physical building and its social/cultural contexts.[48] The identity of a building as a place relies on both a physical site, space and form combined with the people who use, interact with and inhabit it. This usage, interaction and inhabitation has its own history, intertwined with that of the physical/spatial structure, and both have wider geographic as well as temporal contexts. Therefore, the idea of a building as an embodiment of heritage must be considered in terms of this interaction on and beyond its site. Once empty, what is beyond becomes what is present, most immediately in the memories of those who once used the building, and more generally in the community and culture that the building's purpose once catalysed. Its adaptive reuse cannot be a neutral process.

Very few industrial buildings in Geelong are state heritage-listed, though numerous examples exist from every stage of the city's history, and the most recent ex-industrial structures represent new challenges in the evaluation of architectural heritage.[49] The industrial built environment has had a fundamental role in making Geelong's culture, and so an emotional response to the past is contained within the buildings. Industrial heritage, like other forms of heritage, comprises of two irreplaceable dimensions or components: the physical (building) and the social (people), and the challenge when dealing with empty industrial buildings is to make evident the strong bonds and connections that derive from their history of occupancy through individual and collective stories of workers and communities in and around them.[50] In *Buildings Must Die*, Cairns and Jacobs propose that preservation be considered through a dual matrix of *matter* – the materiality of the building, site, landscape – in conjunction with *mattering* – what matters about it.[51] Preservation in this sense is about labouring over what matters before it is neglected, erased or superseded. In *Constructing Industrial Pasts*, Stefan Berger argues that the term "dirty industry" extends meaning beyond the environmental measure of carbon concentration, air, water and earth pollutants, and environmental damage, to an industrial and labour history.[52] Dirty industry is entangled with a dark history of exploitative management of workers that the powerful elite of industry would like to erase; it is the "difficult histories" of labour and the exploitation of people that are subjected to practices of forgetting and erasure. Berger links the environmental "dirty" of industry with the moral "dirty" of difficult histories: 'Deindustrialisation has threatened, in particular, working-class communities with poverty, marginalisation and a sense of being thrown onto the garbage heap of history'.[53] The lack of attention to industrial heritage illustrates a reluctance to engage with difficult histories, despite their pivotal significance for a town,

---

[48] Paz Pozo and Benito Gonzales, "Industrial Heritage and Place Identity in Spain: From Monuments to Landscapes", *Geographical Review* 102, no. 4 (2012): 446–64.

[49] Daniel Out, "Memento Mori" (Master's thesis, Deakin University, 2017); David Rowe, *About Corayo: a thematic history of Greater Geelong* (City of Greater Geelong, 2021). That said, many have a heritage overlay under the local planning scheme.

[50] Benito del Pozo and Pablo Gonzáles, "Industrial Heritage and Place Identity in Spain", *Geographical Review* 102, no. 4 (2012): 446–64.

[51] Stephen Cairns and Jane Jacobs, *Buildings Must Die: A Perverse View of Architecture* (Cambridge, Massachusetts: The MIT Press, 2014).

[52] Stefan Berger, "Pre-conditions for the Making of an Industrial Past", in Stefan Berger (ed), *Constructing Industrial Pasts. Heritage, Historical Culture and Identity in Regions Undergoing Structural Economic Transformation* (Oxford, UK: Berghan Books, 2020), 1–26.

[53] Berger, "Pre-conditions for the Making of an Industrial Past", 10.

city or nation. When heritage practice does engage it is often as alignment to optimistic nationalist narratives, as Berger states, 'The net result was often the silencing of that past, or at least of aspects of that past that could not be presented in triumphalist colours'.[54]

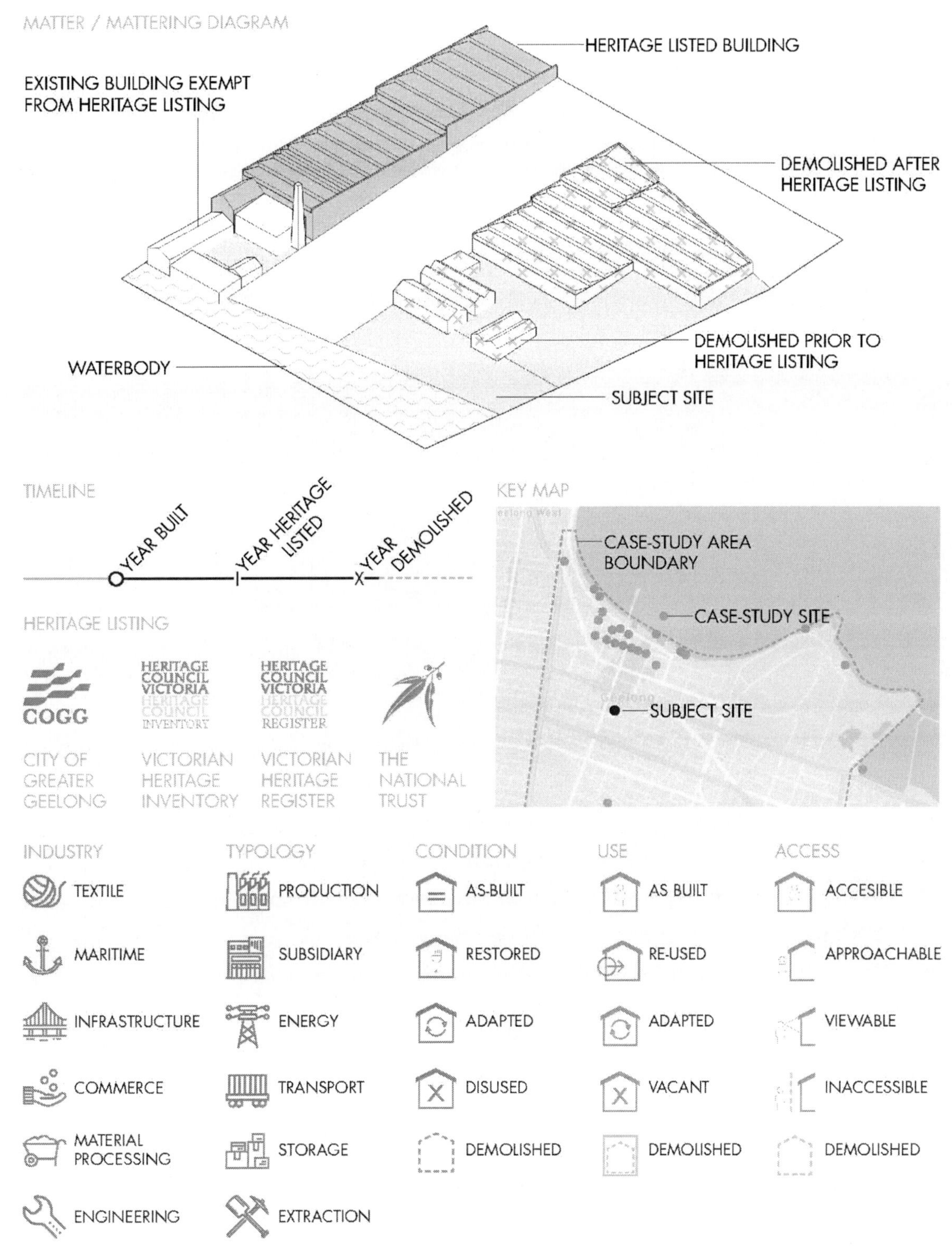

Figure 3.9 Daniel Out, "Memento Mori: An Atlas of Geelong's Industrial Heritage", 2017. Unpublished Master of Architecture thesis, Deakin University, 2017, supervisor Mirjana Lozanovska. Top image shows the method and an application (middle and right).

---

[54] Berger, "Pre-conditions for the Making of an Industrial Past", 5.

The industrial architectural edge of Corio Bay in Geelong may be considered the carrier of an emotional strata of history, inherited by the communities that have worked and lived in and around the industries in Geelong. Rather than presenting a progressive linear narrative of history that conventionally highlights high-profile industrialists, politicians or administrators, attention in this chapter is offered to past industrial workers. Part of the difficulty is in understanding these giant, vast industrial sites and structures; their hangars, chimneys, spheres, ducts and pipes. Beyond the economic value they add to a site (which given the costs of environmental restitution might be negative), what other value do they have? The appeal for architects at least lies in a somewhat picturesque appeal of industrial forms. While some of this appeal might be related to a particularly architectonic appreciation for their expressive yet utterly functional forms (particularly when industrial processes dictate a formal specificity unobtainable when dealing with the vagaries of human inhabitation), there is also a sense of the sublime in industrial structures. This sublimity lies in the genuine sense of awe felt in the presence of not-quite-understood structures of overwhelming magnitude and inexorable purpose. The decay of such structures seems to add to their grandeur. Rust and ruin represent the slow reversion of industrial structures to a nature of greater sublimity than any human creation. However, do these buildings also displace the emotional heritage of the site, the forgotten or disavowed difficult histories of buildings and place? Architectural theorist, Ackbar Abbas argues not all architectural heritage has the 'power to stir memory'.[55] The red brick façade and palm trees of the Ford factory is a "quotation" of Geelong's industrial history, selected from a vast industrial landscape and various typologies of industrial architecture in Geelong. It selectively presents 'the preservation of cultural and urban forms as the preservation of cultural identity'.[56] At another level, this '"history" is no more than decorative' as it masks and effectively obliterates from memory the history of past immigrant workers'.[57]

Figure 3.10 *ORO* installation, 2019. By VacantGeelong team: Mirjana Lozanovska, Anne Wilson, Akari Nakai-Kidd, Cameron Bishop. First presented at *Geelong After Dark 2019*, Town Hall forecourt, Geelong.

---

[55] Ackbar Abbas, "Building Hong Kong: From Migrancy to Disappearance", in Stephen Cairns (ed), *Drifting: Architecture and Migrancy* (Routledge: London, 2004), 129–63.
[56] Abbas, "Building Hong Kong", 134.
[57] Abbas, "Building Hong Kong".

Conclusion

When you take the program out you are left with form. That has a kind of romance.[58]

As a response to an absence of immigrant heritage in Geelong's heritage agenda, one of the later works of the VacantGeelong project was the installation of *ORO* (see Figure 3.10). *ORO* experimented with the inverse practice to that of industrial site activation. It brought a "life-size" projection of past factory workers from their industrial periphery to the Geelong Town Hall forecourt in the cultural centre of town. Their virtual presence was a haunting allegory of their absent history.[59] *ORO* is a round dance where each person holds hands and together the group performs an aligned and 7/8 rhythmic movement. The video projection of the dance of *ORO* animated the interior of one of the three sensory portals, also installed at the site of the forecourt and designed by the VacantGeelong team. Measuring only 2400 × 1200 × 2400, the intimate interior accentuated a corporeally active cultural exchange between life-size dance projection and the audience, who wove their path through its interior. The geo-cultural displacement and in-placement within *ORO* created immersive interiors – made up of past Ford workers (virtual) and attendees (corporeal) of the *Geelong After Dark* festival (2019).

VacantGeelong works highlight what and how heritage can better stir collective memory. Creative processes exploring the embodied memory within the silos, warehouses and chimneys activated the sites to listen to the communities built around them. These works brought about an evolution of new creative methodologies at the crossroads between art and architecture that intersect with theories on the role of architecture in social change. The call for an interval or pause allowed reflection on art and architecture, their relationship with community and vacant industrial buildings, with heritage and with negative perceptions of industrial architecture. The non-measurable and the measurable aspects of vacancy, and the nuances of the meaning of being vacant and vacating, unfolded and extended ways of thinking about time and space. Embodied memory frames ways to perceive both the haunting presence and functional absence of industrial architecture, supplanted by occupation of industrial sites and the theatrical staging of architecture as performative subject rather than passive object; site activations recalibrated the value of vacant industrial architecture.

The decline of industrial towns and cities present a trans-regional and societal challenge. Potential futures have been seen in the vacant buildings and empty spaces of places undergoing such transitions. Geelong's industrial buildings – primarily seen as the raw materials for development and commodification and, ironically in the case of ex-industrial places, as urban ore – might be the physical foundation for revitalisation.[60] The urgency to build a new future for Geelong risks overlooking the emotional heritage and pivotal significance of industrial architecture; and history is strangely absent in urban strategies. We have argued against speedy constructions and propose that engagement with communities – especially past industrial immigrant workers – can bring their emotional narratives to bear upon the buildings, enabling ways to appreciate architecture and its power to stir memory.

---

[58] Paul Katsieris, "Panel discussion" (Vacancy and Preservation: The Architecture of the Post-Industrial City Symposium, National Wool Museum, Geelong, 2017)

[59] Mirjana Lozanovska, Anne Wilson, Cameron Bishop and Akari Nakai Kidd, *ORO*, 2019, first presented at *Geelong After Dark 2019*. See https://architecturevacancylab.deakin.edu.au/oro/. Macedonian participants from Macedonian Social Club: Ilo Najdovski, Venta Pacovska, Cvetko Pacovski, Bogdan Dimitrovski and Ilo Nikolovski.

[60] M. Chusid, "Once is Never Enough", *Building Renovation*, Mar–Apr (1993): 17–20; 10.

CHAPTER 4

FROM IDENTITY TO IMPACT:
THE EVOLUTION OF GEELONG'S DESIGN INNOVATION ECOSYSTEM

TUBA KOCATURK AND RUSSELL KENNEDY

Introduction

This chapter examines the impact of Geelong's UNESCO City of Design designation in cultivating a design innovation ecosystem within a regional context, with a specific focus on the instrumental role played by Deakin University in facilitating and nurturing this ecosystem through collaborative engagements with various stakeholders.

A city's development is an ever-evolving process, marked by its ability to adapt and redefine itself, especially in the context of post-industrial transformation. In this chapter, we embark on a comprehensive exploration of Geelong – a regional city located in western Victoria (see Figure 1.1). Our objective is to unravel the intricate narrative of this journey, tracing the city's transition from a post-industrial town to its distinguished status as a UNESCO City of Design. This transformation serves as a compelling case study that sheds light on the dynamics of urban reinvention, the role of innovation, and the profound influence of design thinking. The chapter offers a multi-dimensional exploration of Geelong's UNESCO City of Design designation, encompassing historical context, the design innovation ecosystem, comparative insights, and practical impacts of design initiatives.

Our examination of Geelong's UNESCO City of Design designation is nested within a mixed framework, incorporating elements from urban studies, design theory, and innovation ecosystem literature. This integrated approach provides a robust foundation for analysing the significance and evolution of the city's ongoing transformation in the context of identity and purposeful reshaping for Geelong as a city that continues to grapple with the decline of traditional industries. At the core of our analysis resides design theory, which elucidates the transformative capacity of design thinking.[1] This theory emphasises the role of design as a powerful catalyst for innovation. The chapter is also firmly grounded in the literature on innovation ecosystems, investigating how they are cultivated, with a focus on collaborative efforts between academia, industry and the broader community.[2] Here, we illuminate the role of Deakin University and its partners in nurturing Geelong's design innovation ecosystem.

Throughout this chapter, our analytical framework sets the stage for an in-depth exploration of Geelong's multifaceted history, UNESCO City of Design designation, and the evolution of its dynamic design innovation ecosystem. This examination encompasses several key dimensions, including a critical appraisal of the significance of Geelong's UNESCO designation, an exploration of its transformation from a post-industrial regional city, and an examination of the collaborative initiatives that have shaped its design innovation ecosystem. We also draw comparisons with other UNESCO Cities of Design and post-industrial cities, thus providing a comprehensive perspective on Geelong's journey. To illustrate the practical impact of Geelong's UNESCO City of Design designation, we present a series of case studies that showcase the city's collaborative design initiatives. Finally, we delve into potential future directions and opportunities for growth and sustainability within the realm of design-driven urban and economic transformation.

A glimpse into Geelong's ongoing transformation

Geelong has undergone a profound transformation in recent years. This metamorphosis, marked by substantial shifts in its urban landscape, extends far beyond the physical realm. It penetrates the very essence of its society, mirroring the interplay between changes in the city's economy and the far-reaching impacts on the city's social fabric. In this scholarly exploration, we embark on a journey that unveils the connections between Geelong's evolving urban environment and the dynamics of its economy and society. Understanding the breadth and importance of Geelong's urban transformation necessitates a historical perspective. The city's history is a rich tapestry woven from diverse threads, with Aboriginal

---

[1] Tim Brown and Barry Katz, "Change by Design", *Journal of Product Innovation Management* 28, no. 3 (2011): 381–83; Richard Buchanan, "Wicked Problems in Design Thinking", *Design Issues* 8, no. 2 (1992): 5–21; Nigel Cross, *Design Thinking: Understanding How Designers Think and Work,* (Oxford; New York: Berg, 2011).

[2] Allan O'Connor, Erik Stam, Fiona Sussan and David B. Audretsch, *Entrepreneurial Ecosystems: Place-Based Transformations and Transitions,* International Studies in Entrepreneurship (2017); Katri Valkokari, "Business, Innovation, and Knowledge Ecosystems: How They Differ and How to Survive and Thrive within Them", *Technology Innovation Management Review* 5, no. 8 (2015): 17–24.

settlement dating back thousands of years. British colonial settlers arrived in the early nineteenth century, and the town was formally established in 1838, its growth spurred by its strategic location on Corio Bay. The early economy of Geelong revolved around agriculture, with wool production and wheat farming taking centre stage.[3] The port, inaugurated in 1851, emerged as a vital conduit for the export of these products, most notably wool, and made a substantial contribution to Geelong's early prosperity.[4]

The twentieth century heralded a significant transformation of Geelong's landscape as the city wholeheartedly embraced the realm of manufacturing. (See also Chapter 8, "Mapping Industrial Vacancy".) Geelong distinguished itself particularly in the domains of automotive and textile production. The establishment of an Australian manufacturing plant by Ford, an iconic moment in the city's history, solidified its position as the epicentre of the Australian automotive industry, profoundly shaping its identity, bolstering economic growth, and providing significant employment opportunities. In the face of shifting global economic currents, Geelong confronted the inevitable decline of these traditional industries. The closure of the Ford plant in 2016 serves as a poignant exemplar of this economic downturn. (See also Chapter 3, "Dialogues Between Space and Time"). Undeterred, Geelong displayed resilience and adaptability. The city charted a new course, steering away from traditional manufacturing and setting sail towards a diversified economic landscape.[5] The emergence of advanced manufacturing and healthcare, and the remarkable growth of Deakin University as a knowledge and research hub have played pivotal roles in this economic renaissance. This reshaping of the economic landscape is mirrored in the city's urban environment. Innovation hubs, research precincts, and a burgeoning service sector now characterise Geelong's transforming urban milieu.

This economic resurgence was paralleled by a wave of urban redevelopment initiatives. The revitalisation of the waterfront precinct (1998), later reinforced by the transformative Geelong Waterfront Safe Harbour Precinct Project, has further enhanced the city's connection to the bay. Simultaneously, cultural precincts – exemplified by vibrant locations like Little Malop Street and Ryrie Street – have infused the city's cultural life with dynamism.[6] These urban projects did more than reshape the city's physical landscape; they rekindled its social fabric. A sense of community and cultural identity began to thrive, reflecting the profound interplay between the city's economic resurgence and its evolving social dynamics.

The interplay of economy and urban transformation in Geelong ushered in a series of societal impacts. The shift towards knowledge-intensive industries attracted a more diverse and educated population, catalysing shifts in the city's social demographics. Simultaneously, a fervent commitment to environmental sustainability has galvanised community engagement, forging a shared commitment to ecological preservation. Nonetheless, this transformation has not been without its challenges. Gentrification, housing affordability and the quest for social inclusion have emerged as critical concerns[7] (See also Chapter 6, "Reimagining Geelong via Systems Thinking"). The continuous challenge lies in striking a delicate balance between preserving Geelong's rich history and heritage while accommodating the imperatives of growth and innovation.

As the city strides forward, it grapples with the complexities of nurturing an inclusive and equitable society. In its journey, Geelong offers not just a case study but a profound narrative of urban transformation in the twenty-first century, one in which the evolution of its urban landscape closely mirrors the unfolding dynamics of its economy and society.

From a post-industrial town to a UNESCO City of Design

Post-industrial cities often find themselves at a crossroad as to whether to find a new identity or embrace their industrial past. After the closure of major manufacturing plants in the region, Geelong has experienced a new growth in areas of engineering, design and material science – a legacy of its manufacturing base – and in emerging strengths such as information and communication technology, and health care. Geelong is also identified as home to important education and research facilities with significant infrastructure, including institutions such as the Commonwealth Scientific and Industrial Research Organisation (CSIRO), The Gordon Institute of TAFE (Technical and Further Education) and Deakin University. A central plank in Geelong's rebuild strategy was the creation of the Geelong Future Economy Precinct at Deakin University, which has created over 1000 jobs, including skilled roles in advanced manufacturing in globally competitive companies, such as Carbon Nexus, LeMond Composites and Carbon Revolution, which is shown to ease the impact of Geelong's manufacturing transition.[8]

Deakin University has played another key role in advancing the design and innovation agenda by initiating the Geelong–UNESCO Creative Cities Network (UCCN) conversation. In 2016, Deakin University's School of Engineering and School of Communication and Creative Arts co-hosted the 2016 International Conference on Design and

---

[3] Leigh Edmonds and Graeme Vincent, *Living by Water: A History of Barwon Water and Its Predecessors* (Barwon Water Authority, 2005).

[4] Ted Henzell, *Australian Agriculture: Its History and Challenges* (Collingwood, Vic.: CSIRO Pub., 2007).

[5] David S. Jones and Phillip B. Roös (eds), *Geelong's Changing Landscape: Ecology, Development and Conservation* (Collingwood: CSIRO Publishing, 2019).

[6] Department of Environment, Land, Water and Planning, *Revitalising Central Geelong Action Plan* (Melbourne, 2016).

[7] Richard Tucker, Meg Mundell, Louise Johnson, Danielle Hitch, Fiona Andrews, Jian Liang, Lukar Thornton, Isabella Bower and Anahita Sal Moslehian, *Creative Strategies for Tackling Locational Disadvantage in Geelong* (Deakin University report prepared for the City of Greater Geelong by HOME Research Hub, April 2021).

[8] Department of Industry, Science and Resources, *Innovation and Science Australia. Australia 2030: Prosperity through Innovation* (Canberra, 2017).

Technology (DesTech) at its Geelong Waurn Ponds Campus. The aim and theme of the conference was to explore intersections between technology, engineering and the creative arts. Published in the proceedings of the DesTech conference was a paper titled: "Building a Case for an International Design Centre in Geelong" that called on the City of Greater Geelong to apply for UCCN status as a City of Design. The paper proposed a two-phase approach to position Geelong as an effective global design stakeholder:

- create a Geelong International Design Centre
- apply for Geelong to join the UNESCO Creative Cities Network as a City of Design.[9]

The proposition gained favourable reception among city administrators, who recognised the potential benefits of a successful application to the UCCN. They believed that achieving the designation of UNESCO City of Design would quickly position Geelong alongside other global locations renowned for their commitment to design as a primary driver of innovation and transformative societal change.

When responding to the UCCN's 2017 call for applications, the City of Greater Geelong described the value of design from their perspective as "an agent of change" with a potential to reshape Geelong from an industrial economy into a burgeoning clever and creative city.[10] It was driven by makers, innovators, and educational/research institutions, underpinned by a desire to engage with UCCN members throughout the Asia–Pacific region and beyond. Geelong was particularly keen to lead collaborations aligned to the UCCN mission with the state of Victoria's design industry. The application committee identified several key partners and stakeholders who would help create benefits across diverse interconnected stakeholders within a "quadruple helix" model of innovation centred around academia, government, industry and community.[11]

The post-designation phase marked a pivotal juncture in Geelong's journey as a City of Design, as it embarked on an introspective exploration to comprehend the significance and implications of this esteemed designation. This process resembled a profound exercise in soul searching, as Geelong sought to establish a design-driven mission befitting its newly acquired status. The objective was to formulate a purpose that would not only honour its historical legacy but also serve as a transformative conduit, seamlessly bridging the gap between the city's past and future endeavours. At the crux of this quest lay a fundamental question: How could design be harnessed as a powerful instrument to propel Geelong towards its lofty aspirations?

The multifaceted value of design

Design, as a multifaceted and fluid concept, encompasses a wide array of disciplines, ranging from architecture and urban planning to industrial and graphic design. The diverse approaches to design offered by various thinkers and practitioners introduce a complex tapestry of perspectives and applications. Design scholar Richard Buchanan's perspective on design serves as a significant exemplar, emphasising design's transformative potential to address complex problems while transcending conventional boundaries and scales.[12] This holistic approach, as Buchanan argues, positions design as a fundamental human activity for shaping the world.

Buchanan's view reframes design, extending its purview beyond aesthetics or the mere creation of physical objects. It characterises design as a versatile problem-solving approach applicable to a broad spectrum of challenges. His framework introduces four distinct orders of design, which shed light on its multifaceted nature.[13] The first order, symbolic and visual communication, adheres to the traditional tenets of design, focusing on crafting visually appealing and meaningful artefacts, encompassing graphic design, industrial design, and other forms of visual communication. The second order, material and technological design, transcends aesthetics to delve into the materials, technologies and systems underpinning the creation of objects, emphasising the functional aspects of design, such as product design and architecture. The third order, service and interaction design, accentuates design's pivotal role in shaping user experiences and interactions, encompassing service design, user interface design and the creation of seamless customer experiences. The fourth and highest order, systemic and complex design, confronts intricate, interconnected challenges with societal and global implications, calling for the application of design thinking to address systemic issues, including urban planning, healthcare systems and environmental sustainability.

Two renowned design leaders, Tim Brown and Barry Katz, offer an alternative, yet complementary lens, rooted in human-centred problem-solving.[14] Their view aligns with Buchanan's viewpoint on tackling systemic and complex design challenges but places a more pronounced emphasis on empathy and user-centred solutions. Both perspectives

---

[9] Meghan Kelly and Russell Kennedy, "Building a Case for an International Design Centre in Geelong" (International DesTech Conference, Geelong, Australia, February 9, 2017).

[10] Tim Ellis, Terry Hickey, Robert Treseder and Russell Kennedy, *UNESCO Creative Cities Network Application* (City of Greater Geelong, 2017).

[11] Elias G. Carayannis, Evangelos Grigoroudis, David F. J. Campbell, Dirk Meissner, and Dimitra Stamati "The Ecosystem as Helix: An Exploratory Theory-Building Study of Regional Co-Opetitive Entrepreneurial Ecosystems as Quadruple/Quintuple Helix Innovation Models", *R&D Management* 48 no. 1 (2018): 148–62.

[12] Richard Buchanan, "Wicked Problems in Design Thinking", *Design Issues* 8, no. 2 (1992): 5–21.

[13] Buchanan, "Wicked Problems in Design Thinking".

[14] Tim Brown and Barry Katz, "Change by Design", *Journal of Product Innovation Management* 28, no. 3 (2011): 381–83.

underline the transformative potential of design as a versatile problem-solving approach applicable across a spectrum of challenges and contexts.

The United Kingdom's Design Council, in its pivotal report, "Design for Innovation" outlines a comprehensive vision for design's capacity to drive innovation and foster economic growth.[15] This perspective accentuates the intrinsic synergy between design and innovation, providing a tangible policy framework for leveraging design to advance societal progress. The process of design thinking, as endorsed by the Design Council, harmonises seamlessly with the innovation process by nurturing creativity, exploring novel opportunities, and conducting rapid prototyping and testing of ideas. The Design Council's approach to "design" seeks to expedite the translation of innovative concepts into tangible products, services, and experiences, recognising that innovation is not a solitary event but a continual process enriched by the infusion of unique (design) methodologies.

Nevertheless, the notion of design as a transformative force, while exhilarating, is not devoid of challenges and complexities. In the context of Geelong, and numerous other cities, defining the boundaries of design can engender ambiguity, leading to questions regarding its scope and practical implementation. Additional complications arise from issues related to inclusivity, accessibility and sustainability, which can pose challenges when implementing design initiatives. Furthermore, the delicate task of balancing the preservation of cultural heritage with the imperatives of innovation and progress adds another layer of complexity. These complexities necessitate thoughtful consideration as cities like Geelong embark on their journey as UNESCO Cities of Design, emphasising the need for a nuanced and inclusive approach to the utility of design as a product, a process, a methodology and a driver of innovation.

How other cities harnessed the power of design

Within the realm of UNESCO Cities of Design, each city adopts a unique approach to its designation, using design as a catalyst for diverse aspects of urban development, social fabric and economic landscape. For instance, Helsinki, Finland, prioritises user-centric and sustainable design; Shenzhen, China, focuses on fostering innovation and entrepreneurship; Montreal, Canada, thrives on the convergence of creativity and culture; and Buenos Aires, Argentina, emphasises design's pivotal role in social and economic development. These diverse strategies, as highlighted by Karl Stocker, reflect the cities' distinct characteristics and their quests for sustainable development within their specific contexts.[16] The journey toward design-led transformation is marked by complexities that necessitate a thoughtful approach, drawing inspiration from global peers while crafting solutions tailored to each unique context and aspiration.

Cities comparable to Geelong in terms of their industrial past have effectively harnessed the transformative potential of design to revitalise their urban identities, repurpose industrial spaces, foster innovation and create sustainable economic opportunities. Turin's journey in Italy involved leveraging its expertise and heritage in the automotive industry to establish itself as a thriving hub for design and innovation. In parallel, Detroit, United States, capitalised on its industrial infrastructure and design legacy to cultivate a vibrant creative community and champion design-driven urban development. Nevertheless, it is essential to acknowledge that the paths of these cities have not been devoid of challenges. Turin and Detroit encountered issues related to the preservation of historical architecture, socio economic disparities and the complexities of gentrification.[17] The rapid pace of transformation raised questions concerning inclusivity and affordability in housing and business opportunities.

Both Dundee, United Kingdom, and Puebla, Mexico, with their unique approaches to design, serve as inspiring examples for cities of similar scale to Geelong in harnessing design's transformative potential to drive economic growth, cultural development and sustainable urban futures. Dundee, a city celebrated for its innovative approach to design, serves as a compelling model for urban revitalisation.[18] Its design-led initiatives have effectively rejuvenated both the economy and the cultural landscape.[19] However, beneath the surface of success, local debates have emerged. The flourishing gaming industry, home to prominent studios like Rockstar Dundee and 4J Studios, exemplifies how Dundee has harnessed design-driven innovation to create sustainable economic opportunities. Yet, this rapid growth has prompted discussions about the social and economic ramifications of the gaming sector. Issues of inclusivity, sustainability and the potential digital divide are among the critical concerns that warrant closer examination.

Puebla, a city similar in size to Geelong, offers an alternative approach to design-driven urban transformation. Puebla places significant emphasis on cultural preservation, urban development and entrepreneurship.[20] Notably, its UNESCO World Heritage site, the historic city centre, showcases the harmonious integration of traditional craftsmanship with contemporary design practices. The city's commitment to safeguarding colonial architecture while promoting design-driven endeavours is commendable. However, this approach has also sparked local debates. Puebla grapples with the

---

[15] Design Council UK, *Design for Innovation*, (2011), accessed July 15, 2023, https://www.designcouncil.org.uk/fileadmin/uploads/dc/Documents/ DesignForInnovation_Dec2011.pdf.

[16] Karl Stocker, *The Power of Design: A Journey through the 11 UNESCO Cities* (Springer, 2013).

[17] Asma Mehan, "The Challenges of 'Comparative Urbanism' in Post-Fordist Cities: The Cases of Turin and Detroit", *Contour Journal* 15, no. 9 (2019): 1–14; 1.

[18] "A City of Design", Dundee, accessed October 10, 2023, https://cityofdesigndundee.com.

[19] "A City of Design", Dundee.

[20] "Puebla", UNESCO Creative Cities Network, accessed October 26, 2023, https://en.unesco.org/creative-cities/puebla.

challenges of preserving heritage while embracing modernity, giving rise to questions regarding authenticity, the impact of tourism, and shifts in the city's cultural and social fabric.[21]

As Geelong embarks on its own design-driven transformation, it stands at a crossroad. Issues such as social equity, cultural preservation, economic sustainability and urban inclusivity are not isolated aspirations; they are tangible challenges that cities like Geelong must address. Can the city harness the invaluable lessons derived from Turin, Detroit, Dundee, Puebla and others? Can Geelong translate these learnings into a blueprint for sustainable urban development, addressing concerns related to environmental impact and resource management? Can it navigate the local and conceptual critiques and infuse them into its own journey?

DesignMind – building an ecology of design

Geelong initiated a strategic effort to utilise design as a catalyst for transformation and cultivate a design innovation ecosystem. In other words, it aspired to create an ecology of design by fostering dialogues across culture, business, science and urban planning. Deakin University, through its DesignMind platform, played a pivotal role in this endeavour. Established in 2019, DesignMind was envisaged as a transdisciplinary design and innovation platform to connect with and facilitate design-related research conversations across the university. It also aimed to externally interface the aligned design and research activities across the university with the Geelong's UNESCO City of Design agenda.

In a nutshell, DesignMind aimed to bridge diverse interpretations of design, emphasising its intrinsic value in health, science, technology, sustainability, heritage and other key innovation domains in Geelong. Through public lectures, workshops and exemplary projects, DesignMind sought to elevate the perceived value of design, making it accessible and relevant across sectors. The goal was to harmonise disparate interpretations of design and position it as a unifying force driving innovation and positive change in various domains. In other words, it served as a facilitator for design dialogues and collaborations that transcended traditional disciplinary and sector boundaries. In this way it worked to foster a shared understanding of design's versatility and adaptability, emphasising its potential to transcend industry-specific limitations and thus contribute to the city's overarching goals of cultural enrichment, sustainability and economic growth. This proactive approach laid the foundation for a comprehensive interpretation of design, promoting its broader adoption as an innovation catalyst.

Four projects are showcased that have been developed in close collaboration with and through the facilitation of DesignMind, each demonstrating how design created value through the integration of multiple knowledge fields and cross-sector perspectives, contributing to an ever-evolving design and innovation ecosystem in Geelong.

Project 1: Experiencing (In)Tangible Heritage Through Extended Reality: Western Beach Park, Geelong

This collaborative initiative, spearheaded by the MInD Lab (Mediated Intelligence in Design Lab) in the School of Architecture and Built Environment, and in partnership with Deakin University's DesignMind, the City of Greater Geelong (CoGG), and DarkSpade, served as a compelling demonstration of the potential for amalgamating design, technology and heritage. The project achieved the prestigious Gold Award at the 2020 Melbourne Design Awards in the Systems – Concept category.[22] Its central focus revolved around the creation of an open-air digital exhibition within Geelong's Western Beach Park, driven by mobile augmented reality (AR) technology. The main innovation was to seamlessly integrate both tangible and intangible heritage data through a dedicated AR application, which could be operated across various platforms, providing location-based storytelling (see Figure 4.1).

The project's inception was marked by the transformation of Western Beach Park in central Geelong, which was previously inaccessible to the public. Because the site's material artefacts held limited heritage value, the project shifted its attention to preserving the intangible aspects of cultural heritage, such as the knowledge of traditions, skills and customs that are passed on to the rest of the community, from generation to generation. These aspects of cultural heritage are recognised by communities as distinct facets of identity. In that regard, the project endeavoured to encourage community engagement in the realm of digital place-making. The developmental phases encompassed tasks such as cataloguing digital exhibition materials, conducting site analysis, evaluating technology, and crafting a conceptual map that governs the interaction between digital narratives, visitor movements and media presentations (See also Chapter 3, "Dialogues of Space and Time," Chapter 5 "Tracing the Transformation of Little Malop Street," and Chapter 9 "The Place of Heritage").

At the heart of this project lay the visitor's narrative experience, which was enriched by location-based technologies, effectively turning visitors into creators and narrators of historical discourse. The application integrated technology into the public realm, ensuring a natural and intuitive experience. The project tackled significant challenges, including the integration of technology within the physical context and the harmonious blending of historical digital (visual, audial and textual) narratives with tangible surroundings. It merged digital immersion with physical exploration, where digital narratives unfolded organically as its users navigated through the site. The project's three thematic narratives were

---

[21] "Puebla", UNESCO Creative Cities Network.
[22] "Melbourne Design Awards 2020", accessed November 2, 2023, https://betterfutureawards.com/MEL20/project.asp?ID=19416.

dedicated to public baths, boat builders and the transformation of Geelong's coastline, to revitalise the history of a location with minimal physical artefacts.

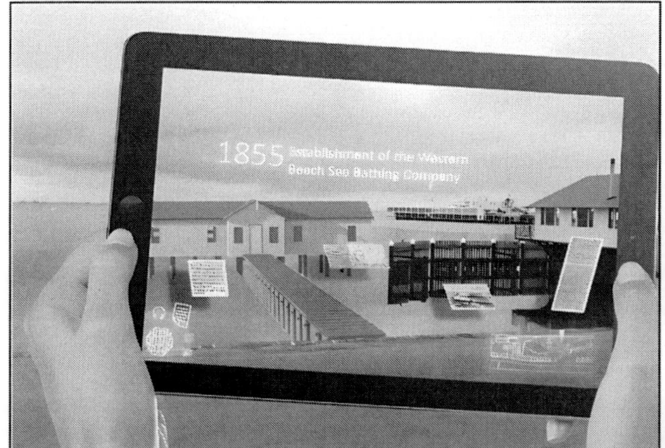

Figure 4.1 Top: The visual impressions of users' experience of location-activated spatial storytelling. © 2020 MInD Lab, Deakin University. MInD (Mediated Intelligence in Design) Research Lab. https://mindlab.cloud. Bottom: The aerial view of Western Beach, indicating the project site, photographed in 2019.

This project underscored the value of adopting a design ecosystem approach, where the synergy between design, technology and heritage converged to create transformative experiences within urban spaces. It embodied the principles of participatory community engagement and storytelling through digital place-making, profoundly influencing the way we interact with our heritage within an urban environment.

Project 2: A circular approach to a pandemic – designing out PPE (personal protective equipment) waste

This project was brought to life through direct facilitation of Deakin University's DesignMind in collaboration with the Institute of Frontier Materials (IFM), Regional Innovation for Circular Economy (RICE), National Indigenous Knowledges Education Research and Innovation (NIKERI) Institute and various schools across Deakin University, as well as professionals in design and the circular economy. This project showcased the power of design and system thinking in addressing environmental challenges posed by PPE (personal protective equipment) waste during the COVID-19 pandemic.

The project's core objective was to reimagine disposable face masks using circular economy principles. It sought to create masks that offered a user-friendly experience, ensured feasibility in production, exhibited aesthetic appeal and embraced a sustainable lifecycle. The team's diverse range of participants included material scientists, architects, product designers, postgraduate students, and early and mid-career researchers. Expert coaches were also engaged to guide the teams in various aspects of design, business strategies, consumer behaviour and entrepreneurship.

The project yielded three distinct face mask designs, each exemplifying circular economy principles. The Spinnaker team focused on using sustainable cellulose-based materials to create masks that were washable, reusable and biodegradable (see Figure 4.2).

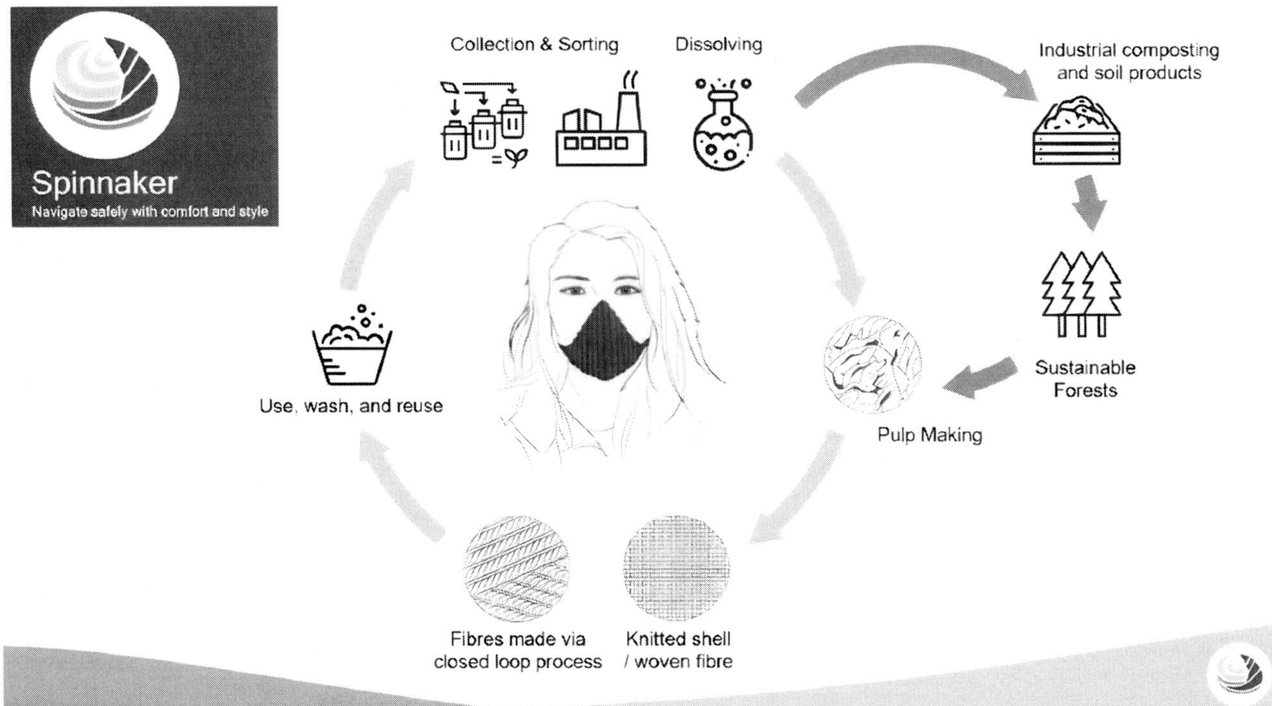

Figure 4.2 A snapshot from the Spinnaker team's presentation of their circular (mask) design and supply chain model, 2021. © 2021 Deakin University.

The Smile Easy team prioritised sustainability by forming a close network of collaborators to minimise energy consumption and ensure recyclability of mask components. The Smart Mask team integrated local Aboriginal culture into their designs to enhance user well-being and cultural identity.

This initiative not only offered innovative solutions to PPE waste but also provided an exemplary case for the value of transdisciplinary design in innovating sustainable and socially conscious solutions.

Project 3: Indigenous Design Charter project – research, development and applications

The Australian Indigenous Design Charter and International Indigenous Design Charter, formulated by Deakin University, hold a pivotal role in Geelong's official application for the UNESCO City of Design designation.[23] An enduring initiative, the Indigenous Design Charter project engages in culturally sensitive professional practice research, endeavouring to establish global best practice protocols for the representation of Indigenous cultures in design. The charter documents cater to both non-Indigenous designers working with Indigenous knowledge and cultural material, as well as Indigenous designers operating beyond their home country. Recognised by several international and national professional bodies, these charters serve as guiding principles for Australian Federal and Victorian State Government procurement policies and education curriculums at secondary and tertiary levels.

The Australian Indigenous Design Charter has been incorporated into the Green Building Council Australia's standard guidelines.[24] Since Geelong received the UNESCO City of Design designation in 2017, the charters have become a mandatory compliance requirement for the Victorian Government and the City of Greater Geelong's public project works including the Geelong civic precinct. Created as a best practice policy and protocols, the Indigenous charters are used as a guide for designers when working on projects involving the representation of First Nations cultures. Endorsed by the City of Greater Geelong, the charter aspires to exert a lasting influence by addressing core issues rather than merely alleviating symptoms, thereby enhancing the lives of Indigenous peoples. Its overarching goal is to elevate the profile of First Nations cultures, fostering self-esteem, pride and a sense of belonging through positive, culturally-led representation and visibility. These aspirations, objectives and values harmonise seamlessly with the ethos of the UNESCO City of Design designation.

---

[23] Russell Kennedy, Meghan Kelly, Brian Martin, and Jefa Greenaway, *International Indigenous Design Charter: Protocols for Sharing Indigenous Knowledge in Professional Design Practice* (Melbourne: Deakin University, 2018).
[24] Green Building Council Australia, *Reconciliation Action Plan 2021*, accessed November 2, 2023, https://new.gbca.org.au/about/publications/reconciliation-action-plan/.

Project 4: Perpetual Pigments

This research application was conducted in collaboration with Deakin University's Institute for Frontier Materials (IFM), researchers from Deakin's School of Communication and Creative Arts, and the NIKERI Institute. The genesis of this collaboration can be traced back to the circular approach to a pandemic project discussed earlier. The Perpetual Pigments project also aligns with circular economy principles, embodying a participatory synergy across the realms of science, design, art and culture.

The Perpetual Pigments project tests the results of a world first research project conducted by Deakin University's IFM. The research received funding through a Sustainability Victoria grant from the Victorian State Government. Framed within the circular economy conversation, IFM has developed a process to extract pigments from discarded textiles and fabrics made from natural fibres. The primary innovation was to produce pigments using green pre-processing and milling technology using minimum energy, time and resources. IFM researchers were able to engineer particles with microparticles while retaining the colour of the waste textile. This outcome enabled them to produce micro-pigments from textiles segregated by colour for a range of applications including pigments for printing/colouring textiles and vegan leather, and for the creation of art.

IFM approached Deakin University's DesignMind to explore various application areas of this innovation. Inspired by the "sustainable colour, continuous culture" concept, six notable First Nations artists were invited to participate in an experiment to produce artworks using the recycled (colour) pigments produced by IFM (see Figure 4.3 in the colour plate section).

Developed with design thinking methodology and framed within a circular economy paradigm, the Perpetual Pigments project introduced an empathy-grounded phase of prototyping and testing to the project by inviting research participation outside of the field of science. Industry research partner Rip Curl further demonstrated the connective ecology of the project.[25] The iconic local brand worked closely with IFM and the exhibition team to produce T-shirts featuring designs printed with the recycled pigments (see Figure 4.4 in the colour plate section).

This research and the collaborative work of renowned First Nations visual artists and textile designers culminated in an exhibition during the 2023 Geelong Design Week.[26] The exhibition showcased the results of participatory research, and the testing of the effectiveness of recycled pigments in visual art practice. The Perpetual Pigments project aimed to address the challenges of recycling textiles considering the complexities of different colours, fibres and blends. It served as a model for cross-disciplinary collaboration and innovation, engaging various stakeholders within the Deakin University community and beyond.[27]

Conclusion

In the arduous ongoing transition from post-industrial town to UNESCO City of Design, Geelong's journey stands as a remarkable testament to the transformative potential of design. Yet, it is imperative to grasp that the UNESCO designation is not a mere accolade for past achievements; it represents the recognition of the potential of a city, a promise into the future, and a commitment to integrating design and creativity into the heart of sustainable development. The title does not signify an endpoint but rather the commencement of a challenging journey. Geelong's attainment of this designation symbolises its aspiration to wield design as a transformative force, allowing for innovation and progress while preserving its rich cultural heritage.

Looking into the future, Geelong readily acknowledges the imperative to disentangle itself from a purely industrial approach to design. This historical perspective, while deeply rooted in the city's past, has also left an indelible mark of irreversible environmental damage (See Chapter 3, "Dialogues Between Space and Time"). Consequently, the city is coming to terms with the realisation that its commitment extends beyond the present, indicating a future where designs are no longer exclusively centred on creating new products but also catering to human well-being and the well-being of the planet. This perspective is not unique to Geelong but is firmly grounded in a global necessity. In this pursuit, design is primed to play an instrumental role in achieving the primary objective of UCCN (UNESCO Creative Cities Network): creating sustainable cities and communities, underscored by the United Nation's sustainable development goal (SDG) 11. The culmination of this awareness has catalysed the initiation of an innovative program in the School of Architecture and Built Environment, at Deakin University, titled "Design for Circular Cities". The program has received formal recognition from the city and has been described by the City of Greater Geelong Council's Mayor, Trent Sullivan, as having 'the potential to chart the course for the future of this designation'.[28]

However, it is crucial to adopt a critical stance even in the face of such commendable efforts and goals. Geelong's commitment to environmental sustainability and innovation, while noteworthy, also carries the weight of formidable challenges. The transition to a circular economy requires immense investments, not just in resources but in terms of shifting societal paradigms and industrial practices. It demands a holistic re-evaluation of how products are conceived,

---

[25] Russell Kennedy, Tonya Meyrick and Jacinta Kay, *Perpetual Pigments - Sustainable Colour, Continuous Culture,* Deakin University, Geelong, Australia, accessed November 14, 2023, https://perpetualpigments.com.au, 12.

[26] Kennedy, Meyrick and Kay, *Perpetual Pigments - Sustainable Colour, Continuous Culture,* 28.

[27] Institute of Frontier Materials (IFM), School of Communication and Creative Arts, School of Architecture and Built Environment, and current staff and alumni of the National Indigenous Knowledges Education Research Innovation (NIKERI) Institute.

[28] Trent Sullivan, "Shining in Design Spotlight", *Geelong Advertiser,* 2023.

manufactured and disposed of, which may face resistance from established industries and consumer habits. Additionally, there is a risk of overreliance on design as a panacea, overlooking the need for broader systemic changes in areas such as governance, policy and cultural norms.

Moreover, the potential to become the first circular city in Australia, in addition to being the first Australian UNESCO City of Design, should not overshadow the complexity and long-term commitment that such a transition entails. Geelong's pursuit of this vision is ambitious and commendable. The success of this endeavour hinges not just on a visionary declaration but on concrete, well-considered actions and a willingness to adapt and learn from both successes and setbacks. This chapter is just one part of the ongoing story. Geelong's ultimate legacy as a circular city will depend on its ability to translate vision into lasting, positive change.

PART 2

ENTWINED HISTORIES

CHAPTER 5

TRACING THE TRANSFORMATION OF LITTLE MALOP STREET:
VISUALISING GEELONG'S PAST THROUGH DIGITAL MEDIA

MD MIZANUR RASHID, SANJA RODEŠ AND CHIN KOI KHOO

Introduction

The preservation and revitalisation of urban heritage is becoming increasingly important in the face of rapid urban development and changing urban landscapes. Collective memories are intrinsically linked to the sense of place, with built heritage serving as a tangible connection to the past. The architecture of a city holds a central position in collective memory, capturing multiple narratives over time. Scholars have recognised the importance of "memoryscapes" in the digital realm for community development and identity formation.[1] Richard and Duif highlight that digital technologies are increasingly used by governments, companies and researchers to capture both tangible and intangible dimensions of memories and their meanings.[2] In the past five years, concepts like digital place-making have gained traction within creative industries and the cultural heritage profession.[3]

The use of digital media and technology to document and represent lost heritage is a promising approach to preserving urban heritage. Digital technologies, such as augmented reality (AR) platforms, are being applied to public spaces to engage urban audiences and enhance the understanding of human perception.[4]

This chapter explores the transformation of Geelong, a city witnessing significant changes as its key industries evolve over time. The once-thriving wool industry of the late nineteenth and early twentieth centuries has given way to sectors such as automotive, cement and aluminium production. Over time, these industries too have been phased out, making room for the emergence of offices, institutions and luxury developments. The city now grapples with a gap in its architectural heritage and historical narrative, leaving untold histories waiting to be revealed. While much of Geelong's central business district is being revitalised and reshaped, certain areas remain voids, including the eastern half of Little Malop Street, which borders Market Square Mall.[5] Geelong's Little Malop Street, once a crucial part of the city's central business district (CBD), illustrates the difficulties in preserving urban heritage amidst rapid urban development and gentrification. This condition was exacerbated by the recent pandemic, with an increase in shop and business closures, deserted streets and buildings, and antisocial behaviour. Leveraging digital tools like Matterport virtual reality (VR) scanning, time-lapse video, and virtual modelling, in conjunction with traditional archival research, presents a diverse array of opportunities for multimedia heritage and storytelling. Establishing a digital repository for Little Malop Street enables the development of a dynamic portrayal of the city's industrial legacy and cultural identity, providing a platform for public interaction with its history and heritage.

In addition, this chapter considers the richness of digital media, which goes beyond media only being a platform, arguing that media are not neutral, but instead frame the interactions between the public, heritage and history. Different digital media that aim to preserve industrial heritage are compared and analysed, each conveying different messages and allowing for different perceptions depending on the medium or the specific digital media employed. By extension, these media implicate digital images, which are often embedded in the digital platform itself. Consideration of media and images in relation to preservation of heritage extends the examination beyond documentation only. We argue that both

---

[1] Paul Basu, "Palimpsest Memoryscapes: The Urban Politics of Memorialization in Post-Partition Kolkata", *Environment and Planning A* 39, no. 10 (Chicago: Springer, 2007), 2421–38; Andreas Huyssen, *Twilight Memories: Marking Time in a Culture of Amnesia* (London: Routledge, 1995); Pierre Nora, *Les Lieux de Mémoire (Vol. 1): La République (Places of Memory: The Republic)*, (Chicago: University of Chicago Press, 1989); James Edward Young, *The Texture of Memory: Holocaust Memorials and Meaning* (New Haven: Yale University Press, 1993).

[2] Gregg Richards and Lian Duif (eds), *Small Cities with Big Dreams: Creative Placemaking and Branding Strategies* (London; New York: Routledge, 2019).

[3] Nicole Basraba, "The Emergence of Creative and Digital Place-Making: A Scoping Review Across disciplines", *New Media & Society* 25, no. 6 (2023): 1470–97.

[4] Nikolaos M. Avouris and Nikoleta Yiannoutsou, "A Review of Mobile Location-Based Games for Learning Across Physical and Virtual Spaces." *J. Univers. Comput. Sci.* 18, no. 15 (2012): 2120–42; Martin Traunmueller, Paul Marshall, and Licia Capra, "Crowdsourcing Safety Perceptions of People: Opportunities and Limitations", in *Social Informatics: 7th International Conference, SocInfo 2015, Beijing, China, December 9–12, 2015, Proceedings 7* (Springer International Publishing, 2015), 120–35; Yuji Yoshimura et al. "Quantifying Memories: Mapping Urban Perception." *Mobile Netw Appl* 25 (2020): 1275–86, https://doi.org/10.1007/s11036-020-01536-0.

[5] Matt Novacevski, "Contested Spaces: Living off the Edge in a City Mall where Design Fuels Conflict", *Conversation,* 2017, https://theconversation.com/contested-spaces-living-off-the-edge-in-a-city-mall-where-design-fuels-conflict-72351.

digital media and images add a new dimension to the discussion. We propose that media and images offer more than simply visuality, and this is further explored by briefly considering image and media theory.

Image, media and perception

Image theory offers a useful lens through which to understand the potential of digital media and technology to document and represent lost urban heritage.[6] Perhaps the most useful understanding of image and media is offered by art historian Hans Belting, who examines the difference between the image and the visual, and proposes that the image is defined by more than its pure visibility; it is "invested, by the beholder, with a symbolic meaning and a kind of mental 'frame'".[7] Belting adopts an anthropological approach towards analysing images; he believes that image *per se* does not exist outside of its relationship with the body, proposing a triangular basis for image analysis, which includes body, medium and image. Image only exists when it is seen and is inseparable from mental image or its mental reflection in human brain – it is both physical and mental. He proposes that "the picture is the image with a medium", or the image is within the picture.[8] This analysis creates a distinction between image and a medium, or media, which allows for a separation of analysis of media (in this chapter – digital media) from the analysis of images.[9]

Images are not passive reflections of reality, but actively shape and construct our perceptions of the world.[10] Reflecting back on media theorist Marshall McLuhan's argument that "the medium is the message", we can also argue that the specific medium (or media) has a relevant role in constructing narratives and perceptions.[11] McLuhan saw the "electric media" as extensions of the human nervous system, and believed that media profoundly influences the psychological condition and the relationship between an individual and society.[12] Although proposed in the second half of the twentieth century, these observations are visionary and more applicable for the current century and its advanced digital media. As such, the use of digital media and technology to create virtual models of lost buildings and streetscapes facilitates image-making and actively (re)constructs our perceptions of urban heritage.

In addition, image theory emphasises the importance of context in shaping our perceptions of images.[13] Images are not neutral in the meanings they convey and are embedded within national and cultural coding. Virtual models of lost heritage must therefore be situated within a broader context of cultural memory and historical narrative to be effective in capturing and revitalising urban heritage. This requires careful consideration of the ways in which virtual models of lost heritage are presented and contextualised, as well as attention to the broader cultural and historical narratives that shape our perceptions of urban heritage.

The use of digital media and technology to document and represent lost heritage can also be understood as a form of remediation, as described by Bolter and Grusin.[14] Remediation refers to the ways in which new media technologies remediate, or refashion, older media forms. In the context of urban heritage, the use of digital media and technology can be understood as a remediation of older forms of representation such as photographs and architectural drawings. By refashioning these older forms of representation into dynamic virtual models, it is possible to create a more immersive and engaging experience of lost heritage, and to create new opportunities for public engagement and participation. By recognising the active role of media and images in shaping our perceptions of urban heritage and cultural identity, and by situating virtual models of lost heritage within a broader context of cultural memory and historical narrative, it is possible to create dynamic representations of urban heritage that engage and inspire public participation in heritage documentation and dissemination.

The methods and techniques of capturing through digital media

Drawing from recent advancements in neuroscience and cognitive psychology, Goldhagen highlights the influential role of the physical environment in shaping memory.[15] These insights, although not ground-breaking, align with a century of research on the interplay between place and memory across academic disciplines. Goldhagen stresses that our contemporary built environments are pivotal in forming autobiographical memories and, by extension, our sense of identity.[16] In *The City of Collective Memory*, Boyer underscores how architecture and city monuments serve as links

---

[6] William J. Mitchell, *Picture Theory: Essays on Verbal and Visual Representation* (Chicago: University of Chicago Press, 1994).

[7] Hans Belting, *An Anthropology of Images: Picture, Medium, Body*, translated Thomas Dunlap (Princeton: Princeton University Press, 2011), 9.

[8] Belting, *An Anthropology of Images,* 3, 4–5, 9–10.

[9] See Sanja Rodeš, "On the Image of the Hurricane Katrina and the Rebuilding of New Orleans", *Architectural Research Quarterly* 25, no. 4 (2021), 337.

[10] Jean Baudrillard, *Simulacra and Simulation,* trans. Sheila Faria Glaser, The Body in Theory (Ann Arbor: University of Michigan Press, 1994).

[11] Marshall McLuhan, *Understanding Media: The Extensions of Man* (New York: McGraw-Hill, 1964).

[12] McLuhan, *Understanding Media*, 5, 7–23.

[13] Roland Barthes, *Image, Music, Text* (New York: Hill and Wang, 1977).

[14] Jay David Bolter and Richard Grusin, *Remediation: Understanding New Media* (Cambridge, USA: The MIT Press, 2000).

[15] Sarah Williams Goldhagen and Andrea Gallo, *Welcome to your World: How the Built Environment Shapes our Lives* (New York: Harper, 2017), 61.

[16] Sarah Williams Goldhagen, quoted in Jay David Bolter and Richard Grusin, *Remediation: Understanding New Media* (Cambridge, USA: The MIT Press, 2000), 83.

between the past and present, fostering community, culture and national identity.[17] Beyond their immediate functions, physical structures acquire intangible meanings over time, enriched by people's interactions within the urban landscape.[18]

The concept of "narrative geography", which explores the interplay between space and narrative, is proposed by Ryan et al.[19] This framework delves into the dynamic relationship between physical spaces and the stories imprinted on them, offering a comprehensive understanding of how narrative and spatial experiences jointly shape our perception of environments. Basaraba advocates for narrative-focused digital place-making, which not only revitalises memories but also has the potential to offer "edutainment" experiences, educating users about heritage in an engaging manner.[20] Digital technologies are increasingly harnessed for creative, artistic and cultural purposes, not only to raise awareness of history and culture, but to brand a city's image.[21]

The convergence of technology and cultural heritage presents both challenges and opportunities for realising the potential of architectural experiences in the digital age. Presently, the ability of new technologies to provide meaningful engagement with intangible cultural heritage, such as virtual heritage experiences in architecture, is significantly limited.[22] There is an argument that the true value of architecture lies in both its tangible and intangible aspects, which become apparent only after physical construction. The intangible essence is valued for its role in facilitating human thought processes, preserving memories and bearing witness to the lives and histories of individuals and communities over time.[23] In summary, the immaterial qualities of architecture significantly contribute to self-understanding and shape perceptions of identity, creating a distinct framework through visualised, place-based experiences.[24]

Current digital media and technologies – such as digital photography/imagery/video, 3D model/render, interactive website and virtual/augmented reality – are considered to provide the new potential to document and visualise historical data, especially for architectural transformation and in the case of lost heritage. The accessibilities and availabilities of digital media have revolutionised the way we preserve and display the heritage of our cities.[25] In this study of Little Malop Street, a historical street with a rich cultural significance, a series of digital media methods have been employed to capture and document its lost heritage and transformation. This chapter outlines four key methods of digital media and imagery that have the potential to enhance this endeavour: time-lapse video, virtual reality scanning and viewing (Matterport), interactive visual timelines and a website. These methods not only provide a visual record of the past but also enable users to engage with the street's history, allowing for a deeper understanding and appreciation of its heritage. These digital media also raise questions around using new and unexplored methods to document and narrate historical knowledge in the present.[26]

Method 1: Time-lapse video

Time-lapse videos have emerged as a simple but powerful tool for capturing the transformation of urban spaces and cityscapes. By condensing hours, days or even years into a few minutes, these videos provide unique perspectives on the changes that occur over time. In the context of Little Malop Street, significant lost and modified buildings have been selected to showcase and compare their evolution and transformation, highlighting their architectural alterations, changes in façades, as well as shifts in functionality and program. This method not only allows for an immersive experience but also serves as an animated visual documentation of the street's heritage that can be accessed and evaluated by future researchers and generations.

Archived images of eight selected buildings with identified heritage value, and recorded videos of the current state of the buildings are the main resources that give form to the overall animated content of the time-lapse video. The selected

---

[17] Christine M. Boyer, *The City of Collective Memory: Its Historical Imagery and Architectural Entertainments*, 1st edn (Cambridge, USA: The MIT Press, 1996).

[18] Boyer, *The City of Collective Memory*, 309.

[19] Marie-Laure Ryan, Kenneth Foote and Maoz Azaryahu, *Narrating Space/Spatializing Narrative: Where Narrative Theory and Geography Meet* (Columbus: The Ohio State University Press, 2016).

[20] Nicole Basaraba, "The Emergence of Creative and Digital Place-Making: A Scoping Review Across Disciplines", *New Media & Society* 25 no. 6 (2023): 1470–97; Zhigeng Pan, Xiaopeng Zhang, Abdennour El Rhalibi, Woontack Woo, and Yi Li (eds), *Technologies for E-Learning and Digital Entertainment: Third International Conference, Edutainment 2008, Nanjing, China, June 25-27, 2008, Proceedings*, Vol. 5093 (Nanjing, China: Springer, 2008).

[21] See Gemma San Cornelio and Elisenda Ardévol, "Practices of Place-Making Through Locative Media Artworks", *Communications* 36 (2011): 313–33; Surabhi Pancholi, Tan Yigitcanlar and Mirko Guaralda, "Public Space Design of Knowledge and Innovation Spaces: Learnings from Kelvin Grove Urban Village, Brisbane", *Journal of Open Innovation: Technology, Market, and Complexity* 1, no. 1 (2015): 13.

[22] Marilena Alivizatou, "Digital Intangible Heritage: Inventories, Virtual Learning and Participation", *Heritage & Society* 12, no. 2-3 (2019): 116–35, doi:10.1080/2159032X.2021.1883950.

[23] Divya P. Tolia-Kelly, Emma Waterton and Steve Watson (eds) *Heritage, Affect And Emotion: Politics, Practices And Infrastructures*, (Routledge, 2016); See also Anna Fielding, "Going Deeper than 'Emotional Impact': Heritage, Academic Collaboration and Affective Engagements", *History* 107, no. 375 (2022): 408–35.

[24] Fielding, "Going Deeper than 'Emotional Impact.'"

[25] Kristin L. Huffman, Andrea Giordano and Caroline Bruzelius (eds), *Visualizing Venice: Mapping and Modeling Time and Change in a City*, (London; New York: Routledge, 2017).

[26] Caroline Bruzelius, "Digital Technologies and New Evidence in Architectural History", *Journal of the Society of Architectural Historians* 76, no. 4 (2017): 436–39.

Figure 5.1 Screenshots captured from the time-lapse video that outline the chronological transformation of the eight selected buildings. © 2023 Md Mizanur Rashid, Sanja Rodeš and Chin Koi Khoo.

buildings are the Bright & Hitchock's building (1902), Albion Hotel (1875), Fire Insurance building (1889), Exchange and Regent Theatre (1928), Prince of Wales Hotel (1967), Richardson's Exchange building (1901), Corio Hotel (1987) and the Union Bank (1912). By juxtaposing archival photographs with videos of contemporary Little Malop Street, the medium blends historical information with the present condition, integrating the non-moving image (photograph) with the moving image (video). The shift in media development from the embedded archival photograph to the moving image is made apparent in this format. Time-lapse video is not interactive, and the user is simply viewing the content. By providing a curated selection of images, including only a selection of buildings rather than the entire street, the time-lapse video proposes a hierarchy and highlights the importance of the selected buildings over the rest of the street. By emphasising the difference between the historical images and their present condition, time lapse clarifies change over time and implicitly suggests the viewer's perceptions (see Figure 5.1).

Method 2: Virtual reality scanning and viewing (Matterport)

Virtual reality (VR) scanning has opened new opportunities for experiencing historical or lost buildings. Through the use of a specialised 360-degree camera and the Matterport VR scanning platform, Little Malop Street can be captured in three-dimensional detail, allowing users to explore the street as if they were physically present. Scanned street and building content in the Matterport VR platform provide an interactive and immersive experience, enabling users to navigate the street, examine existing and previous architectural details via the curated old images and chronological information, and to gain a sense of the historical atmosphere that once prevailed. This method is particularly valuable to compare and evaluate the captured lost heritage (archived images and historical information) and the scanned digital form of the current streetscape of Little Malop Street anytime and anywhere. It is also recording the current streetscapes and buildings in digital form as a digital visual archive for future research and study.

In comparison with the time-lapse video, the Matterport VR platform is highly interactive, and the user is driving their own experience of viewing and attaining knowledge. The viewer chooses which buildings to get more information on and, unlike time-lapse video, can observe the rest of the streetscape. This media is VR based and the photographs are secondary and embedded within the platform, should the user choose to engage. The buildings with embedded archival photographs in this media are the same ones included in the time-lapse video, but they represent and convey the information differently.

There are two modes of the Matterport VR platform for users to experience the interactive visualisation for the past and present of Little Malop Street: Model and Street mode. Figure 5.2 shows the overview for the Model mode of the three-dimensional scanned Little Malop Street with the eight indicative red tags of the selected buildings that will disseminate the archival images of each building with relevant information. When the cursor moves to the red tag of a selected building, a pop-up dialogue box will appear to disseminate the archived images and the relevant chronological information of each image (see Figure 5.3). The Street mode, on the other hand, allows users to access and experience the archival images and relevant chronological information of the eight selected buildings via the first-person view (FPV) with the pop-up dialogue boxes (see Figure 5.4 in the colour plate section). In addition to the overview evaluation of the Model mode, the Street mode provides a complementary effective and immersive experience for users while navigating and browsing the selected buildings with FPV. The two modes of the VR platform demonstrate the methods to experience and evaluate the archival visual content from different perspectives, thus shaping perception and allowing an appreciation for the heritage and history of the Little Malop Street between the past and present.

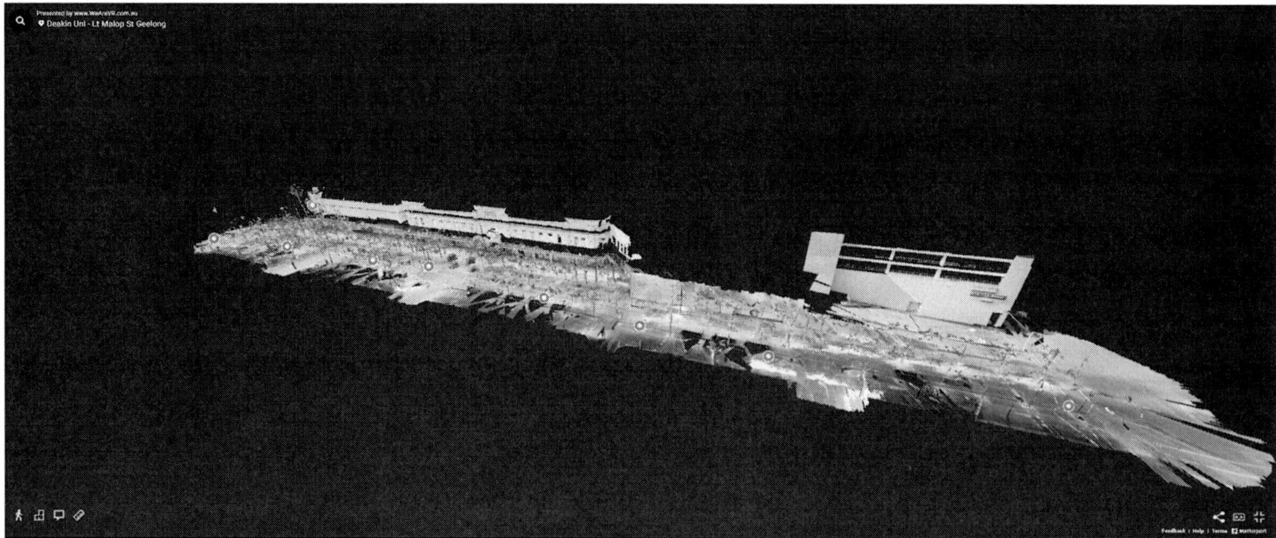

Figure 5.2 Model mode of the overall Little Malop Street with eight indicative tags of the identified buildings in the Matterport VR platform. © 2023 Md Mizanur Rashid, Sanja Rodeš and Chin Koi Khoo.

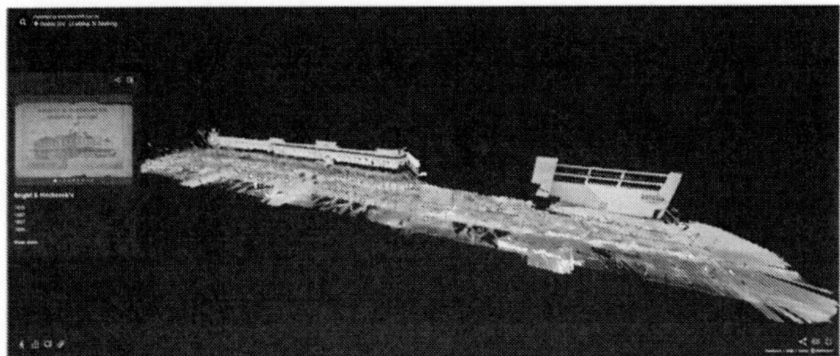

Bright & Hitchock's Building (1902 - 2023)

Rock O'Cashel / Derby's Arm / Albion Hotel (1875 - 2023)

Shops / Fire Insurance / Geelong Advertiser (1889 - 2023)

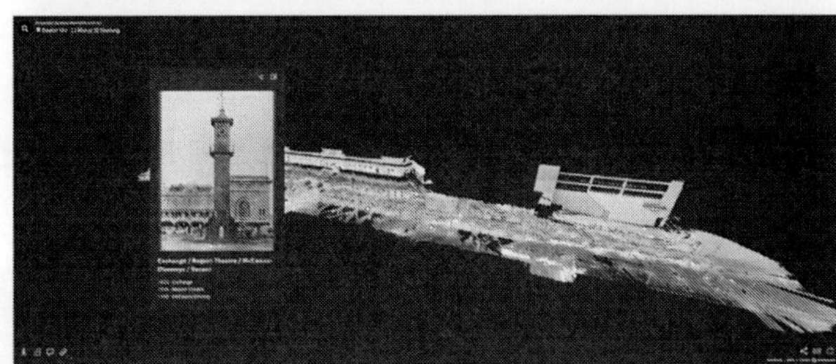

Exchange / Regent Theatre / McEwans - Dimmeys / vacant (1928 - 2023)

Prince of Wales Hotel / Geelong Advertiser building (1967 - 2023)

Richardson Exchange Building / Centrepoint Arcade (1901 - 2023)

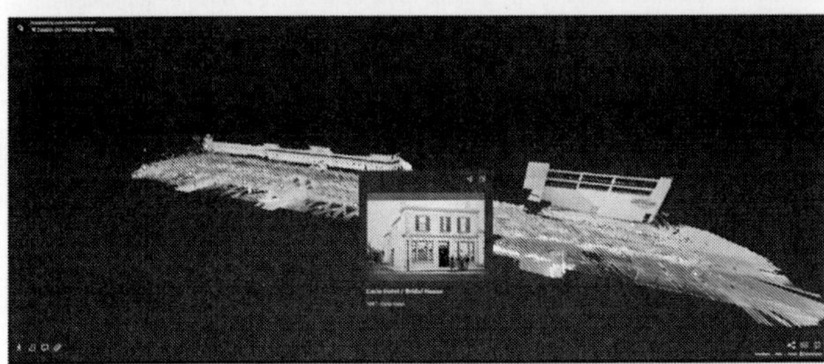

Corio Hotel / Bridal House (1987 - 2023)

Union Bank / Shops & YMCA (1912 - 2023)

Figure 5.3 Model mode of the eight identified buildings with the pop-up dialogue box of archived images and chronological information in the Matterport VR platform. © 2023 Md Mizanur Rashid, Sanja Rodeš and Chin Koi Khoo.

Method 3: Interactive visual timelines

This platform using an interactive timeline represents the history of Little Malop Street in a chronological format from 1889 to recent times. This interactive timeline includes significant architectural changes, especially to the façades, as well as notable cultural and social milestones. Users can interact with the timeline, zoom in on specific periods, and access additional information, such as archived photographs and brief descriptions of each period. By organising the street's history in this manner, an interactive visual timeline provides a comprehensive and dynamic representation of Little Malop Street's transformation over time, enhancing the understanding of its heritage through architectural and urban changes. The timeline organises the images and information according to time periods rather than spatially. In this manner, digitalised archival photographs are integrated into the timeline platform and make it accessible for further historical evaluation and information while the three-dimensional virtual space is not present.

The comprehensive collection of the digitalised archival photographs and drawings is chronologically organised with the interactive visual timeline sliders below each representation of the images and relevant information. Figure 5.5 illustrates a series of screenshots of the timeline from 1838 to 1855 to present succinct and concise information with the included archival visualisations: photographs, paintings, drawings and maps. Users can click on the chronological timeline slider of each historical period to review and evaluate the transition and transformation of Little Malop Street with the images and concise historical information of each period. For instance, Figure 5.6 shows the unfolding archival images and photographs that are represented by the selected timeline screenshots from 1960 to 2000, illustrating the different transformations of the buildings with coloured photographs to reflect the essence of the modernisation of Little Malop Street between the mid and end of the twentieth century.

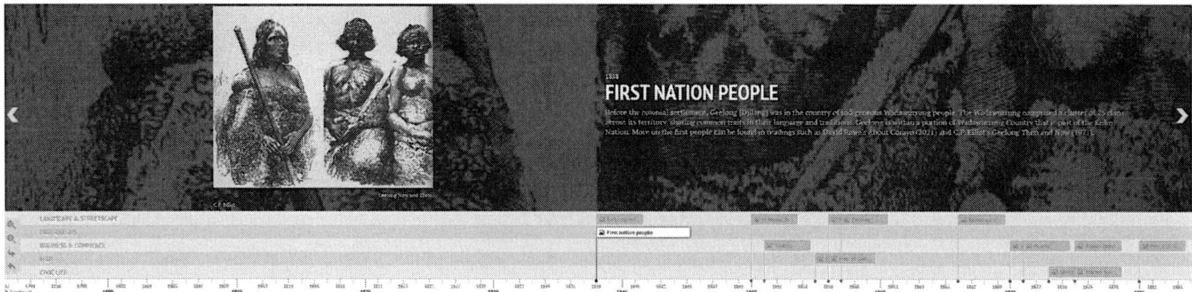

1838

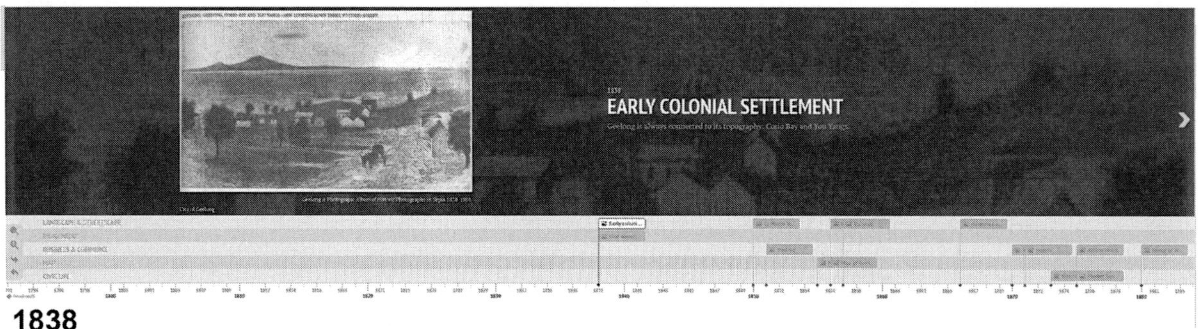

1838

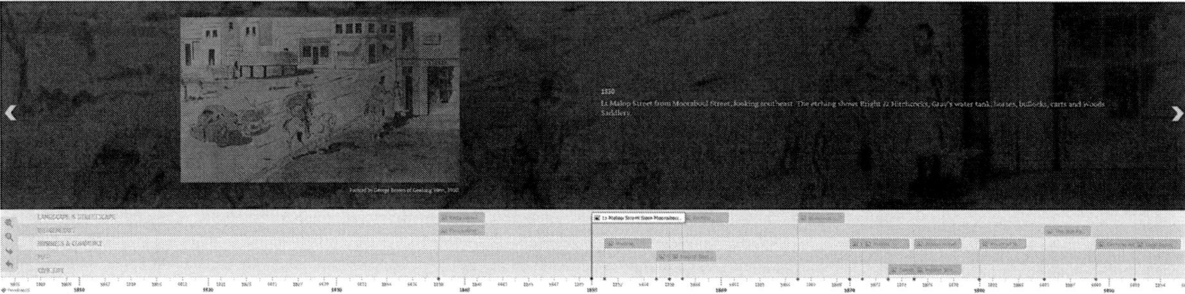

1850

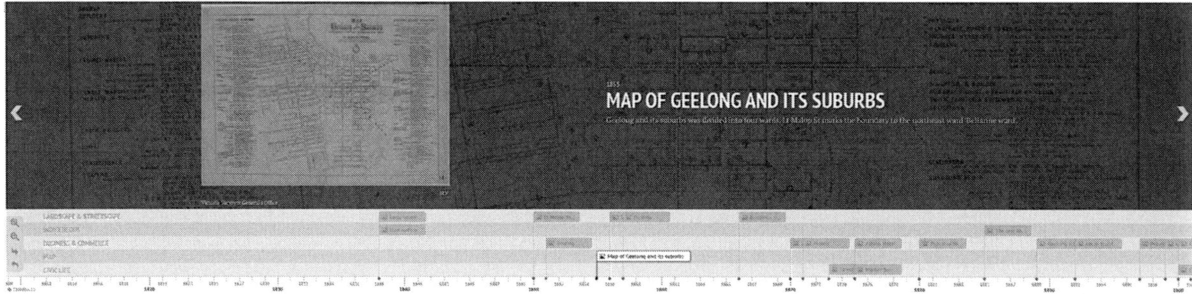

1851

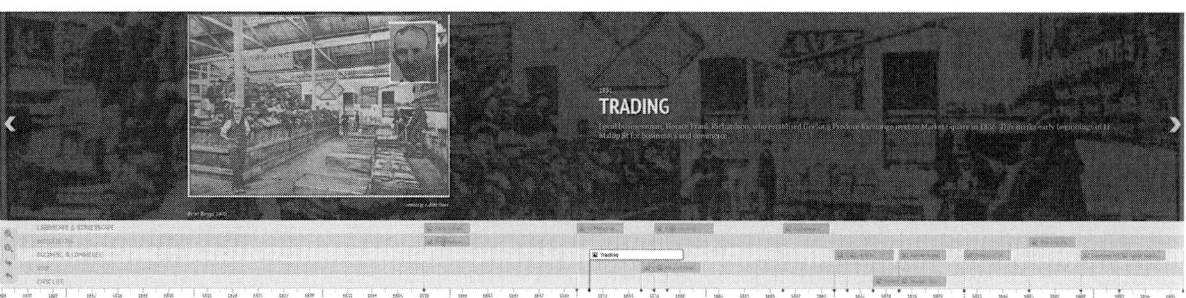

1855

Figure 5.5 Selected screenshots of the chronological timeline from 1838 to 1855. © 2023 Md Mizanur Rashid, Sanja Rodeš and Chin Koi Khoo.

1960

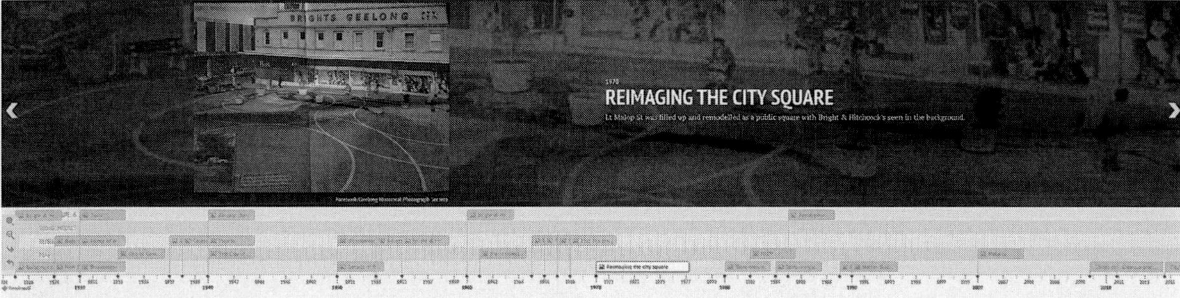

1970

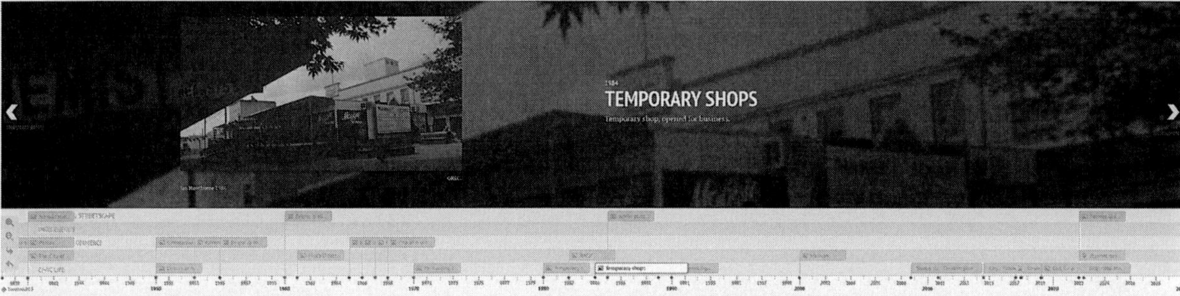

1984

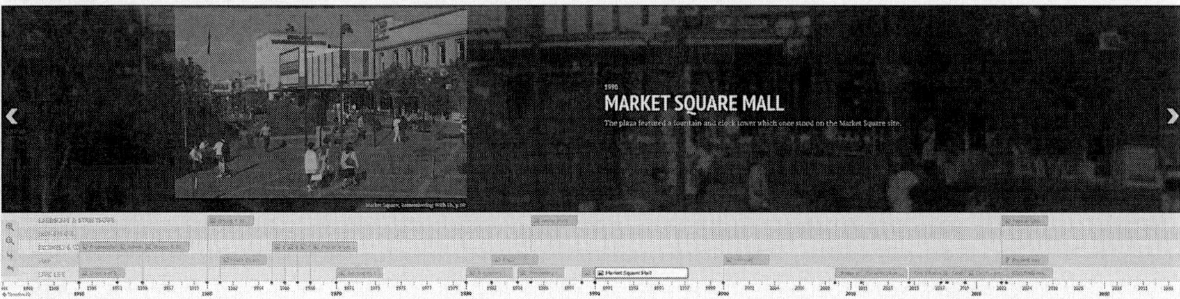

1990

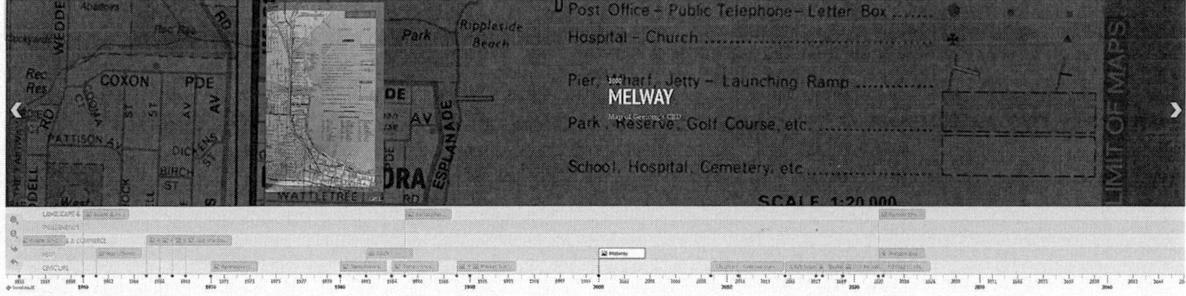

2000

Figure 5.6 Selected screenshots of the chronological timeline from 1960 to 2000. © 2023 Md Mizanur Rashid, Sanja Rodeš and Chin Koi Khoo.

Method 4: Website to represent the different media and user experience

The website serves as an accessible and user-friendly platform for presenting the various interactive media of the lost heritage and the transformation of Little Malop Street. The website incorporates a combination of the digital platforms previously described: media and images, including time-lapse videos, VR scans, and an interactive timeline. Through intuitive navigation, users can explore different sections of the street and/or building façades, view historical images, watch a time-lapse video and access relevant historical information through diverse experiences.

The website (https://www.littlemalop.net) consists of six main sections that include Home, Tracing the Transformation, Explore 360, Timeline, Archive, and Research Team (see Figure 5.7). The Home section includes the content and brief historical overview of Little Malop Street that outlines the street's past, now lost in time, by using various digital media contents and methods. Tracing the transformation displays the loop of the time-lapse video of Little Malop Street. Explore 360 allows users to interact with the VR platform of the street via model and street views to evaluate the three-dimensional scanned Little Malop Street with the pop-up dialogue box of archived images and chronological information. Timeline provides an interactive platform that offers an engaging way to represent the historical visual content and brief information of Little Malop Street in a chronological format from 1889 to recent times. The extensive collection of archival images, drawings, maps and photographs of the street is stored in the Archive section for the purpose of further review and evaluation of the overall collected visual content. Information regarding the research team and the contribution of relevant collaborators is acknowledged in the Research Team section.

Figure 5.7 The screenshots of the selected four sections (clockwise from top): Home, Tracing the transformation, Explore 360 and Timeline from the interactive website of Little Malop Street. © 2023 Md Mizanur Rashid, Sanja Rodeš and Chin Koi Khoo.

The overall content of the website represents the collection via various digital methods that have been discussed previously in this chapter. The website serves as an accessible platform from which to disseminate the content widely for the Geelong community, as well as a general audience. Instead of being a site of fixed content, this website platform is designed to enable constant update and revision of archival information and newly discovered visual components of the street. It is therefore a tool for the future study outcomes of the relevant research.

Discussion of the methods of using digital media and images

The methods discussed in this chapter (time-lapse video, Matterport VR scanning and viewing, interactive visual timelines and a website) demonstrate the potential and actual power of digital media and images to capture the lost heritage and transformation of Geelong's Little Malop Street. Each of the media platforms offers a different experience and connects the public to different layers of information on Geelong, with varying degrees of interactivity. The various digital platforms both communicate the information and direct the experience. Time-lapse video, VR scanning with interactive interface of Matterport, interactive timeline and website offer discreet and engaging ways to document, preserve and share the history and heritage significance of this historic street. By utilising the contemporary media and digital technologies, the importance of history and heritage of Little Malop Street is communicated and made relevant in the present. By employing these methods with relevant digital platforms, the heritage of Little Malop Street can be made accessible to a wider audience beyond academics, historians or heritage experts, fostering a deeper understanding and appreciation of the street's significance, and ensuring its legacy is known. The interactivity and attractiveness of these digital media is a significant element, where for example VR is frequently used within the sphere of entertainment for the general public.[27] Due to the interactivity and attractiveness of this media, the embedded historical content is made further engaging by extension. The popularity of digital media in entertainment also has a potential to bridge the gap between history, heritage and youth, which are arguably main consumers of these digital media and platforms. The potential of VR is already acknowledged in education, as VR can help increase students' engagement and focus.[28] These digital technologies offer new opportunities for engagement and are able to reach different audiences, disseminating information via internet, building on the previously used archives or printed media only.

As digital technology continues to advance, it is crucial to embrace these tools and methods in both heritage documentation and in research, as it allows people to connect with the lost past while embracing future possibilities for Little Malop Street.[29] Although there are challenges in using digital technologies to document historical data via digital images and other media, the benefits for accessibility make it a key tool for historians, conservation architects, researchers, the City of Greater Geelong and the general public.

The use of digital media and technology offers new opportunities for urban planning and design. By creating a digital archive of lost heritage narratives, it is possible to integrate this heritage into the urban landscape in new and innovative ways. For example, virtual models of lost buildings and streetscapes can provide a way to visualise the past and design new buildings and public spaces.[30] This creates a dialogue between the past and present, and a sense of continuity and connection with the past, providing a framework for the future. It can also provide a platform for public engagement and participation in the design process, promoting a sense of ownership and pride in the urban environment.[31]

This chapter explored the potential of digital technology to preserve architectural memories and adapt them to the evolving urban landscape. Building on the belief that architecture offers insights into human nature, values and culture, the project employs digital tools to reconstruct Geelong's urban history for widespread dissemination.[32] The concept of "virtual heritage" facilitates non-invasive monument restoration through immersive multimedia experiences, benefiting conservators, historians, archaeologists and urban designers in capturing and integrating the memory of the place in the future design of the city.[33] Despite the considerable aid provided by three-dimensional virtual models in the process, capturing intangible values remains a notable challenge.

This digital visualisation project adopts a comprehensive approach to this problem by effectively utilising digital technologies to capture both tangible and intangible memories.[34] Understanding a building's significance within the contemporary context, but divorced from traditional interactions, presents a unique challenge.[35] Although architecture inherently encapsulates collective memories, the process of engaging with those is intricate and nuanced.[36] This project itself centres on the concept of "affective heritage", aiming to broaden heritage understanding(s) by meticulously examining historic structures to holistically capture human experiences. The ultimate goal of the project is to bridge temporal gaps, enabling present-day individuals to forge a profound connection with the past, thus shaping collective memory and fostering cultural preservation.

Furthermore, digital media and technology can facilitate the integration of lost heritage into the urban landscape in various ways.[37] This integration can provide a more immersive experience for residents and visitors, promoting a deeper appreciation of the city's history and cultural heritage. It can also contribute to the development of a unique and distinctive urban identity that can attract tourism and investment.[38]

---

27 Ajah Hamad and Bochen Jia, "How Virtual Reality Technology has Changed Our Lives: An Overview of the Current and Potential Applications and Limitations," *Int J Environ Res Public Health*. 2022 Sep; 19 (18): 11278, doi: 10.3390/ijerph191811278

28 Hamad and Jia, "How Virtual Reality Technology has Changed Our Lives."

29 Mohamed Gamal Abdelmonem, "Architectural and Urban Heritage in the Digital Age: Dilemmas of Authenticity, Originality And Reproduction", *International Journal of Architectural Research*, ArchNet-IJAR 11, no. 3 (2017): 5–15.

30 Tomoki Nakaya et al., "Virtual Kyoto Project: Digital Diorama Of The Past, Present, And Future Of The Historical City Of Kyoto", *Culture and Computing: Computing and Communication for Crosscultural Interaction* (2010): 173–87.

31 Eva Eriksson, Thomas Riisgaard Hansen, and Andreas Lykke-Olesen, "Reclaiming Public Space: Designing for Public Interaction with Private Devices" in *Proceedings of the 1st International Conference on Tangible and Embedded Interaction* (2007), 31–38.

32 Peter Scriver and Vikramaditya Prakash (eds), *Colonial Modernities: Building, Dwelling and Architecture in British India and Ceylon* (London; New York: Routledge, 2007).

33 Abdelmonem, "Architectural and Urban Heritage in the Digital Age.".

34 Gregg Richards and Lian Duif (eds), *Small Cities with Big Dreams: Creative Placemaking and Branding Strategies,* (London; New York: Routledge, 2019).

35 Mohamed Gamal Abdelmonem, *The Architecture of Home in Cairo: Socio-spatial Practice of the Hawari's Everyday Life*, (London; New York: Routledge, 2016).

36 Paul Connerton, *How Societies Remember* (Cambridge, UK: Cambridge University Press, 1989).

37 Eugene Ch'ng, "Digital Heritage Tourism: Reconfiguring the Visitor Experience in Heritage Sites, Museums and Architecture in the Era of Pervasive Computing", in *Percorsi Creative di Turismo Urbano (Creative Paths Of Urban Tourism) Conference, Catania* (2011).

38 Lorenzo Cantoni, "Digital transformation, Tourism and Cultural Heritage", in Maria Gravari-Barbas (ed), *A Research Agenda for Heritage Tourism* (Cheltenham, UK: Edward Elgar Publishing, 2020), 235–252; See also Amira Hassan Abdo, "Digital Heritage

Our research demonstrates that digital media and related imagery are a link between the public and heritage, and that media directs the experience as much as it allows for interactivity. The chapter argues that media and imagery go beyond merely documenting; digital media have a potential for curating and shaping history to a degree, depending on the possibilities and limitations of each of the digital platforms that offer a different layer of unique representations to communicate and unfold the historical artefacts and documentations. By deciding on what is being seen and communicated, what is included or excluded, and in what manner (which depends on both the digital media and the person who translates the historical information into a digital platform), the role of digital media to convey history remains that of an active creator, rather than a passive conveyor. Acknowledging the ability of digital media tools to shape history as they document it, media and imagery offer a rich and growing field of potential for urban and cultural heritage and history, and for further research.

The digital media methods and examples discussed in this chapter provide the initial immersive insight and experience for users via the digitalised images and visualisations of the present and lost buildings of Little Malop Street. Each method serves as a unique opportunity to enable users to see, experience and evaluate the historical and cultural content of the heritage against the present environment via the visualised digital images and scanned street views in the VR platform. Instead of the conventional interpretation of traditional archival images, the interactivity and immersive experience that is enabled by the new layer of digital content provides an alternative evaluation of the past and present Little Malop Street, especially in relation to the transformation of the series of architectural façades and programs. By incorporating lost heritage into the urban landscape in innovative ways, it is possible to develop a unique and distinctive urban identity that can attract tourism and investment. For instance, this urban identity will be represented via the integration of the physical environment and a digital media platform, such as the visual/augmented reality app, that offers and encourages visitors and tourists to explore and experience the hybrid content between lost heritage and existing environment.

Conclusion

The case of Geelong's Little Malop Street illustrates the importance of community engagement and participation in the experience of urban heritage from the new perspective of digital media and image manipulation. The creation of a digital archive of lost heritage can serve as a platform for public engagement and participation and introduces an approach for capturing and revitalising the city's past. By creating a space for public dialogue and engagement, it is possible to build community support and awareness for the importance of urban heritage and cultural identity.

The example of Geelong's Little Malop Street highlights the challenges of preserving heritage in the face of rapid urban development and gentrification. However, by creating a digital archive of images of the lost heritage, it is possible to create a dynamic representation of the transformation of the city's built heritage through time, and a platform for public engagement to disseminate the heritage value. The use of virtual modelling and other digital platforms can inform the design of new buildings and public spaces in a way that respects the city's past while embracing its future.

Digital media extends both the possibilities for documenting and narrating history and has the potential to enhance the relevance of history for the public. By using contemporary digital methods to represent and convey historical knowledge, this knowledge is made more present and attractive. The active role of media platforms and related imagery in interpreting historical knowledge and narratives is notable and calls for further considerations. As McLuhan argued, media is "the extension[s] of man [sic]", its increasing embeddedness into historical and cultural narratives is highly relevant for contemporary understandings and documentation of history.[39]

The potential of digital media and technology in documenting, disseminating and revitalising existing urban heritage is still being explored, and further research is needed to understand its full impact and potential. This study of Geelong's Little Malop Street provides a relevant example of how digital media can be used to achieve this potential in the face of rapid urban development and change. By creating a dynamic representation of the city's heritage and cultural identity, and by engaging the public in the interpretation and revitalisation process, it is possible to build a stronger, more resilient and connected urban community.

Applications and its Impact on Cultural Tourism", *Journal of Association of Arab Universities for Tourism and Hospitality* 17, no. 1 (2019): 37–50; Ch'ng, "Digital Heritage Tourism."

[39] McLuhan, *Understanding Media;* Steve F. Anderson, *Technologies of History: Visual Media and the Eccentricity of the Past* (UPNE, 2011). See also Maurizio Forte, "Digital Cities, Neuroarchaeology and Cyberarchaeology" (keynote speech, *26th Conference on Cultural Heritage and New Technology*, CHNT, Vienna, Austria, 2021).

CHAPTER 6

REIMAGINING GEELONG VIA SYSTEMS THINKING

RICHARD TUCKER AND LOUISE JOHNSON

Approaching the reimagining

The approach taken by HOME, a strategic research and innovation centre comprising around thirty academics from the four faculties of Deakin University – Arts and Education; Business and Law; Science, Engineering and Built Environment; and Health – was key to the way the challenges of reimagining the city of Geelong were framed. For each project, a range of academics from specific disciplines were assembled, with all teams and team members committed to working in an interdisciplinary way. This move beyond the focus and remit of one discipline is widespread within the academy and has been impelled by the enhanced complexity of nature and society, generative technologies, demands from funders, the recognition that issues – especially those that span the sciences, the environment, and humanities – are not confined to a single discipline, the drive for innovation and a need to solve larger societal problems.[1] When further discussing the nature of interdisciplinarity, Julie Thompson Klein notes:

> The heightened discourse of problem solving also meant it became linked with the concept of wicked problems that are not isolated to particular sectors of disciplines. They are interdependent, driven by complex cause-effect relationships.[2]

The HOME hub research centre is indeed focused on addressing "wicked problems" in contemporary Australia, particularly those associated with accessing affordable, socially connected and sustainable housing. At the time of writing – two decades into the new millenia – this is one of the key issues in Australia and Geelong, registered in soaring rents, rising levels of homelessness and through a series of public forums involving more than 250 locals where housing access, security and quality emerged as the top priority.[3] HOME members participated in these forums, recording major issues in Geelong as a prelude to designing interventions as a research group. This approach is followed across a range of research projects as HOME members bring together diverse academic expertise and utilise systems thinking tools to address community problems in new ways and co-design feasible but impactful solutions. The research that is reported here is not driven by academic imperatives, but by social ones, with the aim being to make a difference to the communities in which these projects are located, to contribute to Geelong's reimagining as the city confronts issues of accessibility, homelessness and spatial inequality.

This chapter reflects on the impacts, accumulated knowledge, achievements, limitations and future possibilities of three HOME research projects that all seek to reimagine Geelong by improving the lives of groups facing accessibility and social inclusion obstacles. These groups include low-income earners excluded from the housing market, people living with disability or mental illness, and those living in three Geelong suburbs evidenced as amongst the most disadvantaged in Victoria. The three projects are:

- Vital Communities, which provided recommendations for strategic approaches and policy needs to achieve social equity in the areas facing greatest disadvantaged in Geelong.
- Accessible and Inclusive Geelong Feasibility Study, which informed a collective plan of action, supported by a wide range of community stakeholders, to enable Geelong to be accessed, understood, and used to the greatest extent possible by all people.
- Geelong Microvillage, which explored the viability of affordable houses for those with limited funds and a desire for modestly sized homes that minimise consumption of building materials, land and energy, and which integrate and link with their adjacent community.

One important aspect to imagining different "Geelongs" in these projects was the process by which outcomes were generated. Key to all three was the combination of community-based participatory research with a systems thinking framework to better understand the complex inter-relatedness of what shaped the issues in each.

---

[1] Andrew Barry and Georgina Born, *Interdisciplinarity: Reconfigurations of the Social and Natural* (Routledge, 2013); John H. Aldrich, *Interdisciplinarity: Its Role in a Discipline-Based Academy* (Oxford University Press, 2014); Julie T. Klein, *Beyond Interdisciplinarity: Boundary Work, Communication and Collaboration* (Oxford University Press, 2021).

[2] Klein, *Beyond Interdisciplinarity: Boundary Work, Communication and Collaboration*.

[3] Wadawurrung Country, Sally Fisher, Juliet Bennett, Amanda Tattersall, Amy Tong, Katie Moore, Elise Ganley, Isabelle Napier, Molly Jones, Teagan Mitchell, *A Real Deal for Geelong: Community Listening Report for Climate Transition* (2023).

In each of the projects, particular teams were assembled with the appropriate expertise, set of perspectives, an openness to cross disciplinary and methodological boundaries and a commitment to address community-derived problems. As Head notes: 'modern social problems are "wicked" problems because stakeholders disagree about the nature of these problems, about possible solutions and about the values or principles that should guide improvements' before advocating an approach that embraces complexity, uncertainty and divergence.[4] Lawrence further notes that as housing is one such problem, then it is amendable to a "transdisciplinary imagination", which brings together a range of people and their disciplines along with a commitment to utilise but also to go beyond each.[5] The teams associated with each project, identified by their schools/division and disciplines, are detailed in Table 6.1.

Project (participant numbers)	School/Division (participant numbers)	Discipline/Expertise
Vital Communities (10)	School of Architecture and Built Environment (3) School of Health and Social Development (2) School of Exercise and Nutrition Faculty of Science, Engineering and Built Environment (1) Deakin Business School (1) Strategic Partnerships (Research) (1) Externals (2)	Architecture Public health Nutrition Econometrics Human geography Social science
Accessible and Inclusive Geelong Feasibility Study (20)	School of Architecture and Built Environment (6) School of Health and Social Development (9) School of Humanities and Social Sciences (1) Deakin Business School (1) Systems Thinking (1) Externals (2)	Architecture Universal design Public health Disability Human geography STICKE Urban planning Inclusionary design
Geelong Microvillage Project (13)	School of Architecture and Built Environment (1) School of Health and Social Development (3) School of Humanities and Social Sciences (4) Business (3) Systems Thinking (2)	Architecture Public health Human geography Anthropology Tenure forms Economics STICKE

Table 6.1 Teams associated with each project, identified by their schools/division and disciplines

HOME therefore aims to inform change to housing and cities to meet the diverse needs of all people. The interdisciplinarity of our researchers provides the breadth of expertise required to address the system-wide complexities of each place and issue. The processes we utilise are founded on providing a holistic understanding of what can be termed the wicked problem of the interlinked obstacles that prevent cities from being accessed, understood and used to the greatest extent possible by all people and to provide workable solutions. For this we draw on systems thinking.

STICKE, systems thinking and system dynamics in urban planning contexts

Systems thinking is a holistic approach to understanding and solving complex problems. It views the world as a system composed of interconnected and interdependent parts or elements. Instead of analysing individual components in isolation, systems thinking considers the relationships and interactions among these components. Systems thinking is therefore used for addressing complex issues where there are many possible solutions and where intuitive methods have failed to produce satisfactory change. By recognising the immutability of certain factors hindering progress, the approach identifies and evaluates the feasibility of different interventions. System dynamics, which was initially developed by Forrester, is nested within systems thinking and focuses on understanding and modelling dynamic systems over time using computer-based simulation models, such as the one used in the projects described in this chapter.[6]

---

[4] Brian W. Head, "The Rise of 'Wicked Problems' – Uncertainty, Complexity and Divergence", in Brian W. Head (ed) *Wicked Problems in Public Policy: Understanding and Responding to Complex Challenges* (Springer International Publishing, 2022) 21–36, https://doi.org/10.1007/978-3-030-94580-0_2.

[5] Roderick J. Lawrence, "Collective and Creative Consortia: Combining Knowledge, Ways of Knowing and Praxis", *Cities & Health* 4, no. 2 (2020): 237–49, https://doi.org/10.1080/23748834.2020.1711996.

[6] Jay Wright Forrester, "Industrial Dynamics. A Major Breakthrough for Decision Makers", *Harvard Business Review* 36 no. 4 (1958): 37–66; Jay Wright Forrester, *Industrial Dynamics* (Pegasus Communications, 1961).

While in the late 1960s, system dynamics was adapted to urban planning contexts to examine problems emerging from intense and rapid urbanisation, its use in urban planning waned until gaining traction at the turn of the twenty-first century to address sustainability issues, which are often tied to intricate, self-organising systems.[7] Notable successes included air quality management in Santiago de Chile and community development in Northern Mexico.[8]

The literature has increasingly advocated systems thinking for operationalising sustainability in urban contexts.[9] In this, cities are recognised as dynamic systems characterised by constant interactions and changing variables, resulting in non-linear feedback loops. Rather than viewing cities as simple cause-and-effect systems, this perspective emphasises the need for a holistic understanding of the entire system and the relationships among its components.[10]

The wider application of systems approaches in urban planning has been relatively recent.[11] For example, in integrated planning theory it has frequently been employed to promote sustainable urban development.[12] Integrated planning theory and systems thinking approaches are complementary, sharing common principles and objectives: elements of consensus building, participatory design, and the consideration of urban ecosystems in the planning process.[13] A notable outcome of this methodology is Rotterdam's Groenplan, an urban green infrastructure strategy, highlighting the shift towards holistic, participatory planning for urban sustainability.[14]

Similarly, in our research in Geelong, we have applied systems thinking to participatory action research in recognising, understanding and changing the city as a complex urban system from a community-based perspective. By engaging community stakeholders in systems thinking processes, that is, those individuals or groups who have a vested interest or stake in a particular research problem, the approach emphasises the importance of shared visions and co-designing solutions in promoting community-driven action and capacity-building. The method drives a consensus-based approach to assessing the impact of proposed interventions. In this, multiple stakeholder perspectives are used to identify problems, causes, relationships, and potential interventions collectively, empowering community stakeholders to drive and take part in meaningful action.

To facilitate the visualisation of Geelong as a complex urban system, the research team utilised a systems dynamics modelling software known as STICKE (Systems Thinking in Community Knowledge Exchange). STICKE is an approach to addressing complex community issues that involves a deep understanding of a community as a complex system with various interconnected components, such as education, healthcare, environment, housing, and social services. STICKE recognises that communities are not just a collection of isolated parts but are interconnected systems where changes in one area can have far-reaching effects. It emphasises the need to consider these interconnections when addressing community challenges.

STICKE is a software application developed by Deakin University in collaboration with the GLOBE – a World Health Organization Collaborating Centre for Obesity Prevention. STICKE uses visual tools in the form of system maps that help stakeholders grasp the complexity of the issues at hand. These maps are made up of causal loop diagrams

---

[7] Jay Wright Forrester, *Urban Dynamics* (M.I.T. Press, 1969); Peter Hjorth and Ali Bagheri, "Navigating Towards Sustainable Development: A System Dynamics Approach", *Futures* 38, no. 1 (2006): 74–92.

[8] Alfredo del Valle, "Managing Complexity Through Methodic Participation: The Case Of Air Quality In Santiago, Chile", *Systemic Practice and Research*, 12 (1999): 367–80; *Russell L. Ackoff et al., Proceedings Russell L. Ackoff and The Advent Of Systems Thinking,* (1999); Jaime Jiménez and Juan Carlos Escalante, "Community Development through Participative Planning", in *Proceedings of the Conference on Russell L. Ackoff and the Advent of Systems Thinking. A Conference to Celebrate the Work of Russell L. Ackoff on his 80th Birthday and Developments in Systems Theory and Practice* (1999).

[9] Stephen Martin, "Sustainable Development, Systems Thinking and Professional Practice", *Journal of Education for Sustainable Development* 2, no. 1 (2008): 31–40; N. C. Nguyen, O. J. Bosch and K. E. Maani, "Creating 'Learning Laboratories' for Sustainable Development in Biospheres: A Systems Thinking Approach", *Systems Research and Behavioral Science* 28, no. 1 (2011): 51–62; Umberto Pisano, "Resilience and Sustainable Development: Theory of Resilience, Systems Thinking", *European Sustainable Development Network (ESDN)* 26, no. 50 (2012); Joanne Tippett, John F. Handley and Joe Ravetz, "Meeting the Challenges of Sustainable Development-A Conceptual Appraisal of a New Methodology for Participatory Ecological Planning", 0305-9006, 67 no. 1 (2007): 1–98.

[10] T. Irene Sanders, "Complex systems thinking and new urbanism" in Tigran Haas (ed), *New Urbanism and Beyond: Designing Cities for the Future* (New York: Rizzoli, 2008), 275–79.

[11] Kathyrn M. Davidson and Jackie Venning, "Sustainability Decision-Making Frameworks and the Application of Systems Thinking: An Urban Context", *Local Environment* 16 no. 3 (2011): 213–28.

[12] Tan Yigitcanlar and Suharto Teriman, "Rethinking Sustainable Urban Development: Towards an Integrated Planning and Development Process", *International Journal of Environmental Science and Technology* 12 no. 1 (2015): 341–52.

[13] Carey Curtis, "Planning for Sustainable Accessibility: The Implementation Challenge", *Transport Policy* 15, no. 2 (2008): 104–112; Thomas Straatemeier and Luca Bertolini, "Joint Accessibility Design: Framework Developed with Practitioners to Integrate Land Use and Transport Planning in the Netherlands", *Transportation Research Record* 2077, no. 1 (2008): 1–8; Abed Abukhater, "Rethinking Planning Theory and Practice: A Glimmer of Light for Prospects of Integrated Planning to Combat Complex Urban Realities". *Theoretical and Empirical Researches in Urban Management* 4, no. 2 (11, 2009): 64–79; Bauke Devries, Vincent Tabak and Henri Achten, "Interactive Urban Design Using Integrated Planning Requirements Control", *Automation in Construction* 14, no. 2 (2005): 207–13; Christopher Pettit and David Pullar, "An Integrated Planning Tool Based upon Multiple Criteria Evaluation of Spatial Information", *Computers, Environment and Urban Systems* 23 no. 5 (1999): 339–57; Joe Ravetz, *City-Region 2020: Integrated Planning for a Sustainable Environment* (Routledge, 2016); Gemeente Rotterdam, *Groenplan Rotterdam* (Rotterdam, The Netherlands, 2005).

[14] Gemeente Rotterdam, *Groenplan Rotterdam*; Nico Tillie and Roland van der Heijden, "Advancing Urban Ecosystem Governance in Rotterdam: From Experimenting and Evidence Gathering to New Ways for Integrated Planning", *Environmental Science & Policy* 62 (2016): 139–144.

(CLDs) that depict how the variables within a system map are interrelated. Based on the group model building (GMB) methodology, STICKE guides participants through tasks facilitated by trained researchers to examine interdependent causes and effects of a given problem. The methodology consists of three steps: group discussion and map building, map review and development, and confirmation of the systems map and generation of prioritised action ideas. These actions are prioritised based on participants' ratings of their perceived feasibility and impact.

The use of STICKE offers several advantages. Firstly, it enables direct knowledge and experience sharing between individuals with and without lived experience of intractable problems, such as (in our Geelong research) inclusion or accessibility, lack of affordable housing, or locational disadvantage. This knowledge exchange fosters deep and shared understandings of city-scale obstacles to change. Secondly, it allows diverse stakeholders to collaboratively develop a mutually agreed plan of action to overcome these obstacles. This inclusive approach ensures that a broad range of perspectives is considered in such plans. Lastly, STICKE promotes collective impact and sustainability of change by facilitating positive attitude shifts towards those with lived experience of an issue, for instance the homeless or those with disability.

Overall, STICKE serves as a valuable tool for community engagement and problem solving, enabling diverse stakeholders to contribute their perspectives and experiences in an exchange of knowledge that facilitates collective decision-making. It is a process by which new solutions to existing problems can be elicited and new urban spaces imagined.

Vital Communities

In 2019, the City of Greater Geelong (CoGG) established a policy framework for improving the integration and socio-economic development of three areas of the city long burdened by social inequality and inequity – Corio, Norlane and Whittington. Described as the Vital Communities project, the city commissioned the HOME Research Hub to develop strategies for alleviating locational disadvantage in these areas.[15] The research was to engage with existing policies, survey extant academic literature, collate international and national initiatives and engage with local residents to develop strategies for progressing social equity and prosperity across five practice domains: Employment, Education, Housing, Liveability, Health and Well-being. HOME was tasked to address one of the most intractable wicked problems bedevilling all societies – long term socio-spatial disadvantage – in a part of the city that had been subjected to many earlier studies and interventions, most of which had failed. This project therefore involved a reimagining of the causes and possible alternatives to socio-spatial disadvantage.

The assembled research team reflected the range of disciplines and areas of expertise needed to engage with all five domains (see Table 6.1). As a result of the COVID-19 pandemic, in-person interviews and focus groups with residents moved online to discussions with service providers. They were recruited from a list of major providers in the area supplied by CoGG, while a STICKE workshop occurred with CoGG once the results were collated. One of the major limitations of this study was the restricted participation of residents as a result of the pandemic, though most of the service organisations had worked in these areas for years and were very attuned to their situation and needs. From these online discussions, the team offered three main recommendations:

- Recommendation 1: Affirmed the importance of listening to the communities; build on existing local strengths, support, recognise and support the community's ability to design solutions to problems.
- Recommendation 2: Once the listening had occurred, the city should address fourteen priority areas to improve quality of life for residents in Corio, Norlane and Whittington. These included: digital exclusion, disengagement from education, unemployment, Indigenous health and well-being, food security, access to health services, domestic violence, housing stress, neighbourhood revitalisation and public space improvements and place-based stigma.
- Recommendation 3: Address these fourteen priority areas through ten proposed initiatives. The initiatives should be multi-pronged in focus, drawing on cross-sector collaboration, and span practice domains and local issues, recognising the multi-faceted nature of disadvantage and its alleviation.[16]

A STICKE workshop with key decision-makers within the City of Greater Geelong detailed the research process and its recommendations before distilling a set of feasible actions.[17] While again multi-faceted, these suggestions involved affirming the need for genuine consultation with residents and focused interventions along the lines suggested by the project team. One suggestion involved revisiting an existing structure plan for Corio–Norlane that had included a proposal to green the areas and revitalise its neighbourhood shopping centres. Some key recommendations of this research were taken up by the City of Greater Geelong, and that involved wide consultation as part of a reimagining and rebuilding of Labuan Square, a small neighbourhood shopping centre in Norlane.

---

[15] Richard Tucker, Meg Mundell, Louise Johnson, Danielle Hitch, Fiona Andrews, Jian Liang, Lukar Thornton, Isabella Bower and Anahita Sal Mosleahian, *Strategies for Tackling Locational Disadvantage in Geelong* (2021).

[16] Tucker et al., *Strategies for Tackling Locational Disadvantage in Geelong*, 187–188.

[17] Tucker et al., *Strategies for Tackling Locational Disadvantage in Geelong.*

Small interventions 1: Labuan Square

Labuan Square is a 1950s-era neighbourhood strip of shops in Norlane. As a small precinct that has suffered from the competition presented by a larger, drive-through centre and the wider move away from local shopping, it had been a concern for CoGG for some time. In the last twenty years, including in the 2012 Corio–Norlane Structure Plan, the City of Greater Geelong had urged its revival by encouraging businesses to locate there and upgrading retail infrastructure and landscaping. However, it never returned to its 1970s vibrancy and while what remains has been well utilised, it is widely regarded as a neglected and hostile space.

Following a key recommendation of the Strategies for Alleviating Locational Disadvantage in Geelong project team, and in recognition of the more than thirty-nine past "consultations" in this area, many of which had led to little improvement, the City of Greater Geelong embarked on a systematic and wide-ranging community engagement process, overseen by a well-regarded local organisation – Norlane Community Initiatives (NCI). The multi-faceted process by which CoGG elicited community input into the value and redesign possibilities of this centre is a model of genuine consultation. Advertising occurred in print and radio media as well as through the usual council "Have Your Say" portal. NCI utilised six local residents trained as community surveyors to promote the consultation process as well as to conduct one on-site "listening post" exercise (few in number because of pandemic restrictions), organise two community drop-in sessions and deliver 850 postcards into local letter boxes with particular attention paid to residents with special needs.[18] A Project Reference Group, comprising local community service organisations, residents and the CoGG person overseeing the project, met regularly. The CoGG online survey elicited 179 responses, highlighting the issues surrounding the centre as well as nominating agendas for its improvement.

Issues included the centre's apparent abandonment by the government, residents and traders alike; lack of safety; poor mix of shops (many closed or boarded up) and a derelict toilet block. But residents and traders also recorded their regular use of the centre, especially its post office, chemist, medical facilities, small supermarket, take-away food stores and public seating. They bemoaned the loss of shops over recent years – the café, bakery, wholefoods store and opportunity/thrift shop. Furthermore, they noted the opportunity presented by its design, accessibility and landscape – especially the orchard – and urged sustainable landscaping, access to nature, improved appearance, shop activation and safety, as well as more activities and events. The overall reimagining which emerged was for:

> Labuan Square to again be a vibrant, green, attractive, friendly, accessible and safe public space for our neighbourhood with a mix of essential and speciality shops, cafes or eateries, services and activities … a community hub.[19]

The many suggestions for change included an array of pragmatic ideas readily embraced by CoGG and incorporated into both their design plan and funding bids. Therefore, an emphasis on revamped landscaping, including playgrounds, public art and openness to Indigenous plantings and traditions has underpinned the new urban design for Labuan Square. The design was presented to the Community Advisory Committee, the traders' group and for public feedback, most of which was affirmative. The core of the design – developed in close collaboration with the Wadawurrung Traditional Owners Aboriginal Corporation – is the flow of the nearby Cowie's Creek. The movement of the creek from its rocky headwaters, through to an open marshland, finally entering Corio Bay through steep orange cliffs, is now symbolically represented in the new landscape design for the core of the centre. In addition, a $100,000 Place Activation Grant has funded CCTV cameras, better seating and lighting, new planting and a rebuilt toilet block. There is a further bid in the pipeline for a Creating Safer Places Grant to extend this work and to encourage community events and activities. NCI has established a social enterprise café in the centre, while other businesses – such as the supermarket – have renovated and been reactivated.

The case study of Labuan Square is a positive example of genuine community consultation, and engagement with the local Aboriginal community for a reimagining of the design of a neighbourhood shopping centre and a revamping of this centre to better meet the concerns and needs of a long-neglected suburb. The prioritising of this place and the process by which it was redeveloped emerged from the HOME research recommendations and the STICKE process of engaging key decision-makers to embrace its agenda. The result (see Figures 6.1 and 6.2) is a stunning example of how a small part of this "disadvantaged" area could be reimagined with the genuine input of local communities working in partnership with a regional authority.

---

[18] Norlane Community Initiatives (NCI), *Community Engagement and Consultation, Labuan Square Redevelopment* (City of Greater Geelong Department of Planning and Community Development, 2021).

[19] Norlane Community Initiatives (NCI), *Community Engagement and Consultation, Labuan Square Redevelopment.* See also: Mundell, M., Andrews, F., Tucker, R., **Johnson, L.**, & Liang, J. (2024). Public space in the shadow of COVID-19: placemaking for spatial justice in Geelong's 'disadvantaged' neighbourhoods. *Journal of Urbanism: International Research on Placemaking and Urban Sustainability*, 1–24. https://doi.org/10.1080/17549175.2024.2337888cc

Figure 6.1 Reimagining Labuan Square (before), 2019 (Photo Louise Johnson).

Figure 6.2 Reimagining Labuan Square (after), 2024 (Photo Louise Johnson).

Accessible and Inclusive Geelong Feasibility Study

This second case study focused on imagining the changes required to make Geelong an accessible and inclusive city. The research collaboration involved a wide range of stakeholders, including disability advocates and those with lived experience, aiming to create well-designed, sustainable, and connected communities that cater to everyone's needs. The recruitment of these participants was underpinned by the concept of intersectionality in disability studies, which recognises that an individual's experience of disability is not solely defined by their disability itself but is profoundly influenced by other characteristics and circumstances, such as race, culture, gender, sexuality, socio-economic status, and age etc.[20] Thus, exploring the real-life experiences of individuals with disabilities was prioritised, guided by the belief that fostering social inclusion for this group is closely tied to promoting social inclusion for the broader population. This connection arises from the intersection of disability with various other dimensions of diversity (e.g. race, culture, gender and sexuality).

---

[20] Tina Goethals, Elisabeth De Schauwer and Geert van Hove, "Weaving Intersectionality into Disability Studies Research: Inclusion, Reflexivity and Anti-Essentialism", *DiGeSt. Journal of Diversity and Gender Studies* 2, no. 1-2 (2015): 75–94.

The project utilised STICKE to facilitate collective impact and collaboration among stakeholders. Here this systems-based approach prioritised community engagement to support long-term planning, design, and decision-making processes. The identified strategies aimed to provide equal opportunities for spatial and digital connectivity, economic participation, employment, education, housing and community infrastructure.

To meet this project's expansive scope, wicked research problem and fundamental focus on inclusivity, a combination of community-based participatory research with systems thinking was used. This mixed methodology allowed the team to gather a wide range of diverse opinions, viewpoints and ideas, with systems thinking enabling participants to visualise and specify the complex and dynamic characteristics of problems faced by people with disability, and identify intervention points at which a community can change from current frustrations towards a collective plan of action.[21] This approach involved conducting a series of STICKE workshops, which allowed for non-intrusive, broad consultation with community stakeholders, including those with lived experience of disability.

Consultative stakeholder groups were formed to guide the project aims and objectives. These comprised representatives from the research funding bodies, local government planning department officials, disability advocacy organisations, and people with lived experience of disability. Recruitment and participation strived to recognise diversity within the disability community, as many people with disabilities do not have reduced capacity to consent but face challenges related to physical or sensory impairments, age, or environmental and social barriers. The research considered people with disability as active and informed participants in civic decision-making processes, an approach aligning with Article 12 of the UN Convention on the Rights of Persons with Disabilities, which upholds the equal legal capacity of persons with disabilities in all aspects of life.[22]

The success of STICKE in this project relied on having a diverse mix of participants bringing a range of experiences and expertise related to the system being studied. To address the complex issues of accessibility and inclusivity, three workshops were conducted, each focusing on a separate "sub-system": building, planning and building regulations; community infrastructure; and employment and economic participation.

Across the STICKE workshops, participants generated 109 actions to enhance accessibility and inclusivity in their city.[23] Out of these, thirty-seven actions were identified as priorities and ranked based on their perceived impact and feasibility.[24] At this stage of the project, the researchers and consultative stakeholders adjusted the approach to address an important limitation in the participation; the workshops had low representation of people with lived experience of disability, in particular across a wide spectrum of disability, which it was felt compromised the inclusive and participatory intentions of the research. To rectify this issue, three focus groups consisting mainly of individuals with lived experience of disability were held to evaluate the key priority actions developed in the workshops.

The actions identified in the STICKE workshops were evaluated by the focus groups using a semantic differential scale to determine their effectiveness in bringing about systemic change. Participants reached consensus on the evaluations using graphic pictograms placed on a scale. These evaluations closely aligned with those arrived at in the STICKE workshops, confirming the perceived levels of feasibility and impact of the priority actions across the two stages of community consultation.

The research ultimately identified five foundational principles of action informing the implementations of all other actions towards an accessible and inclusive city:

1 adopt inclusive co-design and co-research approaches for the development, implementation and evaluation of actions
2 embed the principles of universal design into the implementation of all actions
3 ensure built environment improvements and provision of affordable and appropriate housing, dedicated services, and employment are available for all, especially in areas with high immediate demand
4 prioritise attitudinal change towards inclusion and access
5 adopt inclusion as a core value for Geelong. Six priority recommendations were made (in relation to regulations, attitudes, information, housing, partnerships and employment), and twenty-eight priority actions (nested within a related a priority recommendation).

And came up with six priority recommendations, which were:

1 Regulations: improve planning legislation and other regulatory measures to define and safeguard access and inclusion within the planning framework.
2 Attitudes: raise awareness of and improve attitudes towards access and inclusion across different policy initiatives, platforms of communication, events, and spaces.

---

[21] Rhonda BeLue, Chakema Carmack, Kyle R. Myers, Laurie Weinreb-Welch and Eugene J. Lengerich "Systems Thinking Tools as Applied to Community-Based Participatory Research: A Case Study", *Health Education & Behavior* 39, no. 6 (2012): 745–51.

[22] United Nations Convention on the Rights of Persons with Disabilities: Resolution by the General Assembly (2007). In (61 ed.).

[23] Richard Tucker, David Kelly, Patsie Frawley, Louise Johnson, Fiona Andrews, Kevin Murfitt and Valerie Watchorn, "Making an Australian Regional City Accessible and Inclusive: A Transdisciplinary Research Approach to Community Participation in Urban", *Urban Policy and Research* (2022), https://doi.org/10.1080/08111146.2022.2103670; Tucker et al., *Accessible & Inclusive Geelong Feasibility Study* (2019).

[24] Tucker et al., *Accessible & Inclusive Geelong Feasibility Study.*

   3 Information: establish a Geelong accessible visitor and information centre run and managed by people with disabilities, with accessibility support staff, as an exemplar of the five principles of action.
   4 Housing: increase the supply of accessible and affordable public and community housing.
   5 Partnerships: increase business groups' collective participation in developing initiatives around inclusion.
   6 Employment: raise expectations and aspirations of employment and economic participation by co-designing work arrangements with people with disability.

Importantly, these actions and recommendations cannot be implemented effectively in isolation but require a combination of interventions at different points within the system. For example, priority recommendation 4, to increase the supply of accessible and affordable public and community housing, addresses a need manifested as a further priority recommendation to improve planning legislation to define and ensure access and inclusion within the planning framework, which in turn had six interrelated priority actions defining how this might be implemented. For example: include a new Access and Inclusion Policy in the principal planning framework and review the Apartment Design Guidelines for Victoria and the relevant provisions in Clauses 55 and 58 of the Victoria Planning Provisions to ensure that they meet contemporary access and inclusion requirements.

This study has had a positive outcome in terms of collaborative structures and attitude transformation among the research team, stakeholders, and participants. These sustained relationships have the potential to implement a series of connected actions to overcome barriers and make Geelong a world-class accessible and inclusive city. Moreover, it is crucial for government, policy leaders, stakeholder organisations, and researchers to continue working closely with people with disabilities to develop, fund, implement and continuously evaluate the recommendations and actions identified in this study.

Nineteen of the priority actions are embedded in the built environment, with two priority recommendations directly addressing how the buildings of a city play a crucial role in determining the level of accessibility and inclusion within the urban environment. The first was increasing the supply of accessible and affordable public and community housing, a recommendation that resonated across all three STICKE workshops. Importantly, it was found that access for people with disability to appropriately designed and affordable housing was at the fulcrum of many other issues across numerous city domains that created obstacles to meaningful living and achieving fulfilled lives.[25] The absence of such housing can be seen as a reflection of systemic shortcomings. This issue is attributed to the conflicting priorities and inadequate coordination among various stakeholders, including public and private developers, designers, architects, occupational therapists, and disability service organisations, as highlighted by Lakhani et al.[26]

While the project aimed to achieve the gold standard of research conducted by and for people with disabilities, it faced limitations due to time constraints and other challenges.[27] In particular, a short lead-in time hindered the establishment of essential relationships, trust-building with underrepresented groups, and the formation of connections within stakeholder networks. There were additional recruitment issues that future projects should anticipate, including difficulties in reaching participants across the full spectrum of disabilities, the economic marginalisation of some participants, and the emotional and time commitments required. Furthermore, the decision to address accessibility and inclusion holistically rather than focusing on specific disability cohorts meant that the research did not explicitly address issues related to marginalised groups such as Aboriginal communities, refugees, and culturally and linguistically diverse populations. In other words, while the research aimed to tackle accessibility and inclusion issues as a whole rather than focusing on certain disability or other groups often excluded from participation in society, such a holistic approach can inadvertently overlook the unique difficulties faced by these marginalised groups.

Small interventions 2: Geelong visitor accessibility centre

The second recommendation of the Accessible and Inclusive Geelong Feasibility Study was building a Geelong visitor accessibility centre run and managed by people with disability, with accessibility support staff, as an exemplar of the five principles of action.[28] The effectiveness of this intervention relies upon its accompanied services, information and supports, the employment of those with lived experience within it and its ability to be accessed across a range of geographies. Such a building was seen to have the power to unlock space in the city where ability and pride can flourish and encourage the improvement of related services.

The initial concept for the building eventually served as the foundation for a co-design research study, which aimed to investigate stakeholder perceptions and experiences regarding the involvement of individuals with disabilities in a co-designed universal designed public building. The Geelong inclusive visitor centre provided the design context for these explorations, with participants recruited from Geelong and its surrounding areas. Employing a phenomenological

---

[25] Richard Tucker, David Kelly, Louise Johnson, Ursula de Jong and Valerie Watchorn, "Housing at the Fulcrum: A Systems Approach to Uncovering Built Environment Obstacles to City Scale Accessibility and Inclusion", *Journal of Housing and the Built Environment* 1 (2021), https://doi.org/10.1007/s10901-021-09881-6.

[26] Ali Lakhani, Heidi Zeeman, Courney J. Wright, David P. Watling, Dianne Smith and Rafikul Islam, "Stakeholder Priorities for Inclusive Accessible Housing: A Systematic Review and Multicriteria Decision Analysis", *Journal of Multi-Criteria Decision Analysis* 27, no. 1-2 (2020): 5–19.

[27] Mike Oliver, "Changing the Social Relations of Research Production?", *Disability, Handicap & Society* 7 no. 2 (1992): 101–114.

[28] Tucker et al., "Making an Australian Regional City Accessible and Inclusive".

approach to data analysis, the study revealed four major themes: the presence of challenges in practicing co-design; the inclusive, accessible, and genuine nature of co-design; the integration of co-design processes throughout all design stages; and the positive outcomes that co-design delivers. The findings strongly underscored the importance of involving people with disabilities in the design of public buildings to enhance universal design, while also shedding light on current practices, challenges and limitations. Furthermore, valuable insights were gained into how co-design processes can optimise the experiences of all participants as well as the outcomes.

Geelong Microvillage Project

From Microvillage to transitional housing for homeless men

Through sustained partnerships between researchers, philanthropy, industry and government, the Geelong Microvillage Project formed a translational quality loop. This progressed from using STICKE to understand community housing needs, to policy/design recommendations, to constructing innovative housing, to assessing and disseminating a new model. The research examined the feasibility of constructing small, cost-effective homes designed for sustainable, socially integrated living. This exploration influenced the creation of a prototype home for individuals experiencing precarious housing situations in Geelong. The prototype was constructed using an innovative and efficient prefabrication system, and this initiative resulted in the construction of seven homes tailored to the needs of homeless men. These homes introduced a novel transitional housing model aimed at breaking the cycle of homelessness. Subsequently, an evaluation of this model was conducted to determine its suitability for nationwide application.

The Geelong Microvillage Project was a collaboration that aimed to address housing affordability and homelessness issues.[29] The project involved HOME researchers, Geelong residents in housing precarity, philanthropy, industry and government. Through partnerships between these varied stakeholders sustained for over five years, and interdisciplinary research approaches to bring together this diverse knowledge and lived experience, the project progressed across six iterative stages:

1 exploring the viability of affordable, small homes for sustainable, socially integrated living, including understanding obstacles to increasing the supply of small, affordable homes using systems thinking
2 synthesising multi-stakeholder inputs to inform planning regulations and policy recommendations
3 co-designing compact, relocatable homes
4 developing and constructing a prototype home
5 constructing transitional housing for people experiencing homelessness based on that prototype
6 evaluating the transferability of this new transitional housing model to other contexts of homelessness.

The Microvillage project was initiated to tackle the challenges faced by pensioners in regional Australia who were struggling with high rents and inadequate housing. Instigated by advocacy groups for these stakeholders, including the Bellarine Tiny Homes Group and Geelong Sustainability, the first stage of the project, lasting two years, evaluated the viability of tiny homes for low-cost housing. The research was funded by two community foundations – the Lord Mayor's Charitable Foundation and the Geelong Community Foundation – and it explored the regulatory, financial and environmental viability of various forms and sizes of transportable small homes.

The project used STICKE to engage diverse stakeholders (experts in the fields of planning, finance, design, other housing-supply stakeholders, and people with lived experience of housing precarity) in collective decision-making to address complex issues within the housing supply system related to housing affordability. STICKE facilitated knowledge sharing, consensus building and a positive attitude shift within the housing sector towards smaller, more sustainable homes and towards those in housing precarity. This project extended the focus of built environment and housing research into a direct engagement with the lived experience of people experiencing or facing homelessness.

While the project determined the obstacles to, and significant limitations of, tiny homes meeting housing affordability challenges, it also identified opportunities for utilising prefabricated, small homes for non-permanent housing.

Small interventions 3: the Independent Living Unit Project

The collaboration was extended to build on the connections between likeminded stakeholders, with shared aims, made during the STICKE process. This brought together Samaritan House, Deakin University architecture students and FormFlow (a local developer of building products, systems and solutions for addressing housing affordability, accessibility and sustainability), and led to the further development and use of FormFlow's prefabrication system in the construction of a prototype compact home. Those experiencing housing precarity contributed to the design of this prototype.

---

[29] Richard Tucker, Ursula de Jong, Louise Johnson, Nicole Johnston, Adrian Lee, Fabienne Michaux, Elyse Warner and Fiona A. Andrews, "Microvillage: Assessing the Viability of Increasing Supply of Affordable, Sustainable and Socially Integrated Small Homes", *Housing Studies* 39, no. 1 (2021): 10, https://doi.org/10.1080/02673037.2021.2014418.

Building upon the success of the prototype, partners secured government grants to install seven of these compact homes as part of the Independent Living Unit Program (ILUP) for men experiencing homelessness (see Figure 6.3 in the colour plate section and Figure 6.4).

Figure 6.4 The exterior design of the ILUs and the outdoor communal area, 2023.

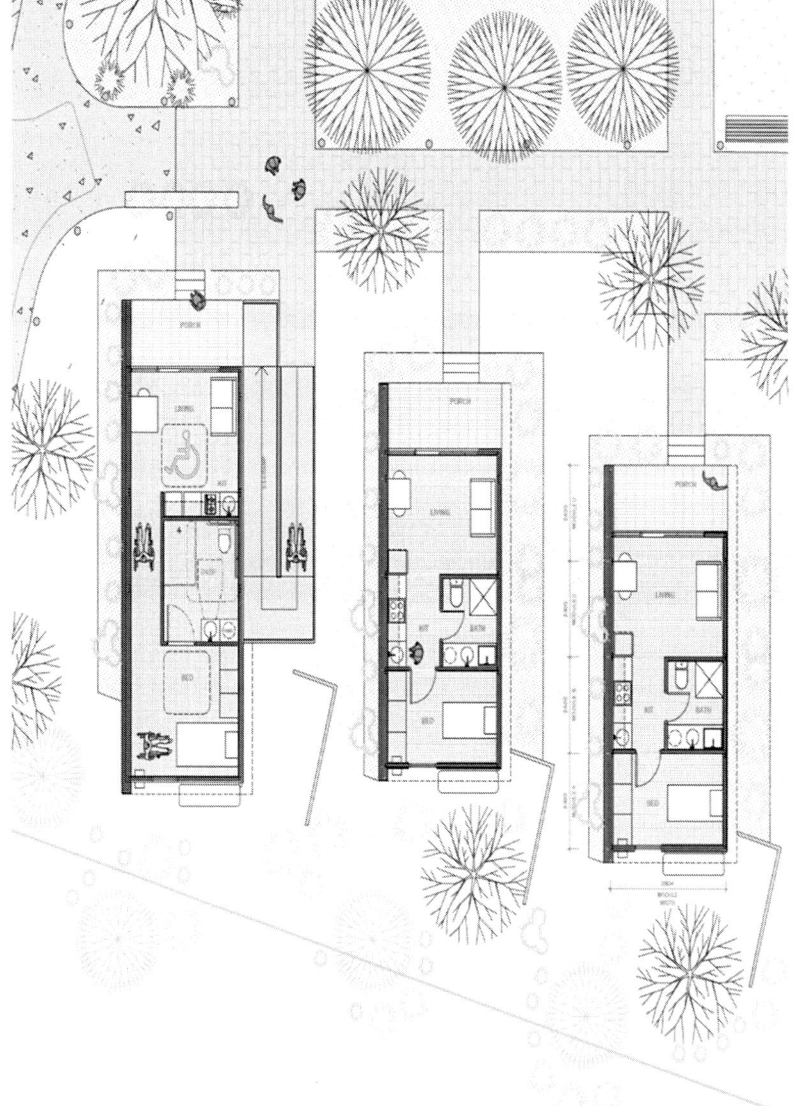

Figure 6.5 Plans of three of the units.

The seven single-storey homes, each comprising a living space, bedroom and bathroom, are arranged in a row across the site (see Figure 6.5). They are deliberately set back 2.4 m from their neighbours so that their front porches address the shared street, but also provide private sitting spaces for the residents. To enhance energy efficiency, the homes incorporate passive solar features, including a north-facing orientation, high ceilings, eaves and a "floating" roof design. This sectional configuration welcomes the winter sun while shielding the homes from the summer sun (see Figure 6.6).

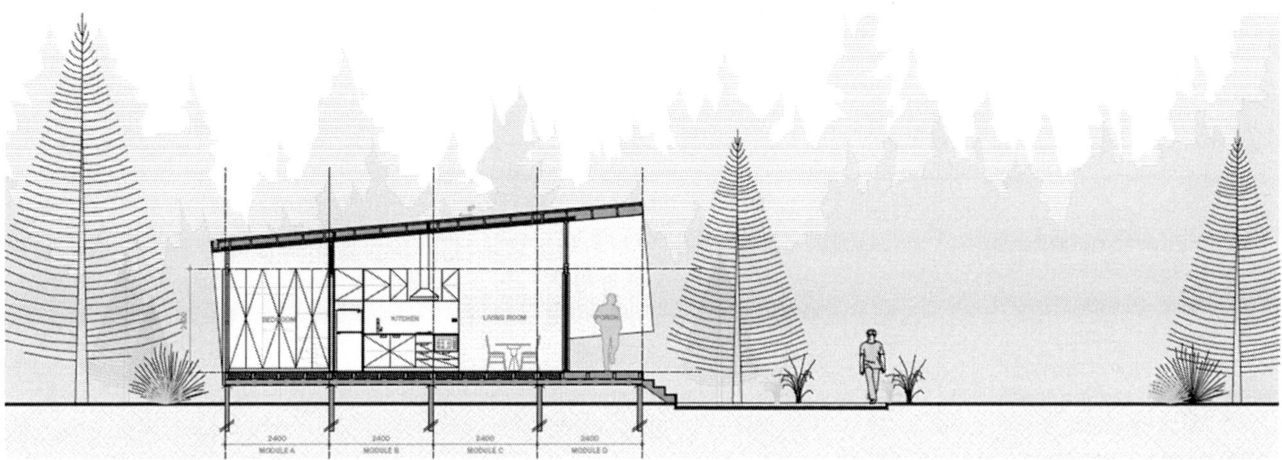

Figure 6.6 Cross-section of one of the units.

Well-placed windows and generous ceiling heights provide these homes with a sense of spaciousness, despite the compact size of the unit. Each unit is constructed from four prefabricated modules, which were assembled off-site. These components were then transported, assembled, and completed with framing and cladding in a single day on the construction site (see Figure 6.7), meaning residents in the adjacent crisis accommodation faced minimum disruption.

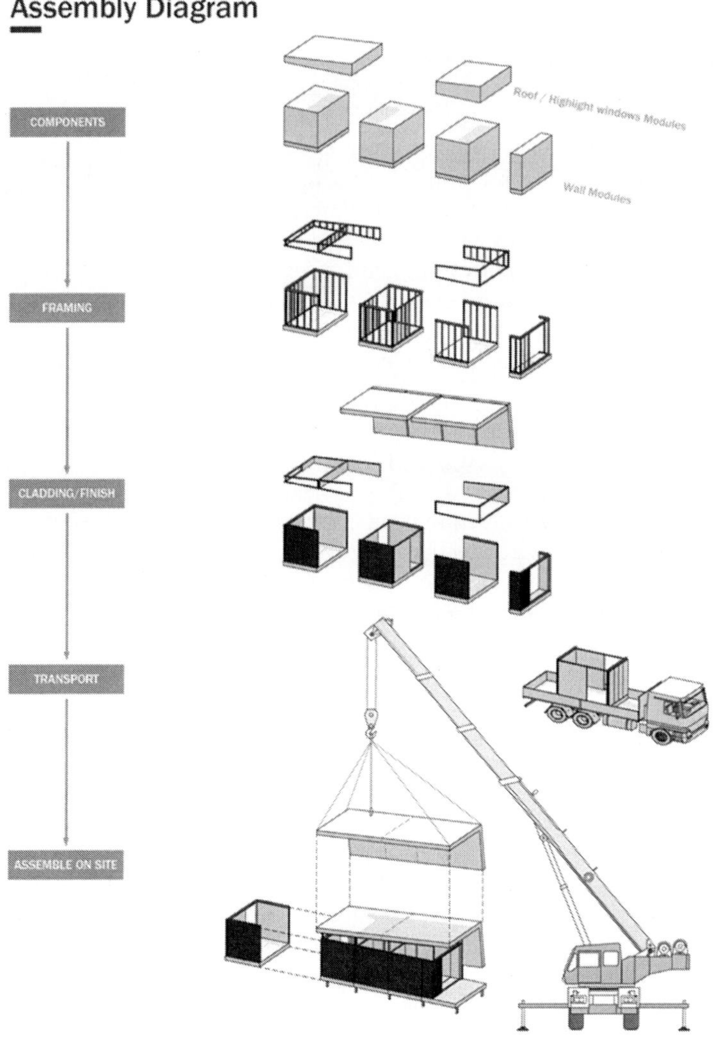

Figure 6.7 How the prefabrication is orchestrated.

The ILUP aimed to provide supported accommodation and transition individuals out of homelessness. Closing a loop from design innovation to design evaluation, the final stage of the research assessed the effectiveness of the ILUP in improving the transitioning process for homeless men and its potential applicability to other housing providers and similar housing contexts.

The evaluation identified eleven aspects of the ILUP's material design that impacted the transitioning process for residents:

- quality of design
- size
- spatial separation with visual connection
- appropriate furnishings
- design for safety
- build quality
- nearby amenities
- semi-open spaces
- quality common areas
- clustered unit arrangements
- location and neighbourhood quality.

Analysis of these factors demonstrated that well-designed transitional housing can be a key factor to the process of housing transition, resulting in self-reported positive short-term outcomes for residents, including:

- reduced levels of anxiety
- enhanced safety and security
- stable and consistent daily routines
- improved hygiene, diet, and overall well-being
- boosted self-confidence and self-reliance in their capabilities
- a sense of worthiness, motivation and empowerment over their life
- increased knowledge of rental market and their rights
- meaningful and deep friendships and a burgeoning sense of community.

The Geelong Microvillage project demonstrates the power of sustained partnerships and interdisciplinary, systems-based approaches in addressing the wicked problems of housing affordability and homelessness. By engaging stakeholders via STICKE, applying the shared knowledge created to inform innovative design and construction methods, then evaluating the housing model created out of this process, the project has made significant strides in transforming the housing landscape for disadvantaged communities in Victoria. In total, twenty researchers, thirty-five community stakeholders, eighteen students, two philanthropic organisations, an industry partner, two housing providers and seven homeless men were brought together via a systems approach to make this meaningful change. The findings and methodologies developed through this project have broader applicability to crisis housing contexts nationally and internationally.

Conclusion

The projects described in this chapter represent a collective and interdisciplinary effort to address complex and pressing challenges in Geelong. These initiatives, undertaken by the HOME Strategic Innovation and Research Centre, exemplify the power of collaboration via systems thinking, and a commitment to creating positive change within communities. The key contribution of these projects lies in their holistic approach, guided by systems thinking, to address wicked problems that affect Geelong and, by extension, other communities facing similar challenges. The projects are not confined by academic imperatives but are deeply rooted in social imperatives, with the primary aim of making a tangible difference in the lives of the communities they serve.

Through interdisciplinary teams assembled from diverse academic backgrounds, the research tackled issues such as accessibility, homelessness, spatial inequality and housing affordability. By embracing an inclusive and community-driven approach, the research emphasised the importance of shared visions, co-designing solutions and the active involvement of community stakeholders.

The utilisation of STICKE provided a visual and collaborative framework for understanding and addressing complex urban and societal issues. It facilitated knowledge exchange, consensus building and the elicitation of innovative solutions.

Notable accomplishments emerged from these research endeavours. For instance, the development of innovative housing solutions for homeless men in Geelong, enabled by a novel prefabrication system, opened the door to identifying how a new kind of transitional housing model aimed at breaking the cycles of homelessness could be adapted to other Australian contexts. Similarly, the Vital Communities project paved the way for social equity and prosperity in disadvantaged areas of the city, bringing about a reimagination of the causes and alternatives to socio-spatial disadvantage. In the case of the Accessible and Inclusive Geelong Feasibility Study, the research promoted social inclusion by recognising the intersectionality of disability with various other dimensions of diversity, fostering meaningful engagement with the community. This project emphasised the need for attitudinal change, inclusion as a core value, and universal design principles to create a truly accessible and inclusive city.

These projects, guided by the principles of interdisciplinarity, community engagement, and systems thinking, have not only enriched the understanding of complex urban issues but also yielded practical and actionable solutions. They provide a model for how collaborative research can lead to real-world transformation, demonstrating that innovation and inclusivity can drive positive change within communities, not only in Geelong but potentially on a broader scale.

In conclusion, while to reimagine a city or places within it is an ambitious, even arrogant, undertaking, what we have shown in these three case studies is that there are tools to elicit community alternatives and real possibilities for these new imaginings to be realised on the ground. The three examples involve inter-related wicked or intractable social problems. But through systems thinking and cross-disciplinary approaches, co-design with communities and working with those with the power to deliver – be it local government, building firms or charitable organisations – does facilitate the articulation and realisation of alternative imaginings that also address real social problems.

CHAPTER 7

AGRICULTURE'S SHADOW CONNECTIONS: TRACING HEAVY INDUSTRIES TO FOOD LANDSCAPES

JOSHUA ZEUNERT

Introduction

Smokestacks, commodity heaps, and behemoth shed arrays may seem a far cry from the agricultural landscapes feeding Australia, and the romantic imagery transmitted by agribusinesses and food retailers.[1] Yet Australian agriculture is critically dependent upon commodity and manufacturing processes from industrial facilities.[2] These linkages between industrial activities and food-producing landscapes are not always easily perceived, clearly articulated, or well understood. The City of Greater Geelong offers an evocative case study of the industry–agriculture nexus, which this chapter presents through the format of a visual essay. It commences by exploring conceptual underpinnings of industrial and agricultural shadow places, their flows and connections. This exposition then links four industrial sites in Geelong representing fertiliser production, grains and oilseeds, food additives, and crude oil by-products. As identified during field work over 2016–2023, the oft-unseen connections between these sites of industrial production are visually traced to local, regional, state, and wider national agricultural landscapes. In doing so, the chapter conveys a material abundance in industrial agri-production systems, their extractive capacity and arresting visual character, contrasting with degradative environmental ramifications and landscape brutality, at-scale. The research highlights and ultimately aims to decouple a production–destruction paradox in food and landscape systems, to compel further research and solution-oriented practices.

To conceal or reveal industry and its flows?

Geelong is the second largest city in Australia's south-eastern state of Victoria, occupying the unceded traditional lands of the Wadawurrung and Kulin Nations since 1837. Acting as an important port, Geelong's history is embedded in both agriculture and industrial modes of production. Matt Novacevski characterises Geelong's traditional built fabric as 'red brick and grit of mills, factories and woolsheds…chimneys, silos and [their] solidity', suggesting the centrality of industry and agriculture to the city's makeup.[3] However, like many Western cities worldwide, deindustrialisation in recent decades has seen the operational loss of a suite of its prior manufacturing icons, such as the Alcoa aluminium smelter (2014), the Ford vehicle plant (2016) and the Cheetham salt works (2002). Further exacerbating the decline of the city's industrial fabric are significant population growth and gentrification, ongoing demolition, conversion and subsumption by urban development and sprawl.[4] New residential encroachment on existing industries can also exert additional pressures on the viability of industrial operations. Despite this backdrop of declining heavy production, some industrial facilities remain in the city, as later explored.

The emergence of modern environmentalism in many Western contexts in the 1960s created awareness of the overburdens and negative ecological impacts of industrial modes of production.[5] This in turn diminished the social capital of industrial activities and stemmed the growth from prior trajectories, as increasing environmental standards imposed legislative requirements curtailing polluting practices.[6] However, instead of decoupling or evolving from the problematic elements of industrial production, Australia (as well as the United States, Canada, the United Kingdom and many European and Western countries) pivoted to source significant proportions of their industrial needs from other

[1] Joshua Zeunert, "An Australian agri-industrial landscape sublime", *Visual Communication* (2024). Doi: 10.1177/1470357224 1258895; Joshua Zeunert, "Bridging Rural and Urban Disconnections: Spatial Graphic Explorations of Australia's Livestock Landscapes", in Raffaele Pernice and Bing Chen (eds), *Urban Regeneration and Rural Revitalization in Australia and China* (London: Routledge, 2024), 110-43.

[2] Joshua Zeunert, "Challenges in Agricultural Sustainability and Resilience: Towards Regenerative Practice" in Joshua Zeunert and Tim Waterman (eds) *Routledge Handbook of Landscape and Food*, (London: Routledge, 2018), 231–52.

[3] Matt Novacevski, "The Post-Industrial Landscape of Geelong", in David S. Jones and Philip B. Roös (eds), *Geelong's Changing Landscape* (Vic.: CSIRO Publishing, 2019), 249–60; 250.

[4] David S. Jones and Phillip B. Roös (eds), *Geelong's Changing Landscape: Ecology, Development and Conservation* (Collingwood: CSIRO Publishing, 2019).

[5] Catalysed by Rachel Carson's 1962 book, *Silent Spring*, (Boston: Houghton Mifflin).

[6] See, for example Paul Brown's and Jane Castle's documentary *Sixty Thousand Barrels: A Citizen's Guide to Toxic Waste Disposal* on industrial practices in Sydney's Botany Bay.

countries; particularly those with less stringent regulations and cheaper workforces.[7] While global trading has existed for many millennia, the extent of contemporary offshore industrial procurement has created dendritic global supply chains that can be challenging to perceive. This is especially the case if separated from concentration nodes such as factories, ports, logistics hubs, rail and truck depots – all typically exhibiting considerable separation distances from residential areas seeking to avoid incongruencies and minimise conflicts.

In addition to offshore procurement of industrial wares, various Western contexts like Australia concurrently undertook obfuscation techniques to conceal remnant domestic industries (e.g. power plants, refineries, mines) and their infrastructural elements (smokestacks, gantries, pipelines, high-voltage powerlines, resource/commodity heaps) from public view. Commonly termed "visual management systems" or "visual impact assessment", these designed and engineered techniques include concealment of viewsheds by natural and/or engineered topography (for example, locating industrial activities in depressions, supplemented with berms and earth banks); using solid screening walls[8]; vegetative screens (dense shrub plantings and/or closely-planted trees); and "naturalised veils" such as restoration ecology (revegetating with pre-colonisation plant species).[9] Visual management and concealment systems can be pragmatically challenging for large and heavy industries.[10] Moreover, they are dishonest, especially if restoration ecology pastes over extractive sites with a denial of history and past uses, with such concealments arguably counterproductive to environmental sustainability and the truth-telling necessary for it.[11]

Offshoring and concealing heavy industries and commodity economies from consumer bases can create an "out-of-sight, out-of-mind" condition. This contributes to the phenomenon that Australian environmental philosopher Val Plumwood characterises as "shadow places" of commodity culture, namely, the 'multiple disregarded places of economic and ecological support, a split between our idealised homeplace and the places delineated by our ecological footprint'.[12] First Nations scholar Tyson Yunkaporta's notion of "outsourced entropy" is congruent, whereby consumers are separated from places of landscape and production violence executed to support their lifestyles.[13]

Shadow places and outsourced entropy are well illustrated by a range of works from environmental photographers documenting, for example, heavy industry's sites of extraction and pollution, such as mines and their tailings. Perhaps most notable is celebrated photographer Edward Burtynsky and his career-long endeavours poignantly revealing human domination over nature and dramatic crescendos of sublime landscape fallout.[14] Other related works include photographer Alex Maclean and his book, *OVER: The American Landscape at Tipping Point*, and environmental historian Cameron Muir's exploration of these themes in an Australian context.[15]

While such works documenting overtly toxic and dramatic industrial sites of industry and mining fallout represent an established tradition, the shadow places of agriculture are less explored. While agricultural landscapes can present as less visually striking than, for example, unnatural colour hues from industrial fallout sites and overt environmental toxification and destruction, the scope of agriculture is spatially unprecedented as a nationally (see Figure 7.1 in the colour plate section) and internationally dominant land use. Thus, a more subtle temporality and "slow burn" of agriculture's shadow processes are particularly insidious due to its extensive spatial remit. Within this realm, photographer George Steinmetz's Feed the Planet project is globally illuminating, as to the extent of agribusinesses manipulation of ecologies and incredible scales of production.[16] The author's own FOOD | LANDSCAPES | AUSTRALIA archive contains 881 videos of Australia's agricultural shadow places, tracing linkages between foods and landscape geographies.[17] However, neither of these works specifically trace linkages between heavy industries and agricultural landscapes.[18]

---

[7] Which can raise social and ethical procurement issues, such as child labour.

[8] Often inscribed with icons that industrial projects may have destroyed, such as flora and fauna.

[9] James Corner, "Terra Fluxus", in Charles Waldheim (ed), *The Landscape Urbanism Reader* (New York: Princeton Architectural Press, 2006).

[10] In a more pragmatic sense, the sheer scale of some large industrial sites, combined with Geelong's subtle topography, port access needed at sea level, and an arcing bay can all challenge and confound attempts at concealment.

[11] Denis Wood, "Unnatural Illusions: Some Words About Visual Resource Management", *Landscape Journal* (1988): 192–205; Joshua Zeunert, 2013. "Challenging Assumptions in Urban Restoration Ecology", *Landscape Journal* 32, no. 2: 231–42; Joshua Zeunert, *Landscape Architecture and Environmental Sustainability: Creating Positive Change through Design* (London/New York: Bloomsbury, 2017); Brett Grimm and Joshua Zeunert, "Short-sighted Visual Character Concerns in Renewable Energy Landscapes: A Case Study of South Australia" in Dimitri Kurochkin, Martha Crawford and Elena Shabliy (eds), *Discourses on Sustainability: Climate Change, Clean Energy, and Justice* (Palgrave Macmillan, 2020), 91–124.

[12] Val Plumwood, "Shadow Places and the Politics of Dwelling", *Australian Humanities Review*, 44 (2008), https://australianhumanitiesreview.org/2008/03/01/shadow-places-and-the-politics-of-dwelling/.

[13] Tyson Yunkaporta, *Sand Talk: How Indigenous Thinking Can Save the World* (Melbourne, Victoria: Text Publishing Company, 2019).

[14] https://www.edwardburtynsky.com/home.

[15] Alex S. MacLean, *Over: The American Landscape at the Tipping Point* (New York: Abrams, 2008); Cameron Muir, "Fifty Shades of Shadow Places: A Photographic Essay", in Christof Mauch, Ruth Morgan and Emily O'Gorman (eds), "Visions of Australia: Environments in History", *RCC Perspectives: Transformations in Environment and Society* 2 (2017): 107–13, doi.org/10.5282/rcc/7914.

[16] https://www.feedtheplanet.earth/index.

[17] https://www.foodlandscapes.com.au/.

[18] https://www.foodlandscapes.com.au/.

Shadow connections in industry and agriculture: A Geelong and Australian case

Figure 7.2 A contrasting bay and waterfront, 2016. If viewed from the immediate city centre and focusing on the redeveloped foreground, Geelong's foreshore and its arcing azure bay and oft-sparkling waterfront provide a range of visual stimuli framing water views (top: facing north from Deakin University's Geelong campus roof terrace, converted from woolstores). However, closer inspection of the bay, reveals large operational and abandoned heavy industries dotting the foreshore arc. Some are visible in the bottom image: bottom left is the grain precinct and centre right is an oil refinery (far right is the topographic trace of the distant You Yangs range). Overcast conditions can blend smokestack and bulk carrier plumes, with grey hues mirrored between sky and water, reinforcing interconnectedness.

The focus of this chapter now transitions to the case of four sites of heavy industry in Geelong, and their interlinked agricultural landscapes. It is suggested that the feature of industrial sites in cities with heavy industry can directly illuminate shadow places and their interconnected webs, especially when – like in Geelong – industrial operations are a central component of the place-fabric (see Figure 7.2). The presence of heavy urban industries helps to defy separations between homeplace, commodity flows, environmental systems, and ecological footprints.[19] In other words, a composition comprising natural setting, heavy industries, and the built environment – as in Geelong's case – can be

---

[19] Plumwood, "Shadow Places and the Politics of Dwelling".

regarded as representative of an economy of mutual recognition.[20] When perceived as such, we may arrive at a more place-informed cultural consciousness of an extractive economy, and its impacts. Furthermore, entropy is palpable in Geelong through the daily rhythms of smokestacks, plumes, container ships, gantries, trucks, freight trains and the like, along with their declining trajectory in flaking, rusting, decaying decline and abandonment.

Linking Geelong's industrial facilities to shadow agricultures

Based on this contextual background and wider research, this chapter has identified several industrial elements in Geelong linking to agriculture, four of which are now discussed.[21] These comprise two primary and two secondary facilities, based on their degree of direct agricultural correlation. The first primary case is the Incitec Pivot facility in North Shore, Geelong (see Figure 7.3). This facility manufactures and distributes agricultural fertiliser, specifically, single superphosphate. This is created based on the raw material of (mined) phosphate rock, chiefly imported from overseas by bulk carrier ships.

The second primary facility centres on a grain and oilseed precinct at North Geelong's port, characterised by a grain elevator and expanse of silos and sheds on Corio Bay (see Figure 7.4). This comprises a grain and oilseed terminal operated by Graincorp, a (barley) malting plant by Malteurop Australia, and (at the time of writing) construction of a new grain storage and export terminal to be operated by CHS Broadbent.

A third facility, albeit of secondary relevance to food landscapes, is Omya Australia's ground calcium carbonates plant in North Shore (see Figure 7.5). Amongst a suite of products manufactured, including some for agriculture, two are specific for the food industry and are included in the use of food preservation.

The final site is the Viva Energy oil refinery in Corio (see Figure 7.6). While this does not chiefly operate for agriculture, it is a fundamental cog in the complex arrangements enabling contemporary Australia's industrial–technological society and its agricultural systems to operate.

To avoid naming specific agribusinesses and sites, as well as for necessary brevity, this chapter now presents a broad conceptual and visual tracing of Geelong's industrial sites to interconnected agri-landscape contexts. Detailed and progeny-specific identification falls outside of its scope, but further research could examine the quantitative tracing of resource and food chains and their specific elements. Imagery and supplementary discussion therefore explore Geelong's four industrial examples through drone photographic linkages made with Australian-based examples of agricultural production utilising and/or producing these industrial components.

As an initial departure point with contextual relevance, Figure 7.7 (in the colour plate section) shows peri-urban food production sites in proximity to Geelong and Melbourne. As a land use and economic activity, Geelong's and Melbourne's peri-urban agriculture largely mirror Geelong's industrial decline.[22] Congruence is also analogous metaphorically, whereby the significant threat to peri-urban food production from Victoria's production-line urban development in 'ever-accelerating cycles of consumption-based mall-and-sprawl urbanism [reflects] planning as though cars continue to roll off the production line'.[23] Loss of peri-urban food supply, especially on agriculturally valuable and inherently-fertile lands for production, represents short-term land planning failing to recognise longer-term interests.[24]

Similar to Geelong's industrial degrowth, Australian agriculture's use of single superphosphate fertiliser has also been declining. This is in-part from its historic overuse and thus decreased agricultural effectiveness, but is exacerbated by the availability of effective fertiliser alternatives, chiefly urea, ammonium phosphate (MAP, DAP) and potassium (potash) fertilisers.[25] Figure 7.8 (in the colour plate section) shows images of fertiliser application to varying Australian agricultural contexts. These images are suggestive of the degree of our dependency on fertiliser – a 2008 estimate in *Nature Geoscience* journal estimated that nearly half of the world's population were supported through nitrogen fertilisers alone – with Australia's fertiliser dependency higher due to low fertility soils and meat-heavy diets.[26]

Fertiliser from Geelong's North Shore facility is primarily used in field pastures (Figure 7.9 in the colour plate section). Resultant plant growth is used directly (i.e. for animals to graze) or indirectly (i.e. harvested and later fed to livestock) as fodder and feed crops for livestock, primarily sheep and cattle, consequently ending up as lamb and beef and their by-products. In other words, Incitec Pivot's North Shore operation primarily links to the agricultural land use classification of "improved pastures", which in turn links to beef and lamb eating, wool, and associated products from

---

[20] Plumwood, "Shadow Places and the Politics of Dwelling".

[21] As part of a wider project: Australian Research Council DE200100529: *Scenario testing for sustainable Australian agricultural landscapes to 2050.*

[22] Beau Beza, Joshua Zeunert and Murray Herron, "Greater Geelong's Planning Future to 2050: Determining Spatial Outcomes Through Agricultural Land Planning", in David S. Jones and Phillip B. Roös (eds), *Geelong's Changing Landscape: Ecology, Development and Conservation* (Collingwood: CSIRO Publishing, 2019), 212–221; Rachel Carey and Sarah James, "Peri-Urban Agriculture in Australia: Pressure on the Urban Fringe", in Joshua Zeunert and Tim Waterman, (eds), *Routledge Handbook of Landscape and Food* (London: Routledge, 2018), 213–27.

[23] Novacevski, "The Post-Industrial Landscape of Geelong", 258.

[24] Joshua Zeunert and Rob Freestone, "From Rural Lands to Agribusiness Precincts: Agriculture in Metropolitan Sydney 1948-2018", in Carla Brisotto and Fabiano Lemes de Oliveira (eds), *Re-imaging Resilient Food Landscapes - Perspectives from Planning History* (Cham, Switzerland: Springer, 2022), 247–72.

[25] CSIRO, "Raiding The $10 Billion Phosphorus Bank", Media release, Ref 98/38, February 19, 1998.

[26] Jan Willem Erisman, Mark A. Sutton, James Galloway, Zbigniew Klimont and Wilfried Winiwarter, "How a Century of Ammonia Synthesis Changed the World", *Nature Geoscience* 1 (October 2008): 637.

Figure 7.3 Incitec Pivot fertiliser facility in North Shore, Geelong, 2017. Bulk carriers unload phosphate rock from overseas, which is combined with sulphuric acid and other components to manufacture single superphosphate fertiliser, which is then distributed to Australian farms, primarily in south-eastern Australia.

Figure 7.4 View of part of the grain precinct at North Geelong port in 2023. Trucks queue to unload grain. The Malteurop facility transforms barley into malt, chiefly for use in beer brewing, but also in spirits, along with malt extracts for other food and beverage products.

Figure 7.5 Omya carbonates in North Shore, Geelong, 2023.

Figure 7.6 The storage tanks and smokestacks of the Viva Energy oil refinery in Corio, Geelong, 2023.

their slaughter and processing. Meat and animal product dietary–agricultural systems are resource and environmentally intensive, supporting less population than plant-based diets.[26]

Geelong's grain facilities represent destination hubs for Australian grain and oilseed growers, particularly in south-eastern Australia, as well as distribution channels for export. Figure 7.10 (in the colour plate section) shows national examples of grain-producing and oilseed-producing landscapes. It is important to note that the direct consumption of grain domestically by Australians is not its primary use, with two-thirds to three-quarters of domestic grain currently consumed by livestock, and much of Australia's total grain harvest being exported.[27] Cropping scenes are characterised by cleared native vegetation for expansive, monocultural fields. These can create soil erosion, acidification, degradation and salinity issues, as well as impact waterways and groundwater through extractions for irrigation, and subsequent eutrophication from nutrient runoff.[28]

Like the mining industry, Australian agriculture is geared to bulk production of raw commodities over value-adding processes such as food and nutrition manufacturing, for example, nutraceuticals and pharmaceuticals. Figure 7.11 (in the colour plate section) shows landscapes relating to these practices in Australia. Industrial-scaled production and processing landscapes characterised by incised and repetitive geometries visibly span remote, regional and urban contexts. While making for arresting visual imagery, their harsh environments are also suggestive of environmental consequences.

Finally, the images in Figure 7.12 (in the colour plate section) are suggestive of oil-dependency in Australian agriculture, albeit these represent a snapshot of a much broader spectrum of use. Crude oil underpins contemporary civilisation and its refining creates petroleum (petrol/gasoline), distillate (diesel), marine (heavy fuel oil), aviation, lubricants and bitumen, amongst others.[29] Diesel is particularly fundamental for Australian agricultural production, fuelling tractors, vehicles, and machinery, while oil derivatives are used for road surfaces (bitumen), and plastics in agricultural storage, for processing and manufacturing. Crude oil by-products fuel the trucks, trains, bulk carrier ships (e.g. grain) and aviation freight planes (such as live animal exports and fresh food exports) during all stages of the food chain. Geelong's oil refinery supplies about half of Victoria's fuel and as such, is a key site enabling agriculture and its shadow places.[30]

The figures in this visual essay aim to highlight how agricultural contexts (Figures 7.7–7.12 in the colour plate section) – be those peri-urban (see Figure 7.7), rural grazing pastures (see Figure 7.9) or grain monocultures (see Figure 7.10) – can reveal complex chains interlinking and connecting sites of industrial production and manufacturing in Geelong (see Figures 7.3–7.6) and across Australia (see Figure 7.11 in the colour plate section). The intention of highlighting these place linkages is first to increase awareness of our heavy dependency for our food supply on sites of industrial production, manufacturing and distribution. Secondly, the imagery seeks to convey how insensitive and brutal modes of production are environmentally impactful, and thus require new and ecologically sensitive practices.

New visions for regenerative futures

To illuminate a greater breadth of industrial, commodity and agricultural shadow places, it is necessary to not only focus on nodes of sites of immediate production, manufacturing and fallout, but concurrently trace material and commodity flows and their connections across these complex chains. Drawing from field research aerial photography, this research traced four elements of Geelong's operating heavy industries: fertiliser, grains and oilseeds, food and agricultural additives, and crude oil by-products. Linkages with spatially extensive Australian agricultural landscapes extending from the peri-urban to the regional were made through aerial photography sourced during field research in the years 2016–23. This highlights the importance of networked and interconnected awareness of place relationships that are critical to evolve ecologically symbiotic practices within local, national and planetary limits.[31]

Tracing industrial–agricultural connections also highlights that deindustrialisation can undermine local and national food-supply security, due to the critical dependence of Australia's commercial food systems on industrial processes to supply the inputs and operational propulsion across all levels of the food chain. The visual emphasis of the research suggests a paradoxical sublime, reflecting awe from an abundance generated by industrial production methods, contrasted with an alarming wake of cumulative landscape and environmental degradation. This represents industrial food systems' wicked paradox: mega-scale industrial systems underpin contemporary society's collective material abundance, while at the same time undermining our sustainability through destroying ecological life webs and the

---

[26] Joseph Poore and Thomas Nemecek, "Reducing Food's Environmental Impacts Through Producers and Consumers", *Science* 360, no. 6392 (2018): 987–92, https://doi.org/10.1126/science.aaq0216; Zeunert, "Bridging Rural and Urban Disconnections: Spatial Graphic Explorations of Australia's Livestock Landscapes"; Zeunert, "Challenges in Agricultural Sustainability and Resilience: Towards Regenerative Practice".

[27] John Spragg, *Australian Feed Grain Supply and Demand Report* (Feed Grain Partnership/JCS Solutions, 2018), https://vstats.substack.com/p/livestock-eat-66-of-grain-in-australia?utm_source=substack&utm_medium=email.

[28] Zeunert, "Challenges in Agricultural Sustainability and Resilience: Towards Regenerative Practice"; Zeunert, https://www.foodlandscapes.com.au/.

[29] Zeunert, "Challenges in Agricultural Sustainability and Resilience: Towards Regenerative Practice".

[30] https://www.vivaenergy.com.au/.

[31] Plumwood, "Shadow Places and the Politics of Dwelling".

carrying capacity of the biosphere.[33] As such, new visions, imaginaries, practices and institutions are urgently needed to evolve new production and consumption systems to transition to intergenerationally sustainable futures.

---

[33] Erisman et al., "How a Century of Ammonia Synthesis Changed the World", 637; Zeunert, "Challenges in Agricultural Sustainability and Resilience: Towards Regenerative Practice".

CHAPTER 8

MAPPING INDUSTRIAL VACANCY

IGOR MARTEK, CHAYAKAN SIAMPHUKDEE AND DIEGO FULLAONDO

Introduction

Geelong is an ugly city. So surmises the casual Melbournian visitor who must pass through its dilapidated northern industrial fringes, before emerging on its southern flanks on their way to their true destination, the beautiful beaches of the Bellarine Surf Coast. This assessment appears harsh, but it is what the author, Igor Martek, thought when as a child his father would take him on summer holidays for two weeks of camping along the Great Ocean Road. Martek further recalled:

> We never stopped in Geelong. All I understood of the city was the view from the car as we drove along the Princes Highway – abandoned grain silos, run-down public housing estates and grotesque factories. Many decades later, when I came to live and work in Geelong, my first impressions were the same (see Figure 8.1).

Figure 8.1 Ford factory site, Geelong, 2023.

Of course, Geelong is genuinely charming. Geelong's industrial gateway is what outsiders experience. However, for locals Geelong is the Barwon River – meandering, picturesque, adorned with ribbons of green, and overlooked from its embankments by well-to-do homes. Closer to town, there are charming cottages, now gentrified, while further on, there are new estates of young families, bike trails, rolling hills, wineries and the sea.

Geelong's northern frontier is an anomaly. While providing an indelible visual experience of towers, pipes, smokestacks and conveyor belts to the transient passing through, it remains ignored if not wholly unseen by resident Pivotonians (Pivotonian is a nickname for Geelong's residents when the city was called the "Pivot City"). This northern area comprises portions of four suburbs: Corio, North Shore, Norlane, and North Geelong. The northern boundary is School Road, running to the prestigious Geelong Grammar School. The southern boundary is Osborne House on Swinburne Road. The western boundary is Princes Highway; more precisely, Princes Highway, then veering south down Station Street, west along North Shore Road, to pick up Princes Highway again as it heads into town. The eastern boundary is Corio Bay (see Figure 8.2). The vast industrial wasteland of Corio Bay ironically sits between Geelong

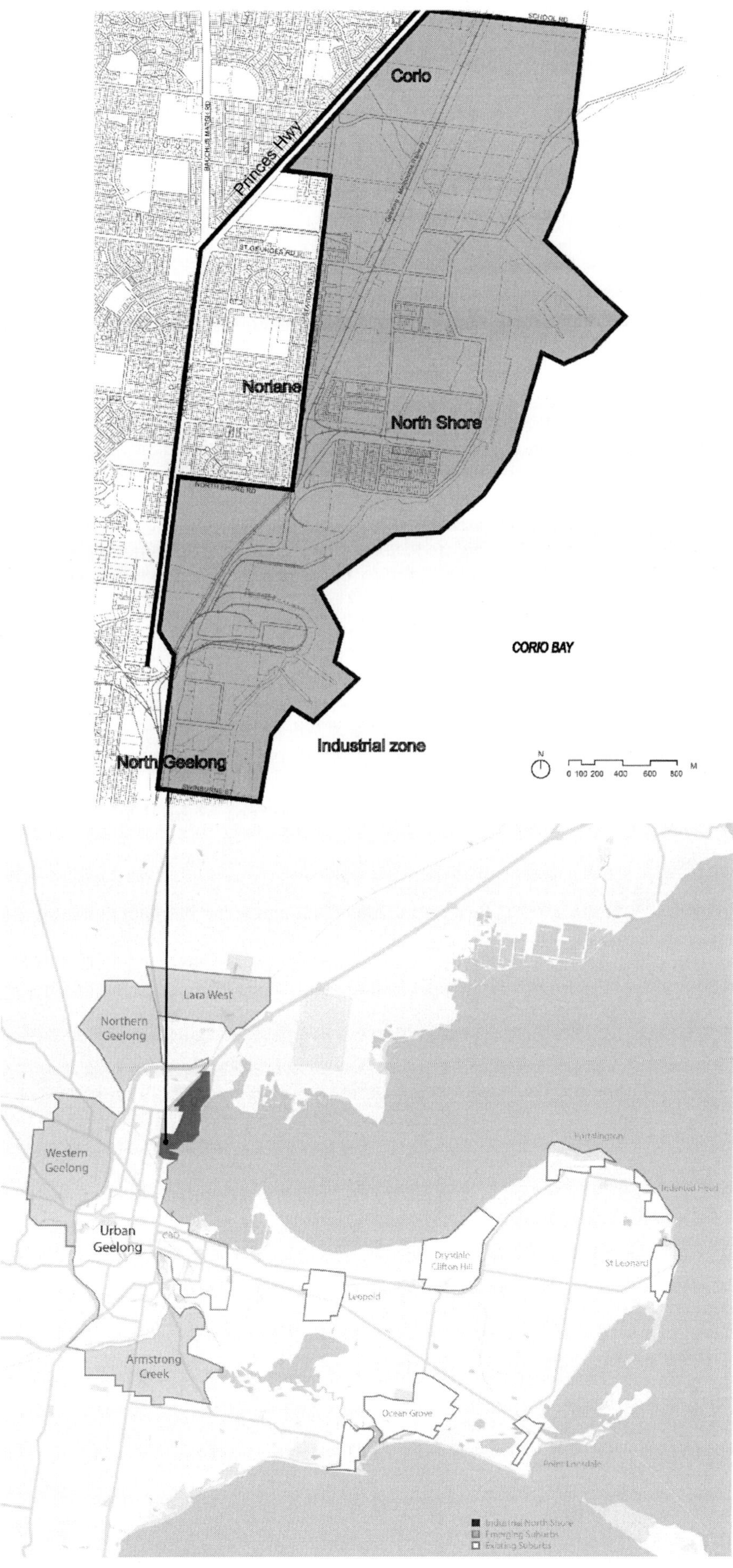

Figure 8.2 Geelong's industrial North Shore located in the wider Geelong region, 2023.

Grammar School, until recently Australia's most expensive school with an annual tuition fee of $43,000, and Norlane – Victoria's most disadvantaged suburb.[1] What then is the point of reflecting on Geelong's industrial North Shore? The answer lies in imagining its future. The past holds the key to understanding the present conditions while laying out the basis for an alternative interpretation (See Chapter 3, "Dialogues Between Space and Time"). The North Shore stretches across six kilometres of prime waterfront real estate. That real estate sits just north of Geelong central business district (CBD) proper, en route to Melbourne, along one of the fastest growing urban corridors in Australia. And yet, for the moment, there are only little transformations happening in the area. Presently, the action is elsewhere. Geelong is the fastest growing of Victoria's regional cities. In 2004, Geelong's population was 150,000; in 2020, it was 200,000.[2] By 2050 it is projected to soar to 500,000 with the growth of four new suburbs: Armstrong Creek, Western Geelong, Northern Geelong, and Lara West (see Figure 8.2).[3] Other targeted development areas east of Geelong on the Bellarine Peninsula include Leopold, Ocean Grove, Drysdale, Portarlington, St. Leonards, and Point Lonsdale.[4]

The current growth model facilitates new suburbs sprawling out from the current urban periphery onto adjacent farmland, without addressing or accommodating existing legacies. The task of absorbing Geelong's expanding needs is given over to developers who have a carefully honed business model of solutions predicated on a *tabula rasa* paradigm in which history begins when they break ground. What had been before, save perhaps for an identified impressive gum tree or creek bed, is of no concern. Indeed, we see new houses inserted into new subdivisions with no intention to harmonise with the existing natural and built landscape. When the current development corridors are saturated, attention will inevitably turn to the North Shore to utilise its prime location and assets. The challenge of Geelong's industrial North Shore is that it has a history; a history that is announced through its massive artefacts of concrete, brick and steel. How then can we address these histories and legacies in the post-industrial landscape?

This chapter documents the industrial heritage of Geelong's North Shore. This is not a proper history, but rather an inventory of the locale's industrial footprint – a beginning from which a substantive history may be woven. First, it examines the pre-colonial setting and the arrival of colonial-settlers. Then it historically reviews the industries in North Shore, from the late nineteenth century to the present, giving an insight into the area's industrial legacy and the importance of addressing its vacancy. The discussion concludes by examining the current state of North Shore's developments, its challenges and redevelopment opportunities. At the same time, it offers a warning: those indifferent to the past betray an indifference to the future. Lucretius in 50 BCE reflected that 'Consider how that past ages of eternal time before our birth were no concern of ours. This is a mirror which nature holds up to us of future time after our death'.[5] Only by an appreciation for what has gone before, can we be properly equipped to build a better tomorrow.

Pre-colonial Geelong and the arrival of settlers

The Wadawurrung are the Aboriginal people who have inhabited the Geelong and surrounding regions, stretching north beyond Ballarat, for some 65,000 years. Together with four other peoples who speak different but related languages, they make up the Kulin Nation. These are the Dja Dja Wurrung (Bendigo area), the Taungurung (Lake Eildon area), the Woiwurrung (Yarra Ranges area), and the Boonwurrung (Moe area).[6] The Wadawurrung consists of twenty-five clans, each led by an elder; each is associated with a geographic locality. For example, the Bengalat Balug clan lived in the vicinity of Indented Head, east of Geelong.[7] The Wadawurrung subsisted by fishing, cultivating yam daisy, hunting, and gathering.[8]

North Shore was rich in resources with food, water and medicine readily available.[9] The Aboriginal people found shellfish and set fish traps along the rocky shores. Indigenous flora and fauna at Cowies Creek were used for medicines.[10] These activities constantly shaped the landscape by an attentive management regime in relation to vegetation and

---

[1] Tim Piccione, "Australia's Most Expensive Private Schools Revealed", *The Canberra Times*, 2023; Craig Butt, "The Top 20 Most Advantaged and Disadvantaged Suburbs in Victoria", *The Age*, 2023.

[2] "Geelong Population", Population Australia, https://www.population.net.au/geelong-population/.

[3] City of Greater Geelong, *Northern and Western Geelong Growth Areas Framework Plan* (Geelong, Victoria, 2019).

[4] City of Greater Geelong, *Northern and Western Geelong Growth Areas Framework Plan*.

[5] Lucretius, *De Natura Rerum (on the Nature of Things)*, ed William Leonard, vol. 3, 2 (50 BCE), 992.

[6] Luise Hercus, "Aboriginal Languages and Clans: An Historical Atlas of Western Central Victoria 1800-1900. Monash Publications in Geography No. 37," (JSTOR, 1992).

[7] Ian Clark, *Scars in the Landscape: A Register of Massacre Sites in Western Victoria, 1803-1859* (Aboriginal Studies Press, 1995).

[8] David Rowe, "Theme Two: Peopling Greater Geelong", in *About Corayo: A Thematic History of Greater Geelong* (Geelong, Victoria: City of Greater Geelong, 2021), 66–7; "3214: Cowies Creek Environmental Loop", City of Greater Geelong, https://www.geelongaustralia.com.au/walks/article/item/8d2ff1eebbbe245.aspx, accessed October 2023.

[9] Rowe, "Theme Two"; Uncle Bryon Powell, Tandop David Tournier, David S. Jones and Phillip B. Roös, "Welcome to Wadawurrung Country", in David S. Jones and Phillip B. Roös (eds), *Geelong's Changing Landscape: Ecology, Development and Conservation* (Collingwood: CSIRO Publishing, 2019), 44–84; Robert Henderson and David Johnson, *The Geology of Australia*, 3rd edn. (Cambridge, New York: Cambridge University Press, 2009).

[10] More information on the natural flora and fauna can be found on the local guide website on Cowies Creek Environmental Loop and Uncle Bryon Powell et al.'s "Welcome to Wadawurrung Country"; "3214: Cowies Creek Environmental Loop", City of Greater Geelong; Uncle Bryon Powell et al., "Welcome to Wadawurrung Country".

animals.[11] There were signs of Aboriginal industry integral to the natural environment itself, where men, women and children each participated in their own roles to reshape the landscape.[12] Men went hunting and scaled trees for possums; women served the family and raised children; children gathered gums and knocked down birds.[13] The Wadawurrung were known to make hunting tools and utensils as well as personal ornaments, clothing and weapons. The productions of these items hint at North Shore as a productive landscape despite no recorded permanent structures or settlements remaining. Such approaches to land management contrast with the developments after the colonial settlements. (See Chapter 2, "Colonial Recollections of Aboriginal Cultural Landscapes in Djilang, Wadawurrung Country".)

At the time of the first British arrivals in 1802, the Kulin population is estimated to have been about 20,000.[14] The first non-Aboriginal people recorded in the Geelong area arrived on the brig *HMS Lady Nelson*. They anchored outside Port Phillip Bay. On 1 February 1802, the commander, Lieutenant John Murray, sent a boat of six men through the Heads to investigate the region, returning 4 February. Murray subsequently sailed into the Bay, explored the Geelong foreshore, and claimed it for Britain on 14 February. In January 1803, the future site of Geelong was mapped by the Surveyor-General, Charles Grimes. In October that year, Lieutenant-Colonel David Collins attempted to establish a penal colony at Sullivan Bay (near present day Sorrento on the Mornington Peninsula). However, being dissatisfied with the site he sent out a party, led by James Tuckey, to find a more favourable location. It was at this time, between 22 and 27 October 1803, on the north shore of Corio Bay, that an encounter between Aboriginal people and the British took place, resulting in the first Aboriginal death in Victoria by non-Aboriginals.

The explorers Hamilton Hume and William Hovell reached Corio Bay by an inland route on 16 December 1824. It is they who report "Djillong" (from which Geelong is derived) and "Corayo" as being the Aboriginal people's name for the area and the bay. By March 1836, three squatters, David Fisher, George Russell and James Strachan, having arrived on the *Caledonia*, settled the area. Geelong was surveyed three weeks after Melbourne by Henry Smythe and registered as a British colonial town on 10 October 1838. At that time, Geelong comprised eighty-two houses and a non-Aboriginal population of 545. By 1841, a regular schedule of steamers plied the bay between Geelong and Melbourne, and wool was being exported to England.

The Aboriginal population declined due to European diseases and dispossession of the country brought to the area by British colonial settlers and surveyors. After altercations with British colonial settlers, clans were sent to protectorates at other locations such as the junction of Moorabool and Barwon River and Point Lonsdale.[15] When Captain Foster Fyans was commissioned as Police Magistrate in 1837, he set up missions to manage the protection of Aboriginal people and distribute food and clothing. The system lasted eleven years, from 1838 to 1848, before lapsing due to lack of funding. As Professor Ian Clark reports:

> All the Aboriginals within 30 miles of Geelong were assembled, amounting to 297 men, women, and children. Each received a blanket and portions of flour. In 1858 Fyans considered that no more than 20 of these 297 people were alive.[16]

A colonial government census of 1861 reported only seven Aboriginal people remaining in the Geelong region.[17]

The decline of conditions for Aboriginal people was only slowly reversed. In 1962, Aboriginal people in Victoria were given the right to vote. In 1976, Aboriginal people were granted the right to make claims on Crown land. In 1992, the High Court of Australia rejected the doctrine of *terra nullius*, stating that native title endures on lands where it has not been extinguished.[18] On 21 May 2009, the Wadawurrung Traditional Owners Aboriginal Corporation (WTOAC) was accorded Registered Aboriginal Party status. The WTOAC trace their ancestry to John Robinson (1846–1919), who had two children by Esther, his wife from Skipton, and a further five children by Margaret from Woolsthorpe. Today, the Wadawurrung are represented by the descendants of Robinson's seven children.[19] Victoria's *Aboriginal Heritage Act 2006* 'recognises Aboriginal people as the primary guardians, keepers and knowledge holders of Aboriginal cultural heritage'.[20] Under the Act, the WTOAC are responsible for providing advice on cultural heritage that might be impacted by any developments taking place in Geelong, and its industrial North Shore.[21]

---

[11] William Gammage, "Gardens without Fences? Landscape in Aboriginal Australia", *Australian Humanities Review* 36 (July 2005): 1–7.

[12] Rowe, "Theme 2", 69–70.

[13] Rowe, "Theme 2".

[14] Gary Presland, *Aboriginal Melbourne: The Lost Land of the Kulin People* (Ringwood, Victoria: McPhee Gribble, 1994).

[15] More details of the Wadawurrung relocation can be found in Ian Clark's *Scars in the Landscape*, 172, and Rowe's "Theme 2", 68–70.

[16] Ian D Clark, *Aboriginal Languages and Clans: An Historical Atlas of Western and Central Victoria, 1800-1900*, (Melbourne: Monash Univerity, Department of Geography and Environmntal Science, 1990).

[17] "Djillong Timeline", Wadawurrung Traditional Owners Aboriginal Corporation, https://www.wadawurrung.org.au/history.

[18] "Djillong Timeline", Wadawurrung Traditional Owners Aboriginal Corporation.

[19] "History", Wadawurrung Traditional Owners Aboriginal Corporation, https://www.wadawurrung.org.au/history.

[20] Victorian Government, *Aboriginal Heritage Act 2006*, https://www.legislation.vic.gov.au/in-force/acts/aboriginal-heritage-act-2006/027.

[21] "Wadawurrung Traditional Owners Aboriginal Corporation" Victorian Aboriginal Heritage Council, https://www.aboriginalheritagecouncil.vic.gov.au/wadawurrung-traditional-owners-aboriginal-corporation.

The industrial buildings of Geelong's North Shore

The industrialisation of Geelong began on the Barwon River, whose waters were utilised by wool mills and tanneries, and by the 1850s, in textile and paper mills. Smaller industries flourished on the waterfront, expanding westward.[22] Industries in North Shore began with agricultural activities such as piggeries and sheep farming. Their activities led to the establishments of abattoirs and freezing works along the water.[23] While these industries formed along Corio Bay, the geographical advantages of North Shore were soon recognised by the authorities as they sought better access during the Victorian gold rush from 1851 to the late 1860s.[24]

On 8 February 1853, the Victorian Government approved the establishment of the Melbourne and Geelong Railway Company. Due to a shortage of labour exacerbated by the gold rush, one hundred prisoners were hired out by the government for the construction of the railway line at the rate of 5 shillings per day. They were housed in hulks anchored in Corio Bay. The railway opened on 25 June 1857, becoming one of the first private lines, and the first linking two major cities in Australia.[25] In 1864, a wharf was built at the mouth of Cowies Creek (separating the present North Geelong from Norlane), making possible the free flow of goods to and from the Bay and into and out of Melbourne. In 1893, the Hopetoun Channel was carved into the shallow Corio Bay to accommodate the approach of deep draught ships. Trade in heavy volumes was now possible between Geelong, Britain, and the rest of the world.[26] Geelong's North Shore area thus emerged as a hub for diverse industrial activity, accommodating agricultural production and exports to heavy manufacturing industries (see Figure 8.3).

Figure 8.3 North Shore station, phosphate works, The Esplanade, 2023.

From the 1850s to 1890s, North Shore's landscape underwent a series of transformations to accommodate the rising industries. The Geelong Gas Company was established in 1854.[27] Engineering works – such as Cowies Creek wharf, Hopetoun Channel, and railways – provided the logistical infrastructure that drew in numerous activities predicated on agricultural and livestock produce: wheat, wool and mutton.[28] Jackson's meat packing and freezing works was founded

---

[22] Peter Begg, *Geelong - the First 150 Years* (Globe Press, 1990).

[23] City of Greater Geelong, *3214: North Shore Walk*.

[24] Discovery of gold at Ballarat in 1851 sparked Victoria's richest gold rush – thousands of people came to Victoria in the hope of finding a lot of gold and becoming rich quickly. "Custodians of the Bay, a Brief History of Geelong Port", Port of Geelong, 2018, https://geelongport.com.au/custodians-of-the-bay/, 8–9.

[25] Tim Lilley, "Building Rail, Building Victoria: A History of the Melbourne-Geelong Railway", University of Melbourne, https://blogs.unimelb.edu.au/shaps-research/2019/06/28/building-rail-building-victoria/.

[26] Begg, *Geelong - the First 150 Years*.

[27] The company supplied energy for Geelong city's streets from 1860 until the establishment of the Electric Lighting and Traction Company in 1899 and its Power Station A in the CBD. David Rowe, "Theme Five: Building Greater Geelong's Industry and Workface", in *About Corayo: A Thematic History of Greater Geelong* (Geelong, Victoria: City of Greater Geelong, 2021), 633–634.

[28] Adrian Patrick Regan, "Re-Manufacturing the City: Geelong 1945-1993" (Thesis, Monash University, 2014); Mirjana Lozanovska and Akari Nakai Kidd, "'Vacant Geelong' and Its Lingering Industrial Architecture", *arq: Architectural Research Quarterly* 24, no. 4 (2020).

in 1864, located beside the Cowies Creek wharf.[29] The Oriental Timber Corporation of Australia had its mills operating in 1908 with a log pond at Cowies Creek.[30] These developments led to the North Shore becoming an industrial powerhouse in the twentieth century.

In 1905, the Geelong Harbour Trust was founded.[31] The organisation would manage and regulate Geelong's maritime traffic, from landing or shipping of merchandise, arrivals and departures of vessels, to wharfage rates.[32] Their activities attracted international manufacturers to base their production facilities in the North Shore area, earning Geelong its nickname as the "Pivot City" as on it 'hinged the commerce of the whole western half of the colony'.[33] Mills and factories dominated the landscape. Federal Woollen Mills (1915), Cresco Fertilizers (1923) and the Phosphate Co-operative of Australia (1924), among other enterprises, appeared in the early twentieth century (see Figure 8.4).[34] Geelong's North Shore remained a hive of industrial activity well into the 1960s. Each new enterprise brought Geelong a huge influx of population, talents, skilled and non-skilled labourers, and migrants.[35] The rapid rate of production saw the development of the emerging suburbs of Norlane, North Geelong and Corio.[36]

Figure 8.4 North Shore area, looking across Osborne Park to North Shore, Geelong, 1933.

The 1920s saw a seismic shift from agriculture to chemicals and heavy industries. Both Cresco Fertilizers and the Phosphate Co-operative Company of Australia were concerned with superphosphate productions to serve the expanding needs of the Victoria's Western District farmers,[37] (See Chapter 7, "Agriculture's Shadow Connections"). Geelong's most iconic company, the Ford Motor Company of Australia, was established in 1925. Ford's criteria for choosing the location of an assembly plant were that the site be near a large city, adjacent to a deep-water port to bring kits in, and with access to a reliable supply of labour.[38] Norlane offered just such a site, and a 40-hectare plot was acquired on which the Ford Geelong plant was built. The plant became a marvel for its architectural merits and construction processes.

---

[29] David Rowe, "Theme Three: Transport and Communications", in *About Corayo: A Thematic History of Greater Geelong* (Geelong, Victoria: City of Greater Geelong, 2021), 253.

[30] Rowe, "Theme Five", 543; Rowe, "Theme Three", 293.

[31] Port of Geelong, *Custodians of the Bay*, 12.

[32] "Port of Geelong Authority (known as Geelong Harbor Trust Commissioners 1905-1981)", Public Record Office of Victoria, accessed November 30, 2023, https://researchdata.edu.au/port-geelong-authority-1905-1981/492509.

[33] Geelong Publicity Commission (GPC), *Beginnings, Geelong: Advantages and Prospects*, (Geelong: GPC, 1930), 14.

[34] "Former Federal Woollen Mills", Victorian Heritage Database, accessed November 30, 2023, https://vhd.heritagecouncil.vic.gov.au/places/11489; Rowe, "Theme Five", 643; Rowe, "Theme Five", 543.

[35] Regan, *"Re-Manufacturing the City"*; Mirjana Lozanovska et al., "Forum: Industrial sites and immigrant architectures. A case study approach", *Fabrications* 29, no. 2, 265; Warwick Eather, *A Human Commodity: Post-War Immigration, Employment and Ford Geelong, 1945-60*, Occasional Paper 1, (Geelong: Centre for Australian Studies, School of Humanities, Deakin University, 1990); GPC, *Geelong: Advantages and Prospects*; Louise Johnson, "The Geelong Suburban Dream: Origins, History and Future", in David S. Jones and Phillip B. Roös (eds), *Geelong's Changing Landscape: Ecology, Development and Conservation* (Collingwood: CSIRO Publishing, 2019), 216–27.

[36] Johnson, "The Geelong Suburban Dream", 218.

[37] Roger Southern Research, "Cresco and Geelong" (2017).

[38] GA, "New Era for Geelong. City and Port to Benefit"; GPC, *Geelong: Its Advantages and Opportunities*, 50.

Divided into sections of 48 ft × 26 ft, its concrete floor was constructed with 'eight inches of blue metals of various grades, over which is $4^1/_2$ inches of reinforced concrete'.[39] The specification gives a smooth surface that can withstand contraction and absorption. It has been estimated that a 1000 tonnes of steel framework was needed for the plant.[40] At the time, Australian factories resisted to a wind resistance of 20 lb, but the Ford Geelong plant achieved a capacity of 30 lb.[41] Its steel framing structures were embedded in a concrete base with north-facing windows for maximum sunlight. The exterior was built from the finest red bricks, selected and delivered from kilns in Melbourne's eastern suburb of Box Hill. Bricklayers were paid at a premium daily rate instead of the usual rate based on number of bricks laid per day to ensure the quality and timeliness of its construction.[42] With nearly 300 workers on site, excluding railway workers who transported building materials directly to the site, the Ford Geelong plant was completed in two years, an amazing accomplishment in both scale and craftmanship[43] (See Chapter 3, "Dialogues Between Space and Time").

Ford's Geelong plant accelerated the area's developments, with its increasing demands.[44] Energy (gas) supply and sewage were supplied for its production.[45] In 1980, Ford employed over 4200 people, performing full design and manufacture of cars. Twenty-five different car models were manufactured over time, in addition to war-time military vehicles. It became the development centre for Africa and the Asia–pacific region. More than four million Ford Falcons alone were assembled between 1960 and 2016 at its Geelong plant. However, globalisation and foreign competition led to a collapse in profitability. On 26 September 2016, Ford closed its Geelong operations. Since then, the site has only found interim use as a COVID-19 pandemic vaccination hub.[46]

The 1930s and 1940s saw more arrivals of international companies and manufacturers, such as Pilkington Brothers Glass and International Harvester.[47] Proximity to Ford encouraged synergies in their productions. The increased demands during the Second World War helped these manufacturers to expand their production capacity.[48] Pilkington grew to become Australia's first supplier to manufacture laminated glass and a premier automotive glass manufacturer, employing 500 personnel in 1980.[49] However, Pilkington's contracts were discontinued after a Chinese glass manufacturer secured deals with Ford and Holden in 2007, leading to its shutdown.[50] Similarly, the International Harvester factory grew from its occupation on forty-five acres of land and employment of 2600 people in 1939 into the largest iron foundry in the Southern Hemisphere, servicing one quarter of the Australasian tractor market.[51] It produced 300 tractors and numerous other trucks and agricultural vehicles every month until its closure in 1982 after the collapse of the agricultural sector in the 1970s.[52]

From the 1950s to 1960s, North Shore saw the rise of Royal Dutch Shell. The Geelong oil refinery became the first refinery in post-war Australia. It became operational on 18 March 1954. One thousand people were involved in its construction, and sixty acres of housing were also built to accommodate employees.[53] The refinery has the capacity to process 7.5 billion litres of crude oil annually. Its accomplishments include introduction of unleaded petrol, 1985; construction of a catalytic cracking unit, 1992 (the largest construction project in Victoria at the time); production of ultra-low sulphur fuels, 2004; cutting benzene emissions by one-quarter, 2006; and a recycling initiative reducing

---

[39] Geelong Advertiser, *Geelong Advertiser: Setting up of the Ford Motor Company in Geelong 1925-1934* (Geelong, Victoria: Geelong Heritage Collections).

[40] Geelong Advertiser, *Geelong Advertiser: Setting up of the Ford Motor Company in Geelong 1925-1934*, 14.

[41] Geelong Advertiser, *Geelong Advertiser: Setting up of the Ford Motor Company in Geelong 1925-1934*, 14.

[42] Geelong Advertiser, *Geelong Advertiser: Setting up of the Ford Motor Company in Geelong 1925-1934,* 13.

[43] Mirjana Lozanovska and Akari Nakai Kidd, "'Vacant Geelong' and its Lingering Industrial Architecture", *Architecture Research Quarterly (ARQ)* 24, no. 4 (2020): 353–68.

[44] Ford purchased more land capacity in 1946, 1961, 1966 and 1970, totalling its area to 66.01 hectares. Ford Motor Company of Australia, "Ford Australia Geelong Site", *50 Years of Going with Ford 1925 – 1975*, (Geelong, Victoria: Geelong Historical Record Centre).

[45] "New Sewerage Area", *Geelong Advertiser: Setting up of the Ford Motor Company in Geelong 1925-1934*, (Geelong, Victoria: Geelong Heritage Collections), 12.

[46] Begg, *Geelong - the First 150 Years*; Danny Lannen, "Ford Geelong Workers Decline Broadmeadows Plant's Farewell to Stay Home", *Djilang Advertiser*, 2016; David Morley, "The History of Ford's Geelong Factory", https://www.carsguide.com.au/car-advice/the-history-of-fords-geelong-factory-86011; Kian Heagney, "Old Ford Factory Making History Again as Mass Vaccination Hub", https://www.whichcar.com.au/car-news/old-ford-factory-geelong-covid-19-vaccination-hub.

[47] Pilkington's origins date from 1826 in England and began its shipments of glass to Australia in 1856. Demand was high enough to entice the opening of a plant in Geelong in 1936. R D Lynch, "Introduction", *History of Pilkington Brothers (Australia) Pty Ltd - Geelong Plant*, Investigation for Social Science II, (1970), 1.

[48] Pilkington, *The end of a long era for Pilkington*, 2009, https://www.glassonweb.com/news/end-long-era-pilkington.

[49] Geelong Pilkington glass plant was able to process and supply safety glasses to 95% of all land transport with safety glass including cars, trucks and all army vehicles, trains and farming equipment (tractors, graders, mobile cranes). Lynch, "Introduction", 1.

[50] Pilkington, "The End of a Long Era for Pilkington".

[51] International Harvester, *History and Development of International Harvester, Australia*, (Australia: International Harvester Printing); "International Harvester Geelong Factory", Intown, accessed November 30, 2023, https://intown.com.au/events/gallery/international-harvester-geelong-factory.htm; Maree Hedson, *History and Development of International Harvester – Geelong Plant* (August 1988).

[52] "International Harvester Geelong Factory", Intown.

[53] The workers also comprised of migrants from fourteen European countries, such as Holland, Italy, Lithuania, Latvia, Britain and France. "Constructing the Geelong Refinery: A History", Viva Energy, accessed November 30, 2023, https://www.vivaenergy.com.au/blog/innovation/constructing-the-geelong-refinery-a-history.

Geelong's water consumption by 5%, 2008. The Geelong refinery remains one of only two oil refineries still operating in Australia.[54]

North Shore's vacant buildings

The foregoing discussion makes plain two key conclusions. First, Geelong's North Shore was, for a long while, a powerhouse of industry. Second, that momentum is now gone. The legacy is threefold. A significant residue of industry remains. The Geelong refinery (formerly Shell, now operated by Viva Energy) is most prominent, supplying about half of Victoria's fuel.[55] Today, the Incitec Pivot fertiliser facility, Boral Cement, and Midway Limited's woodchipping mill occupy the former International Harvester site.[56]

New activities have also appeared. In 2008, the Malteurop Australia malting plant was set up on Crowle Street, North Shore. With an annual capacity of 200,000 tonnes, it is one of three global malt production hubs and it expects that its settlement in Geelong will provide growth and access to more port facilities, infrastructure systems, and skilled human resources.[57] Notably, since 23 October 2022, the *Spirit of Tasmania* sails from Corio Quay.[58] Its strategic terminal relocation from Station Pier in Melbourne to Geelong hopes to accommodate bigger ferries, which will accelerate Geelong's businesses and regional growth.[59]

This history of the industrial sector clearly demonstrates the rise and fall of manufacturing in the area. However, the more dramatic consequence of past industry shutdowns is the abundance of now unoccupied land and abandoned buildings. There is a middle ground between ongoing businesses and empty land. A desktop real estate search has revealed twenty-four factories/warehouses listed for sale or lease in North Shore, at the time of writing (2023). The land areas are substantial at 21,500 m^2. These are fully serviced properties. However, the full extent of vacant dormant industrial space is far greater.

A survey (see Figure 8.5 in the colour plate section) conducted as part of the VacantGeelong project in the School of Architecture and Built Environment at Deakin University reveals the degree of vacancy (See Chapter 3 "Dialogues Between Space and Time"). From 2015 to 2017, this survey was conducted by students, led by VacantGeelong academic staff from the school (including the authors – Diego Fullaondo as map coordinator and supervisor; and Chayakan Siamphukdee as then student member).[60] Its aim was to document and record the vacancy of industrial buildings onto a map. Here the map is used as a visual tool to methodically collate data and represent the findings.[61] The scope of the survey was limited to Geelong as a region around Corio Bay and the Barwon River.[62]

With reference to Figure 8.6 and the two-year period of investigation, inventory of vacant industrial space in the North Shore area, it is evident that:

- North Geelong has thirty-four vacant industrial properties, with a cumulative undercover area of 37,727 m^2
- Corio has eighteen properties with a total vacant space of 39,921 m^2
- North Shore has eight buildings with 9518 m^2
- Norlane adds a final three buildings with 1135 m^2.

The total combined vacant inventory is sixty-three buildings, offering an undercover space of 88,301 m^2, capable of accommodating 482,161 m^3 of machinery and goods. This raw data of vacant architecture in the North Shore area, consolidates North Shore's deeply connected past to industries. It shows a concentration of industrial vacancy that is far greater than the rest of the region surveyed (see Figures 8.7 and 8.8).

---

[54] "Australian Oil Refineries", Australian Institute of Petroleum, accessed 30 November 2023, https://www.aip.com.au/sites/default/files/download-files/2017-09/At%20a%20Glance%20Australian%20Oil%20Refineries.pdf; Viva Energy Australia, "Geelong Refinery - Our History", accessed November 30, 2023, https://www.vivaenergy.com.au/operations/geelong/history.

[55] Shell was acquired by Australian enterprise Viva Energy. "Operations – Geelong", accessed November 30, 2023, Viva Energy Australia, https://www.vivaenergy.com.au/operations/geelong.

[56] "Innovation on the Ground", Incitec Pivot, https://www.incitecpivot.com.au/; "International Harvester", Intown.

[57] "Presentation of Malteurop Australia Pty Ltd", Malteurop, accessed November 30, 2023, https://www.malteurop.com/en/australia.

[58] "Introducing Spirit of Tasmania Quay", Spirit of Tasmania, accessed November 30, 2023, https://www.spiritoftasmania.com.au/geelong-terminal.

[59] Judy Augustine, "How Spirit of Tasmania's New Home is Taking Shape", *Geelong Advertiser*, accessed November 30, 2023, https://www.geelongadvertiser.com.au/news/geelong/how-spirit-of-tasmanias-new-home-is-taking-shape/news-story/762cd89d5ee147882004df2f18a8677d.

[60] Mirjana Lozanovska et al., *Iconic Industry: Exploring the Industrial Built Fabric of Geelong*, (Geelong: Deakin University, 2017), 5.

[61] Diego Fullaondo, "What is a Map?", *Drawing Bazaar*, (Madrid: Escuela de Arquitectura Universidad Europea de Madrid, 2015), 61–65.

[62] Lozanovska et al., *Iconic Industry*, 6.

No.	Address	Type	Suburb	Area M2	Volume M3
1	14 Rooney Rd, North Geelong	com	North Geelong	292	1,168
2	155 Melbourne Rd, Rippleside, North Geelong	com	North Geelong	65	260
3	196 Melbourne Rd, Rippleside, North Geelong	com	North Geelong	170	640
4	197 Melbourne Rd, Rippleside, North Geelong	com	North Geelong	170	640
5	203 Melbourne Rd, Rippleside, North Geelong	com	North Geelong	170	680
6	End Building Liverpool St, Rippleside, North Geelong	ind	North Geelong	82	330
7	Federal Mill Complex 3, Mackey St, North Geelong	ind	North Geelong	10,500	63,000
8	Chimney Federal Mill Complex, North Geelong	ind	North Geelong	2,120	12,720
9	Silo Federation Mill Complex, North Geelong	ind	North Geelong	90	360
10	23-36 Corio Quay Rd, North Geelong	ind	North Geelong	11,000	66,000
11	58-60 Cowie Street, North Geelong	empty plot	North Geelong	456	1,824
12	14 Cadman Terrace, North Geelong	iw	North Geelong	328	2,624
13	16 Cadman Terrace North Geelong	iw	North Geelong	256	1,024
14	18 Cadman Terrace, North Geelong	iw	North Geelong	737	8,844
15	20 Cadman Terrace, North Geelong	iw	North Geelong	620	2,480
16	34 Edols Street, North Geelong	iw	North Geelong	273	2,184
17	9 Cowie Street, North Geelong	iw	North Geelong	1,235	9,880
18	11 Cowie Street, North Geelong	iw	North Geelong	1,235	9,880
19	56 Cowie Street, North Geelong	iw	North Geelong	113	1,050
20	15 Saunders Street, North Geelong	iw	North Geelong	1,472	11,776
21	5 Ryeland Court, North Geelong	iw	North Geelong	1,490	11,920
22	3 Rooney Rd, North Geelong	iw	North Geelong	357	2,856
23	6 Rooney Rd, North Geelong	iw	North Geelong	300	2,400
24	15 Rooney Rd, North Geelong	iw	North Geelong	372	2,976
25	21 Rooney Rd, North Geelong	iw	North Geelong	264	2,112
26	23 Rooney Rd, North Geelong	iw	North Geelong	532	4,256
27	10 Freedman Street, North Geelong	iw	North Geelong	296	2,368
28	8 Naughton Ave, North Geelong	iw	North Geelong	336	2,688
29	9 Naughtons Ave, North Geelong	iw	North Geelong	518	4,414
30	201 Melbourne Rd, Rippleside, North Geelong	off	North Geelong	390	1,560
31	10 Naughtons Ave, North Geelong	iw	North Geelong	357	2,856
32	11 Naughtons Ave, North Geelong	iw	North Geelong	522	4,176
33	18 Naughtons Ave, North Geelong	iw	North Geelong	306	1,224
34	20 Naughtons Ave, North Geelong	iw	North Geelong	303	2,424
			TOTAL	**37,727**	**245,594**

No.	Address	Type	Suburb	Area M2	Volume M3
1	Unit Adjacent Formula Uno Prices High, Corio	com	Corio	400	1,600
2	84-86 Station St, Corio	com	Corio	370	1,480
3	3 Labuan Sqr, Corio	com	Corio	160	640
4	5A Squr: having moon laser, Corio	com	Corio	115	460
5	7 Lauan Aqur, Corio	com	Corio	115	460
6	10 Lauan Sqr, Corio	com	Corio	92	366
7	11 Labuan Sqr, Corio	com	Corio	160	640
8	15 Labuan Sqr, Corio	com	Corio	95	380
9	23 Lowe St, Corio	ind	Corio	3,160	18,960
10	35 Lowe St, Corio	ind	Corio	31,120	124,480
11	189 Station St, Corio	iw	Corio	574	3,444
12	218 Station St, Corio	iw	Corio	460	2,760
13	86-92 Station St, Corio	iw	Corio	595	2,380
14	108-110 Station St, Corio	ws-iw	Corio	290	1,160
15	94-104 Station St, Corio	ws-iw	Corio	800	4,800
16	62-64 Station St, Corio	ws-iw	Corio	215	860
17	244 Princes Highway, Corio	off	Corio	500	3,000
18	208 Station St, Corio	off	Corio	700	2,800
			TOTAL	**39,921**	**170,670**

No.	Address	Type	Suburb	Area M2	Volume M3
1	1-9 Seaside Pde, North Shore	ind	North Shore	97	291
2	143-145 The Esplanade, North Shore	ind	North Shore	4,456	26,736
3	24-26 Seaside Pde, North Shore	iw	North Shore	500	3,000
4	43 Seaside Pde, North Shore	iw	North Shore	500	3,000
5	64 Seaside Pde, North Shore	iw	North Shore	70	420
6	23 Seaside Pde, North Shore	iw	North Shore	240	1,440
7	16 Coonil Cres, North Shore	ws-iw	North Shore	445	2,670
8	28-30 Seaside Rd, North Shore	off	North Shore	3,210	19,260
			TOTAL	**9,518**	**56,817**

No.	Address	Type	Suburb	Area M2	Volume M3
1	49 Morghan Street, Norlane	iw	Norlane	397	3,176
2	51 Morgan Street, Norlane	iw	Norlane	337	2,696
3	17 The Blvd, Norlane	school	Norlane	401	3,208
			TOTAL	**1,135**	**9,080**

			Grand TOTAL	**88,301**	**482,161**

Figure 8.6 Inventory of vacant industrial space in the North Shore area. Type of buildings surveyed: com (commercial); ind (industrial factories); iw (industrial warehouse); ws (workshop); off (office). Source: Diego Fullaondo and Chayakan Siamphukdee, Industrial Vacancy in Geelong 2015–2017, 2017.

Summary of Architectural Vacancy in Geelong (including CBD)

Building Status	Commercial	Offices	Warehouses	Industrial	Other	TOTAL
Vacant (n°)	29	13	98	42	3	185
Part-Vacant (n°))	0	6	6	4	0	16
Refurbishing (n°)	1	1	0	1	0	3
TOTAL (n°)	30	20	104	47	3	204
VACANT + PART VACANT (n°)	29	19	104	46	3	201
TOTAL Vacant Area (m²)	6482	18914	67103	102013	1162	160087

Figure 8.7 Summaries of architectural vacancy (2015–2017) in Geelong (including CBD). Source: Diego Fullaondo and Chayakan Siamphukdee, Industrial Vacancy in Geelong 2015–2017, 2017.

Summary of Architectural Vacancy in Geelong CBD

Building Status	Commercial	Offices	Warehouses	Industrial	Other	TOTAL
Vacant (n°)	62	9	10		4	85
Part-Vacant (n°))	25	10				35
Refurbishing (n°)	5	1				6
TOTAL (n°)	92	20	10	0	4	126
VACANT + PART VACANT (n°)	87	19	10	0	4	120
TOTAL Vacant Area (m²)	33161	12357	2623	0	1215	49356

Figure 8.8 Summaries of architectural vacancy (2015–2017) in Geelong CBD. Source: Diego Fullaondo and Chayakan Siamphukdee, Industrial Vacancy in Geelong 2015–2017, 2017

North Shore has a higher grand total of industrial vacancy area than Geelong's CBD. In 2017, the CBD's architectural vacancy area totalled 49,356 m², including all surveyed building typologies (commercial, offices, warehouses, industries and others) together. Industrial buildings in the CBD accounted for 2623 m² or 5% of its entire architectural vacancy area, meaning vacancy in the CBD was not of an industrial typology. However, the industrial vacancy in the CBD, was equivalent to 6% of North Shore's industrial vacancy.

North Shore contributed 45% (out of 195,674 m²) of Geelong's total architectural vacancy in 2017. This value made industrial architecture the biggest contributor to Geelong's overall architectural vacancy. Those vacant sites in North Shore present opportunities for redevelopment, especially when their underutilised spaces or areas are not simply wasted structures. They are also imbued with history and collective memories that makes North Shore a place with legacies (see Figure 8.9).

Where to from here?

Geelong has experienced two major redevelopment schemes: Vision I and Vision II. Vision I (1996) by Keys Young and Urban Initiatives, in collaboration with the City of Greater Geelong, focused on redeveloping the waterfront, resulting in improved public spaces manifest in a skate park, playground and the much photographed "sail fins", "totems" and "carousel building".[63] Notably, Westfield Geelong shopping centre (formerly the Melbourne Electric Supply Company building or Power Station A) extended its structure with its controversial overpass bridge, straddling Yarra Street, which now obscures views of Corio Bay.[64] Vision II (2011) undertook a wider stakeholder approach, including, among others, the City of Greater Geelong Council, State Government of Victoria, Deakin University, and a consortium of business interests to its projects.[65] Six projects emerged, some of which are still ongoing: Green Spine,

---

[63] City of Greater Geelong, *Central Geelong Waterfront Masterplan 2011*, (City of Greater Geelong, Geelong, 2011).

[64] "Projects", Urban Initiatives, accessed November 30, 2023, https://www.urbaninitiatives.com.au/projects/; Chayakan Siamphukdee et al., "Background and Literature Report on Re-Development of Geelong's Industrial North Shore", (2022).

[65] Initiative collaboration with Deakin University, School of Architecture and Built Environment: https://dro.deakin.edu.au/articles/educational_resource/Vision_2_original_design_work_-_thematic_concepts/20831425.

Year	Company	Image
1954	Geelong Gas Company	
1860	Hopetoun Channel	
1899	Jackson Corio Meat Packing Co.	
1923	Cresco Fertilizer	
1910	Federal Woolen Mills	
1924	Phosphate Cooperative of Australia	
1925	Ford Motor Company	
1928	Distillery Corporation	
1937	Pilkington Bros. Glass	
1940	International Harvester	
1954	Shell Refinery	
1954	Grain Elevators Board	

Figure 8.9 Summaries of North Shore's industries. Source: Igor Martek and Chayakan Siamphukdee, 2023.

Laneways, Urban Heart, Postcode 3220, Transport Arrivals, and Student CBD Accommodation (See Chapter 12 "The A + B Studio").[66] However, these plans are not concerned with industrial buildings.[67]

At the Point Henry peninsula, east of the Geelong CBD, Alcoa's decommissioned aluminium smelter plant is transitioning to become a 'sustainable community and tourist destination'.[68] Most industrial structures were disassembled, leaving only the most prominent features: the vacant 575-hectares of Alcoa's plant and a water tank.[69] The plan is to allow the area to be naturally restored as wetlands and grasslands, while waiting for future developments. This approach of nature recuperation contrasts with the rapid sprawls in Geelong's hinterlands (See Chapter 11, "Radical Pedagogies").

The key takeaway regarding Geelong's redevelopment efforts is that they have been state-led in respect of central Geelong, while left to private investors elsewhere. The Australian Bureau of Statistics, WorkSafe, the National Disability Insurance Agency, and Victoria's Transport Accident Commission were relocated to Geelong's CBD.[70] Private capital was involved at Deakin University's Waterfront Campus and the Market Square redevelopment in the CBD. Beyond the CBD, the private sector undertook some redevelopment schemes. Little Creatures Brewery in South Geelong, Fyansford Paper Mill, and the Woolstores in Newtown adopted sensitive adaptation approaches, which are positive for protecting Geelong's industrial heritage.[71] These examples remain few when assessed against the peripheral suburban sprawl. The vacancy at hand raises one question - how the authorities would address or assist the regeneration of areas near disused industrial sites. No comprehensive plan so far has been proposed for the North Shore, except for the masterplan "Pivot City Innovation District", at the southern boundary of the North Shore area, by the developer Hamilton Group. Based in Geelong, it has won multiple awards for redeveloping three of Geelong's iconic sites, including North Geelong's Federal Mills (33 Mackey Street, North Geelong) and the former Pilkington Brothers Glass factory Glass House (11 Mackey Street, North Geelong) (see Figure 8.10). The Pivot City Innovation District has won awards for urban regeneration for sensitively adapting heritage buildings and their surroundings into offices, leisure spaces, and green walking paths.[72] Integrated, these past industrial sites present the transformation possibilities of industrial zones; the area is successfully rebranding its image as a centre for business incubation.[73]

While these projects highlight (a part of) North Shore transforming with the rest of Geelong, its transformation is not without objections. The City of Greater Geelong is content to maintain the status quo on the North Shore. The final part to the Pivot City Innovation District is a 10,000 m^2 waterfront development with 440 car parks at 44 Mackey Street, North Geelong.[74] The project would be housed in Geelong's Power Station B, which operated from 1934 to 1970.[75] The project's strengths are found in North Shore's assets: the Bay, five minutes to the CBD, fifty-five minutes to Melbourne, 500 m to North Geelong station, and 5000 m^2 of nearby green spaces.[76] Despite these appeals, the project appears to be meeting with objections from numerous stakeholders.[77] The City of Greater Geelong's position regarding the project is that the Power Station site should remain a buffer between North Shore proper and the CBD. The City of Greater Geelong's position regarding the development of the North Shore area may well be as stated by Kirsch and Blackley:

---

[66] The "Green Spine" improves the city's mobility and biodiversity with natural plants and flora. 'Laneways' hopes to increase the permeability across the city blocks towards its redeveloped waterfront. "Urban Heart" attempts to densify the CBD area. David Jones and Helen Meikle, "Reinventing D'Jillong: Current Regeneration Initiatives Challenging the Identity and Place of Geelong" (paper, 6th State of Australian Cities Conference, 26-29 November 2013, Sydney, 2013).

[67] Siamphukdee et al., "Background and Literature Report"; Hisham Elkadi, "Smart Integrated Ecological Approach for Geelong, Australia", *Africanus* 26, no. 1 (1996); David Jones and Helen Meikle, "Reinventing D'jillong: Current Regeneration Initiatives Challenging the Identity and Place of Geelong".

[68] Alcoa established an aluminium smelter on the peninsula in 1963, and it continued operations for five decades until its closure in 2014. "Point Henry: About the Project", Alcoa, accessed November 30, 2023, https://www.alcoa.com/australia/en/point-henry/about-project.

[69] "Point Henry: About the Project", Alcoa.

[70] Committee for Geelong, Geelong, *Australia's Gateway Cities: Gateways to Growth* (Committee for Geelong, 2019), https://www.committeeforgeelong.com.au/wp-content/uploads/2019/11/Australias-Gateway-Cities-Report-and-Appendices.pdf, 9.

[71] Rowe, "Theme Five", 529; "Geelong's Little Creatures Brewery", Architecture & Design accessed November 30, 2023, https://www.architectureanddesign.com.au/projects/transport-industrial/geelong-s-little-creatures-brewery; "The Woolstores: 400 Pakington St, Newtown", Hamilton Group, https://hamilton.net.au/400pako; Fiona Gray et al., "Milling it Over: Geelong's New Life in Forgotten Places", *Historic Preservation* 29, no. 2, (Australia ICOMOS, 2017), 58–69; John Rollo and Yolanda Esteban, "The Promise of Vision-Making a City: A Perpetual Journey", in David S. Jones and Phillip B. Roös (eds), *Geelong's Changing Landscape: Ecology, Development and Conservation* (Collingwood: CSIRO Publishing, 2019); Louise C Johnson, Sally Weller and Tom Barnes "(Extra) Ordinary Geelong: State-Led Urban Regeneration and Economic Revival", in *Ordinary Cities, Extraordinary Geographies: People, Place and Space* (2021), 85–109.

[72] "Pivot City Innovation District", Hamilton Group, accessed November 30, 2023, https://www.pivotcity.com.au/.

[73] "Pivot City Innovation District", Hamilton Group.

[74] "Pivot City Power Station (44 Mackey St, North Geelong)", Hamilton Group, accessed November 30, 2023, https://hamilton.net.au/powerstation.

[75] Rowe, "Theme Five", 636.

[76] "Pivot City Power Station (44 Mackey St, North Geelong)", Hamilton Group.

[77] Marisa Wikramanayake, "Hamilton Pushes on Geelong Pivot City Stage", *Urban Developer*, https://www.theurbandeveloper.com/articles/geelong-planning-scheme-amendment-pivot-city-power-station-hamilton-group-plans-filed.

'In relation to the Port, the Committee concludes that protecting its ongoing operation is the primary land use planning consideration, consistent with the relevant policies in the Greater Geelong Planning Scheme.'[78]

How long that position can endure pressures for redevelopment remain to be seen. The redevelopment will likely determine whether Geelong maintains its past or loses it. However, there are constraints in place: a raft of national and state levels legislation with jurisdiction over the North Shore area and guidelines that are consoling, but insufficient.[79]

Legislative measures for developing the existing site appeal to tangible (built and natural) and intangible (cultural) heritage. The Commonwealth's *Environmental Protection and Biodiversity Conservation Act 1999* and Victoria's *Planning and Environmental Act 1987* oversee the site's (nationally and internationally important) natural elements: soil, water, plants, and animals and their habitats.[80] Heritage-concerned Acts protect culturally significant buildings and items. Industrial buildings with architectural merits (i.e. façade of Ford Geelong plant and the Federal Woollen Mills) are listed on the Victorian Heritage Register and protected under Victoria's *Heritage Act 2017*. Meanwhile, Aboriginal heritage provides another layer of narratives that add nuances and spiritual dimensions to the place. From scar trees and native plants, the natural attributes inform Aboriginal narratives and culture. Natural elements and values, which had been misunderstood or ignored in earlier heritage assessments, are becoming more informed.[81]

Guidelines have been recognised but not yet incorporated under the planning scheme and have no force in the Victorian Civil and Administrative Tribunal (VCAT). The Greater Geelong Municipal Heritage Strategy (2017–2021) set outlines for (i) understanding existing heritage and context and (ii) building designs (setbacks, massing, bulk, and finishes) to be sympathetic.[82] Mock heritage is to be avoided.[83] Similarly, both the Burra Charter and Nizhny Tagil Charter (the latter, with its focus on industrial built heritage) provide principles and recommendations for conserving a place and its heritage.[84] Their emphasis on the importance of the entire environment for its cultural significance and the value of the past as an asset for future generations appear to have been used to discourage the reuse of the existing vacancy, or "brown" sites.[85] Instead, developments on new "green" sites were accelerated, avoiding the site's unique complexities, despite prospects of a unique hybrid industrial landscape, celebrating its past, present and emerging industries. The celebration of heritage with the creative industries and business incubation exhibited at the Pivot City Innovation District showcase a potential to deal with vacancy. However, it does raise important questions around how the collaboration between public and private sectors can be forged. With the rapid growth of Geelong CBD, will North Shore be able to develop synergies that complement both its existing and burgeoning industries?

Conclusion

The conjecture posed in this chapter is that Geelong's North Shore comprises highly desirable real estate, being proximate to Corio Bay, the CBD, and major logistics infrastructure linkages. The abundance of vacant land and buildings make it ripe for redevelopment, but the area is constrained by local, regional and state jurisdictions, and stakeholder interests. Without carefully articulating the history of North Shore, the rapidly burgeoning insensitive developments will obliterate North Shore's legacy, which is embedded in its industrial buildings and landscape, as Karl Marx put it:

> The multitude of productive forces accessible to men [sic] determines the nature of society, hence, that the history of humanity must always be studied and treated in relation to the history of industry and exchange.[86]

---

[78] M. Kirsch and S. Blackley, "Advisory Committee Report Redevelopment of 50 Mackey Street, North Geelong", (2020).

[79] State legislation are: *Environmental Protection and Biodiversity Conservation Act 1999* and *Aboriginal and Torres Strait Islander Heritage Protection Act 1987*. State legislation includes *Planning and Environmental Act 1987, Aboriginal Heritage Act 2006, Aboriginal Heritage Regulations 2007, Aboriginal Heritage Amendment Act 2016*, and *Heritage Act 1995 and Heritage Act 2017*. "Geelong Heritage Strategy 2017-2021", City of Greater Geelong (Geelong, City of Greater Geelong, 2017), accessed November 30, 2023, https://www.geelongaustralia.com.au/common/Public/Documents/8d5010363a10469-finalcoggmunicipalheritagestrategysep 2017.pdf , 7.

[80] Department of Climate Change, Energy, the Environment and Water, *Environment Protection and Biodiversity Conservation Act 1999*, https://www.dcceew.gov.au/environment/epbc.

[81] Cultural blindness had been an issue for Aboriginal heritage because of how Aboriginal natural forms differ from the built forms (architectural aesthetics and scale) or made items. Ed Wensing, "Aboriginal and Torres Strait Islander Australians", in Susan Thompson and Paul J. Maginn (eds), *Planning Australia: an Overview of Urban and Regional Planning*, 2nd edn (Cambridge University Press, 2012), 254–75; Steven Rowley, *The Victorian Planning System: Practice, Problems and Prospects*, (NSW: The Federation Press), 256–57.

[82] "Heritage Strategy 2017-2021", City of Greater Geelong.

[83] "Heritage Strategy 2017-2021", City of Greater Geelong.

[84] The Burra Charter is a document adopted by ICOMOS Australia for best practices of heritage conservation. "Burra Charter", ICOMOS (Australia), accessed November 2023, https://australia.icomos.org/wp-content/uploads/The-Burra-Charter-2013-Adopted-31.10.2013.pdf; The Nizhny Tagil Charter for Industrial Heritage is a document adopted by the industrial heritage expert consultant to ICOMOS, TICCIH (The International Committee for the Conservation of Industrial Heritage). "The Nizhny Tagil Charter", TICCIH (2003), accessed November 2023, https://ticcih.org/about/charter/.

[85] "Burra Charter", ICOMOS (Australia); "Nizhny Tagil Charter", TICCIH.

[86] Karl Marx, Friedrich Engels and Samuel Moore, *Manifesto of the Communist Party* (Foreign Languages Press Peking, 1972).

While the site has been well-overprinted by British, European and other immigrant cultures, there are also Aboriginal industrial narratives to consider. These traces hold wisdom and knowledge to respectfully manage the land with an alternative sensitivity, one which is well-integrated with the landscape itself. One might invoke a post-colonial perspective to resolve their individual and collective legacies but as the Aboriginal poet Bobbi Sykes writes: 'Post-colonial…? What! Did I miss something? Have they gone?'[87] The multiplicity of industrial histories and cultures give North Shore its intricacies and complexities to address its industrial legacies and vacancies.

Figure 8.10 Geelong Vintage Market, Mackey Street, 2023. No comprehensive plan has so far been proposed for the North Shore, except for the masterplan "Pivot City Innovation District", at the southern boundary of the North Shore area. This image depicts changes wrought at the former Pilkington Brothers Glass factory Glass House.

These industrial histories are key to rethinking, redefining and reusing the existing architecture and conditions and incorporating them as a revitalising strategy in "place-making". In doing so, the memory is preserved while making a practical business argument that responds to redevelopment opportunities and the demands of social facilities. Redevelopment will inevitably arrive on the North Shore. It should be welcomed if it brings a dignified history of the area with it. Let that history reconcile us to the past and maintain the beauty that is Geelong.

Acknowledgements

This chapter acknowledges the contributions from the VacantGeelong survey and unpublished papers by Diego Fullaondo and Robert Fuller. At the VacantGeelong team included the School of Architecture and Built Environment's Dr Mirjana Lozanovska, Dr David Beynon and Dr Diego Fullaondo and the School of Communication and Creative Arts' Dr Cameron Bishop and Dr Anne Scott Wilson. Projects are supported by Creative Victoria and the City of Greater Geelong. The vacancy survey (2015–17) included the works of staff from the School of Architecture and Built Environment: Diego Fullaondo (coordinator), and supervising staff Drs Mirjana Lozanovska, Robert Fuller, Cristina Garduño Freeman, Akari Nakai Kidd and Angela Kreutz; and Master of Architecture students: Colin Van den Brandt, Aditya Godbole, Hazirah Hanisah Harun, Jonathan Tan Ern Wei, Arshadl Ibad Mohd Faudzi and Angelina Chan Yee Ching. Their work has led to a substantial new understanding of Geelong's vacancy that underpins this chapter. The tables in Figures 8.6–8.8, which resulted from their creative outputs, were collated by Diego Fullaondo and Chayakan Siamphukdee. The work was presented in the *Iconic Industry* exhibition (National Wool Museum, Geelong, August–September 2017).

---

87 Bobby Sykes, quoted in Linda Tuhiwai Smith, *Decolonizing Methodologies: Research and Indigenous Peoples* (Zed Books, 1999).

CHAPTER 9

THE PLACE OF HERITAGE IN A REIMAGINED GEELONG

URSULA DE JONG AND CHAYAKAN SIAMPHUKDEE

Introduction

March–April 2020: sounds of explosives echo across the Barwon River valley, Geelong, western Victoria, Australia. The cluster of monumental silos at Fyansford fall. Crumbled in an instant. The demolition sends shock waves across the area and leaves clouds of dust hanging over the cliff where the former industrial complex once stood.

Operating since 1902, the former Fyansford cement factory served as an important lime quarry for Geelong.[1] It became a landmark in the landscape and operated until the late 1990s. After its closure, the factory was adapted as a local industrial museum, before falling into disrepair and disuse. In 2018 the silos were painted by the widely acclaimed Geelong-born mural artist RONE, and thus became a destination before their eventual demise (see Figure 9.1 in the colour plate section).[2] While hundreds of signatures petitioned against their demolition, the protest was rendered mute by an exclusionary decision-making process.[3] The demolition of this industrial landmark signifies a critical stage in the reimagining of heritage in the future city of Geelong. The structures were demolished in the name of progress, despite the integral agenda for heritage in Geelong's urban renewal strategies. The site where the Fyansford silos once stood was left empty before being developed for new housing. The silos could have formed the centrepiece of the new development, anchoring it to the historic past in the present and providing an authentic identity for the contemporary residential estate.

In the nineteenth century, Geelong, the second city of Victoria, came to the fore through its industries (see Chapter 8, "Mapping Industrial Vacancy"). Industry flourished throughout the nineteenth century and the first half of the twentieth century. The sudden collapse of its iconic wool industry left the multitude of substantial woolstores in the heart of the city vacant. In the twenty-first century, heavy industries from glass manufacturing, aluminium smelting and car production also closed.

The demise of its industries signalled the beginnings of the city of Geelong's identity struggle. Yet, as the city seeks to redefine itself, these buildings and structures present an opportunity for a rich dialogue between the past, present and future. Geelong has gone through multiple phases of transformation as an industrial city, now it is metamorphosing again as it confronts deindustrialisation.[4]

In these circumstances it is critical to review our understandings of heritage and assess the diverse approaches that the city has taken to the adaptive reuse of its industrial stock. With the end of heavy industry, the model of a proud industrial city was rethought, and the self-vision redirected towards a commercial hub and leisure destination encompassing a "smart and creative city" (see Chapter 4, "From Identity to Impact: The Evolution of Geelong's Design Innovation Ecosystem"). Deindustrialisation has provided the catalyst to work with existing buildings marked as redundant and identified as potential building resources. Adapting these industrial buildings has proven challenging for Geelong's municipal councillors and officers, for the community, and for building professionals, from architects to planners and heritage consultants, as they consider new uses for empty or decaying structures endowed with rich and complex histories.

In this chapter we review our understandings of heritage – tangible and intangible – and its place in Geelong through selected case studies of historically significant industrial buildings. We consider how these have been treated through three frameworks – "lost through demolition", "loss through façadism", and "living through respectful adaptive reuse" – and examine how their values have been impacted.

---

[1] David Rowe, "Theme 5: Building Greater Geelong's Industries and Workforce", in *About Corayo* (Geelong, Victoria: City of Greater Geelong, 2021), 536–38; for the history refer to "Cement works at Fyansford, Geelong", (July 20, 1912) in *The Bacchus Marsh Express* (Vic: 1866 - 1943), http://nla.gov.au/nla.news-article90575191.

[2] Tamara McDonald, "Geelong-born street artist Rone breathes life into Fyansford silos", *Geelong Advertiser*, December 8, 2017, https://www.geelongadvertiser.com.au/news/geelong/geelongborn-street-artist-rone-breathes-life-into-fyansford-silos/news-story/3941e67e31451c83f9a0bd501c8c6685; Rone (Tyrone Wright), *Geelong Cement Silos*, 2018, archival pigment print, Geelong Art Gallery, https://www.geelonggallery.org.au/rone/didactic/geelong-cement-silos .

[3] Tamara McDonald, "Community rallies to save Fyansford silos from demolition despite structural concerns", *Geelong Advertiser*, February 16, 2020, https://www.geelongadvertiser.com.au/news/geelong/community-rallies-to-save-fyansford-silos-from-demolition-despite-structural-concerns/news-story/82528186295c9faaf143e17604e08646.

[4] The authors wish to acknowledge the VacantGeelong project which since 2015 has raised awareness of industrial architecture and heritage in Geelong, (led by Professor Mirjana Lozanovska, https://architecturevacancylab.deakin.edu.au).

What is revealed is a complex relationship that Geelong city has with its heritage. In its self-reinvention or reimagination, Geelong has witnessed major losses as well as sensitive interventions. The selected examples demonstrate an inconsistent approach to Geelong's industrial heritage across time. Despite aspirations articulated and enshrined in policy from the 1970s through to the 2020s, no holistic approach to dealing with the city's heritage has been implemented. Understanding the various approaches taken in our case study projects is critical to teasing out the place of heritage in the city of Geelong, as it tackles architectural vacancy and comes to terms with the role of heritage and its legacy in its evolving identity.

Heritage is complex and deeply connected to history, identity and politics. The built environment can be encompassed by the term "cultural heritage", which implies a shared bond, as well as our belonging to a community. Historian Graeme Davison defined heritage as 'what we value in the past'.[5] The "what" includes the tangible and intangible. Architecture can have both tangible and intangible qualities; the physical materiality of the built envelope tells stories and holds memories, echoes of lived experience; expresses technology and craftsmanship; function and purpose. Geelong's historic industrial structures engender reflective histories and invite interpretation. Our case studies, whether through absence and/or presence, reveal traces of the past.

This chapter uses the Burra Charter, a national charter that establishes principles for the management and conservation of cultural sites in Australia, as a reference point for its critical analysis of the place of heritage in a reimagined Geelong.[6] Conservation and heritage professional, Richard Mackay reminds us that:

> The Burra Charter offers a framework for heritage management in which multiple—sometimes conflicting—heritage and other values can be understood and explicitly addressed. The charter's success stems from its flexibility in accommodating evolving notions of heritage, changing economic and political circumstances, and vastly different types of place. The Burra Charter has been amended in 1999 and 2013 in response to developing practice and awareness of intangible attributes and the legitimate expectations of associated communities.[7]

Background: The City By The Bay

Deindustrialisation in the mid-1970s triggered a major shift in Geelong's vision for itself and its accompanying policies. The city that had proudly advertised its strengths as a place for a productive work life within major industries in the state, particularly the wool and automobile sector, shifted its focus after the 1972 global oil crisis. The City of Greater Geelong Council and the Geelong Regional Commission conducted local surveys and undertook studies of international precedents for urban revitalisation models.[8] North American and European examples were successful in their festive towns, whereby former industrial buildings were converted into markets or "adaptively reused" into specialty shops or museums.[9] These models inspired the authorities to adopt the vision the "City By The Bay", which ambitiously rebranded the city from an industrial centre to a tourist paradise and leisure destination.[10]

The City By The Bay vision identified three aspects that define the city of Geelong. First, the Corio foreshore. The city (see Figure 9.2) is built on a north-facing slope, facing Corio Bay and the You Yangs, giving it spectacular scenic views.[11] Redeveloping the foreshore into a waterfront precinct would complement existing leisure facilities at Eastern Beach. Second, the former extensive industrial precinct that stretches along the foreshore at Western Beach Road provided a stock of buildings that could potentially be adaptively reused. These included multiple historically significant buildings, variously recognised by the National Trust of Australia (Victoria), state heritage legislation and local heritage overlays. Third, the city's commercial zone, which runs along Moorabool Street, the city's main street on the north–south axis, was still active. The redundant industrial zone to the north was deemed as a possible expansion of the commercial zone, which would regenerate the city's economy while strengthening the connection between the city centre and its picturesque foreshore.

---

[5] Graeme Davison, "Chapter 1: The Meaning of Heritage", in Graeme Davison and Chris McConville for the Monash Public History Group (eds), *A Heritage Handbook* (North Sydney: Allen & Unwin, 1991).

[6] The Burra Charter (2013) is available at https://australia.icomos.org/wp-content/uploads/The-Burra-Charter-2013-Adopted-31.10.2013.pdf.

[7] Richard Mackay, "Values-Based Management and the Burra Charter: 1979, 1999, 2013.", *The Getty Conservation Institute publications*, accessed June 6, 2023, https://www.getty.edu/publications/heritagemanagement/part-two/8/; Erica Avrami et al., *Values in Heritage Management: Emerging Approaches and Research Directions* (Los Angeles: The Getty Conservation Institute, 2019).

[8] Geelong Regional Commission, *The City By The Bay*, (Geelong, Victoria, 1981).

[9] Geelong Regional Commission, *The City By The Bay;* Geelong Regional Commission, *The City By The Bay – Link*, (Geelong, Victoria, 1988), 18; Robert Freestone, "An Historical Perspective" in Susan Thompson and Paul Maginn (eds), *Planning Australia: An Overview of Urban and Regional Planning* (Cambridge: Cambridge University Press, 2012), 73–97.

[10] San Francisco's Ghirardelli Square, Boston's Quincy Market, and London's Covent Garden Market inspired planning in Australia with urban regeneration programs through reclamation of industrial buildings. Geelong Regional Commission, *The City By The Bay*, 50.

[11] The You Yangs are a series of granite hills that rise to 319 m above the flat and low-lying Werribee Plain in southern Victoria, Australia, approximately 22 km north of Geelong. They comprise a body of granite, surrounded by basaltic lava flows, that was an island in the sea during the Miocene epoch.

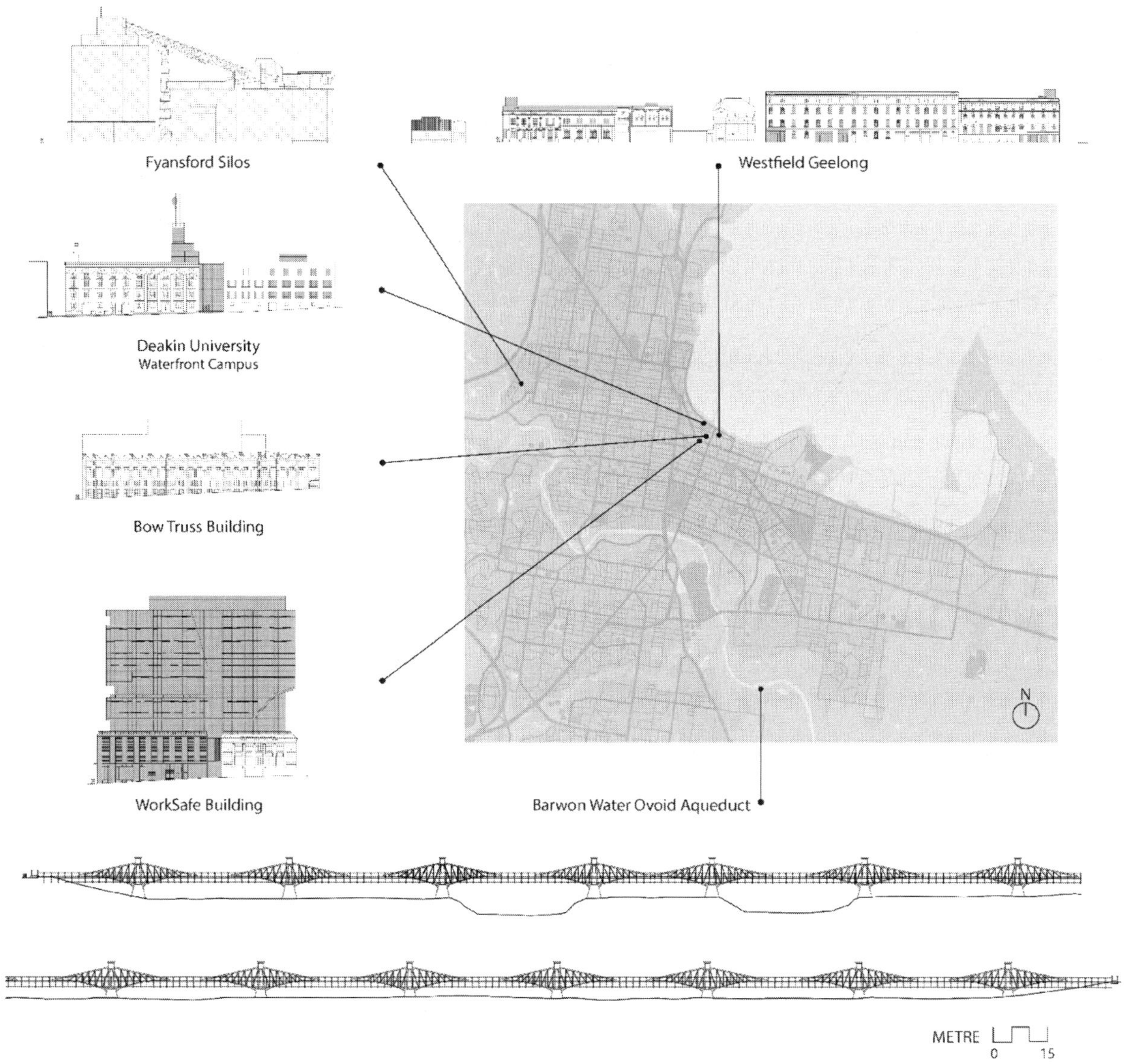

Figure 9.2 Location of the city and precinct for our chapter with all case studies drawn to the same scale (anticlockwise from top: Westfield Geelong, Fyansford silos, Deakin University Waterfront Campus, Bow Truss Building, WorkSafe building and Barwon Water Ovoid Aqueduct). Many buildings located near the foreshore; others located near the Barwon River. Source: Chayakan Siamphukdee and Ursula de Jong, 2023.

These three aspects underpinned the City By The Bay's vision to rebrand Geelong by utilising the existing building fabric:

> Geelong's empty, quiet woolstores could have new life breathed into them as a result of the redevelopment. A hundred years ago these vast buildings were the backbone of the region's economy and played a crucial role in the development of the rich Western District. The woolstores area has been recognised for some time as needing redevelopment, but successive schemes never got off the ground.[12]

Geelong would become 'An old town born again'.[13]

Lost through demolition: The Bow Truss Building (1990) and Fyansford silos (2020)

The demolition of the Bow Truss Building in 1990 demonstrated that the place of heritage in Geelong was far from protected, despite a commitment to utilise heritage structures in the rebranding of the city in a post-industrial transformation. The Bow Truss Building (see Figure 9.3) was considered the most unique structure stemming from Geelong's industrial past as the wool capital of Victoria. Architectural historian Miles Lewis described the building as

---

[12] Geelong Regional Commission, "Woolstores", *Geelong Advertiser*, special edition, printed November 6, 1981, 2.

[13] Garry Brennan, "Geelong – An Old Town Born Again", *Geelong Advertiser*, special edition, printed November 6, 1981, 3.

a most 'exotic' structure.[14] Constructed in a unique concrete method known as the Considère system, the building had a distinctive roof profile as suggested by its name.[15] Lewis writes:

> The top floor of the building, as usual in such structures, was the show floor where wool could be inspected by buyers, and it was designed to have as much natural light as possible. It was lit by a sawtooth facing southwards, the trussed window frames and the roof panels of which were most elegantly made in precast concrete. These precast sections were slung between a series of parallel trusses, also of reinforced concrete, with a clear span of about 54 metres.[16]

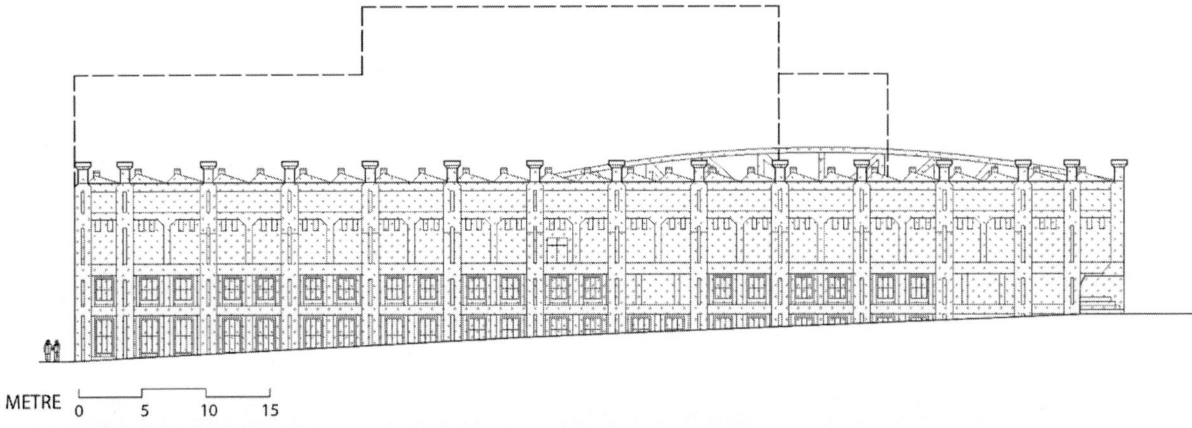

Figure 9.3 Bow Truss Building (demolished 1990). Source: Chayakan Siamphukdee, 2023.

This remarkable structure was by 'a very big margin the largest reinforced concrete roof span in the world'.[17] The unique construction also gave the building a distinctive profile, which could be seen from the west. The building was suggested for World Heritage listing multiple times by individuals, advocate groups and authorities. It was listed under the Victorian *Historic Buildings Act 1981* for state level protection, with further lobbying efforts by the National Trust of Australia for potential federal level protection. Its rare construction method made it one of only two such structures in Australia.[18] However, neither its distinctive nor rare character resolved the dispute as to the most appropriate approach to redeveloping the disused site. Vigorous campaigning was in the end unsuccessful, with the state government stepping in and overriding its heritage listing. The Bow Truss Building was demolished in 1990.

While the cause for preservation appeared watertight, discrepancies in engineering reports of structural investigations into the building's integrity, combined with the strong urge for new development, along with the influence of money and politics, overruled the architectural, industrial and historical significance values of this site.[19] The actual process of demolition of the Bow Truss Building took much more effort and much longer than expected, disproving earlier reports stating that the building was unstable and unsafe. The site then became an open-air car park before a modern multi-storey office building was constructed on the site in 2009. All that remains of this architectural landmark is a memorial installation piece erected along the building's lesser-known public thoroughfare. The loss is palpable. Lewis argues that the Bow Truss Building 'could have been enlisted as Australia's first UNESCO heritage place if not for its demolition'.[20] Little was learned from the demolition of the Bow Truss Building in 1990. The demolition of the Fyansford silos (see Figure 9.4) in 2020 makes manifest that heritage in Geelong is still at risk, and that heritage is seen as a liability rather than an opportunity when it comes to redevelopment.

---

[14] Miles Lewis, "Building Forms and Structures", in Miles Lewis (ed)*, Two Hundred Years of Concrete in Australia* (North Sydney: Concrete Institute of Australia, 1988), 18.

[15] The method was conceived by the French engineer Armand Considère. Miles Lewis, *Two Hundred Years of Concrete in Australia*, 18.

[16] Miles Lewis, *Two Hundred Years of Concrete in Australia*, 18.

[17] Miles Lewis, *Two Hundred Years of Concrete in Australia*, 18.

[18] Miles Lewis, *Two Hundred Years of Concrete in Australia*.

[19] Allan Willingham, "The Life and Death of the Bow Truss Woolstore: Catch 22 on Corio Bay", *Victorian Historical Journal*, 61, no. 2–3 (August 1990): 96–120; Leith Young, "From the Archives, 1990: Fury as historic Geelong woolstore demolished", originally printed in *The Age* on April 28, 1990, https://www.theage.com.au/national/victoria/from-the-archives-1990-fury-as-historic-geelong-woolstore-demolished-20210423-p57lsx.html.

[20] Miles Lewis, interview by Bronwyn Hanna in the Burra Charter oral history project, TROVE //nla.gov.au/nla.obj-219735175/listen/1-3760.

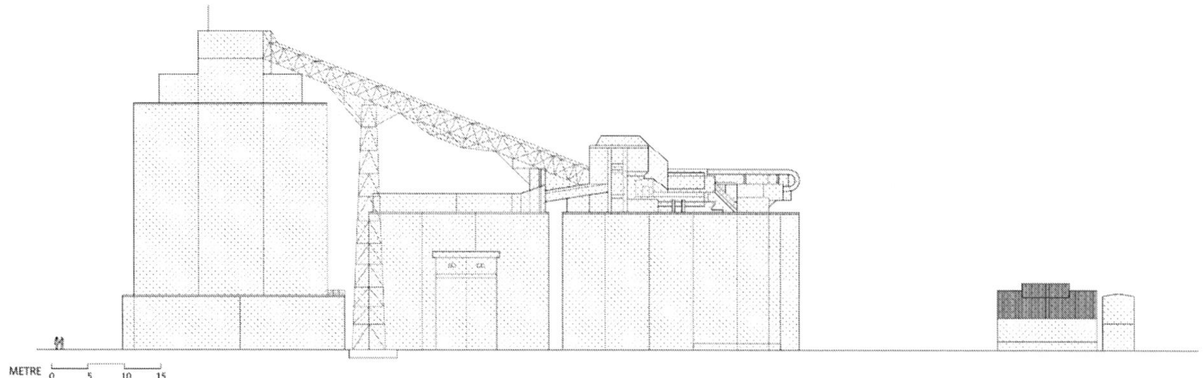

Figure 9.4 Fyansford silos (demolished 2020). Source: Chayakan Siamphukdee, 2023.

Loss through façadism: Westfield Geelong (1980) and WorkSafe building (2019)

Façadism – the practice of preserving only the façade of a building – has long been debated for its lack of sensitivity to cultural heritage and a building's strength, utility and beauty.[21] In Westfield's case it was argued that façadism was the only practical and time-efficient solution to keep parts of the existing built envelope. Preserving the buildings' skins has ensured that Geelong has been able to maintain the partial presence of its oldest structures from its heyday as a wool capital at street level. However, façadism detrimentally affects the integrity of the buildings and their surroundings. The 1980 Westfield strategy was again employed at the WorkSafe building in 2019 without acknowledging the detrimental impacts of façadism. The erasure of interiors represents the loss of a building's integrity and its soul. This skin-deep representation of heritage values poses critical questions around how Geelong continues to engage with its significant architectural legacy.

Westfield Geelong, originally developed as Bay City Plaza, involved the redevelopment of not one but multiple industrial buildings. Myer successfully acquired multiple buildings in Geelong's oldest city block from the 1980s.[22] This allowed for the redevelopment of the block into a shopping centre, fulfilling a key strategy to revitalise Geelong's central business district (CBD).[23] It involved transforming a historic woolstore complex, a former office, tram depot, a power station and laneways, stretching across the entire city block on Brougham Street.[24] At the corner of Moorabool and Brougham Streets, the Stratton and Co. woolstore complex was the first masonry building along the Corio foreshore, signifying the beginnings of the wool industry in Geelong.[25] It was continuously extended until 1955. The scale of its quarter-block size highlights the intrinsic nature of the wool industry to Geelong's historical development. The Blakiston building served as an office and a stable for a local transporting company, operating from the late nineteenth century until the 1980s.[26] The tram depot, located behind an ornate building, operated from 1912–56.[27] The building at the south-west intersection of Brougham and Yarra Streets was Geelong Power Station A, run by the state until the mid-twentieth century when its generators became outdated.[28] The building was extended multiple times over its life, with the most distinctive feature being its landmark chimney, which stood until its demolition for the shopping complex redevelopment. These buildings played an important role in Geelong's history, marking different phases of the city's development.

---

[21] Johnathan Richards, *Façadism* (London, New York: Routledge, 1994); Robert Bargery, "The Ethics of Façadism", (Cathedral Communications, 2005), accessed July 4, 2022, https://www.buildingconservation.com/articles/facadism/facadism.htm; National Trust of Australia (Victoria), Facadism Discussion Paper 2023, (Victoria, 2023), https://www.nationaltrust.org.au/wp-content/uploads/2023/08/NTAV_2023-Facadism-Policy.pdf; Heritage Victoria Council, Adaptive Reuse of Industrial Heritage: Opportunities & Challenges, 2013, https://heritagecouncil.vic.gov.au/research-projects/industrial-heritage-case-studies/ , accessed 19 June 2023.

[22] Myer is an Australian mid-range to upscale department store chain, trading across Australia.

[23] Chayakan Siamphukdee and Ursula de Jong, "Adaptive Reuse: The Case of Geelong's Westfield, where Architectural, Urban and Heritage Practices Intersect", in Julia Gatley and Elizabeth Aitken Rose (eds), *Proceedings of the Society of Architectural Historians, Australia and New Zealand*: 39, *Ngā Pūtahitanga /Crossings* (Auckland: SAHANZ, 2023), 1–16.

[24] Siamphukdee and de Jong, "Adaptive Reuse: The Case of Geelong's Westfield"; David Rowe, "Theme Five: Building Greater Geelong's Industries & Workforce", in *About Corayo* (Geelong, Victoria: City of Greater Geelong, 2021), 550–51.

[25] Anne Cahir, "Former Strachan Murray & Shannon,", *The Bay, Barwon and Beyond: Heritage Places of Geelong* (Melbourne: Heritage Council Victoria, 1997), 56.

[26] David Rowe, "Theme Three: Transport and Communications", in *About Corayo*, (Geelong, Victoria: City of Greater Geelong, 2021), 238; N. Houghton, "From the Archives", *Investigator* 24, no. 4 (Geelong, Victoria: Geelong Historical Society December 1986): 145.

[27] Rowe, "Theme Five: Building Greater Geelong's Industries & Workforce", 238.

[28] National Trust of Australia (Victoria), *Former Melbourne Electric Light Company - Geelong Woolstores Historic Area*, on Victorian Heritage Database, available on https://vhd.heritagecouncil.vic.gov.au/places/68194; Rowe, "Theme Five: Building Greater Geelong's Industries & Workforce", 636.

Figure 9.5 Westfield Geelong – façadism with new additions and alterations in grey. Source: Chayakan Siamphukdee, 2023.

Shifting away from production and industrial use to commercial purposes, the buildings were remodelled for retail operations and to accommodate tourism and a visitor economy that resulted in a total reinvention of this historic urban block. Yet the vision was for this redevelopment to reclaim the old buildings while respecting their original character.[29] Public consultations were held in the 1970s to consider how the new structures would relate to the existing built environment, and the planning scheme established controls such as height limitations to respect the industrial buildings.[30] These measures allowed the retention of the picturesque qualities of Geelong's industrial streetscapes, but little was articulated for the interiors of these buildings. Thus, the façades along Brougham Street (and that of the Stratton and Co. woolstore complex along Moorabool Street) were largely preserved. However, the buildings were gutted – so nothing of the interiors remained (see Figure 9.5).

In its promotional leaflet outlining how the historic buildings had been designed to cater for commercial needs, Westfield boasted that it was Victoria's most modern shopping centre.[31] The design prioritised the practicality of the stores' needs over the architectural character of the industrial buildings: the interiors were modernised, featuring smooth and glamourous surfaces. Such wholesale demolition of the interiors neglected the architectural aesthetics of the industrial buildings and ignored their open plan nature, which could have readily accepted building conversion for new uses. As the interiors of the woolstore complex, stable and tram depot merged into one, their internal spaces and volumetric qualities were homogenised into a single uniform space. The presence of the past was rendered invisible.

The preserved façades too were mutilated: blocked windows are merely decorative; new openings to accommodate cars have been punched into walls, new brick tops and cornices have been added, signage has been ghosted. Behind the façades are vast car parks catering to thousands of shoppers, visitors and tourists. The Westfield redevelopment maintained its building–height ratio in the CBD streetscape; however, its presence demonstrates at most a superficial understanding of heritage. Adaptive reuse has been misunderstood and minimalised. With only the façades left to hint at the histories and narratives of place, the aspiration to breathe new life into the existing architecture falls short on two counts: the heritage values of the old have been lost and no fine contemporary architecture complements the existing structures (see Figure 9.6).

The WorkSafe building

The WorkSafe building (2019) mimics Westfield in its approach to façadism. Designed by architects Peckvonhartel, the project incorporates the historic Dalgety & Co. building.[32] The interior of the original shipping office was demolished and a tower of fourteen stories inserted into the old fabric. The base of the tower "wrapped" by the corner façades, provides some sense of familiarity at street level. But like Westfield, the façades are left as mere skins for the original three floors.

---

[29] Geelong Regional Commission, *The City By The Bay*, 2–3.

[30] Geelong Regional Commission, *Geelong Central Area Study - Preferred Strategy: Public Discussion Paper*, (Geelong, Victoria, 1979).

[31] Bayside City Plaza Report, 1979/80, available at Geelong Heritage Collections.

[32] Peckvonhartel, accessed June 23, 2023, https://www.pvh.com.au/.

Figure 9.6 Westfield Geelong, Geelong, Brougham Street: new insertions disrupting the original façade of the Blakiston building. 2023.

The building won numerous awards for its sustainability ratings.[33] These energy ratings in building design are claimed to be innovative responses to users' energy consumption, emphasising ways to reduce the carbon footprint. However, with a program of extensive demolition, embodied energy was not addressed.[34]

The architects claim to relate to the existing built fabric through preserving, celebrating and complementing it. The redevelopment of the building and tower as an office space recalls the building's previous life as an office building for the wool merchant and shipping agent Dalgety & Co. The façade treatment at WorkSafe appears to function sympathetically with existing architectural elements, such as the fenestration. However, the overall approach is not integrated. Preserving some of the original interiors would have enabled workers and visitors to experience the character and qualities of the old architecture, even within altered conditions to meet the current needs and legal requirements. With the historic building reduced to a façade, any opportunity to generate creative dialogues between the existing and the new vanished. The architects' considerations of the heritage values of the historic building and its site are highly questionable.

While the WorkSafe building has taken a bold stance with a tower, a large-scale imposing glass structure towering over the existing form (see Figure 9.7), its design sources and materiality appear as imitations of the old. Classic rhythms are visible from both Malop Street (south) and Gheringhap Street (west). The extension facing Malop Street adopts repetitive horizontal slats of fake stonework; whereas the exterior of the building's car park (first three stories) on Gheringhap Street copies the façade's columnar rhythm, after creating a small gap to distinguish new from old. We argue that a far more carefully considered design approach was called for. These new structures contribute little to the architectural qualities of the old, to forging any innovative engagement with the preserved façade, or to contributing to contemporary design in the city.

---

[33] These included: a '6 Star Green Star rating for design and construction – the highest rating from the Green Building Council of Australia', 'the first multi-storey Victorian commercial office building outside the Melbourne CBD to achieve this rating' with 5.5 star NABERS Energy rating for the base building, 5.5 star NABERS Energy rating for the WorkSafe tenancy, and 4 star NABERS Water rating', and 'highest rating from the International WELL Building Institute'. Accessed June 4, 2023 https://www.nabers.gov.au/news/case-study-1-malop-street-geelong-vic#section-target-3.

[34] The architects proudly state that 'this landmark heritage building was developed into a world class building attracting WorkSafe as the anchor tenant.' "1 Malop Street", Peckvonhartel, accessed June 4, 2023, https://www.pvh.com.au/project/02-malop-street-geelong-2/.

Figure 9.7 WorkSafe building – old and new architecture, 2023. Note Gheringhap Street (west) elevation clearly visible; Malop Street (south) elevation is behind the palm tree.

The scale and architectural style of the new tower severely impact the historic site as well as the streetscape and the city block. This development raises serious questions around appropriate approaches to adaptively reusing the city's architecture mindful of place. The fourteen-storey tower redefines Geelong's skyline by destroying a traditionally low-rise cityscape. With its height, the tower gives the occupants premium vistas over Corio Bay and to the You Yangs –

but in the process disconnects them from place. This isolated tower redefines Geelong's skyline through disruption. This new height sets a precedent for new constructions in the CBD introducing a sense of verticality into a city that has long been low and horizontal. The city could have made a decision to develop as a medium density city – honouring its heritage whilst accommodating future needs. It could have consciously decided to distinguish itself from Melbourne (and other Australian capital cities) and thus become a distinctive regional city.

Living through respectful adaptive reuse: Deakin University Waterfront Campus (1990s) and the Barwon River Ovoid Sewer Aqueduct (2023)

The previous two sections document the loss of Geelong's significant heritage buildings through demolition and façadism, leaving only traces of the city's heritage. Case studies of Deakin University's Waterfront Campus (1990s), and the Barwon River Ovoid Sewer Aqueduct (2023) provide the opportunity to analyse adaptive reuse approaches to heritage buildings and structures at different levels of heritage classification and in different settings.

Deakin University's Waterfront Campus

Previously known as the Woolstore Campus, Deakin University's Waterfront Campus (see Figure 9.8) showcases a sensitive adaptation and interpretation of the city's heritage. The project was conceived in the 1990s after a design competition won by the architectural firm McGlashan Everist, who proposed the adaptive reuse of a vast area of the neglected brick woolstores. The scheme integrated various uses into the complex, including university administration and chancellery, the School of Architecture and Building, information technology services, the student union, a cafeteria, a library, as well as a Great Hall for the conferring of degrees, capable of seating 1500 people and acoustically tuned for symphony orchestras.[35]

Figure 9.8 Deakin University Waterfront Campus (Woolstore Campus) – detail of conserved and adaptively reused Woolstore, exterior view, 2023.

---

[35] Architecture Australia, "President's Award for Recycled Buildings", in *Architecture Australia*, November 1997, https://architectureau.com/articles/presidents-award-for-recycled-buildings-1/.

The project won the prestigious Australian Institute of Architect's (AIA) President's Award for Recycled Buildings. The jury comments are highlighted here to provide the professions assessment of this successful adaptive reuse project. The design of the Waterfront Campus realised the latent potential of the existing architecture through a creative approach addressing competing challenges, the 'sensitive scheme [thus] retains the quality of the woolstores as well as instilling the building with a new rigor and purpose'.[36] Preserved columns, beams and floors acknowledge the past use as a woolstore, and lift shafts and their workings are retained as subtle reminders of the industrial heritage of this campus. Recycled timbers were repurposed and finely crafted for seats, staircases and library fittings. The openness of the complex of well-considered buildings accommodates the new functions and demands of an educational institution, 'with superb space and light quality throughout'. The jury further considered that 'the connection between the city, the university and the sea is beautifully expressed through the devices of the courtyard entry, the internal street and … framed views of the pier and water'.[37] Here, respect for heritage and the original use coincided with a commitment by McGlashan Everist to meet the contemporary needs of a university.

From the exterior, the transformation of the woolstores appears minimal with new window frames and additional openings where required, but the integrity of the whole is respected. In contrast the interior underwent significant alterations. For example, the creation of an internal University Court involved removing a substantial part of the three-storey warehouse. The project facilitated 'both the open expressions of the structural systems of the woolstores complex and the penetration of light to otherwise dark and claustrophobic spaces'.[38] Architecturally, McGlashan Everist undertook to mediate heritage and contemporary architectural expression. They were facilitated in this aim because these woolstores were not on the Victorian Heritage Register – instead they had only to comply with local heritage overlays, which provided greater freedom for design expression. Thus, despite its subtractive nature, the courtyard reconfigures the woolstores' essential scale, mass and form while not destroying the overall integrity. The strategic removal of elements allowed the design to expose construction details, which would have otherwise been omitted by the building's repetitive functional expression. In working within a heritage precinct for Deakin's Waterfront Campus, the architects clearly understood that the process was 'one of adaptation, not preservation'.[39] Their work creatively tackled strict conservation controls that are often associated with heritage legislation. For them, "success" in this project:

> depend[ed] partly upon the architectural image which must transform warehouse to university, whilst respecting the expectations of conservation. Clearly these two intentions will not always coincide, but we should seek to resolve conflicts without compromising university values and requirements.[40]

Combining experience with educational master planning, a creative approach to heritage, and crafting well considered buildings that address competing challenges of aesthetics, problem solving, planning and cost effectiveness resulted in an exemplary industrial adaptive reuse project.

Barwon River Ovoid Sewer Aqueduct

The 756 m state heritage-listed aqueduct, which crosses the Barwon River flood plain in fourteen spans (see Figure 9.10), presents very different challenges to those of Geelong's woolstores. It was constructed in 1912–15 to the design of Sydney engineer Edward Giles Stone using the Considère reinforcing system (also used in the Bow Truss Building). Built for the Geelong Waterworks and Sewerage Trust to support the effective and hygienic functioning of the burgeoning industrial city, the aqueduct was part of the system delivering wastewater to an ocean outfall on Bass Strait at Black Rock, east of Breamlea (see Figure 9.9).

Requiring increasingly untenable repairs and presenting operational risks, the aqueduct was decommissioned in 1992. The ongoing prospect of falling concrete eventually forced closure of the river in the area in 1995. It was fenced off and left to deteriorate for decades.

When in 2020 it was controversially proposed to demolish the four spans directly over the river, the community vigorously protested.[41] Later that year Heritage Victoria made the decision to grant a permit to demolish these four spans of the aqueduct, and the heritage conservation architecture practice, Lovell Chen, reported that 'the long-running

---

[36] Architecture Australia, "Presidents Award for Recycled Buildings".

[37] Architecture Australia, "Presidents Award for Recycled Buildings".

[38] Allan Willingham, *Deakin University Woolstores Conservation Plan*, May 1994, 20.

[39] Allan Willingham, *Deakin University Woolstores Conservation Plan*, 14.

[40] Allan Willingham, *Deakin University Woolstores Conservation Plan*, 14.

[41] In 2020 Rod Charles, on behalf of the Friends of Barwon River Ovoid Sewer Aqueduct submitted to Heritage Victoria (the protector of places on Victoria's Heritage Register) that 'this highly significant engineering masterpiece is so important to what remains of Australia's engineering heritage architecture that every endeavour must be explored to retain the entire structure for our nation's collective benefit to admire and enjoy this magnificent visually stunning place'. "Friends Solution", Friends of Barwon River Ovoid Sewer Aqueduct, 19 June 2020, accessed June 2023, https://friendsofbarwonriverovoidseweraqueduct.files.wordpress.com/2020/06/submission-by-friends-of-barwon-river-ovoid-sewer-aqueduct.pdf.

challenge to determine the future of the Barwon River Sewer Aqueduct, and restore public access to the Barwon River, has been resolved'.[42]

Figure 9.9 Photo of Barwon River Ovoid Sewer Aqueduct in the landscape, 2008.

In January 2022, it was announced that traditional owners, the Wadawurrung Traditional Owners Aboriginal Corporation and Barwon Water would collaborate on the Porronggitj Karrong project, to deliver a new community, cultural and recreational precinct that acknowledged Aboriginal culture and heritage as well the European heritage values of the aqueduct.[43] Lovell Chen noted that, in this case:

> Balancing the many overlapping cultural values, public interests, heritage and environmental considerations, and practical and economic realities, has been the challenge. Nevertheless, the quarter-century closure of the river needed resolution: there was growing interest in restoring access to recreational water users and traditional owners.[44]

As major infrastructure that supported Geelong city's development and future growth, the problem of the Barwon River Ovoid Sewer Aqueduct significantly broadened considerations around the adaptive reuse of historic structures. Here, in dealing with a landscape rather than a city block, particular critical questions arose around "whose heritage?". There is much to learn in this space from Aboriginal professionals, in relation to how cultural heritage plays a foundational role in people's lives, including health, design, place-making, tourism and the natural environment.[45] Here there is a real opportunity to acknowledge, respect and address Traditional Owner culture and living heritage, as well as European engineering heritage and the industrial development of Geelong. Memory and history, contested values, and conservation versus cultural heritage come to the fore. Heritage practices were challenged at multiple levels and policy

---

[42] Lovell Chen, "News: Resolution for Barwon River Aqueduct", March 2021, accessed June 4, 2023, www.lovellchen.com.au/lc/news-resolution-for-barwon-river-aqueduct/.

[43] "Kim-barne wadawurrung Tabayl (Welcome to Wadawurrung Country)", Wadawurrung Traditional Owners Aboriginal Corporation, accessed October 23, 2023, https://www.wadawurrung.org.au/; "Traditional owners and Barwon Water collaborate on Porronggitj Karrong Project", VicWater, 2022, https://vicwater.org.au/2022/01/25/traditional-owners-and-barwon-water-collaborate-on-porronggitj-karrong-project/.

[44] Lovell Chen, "News: Resolution for Barwon River Aqueduct".

[45] Anika Valenti et al., *State of Victoria's Aboriginal Cultural Heritage Report 2016-2021* (Melbourne: Victorian Aboriginal Heritage Council, 2021).

implementation called into question. State and regional decision makers found themselves in conflict with the many local communities. State heritage legislation took priority because of the Victorian Heritage Register listing of the aqueduct, which meant that Heritage Victoria was charged with the final decision, after taking into account Geelong city's views and policies, and any submissions by local and Victorian communities potentially affected by this decision. No matter what the decision, it could not please everyone. Yet Lovell Chen reported the final decisions with some level of optimism:

> The remaining structure will be stabilised, and the present safety fence removed and replaced at a greater distance. A heritage interpretation plan will be developed, engaging the community, Wadawurrung Traditional Owners and other stakeholders. Removal of the river spans will allow the Barwon to open once again.[46]

Figure 9.10 Barwon River Ovoid Sewer Aqueduct over the Barwon River, aerial view, circa 1930–1940.

Here loss through demolition, adaptive reuse and reclamation acknowledge the inevitable changes and creative vision demanded by a city's growth over time. Barwon Water, in partnering with Wadawurrung Traditional Owners Aboriginal Corporation on the Porronggitj Karrong project have pledged to improve the safety of the heritage-listed Ovoid Sewer Aqueduct and provide the people of Geelong and surrounds with access to the Barwon River and sixty-six hectares of surrounding land (see Figure 9.10).[47] From mid-2022 to 2023, Barwon Water collected community stories and memories about the aqueduct and surrounding area. Works will begin on site sometime in 2024 to stabilise the aqueduct, install a permanent propping structure, and to remove the four aqueduct spans (as the land is a floodplain the time needed to do the works will partly depend on rainfall and the bogginess of the ground). There is a commitment to engage with the community on the draft Healthy Country Plan, and on the themes for the Heritage Interpretation Plan for the aqueduct. Once the site is made safe, Barwon Water plan to progressively open it to the community sometime in 2025, subject to works being completed. Opening of the Barwon River at the aqueduct will take place following the completion of works on the aqueduct, and once the gazetted exclusion zone has been removed by the Corangamite Catchment Management Authority (CCMA).[48] Here we are confronted by the role of decay and decomposition as an integral part of conservation and preservation.[49] The Barwon River Ovoid Sewer Aqueduct illustrates cultural geographer Caitlin DeSilvey's argument: How can we live with and through entropy that presents an entirely new relationship with our notions of heritage?[50] The heritage approach to the Barwon River Ovoid Sewer Aqueduct of demolition plus managed decay ensures that this engineering masterpiece will all but disappear over time, leaving just traces in the landscape.

---

[46] Refer to submission-by-friends-of-barwon-river-ovoid-sewer-aqueduct.pdf 19 June 2020; Lovell Chen, "News: Resolution for Barwon River Aqueduct".

[47] https://vicwater.org.au/2022/01/25/traditional-owners-and-barwon-water-collaborate-on-porronggitj-karrong-project/.

[48] "Porronggitj Karrong and Aqueduct", Barwon Water, accessed October 23, 2023, https://www.yoursay.barwonwater.vic.gov.au/aqueduct.

[49] Caitlin DeSilvey, *Curated Decay: Heritage Beyond Saving* (Minneapolis: University of Minnesota Press, 2017).

[50] Ross J. Wilson, "Book Review of DeSilvey, *Curated Decay*", *International Journal of Heritage Studies* 24, no. 6 (2018): 687–90.

Heritage in a post-industrial city

Our case studies demonstrate very different approaches to Geelong's industrial heritage, from demolition to façadism to sensitive adaptive reuse to managed decay. This has led to unplanned incremental change over fifty years. Traces of the past remain in memories, stories, fabric, interpretations, and lived experience, inscribed in place.

The City By The Bay vision ambitiously redirected Geelong from its industrial past towards the concept of "festival city", to embrace commerce and tourism. In so doing, Geelong would be comparable with other worldly cities that utilised their existing assets – natural and built – to create a post-industrial economy. The place of heritage is integral to such a reimagination, being much more than a backdrop to (re)development. Geelong's industrial landscape stretching along Corio Bay is recognised as a unique setting with picturesque qualities. It has long accommodated the city's needs and growth and has the ability to adapt to a post-industrial economy. While the The City By The Bay vision began articulating the value, role and place of this industrial legacy in the city's new economy, the city of Geelong itself has struggled to come to terms with its complex heritage and the role of heritage in the city's future identity.

The 1970s vision anticipated the inevitability of change and considered measures to ensure that each transformation acknowledged existing structures – but not in very useful or appropriate ways. Strategies included height controls and the protection of architectural elements such as the façades. Over the following decades, tighter heritage and planning controls were enacted such that by end of the century, the heritage overlay, HO1638: Woolstores Industrial Heritage Area (2000) introduced specific requirements. It stipulated tighter parameters, such that development was to maintain views to and from the Woolstores Industrial Heritage Area; to retain the streetscape qualities of the area that is dominated by three-storey and four-storey Victorian warehouses with varying street setbacks and minimal separation between buildings; to retain the special character of the area's nineteenth-century and early twentieth-century commercial and industrial buildings; and to retain the cohesion and integrity of this architecturally significant area. The use of traditional construction materials and the contemporary interpretation of traditional building design within the area were encouraged.[51]

However, these "controls" have proven to be too weak – the terminology is open to interpretation, and "encouragement" invites noncompliance. The multiple demolitions and loss of unique architectural and urban fabric, exemplified by our case studies, also suggest that the heritage values of the city's industrial structures and precincts need to be understood more holistically. The demolition of the Bow Truss Building (1990) and the Fyansford silos (2020) and partial demolition of the Ovoid Sewer Aqueduct (2023), demonstrate not only a loss of the city's significant industrial heritage but highlight the tension that exists between the processes protecting Geelong's historic built legacy and those setting the rebranding agenda for Geelong. Instead of embracing the heritage overlay guidelines and consistently applying them to the conservation, redevelopment and refurbishment of the woolstores as they came up for development, the city vacillated and considered each project application separately, so that an inconsistent ad hoc approach become the norm. In 2019, voices from the Greater Geelong community highlighted the importance of caring for heritage. Key themes around identity, culture and place character emerged from a community consultation exercise on the future of Geelong: 'our heritage reminds us of who we are'; 'our history and heritage, our unique values and culture binds us'; for 'the region and City to develop' they wanted to hold onto 'Geelong's character, both physically and as a sense of place'.[52] A holistic approach to heritage and city planning is still needed.

Heritage: Challenges and opportunities for transforming Geelong

The city of Geelong has found that working with heritage structures in a future-focused program is both a challenging and critical task. The place of heritage in Geelong's future continues to be considered and discussed as the city pursues its experimentation to reframe itself as a post-industrial city. The selected case studies show that this appears to be on a project-by-project basis rather than encompassed by a city-wide aspiration and perspective, and that has led to inconsistent approaches.

The rezoning of multiple industrial buildings and sites for the complex known as Westfield Geelong demonstrates how places of heritage can become banal commercial places. The city planners, architects, designers and developers failed to understand the values and qualities of Geelong's industrial heritage. Here heritage was seen as an impediment to development rather than an opportunity for repurposing the redundant vacant buildings. The preferred modern shopping mall aesthetic blinded all to the potential of these buildings. The city's disregard for heritage opened the door to what Rem Koolhaas has called "Junkspace" aesthetics, bland banal modern spaces designated as 'equally smooth, all-inclusive, continuous, warped, busy, atrium-ridden…'.[53] "Meaningless spaces" replaced the individual historic

---

[51] Heritage Overlay 1638 was introduced in 2000. See David Rowe and Wendy Jacobs, *Former Dennys Lascelles Woolstore (20 Brougham Street, Geelong)* (Geelong: City of Greater Geelong, 2017), 2.

[52] City of Greater Geelong, *Our Heritage Our Collections: Strategic Report on the Use and Management of the City of Greater Geelong's Heritage Collection*, (Geelong, Victoria, 2020).

[53] Junkspace, coined by Dutch starchitect Koolhaas, in his manifesto *Junkspace*. Rem Koolhaas, "Junkspace", research article, *October,* 100 (Spring 2002): 182.

character-filled structures.[54] Koolhaas's Junkspace is essentially a critique of new architecture, but it is particularly relevant when assessing architectural design interventions, such as the remodelling and retrofitting of the heritage structures for Westfield.

Westfield and WorkSafe have reclaimed disused blocks in Geelong's CBD at the expense of heritage. The developments of a shopping centre, Westfield Geelong, and an office tower, the WorkSafe building, subjugated the past character of the heritage precincts they usurped, in contrast to the transformations of the Deakin University Waterfront Campus, which embraced the heritage of its woolstores in a different approach to adaptive reuse.

Current heritage practice in Australia, as outlined by the Burra Charter, identifies five attributes, 'aesthetic, historic, scientific, social or spiritual value' as key 'for past, present or future generations'.[55] These attributes recognise the multi-layered richness of heritage, as well as how cultural significance is integral and embedded in place itself. The notion of place includes a single structure or building, as well as a precinct or streetscape, as it can express through fabric 'all the physical material of the place including elements, fixtures, contents and objects'.[56] What this calls for then is a holistic consideration of the entire environment, both built and natural. It is necessary to be able to articulate and appreciate the complexity of our urban environment to enable opportunities for design interventions to work with place, with context, with heritage – to complement and/or to contrast.

The 2023 *Central Geelong Framework Plan: A plan for the heart of Djilang*, published by the State Government of Victoria's Department of Transport and Planning, clearly sets the agenda till 2050, with population and jobs growth accommodated in planned towers. The rationale for developing the city as a low-rise medium density city has not been contemplated.[57] The state framework for the city of Geelong has imagined it as another Melbourne-like metropolis, rather than a smaller city addressing its unique industrial heritage, embracing medium density and building with climate change.

The Burra Charter acknowledges that values can change over time along with use. It recognises that new information on the structure and its role in the community could affect the understanding of the larger place itself. The Burra Charter is therefore cautious in its approach to change, advising: 'Do as much as necessary to care for the place and to make it useable, but otherwise change it as little possible so that its cultural significance is retained'.[58] This recommendation may appear restrictive, but it demands a thorough investigation of the place before any modification is embarked upon to avoid the loss of cultural significance.

The Burra Charter recommendations were implemented in the reuse of Deakin Waterfront Campus that incorporated new functions into the existing structures. In this case conservation and adaptive reuse approaches were instigated to extend the lives of the buildings while keeping and highlighting material traces of the past, embedding triggers for memories and stories. Here the existing conditions were considered as strengths. High quality and appropriate new design was introduced into the historic woolstores by McGlashan Everist in the 1990s; it continues to undergo modifications to accommodate changing education and public needs.

Reducing a significant building to a mere shell, points towards an attitude of indifference. Integrity or the building's "honesty" is more than a set of principles of design, it is the ability to convey the relationships between plan and section that lie behind the façade.[59] Demolition and façadism render a building obsolete from every possibility; they also make concepts such as *genius loci* and sense of place redundant. The Burra Charter recommends a more cautious approach to deliver an informed understanding of the integrity of these historic industrial structures and of the relationships with their urban settings.

Heritage as a dynamic living concept

The demise of its major industries and subsequent architectural vacancy has provided a new opportunity for Geelong city to rethink what it can be. Urban researchers John Rollo and Yolanda Esteban note that developments in Geelong have been driven by two key documents: *Geelong, City By the Bay* and *Greater Geelong: A Clever and Creative Future*.[60] These reports are consistent in their ambitions for the city, vis a vis their aspirations for the city's well-being, and the economic and social agendas.

---

[54] As Koolhaas states in his manifesto: 'History corrupts, absolute history corrupts absolutely. Color and matter are eliminated from these bloodless grafts: the bland has become the only meeting ground for the old and new… Can the bland be amplified? The featureless be exaggerated? Through height? Depth? Length? Variation? Repetition? Sometimes not overload but its opposite, an absolute absence of detail, generates Junkspace.' Koolhaas, *Junkspace*, 182.

[55] ICOMOS(Australia), *Burra Charter* (2013).

[56] ICOMOS(Australia), *Burra Charter*, 2.

[57] Department of Transport and Planning, *Central Geelong Framework Plan: A Plan for the Heart of Djilang*, (Victoria, 2023).

[58] ICOMOS(Australia), *Burra Charter*, 1.

[59] Sherban Cantacuzino, "Chapter 8. Assessing Quality: the Pertinent Criteria for Designing Buildings in Historic Settings", in John Warren, John Worthington, and Sue Taylor (eds), *Context: Building in a Historic Setting* (Oxford: Architectural Press, 1998), 83–94.

[60] John Rollo and Yolanda Esteban, "Chapter 11: The Promise of Vision-Making a City: A Perpetual Journey", in David S. Jones and Phillip B. Roös (eds), *Geelong's Changing Landscape: Ecology, Development and Conservation* (Collingwood: CSIRO Publishing, 2019), 298–302.

The 2023 *Central Geelong Framework Plan* lists its objective vis a vis Geelong as 'a connection to place'[61]; mentions the need 'to respect and protect building heritage'[62]; discusses heritage and urban fabric[63]; highlights opportunities and challenges[64], names Deakin's Waterfront Campus as an 'excellent example of adaptive reuse', touches on 'protecting heritage buildings and places'[65]; and addresses 'ESD'[66] and 'design excellence'[67]. Adaptive reuse is encouraged over demolition and rebuilding.[68] Design measures such as building heights, plot ratio and spacing between buildings are also considered, demonstrating the authority of the state government to control development. While these design considerations are helpful to maintain certain qualities of place, a holistic approach encompassing the entire city is required.

The intentions to adaptively reuse Geelong's woolstores for cultural and tourism purposes had the potential to ground the city in a meaningful evolution.[69] While heritage is implicit in the expressed visions, the critical frameworks and official guidelines have been found wanting.

Geelong's industrial built heritage is variously protected by state and local heritage overlays, and some buildings are considered to be of contributory value to precincts and/or streetscapes. Thus, the broad spectrum of high quality appropriate adaptive reuse strategies should be considered when envisioning the future city.[70] It is worth considering how heritage is an asset to a city; how heritage can offer contemporary practice an opportunity to critically reflect on the culture and identity of place.

Heritage can be progressive. While it is embedded in the architecture that may become temporarily vacant, it provides layers of collective memories, bonding the community together. This collectiveness shapes concepts of "place" and identity. Heritage is not simply about revering something old, reminiscing about the past, or nostalgia.[71] It can be an inspiration for architectural designs and new uses, consolidating the unique qualities of place, while also addressing multiple stories, including difficult ones.

The transformation of Geelong continues apace. More high-rises are planned for the CBD. Further woolstores are threatened with inappropriate development. It is time for a heritage reset. Lessons must be learned from our selected case studies of demolition, façadism and adaptive reuse, as the city's aspiration to reinvent itself continues. Addressing present needs while respecting the past is a delicate balance. Heritage must be understood as more than the history of a setting. It is dynamic, living. Heritage is an intrinsic part of the process of place-making itself. It requires a creative and consistent response. Addressing, respecting and honouring Geelong's heritage must be a conscious and progressive process as the city seeks to (re)define its identity on an evolving transformative journey.

---

[61] Department of Transport and Planning, *Central Geelong Framework Plan,* 7.

[62] Department of Transport and Planning, *Central Geelong Framework Plan,* 8, 37, 50, 62.

[63] Department of Transport and Planning, *Central Geelong Framework Plan*, 21.

[64] Department of Transport and Planning, *Central Geelong Framework Plan*, 25.

[65] Department of Transport and Planning, *Central Geelong Framework Plan*, 116.

[66] Department of Transport and Planning, *Central Geelong Framework Plan*, 126, 127.

[67] Department of Transport and Planning, *Central Geelong Framework Plan*, 27, 160, 161.

[68] Department of Transport and Planning, *Central Geelong Framework Plan*, 127.

[69] This can be found in the comprehensive report, *The City By The Bay*, in the attempt to address the potential of the city as a tourist-leisure centre. Geelong City Council, *The City By The Bay*.

[70] For instance, in 2021, Liverpool in the UK was stripped of its UNESCO heritage status by the United Nations' heritage committee because the 'outstanding universal value' of its historic waterfront had suffered irreversible loss due to years of new building, after years of warning against disruptive changes, including emerging high-rises. Josh Halliday, "UNESCO Strips Liverpool of its World Heritage Status", *The Guardian*, https://www.theguardian.com/uk-news/2021/jul/21/unesco-strips-liverpool-waterfront-world-heritage-status.

[71] Graeme Davison, "The Meaning of Heritage".

Deanne Gilson, *Karringalabil Bundjil Murrup*, Manna Gum Tree (The Creation Tree of Knowledge) 2020, ochre, acrylic on linen, Purchase 2021, Deakin University Art Collection, image © and courtesy of the artist.

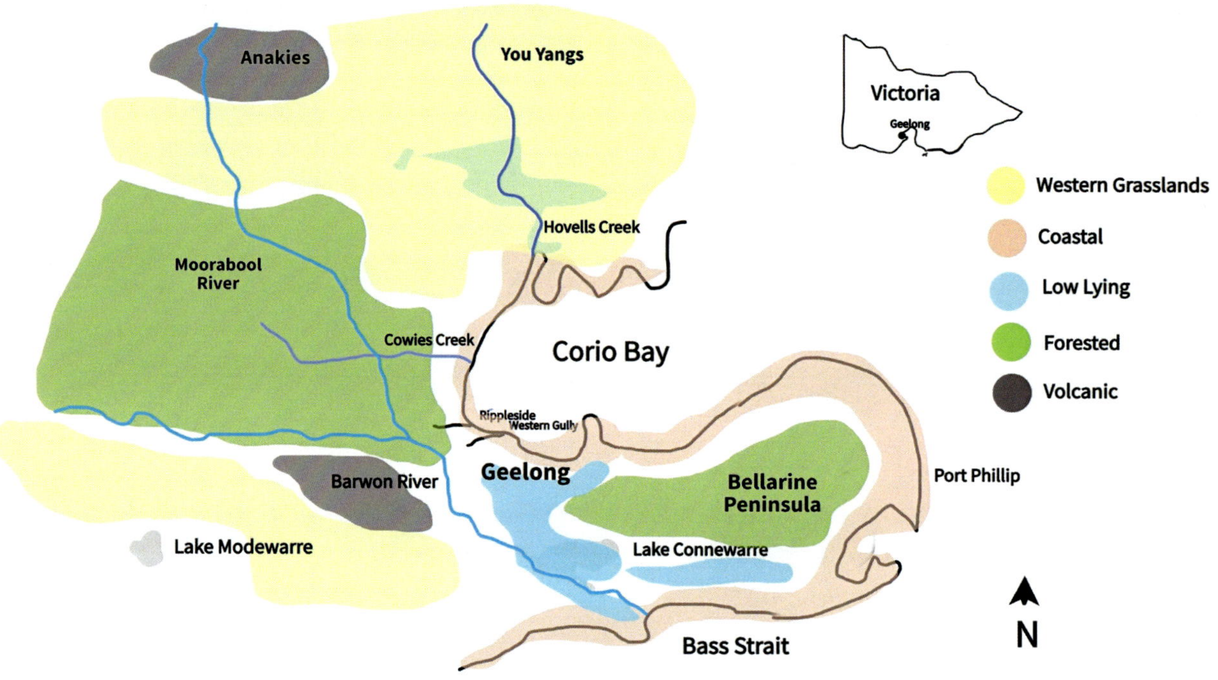

Figure 2.1 Djilang natural landscapes of the site location.

Figure 3.4 Robert Mihajlovski, *The Last Industrial Museum II*, 2017 (series, *So Long Geelong*). Mixed media on canvas 70 × 120 cm. VacantGeelong Open Studio, North Geelong. © and courtesy of the artist.

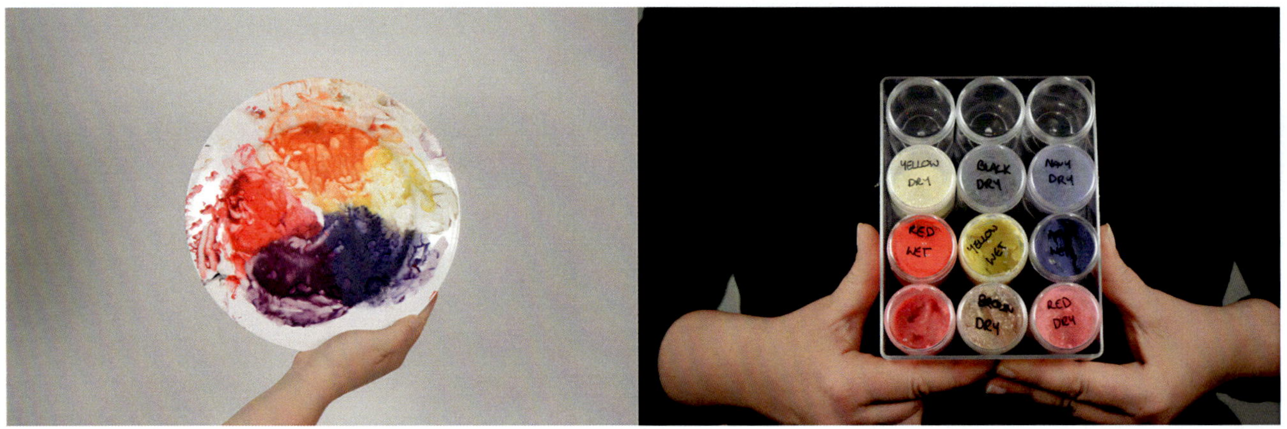

Figure 4.3 Paint pallet by Wadawurrung woman Nikki McKenzie. © 2023 April Brown. Reprinted with permission.

Figure 4.4 Fabric designs by Gamillaroi woman Elly Chatfield with Jacinta Kay. © 2023 April Brown. Reprinted with permission.

Bright & Hitchock's Building (1902 - 2023)

Rock O'Cashel / Derby's Arm / Albion Hotel (1875 - 2023)

Shops / Fire Insurance / Geelong Advertiser (1889 - 2023)

Exchange / Regent Theatre / McEwans - Dimmeys / vacant (1928 - 2023)

Prince of Wales Hotel / Geelong Advertiser building (1967 - 2023)

Richardson Exchange Building / Centrepoint Arcade (1901 - 2023)

Corio Hotel / Bridal House (1987 - 2023)

Union Bank / Shops & YMCA (1912 - 2023)

Figure 5.4 Street mode of the eight identified buildings with the pop-up dialogue box of archived images and chronological information in the Matterport VR platform. © 2023 Md Mizanur Rashid, Sanja Rodeš and Chin Koi Khoo.

Figure 6.3 The Independent Living Unit Project at Samaritan House in Geelong, 2023.

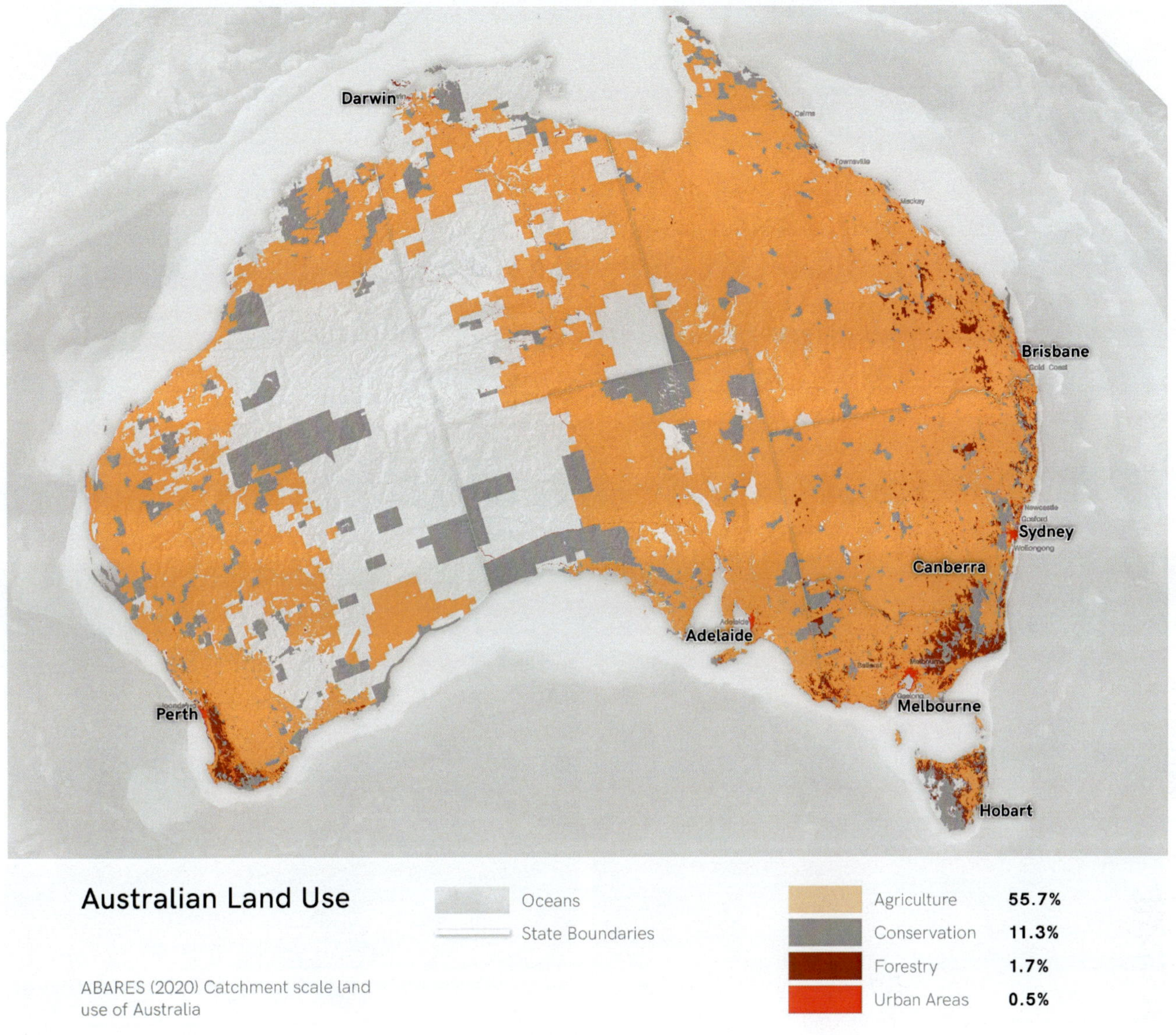

Figure 7.1 Impacts stemming from the sheer spatial extent of agricultural activity in Australia is unparalleled by other land uses.

Figure 7.7 Examples of peri-urban food production in proximity to Geelong and Melbourne, 2021–23. Top: harvesting salad leaves in a small portion of a larger Bacchus Marsh field. Centre left: plastic protection being laid across market garden fields in Cora Lynn. Centre right: growing cauliflowers in Werribee. Bottom left: irrigated pastures for cattle in Point Wilson. Bottom right: irrigated pastures for cattle in Eynesbury.

Figure 7.8 Application of fertiliser in Australian agri-landscapes, 2021–23. Top: sugar cane fields near Helens Hill, QLD. Centre left: a fertiliser heap for spreading in fodder fields near Hamley Bridge, SA. Centre right: an excavator amidst fertiliser in Kununurra, in WA's Ord River Irrigation Area. Bottom left: a tractor spreads fertiliser on a vineyard near Wilyabrup, WA. Bottom right: heaps of fertiliser are deposited in vast hay fields near Jeparit, Vic.

Figure 7.9 Examples of "improved pastures" for livestock feed crops, which are the primary receptacle of single superphosphate fertiliser, 2021–23. Top: beef cattle directly graze pasture at Werris Creek, NSW. Centre left: a centre-pivot irrigated field in Tintinara, SA. Centre right: a 430-m radius centre-pivot field in Kavina, Vic. Bottom left: cattle directly graze pasture as a tractor ploughs, near Pemberton in WA. Bottom right: sheep graze a centre-pivot irrigated pasture near Keppoch, SA.

Figure 7.10 Grain-producing and oilseed-producing landscape examples in Australia, 2021–23. Left to right: grain cropping and an eroded creek line near Jerramungup, WA; burning grain stubble in Lake Bolac, Vic.; land clearing for cropping, near Mount Hope, NSW; interchanging cotton and canola fields use extensive dams to hold irrigation waters diverted from the Murrumbidgee River near Hay, NSW; harvested crop fields are grazed by sheep in Cope Cope, Vic.

Figure 7.11 Food additives, raw materials, food processing and nutraceutical facilities in agriculture, 2021–23. Clockwise from top: a gypsum facility near Ceduna, SA; a saltworks in Port Hedland, WA; a beta-carotene facility in Yallabatharra, WA; microalgae facility near Ayr, QLD.; a food manufacturer in Shepparton, Vic.; processing tomatoes in Shepparton.

Figure 7.12 Examples of oil by-products acting as the lifeblood of Australian agriculture, 2021–23. Left to right: tractors receive brassica harvests in Werribee; harvesting grain by tractor in WA's remote Ord River Irrigation Area; growing fodder and fruits in remote central Australia in Ali Curung, NT involves long freight routes; a feed truck distributes grain at an NSW cattle feedlot near Eugowra; road trains are the central means of freight and agricultural movement in Australia.

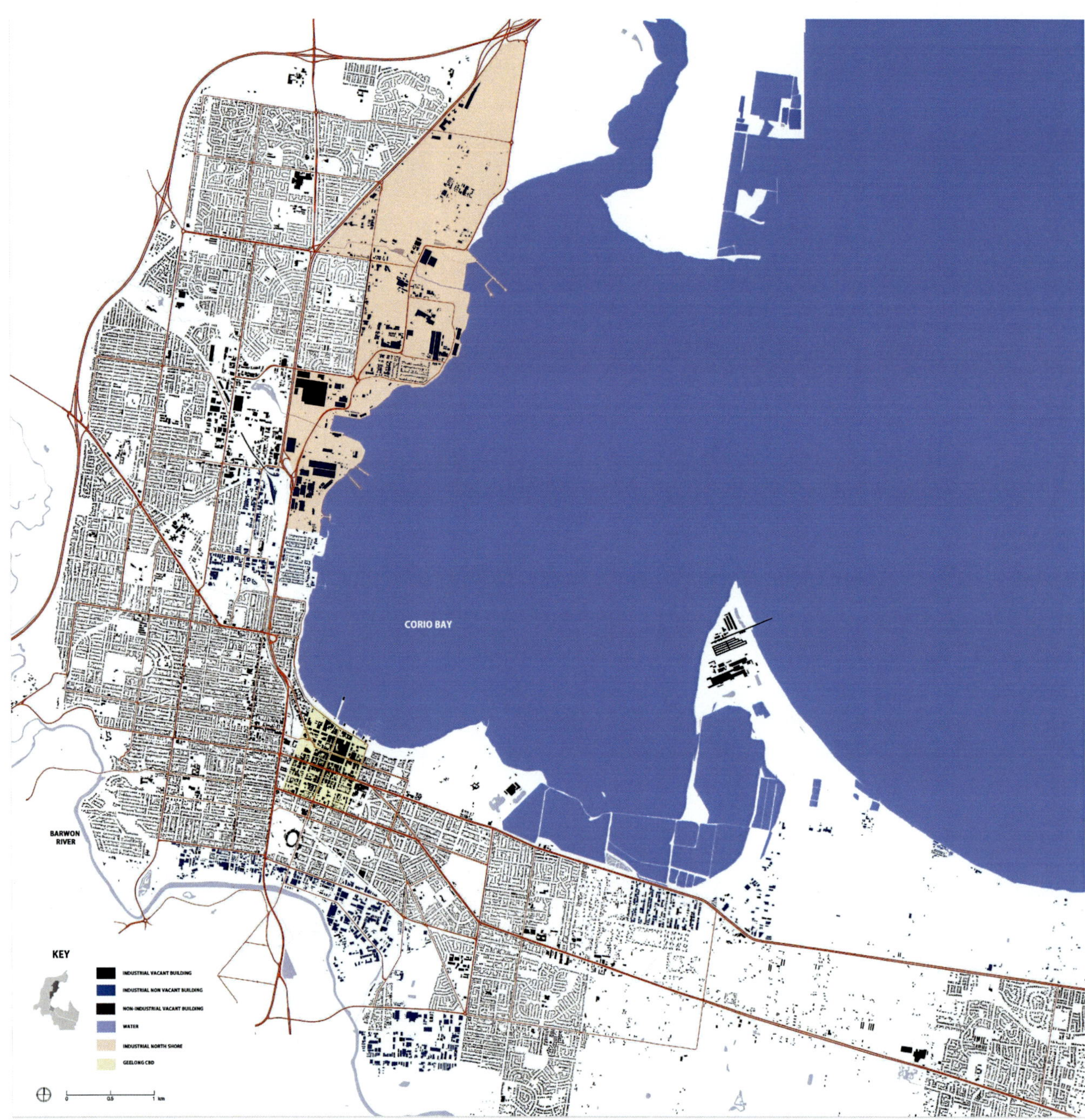

Figure 8.5 Map of industrial vacancy (2015–2017): Geelong (including CBD) and Geelong CBD. Vacant industrial buildings are shown in black; Industrial buildings are shown in blue; other buildings are shown in grey. North Shore highlighted in orange, and Geelong CBD in yellow. Source: Diego Fullaondo and Chayakan Siamphukdee, Industrial Vacancy in Geelong 2015–2017, 2017.

Figure 12.8 Base image: Wilbraham Liardet, *View of Geelong,* 1948, Geelong Gallery Collection. Montage by Julie Pham: progressive Photoshop build-up of *View of Geelong* 2019, 2050, 2100.

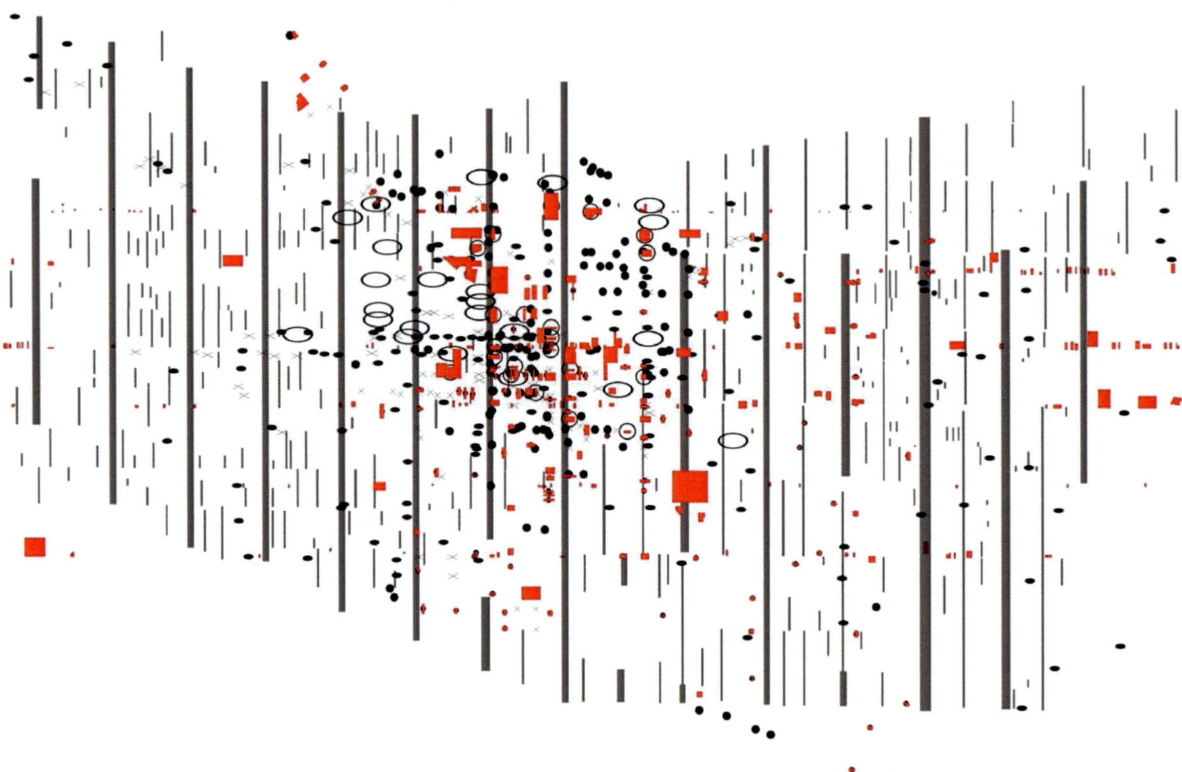

Figure 11.10 From layering to rhizome: data exploration of vertical street patterns, combined vacancies with overlapped spots marked. Layered drawing by Angelina Chan Yee Ching.

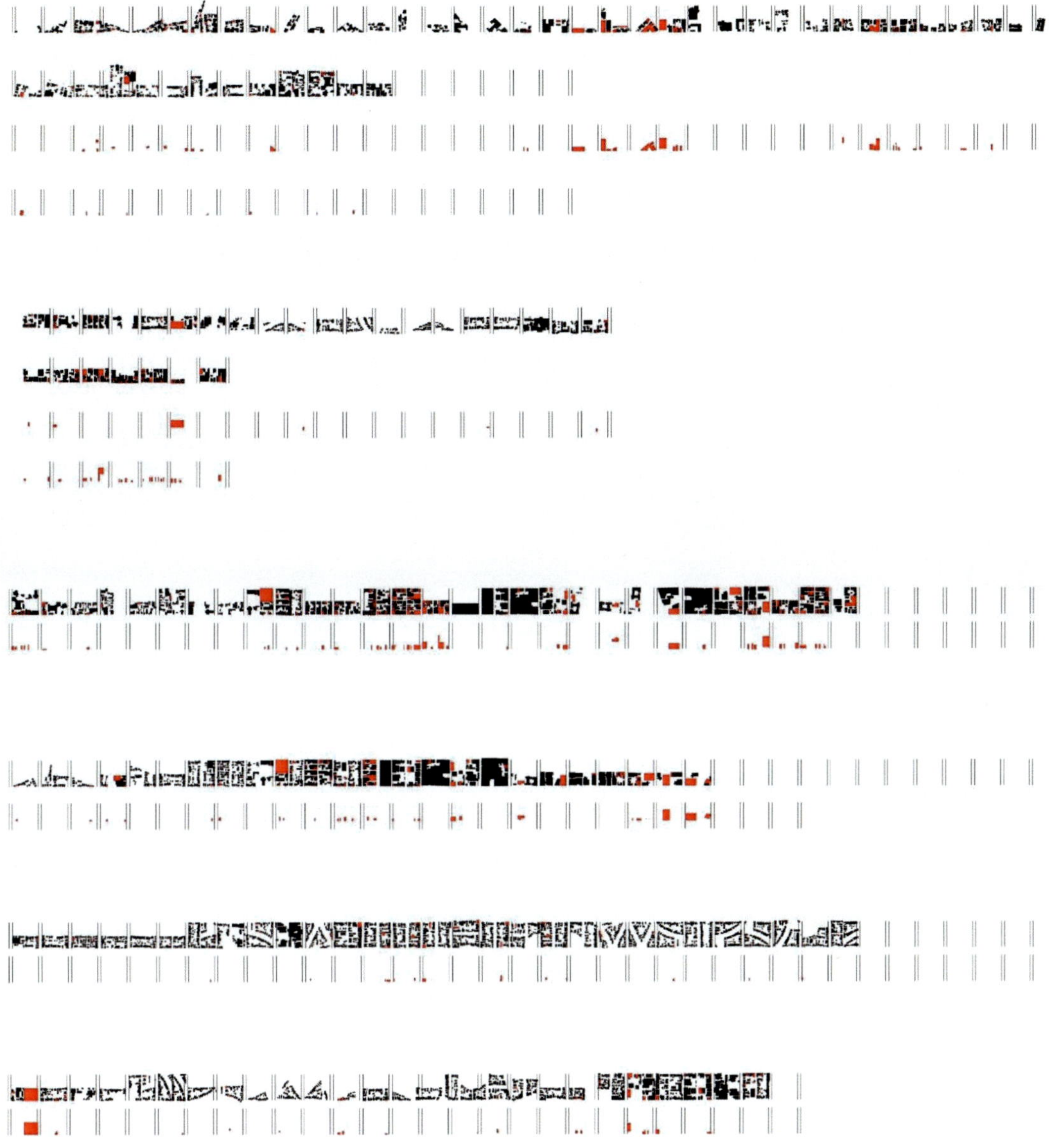

Figure 11.8 Drifting: unfolded drifting routes indicating spatio-temporal experience of vacant sites in Geelong CBD. Drawing composed by Angelina Chan Yee Ching.

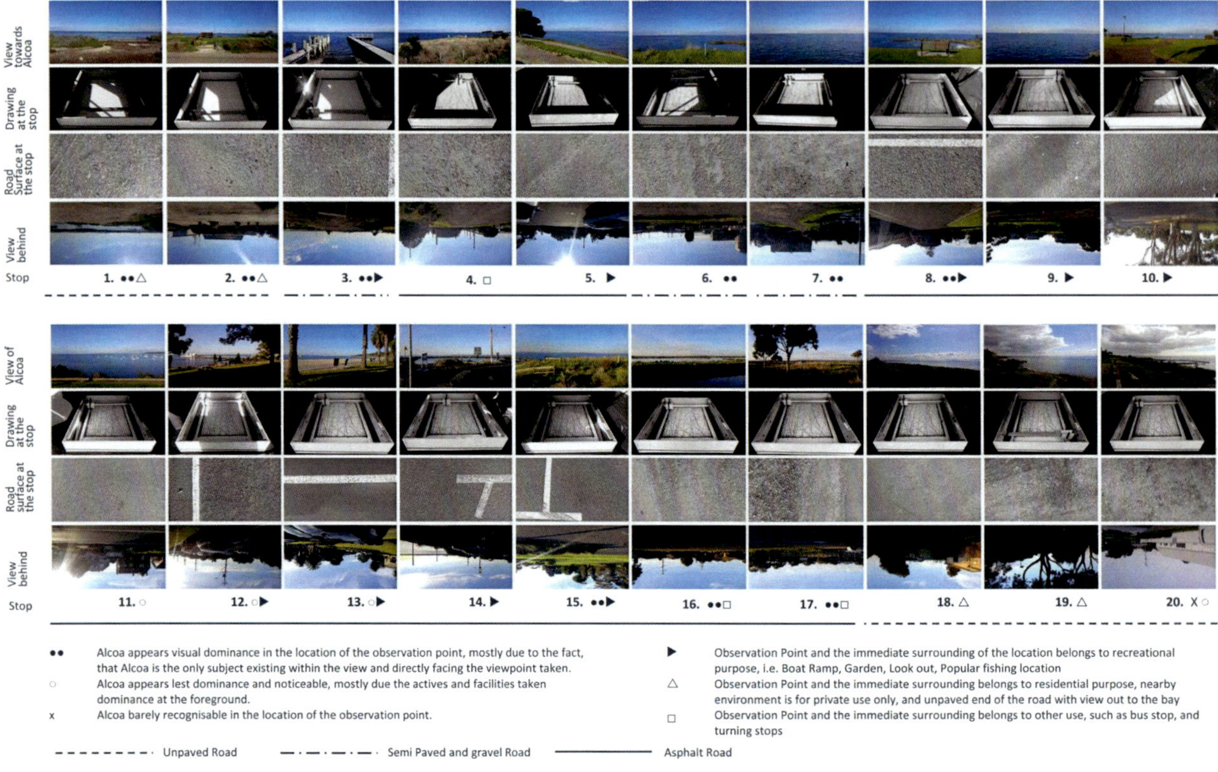

Figure 11.6 Collation table of photography taken in Journey 1 showing summative findings and images of the view towards Alcoa, the drawing machine, road surface and the view behind at each stopping. Composition by Evelyn Jing Pan.

Figure 10.4 William Duke, *Geelong from Mr Hiatt's Barrabool Hills,* 1851. Painting depicts a view of Corio Bay and the early settlement of Geelong and surrounds from the western hills. In the middle ground, the darker green vegetation lining the Western Gully can be deciphered. Victorian Collections.

Figure 9.1 Murals on Fyansford silos by RONE before their demolition in 2020. RONE, *Geelong Cement silos*, 2018–20. Archival pigment print. Geelong Gallery. Gift of Adelaide Brighton Limited. © 2020 RONE.

Figure 13.1 Robert Mihajlovski, *Factory I*, 2017 (series, *So Long Geelong*). Oil, mixed media on canvas 90 × 120 cm. VacantGeelong Open Studio, North Geelong. © and courtesy of the artist.

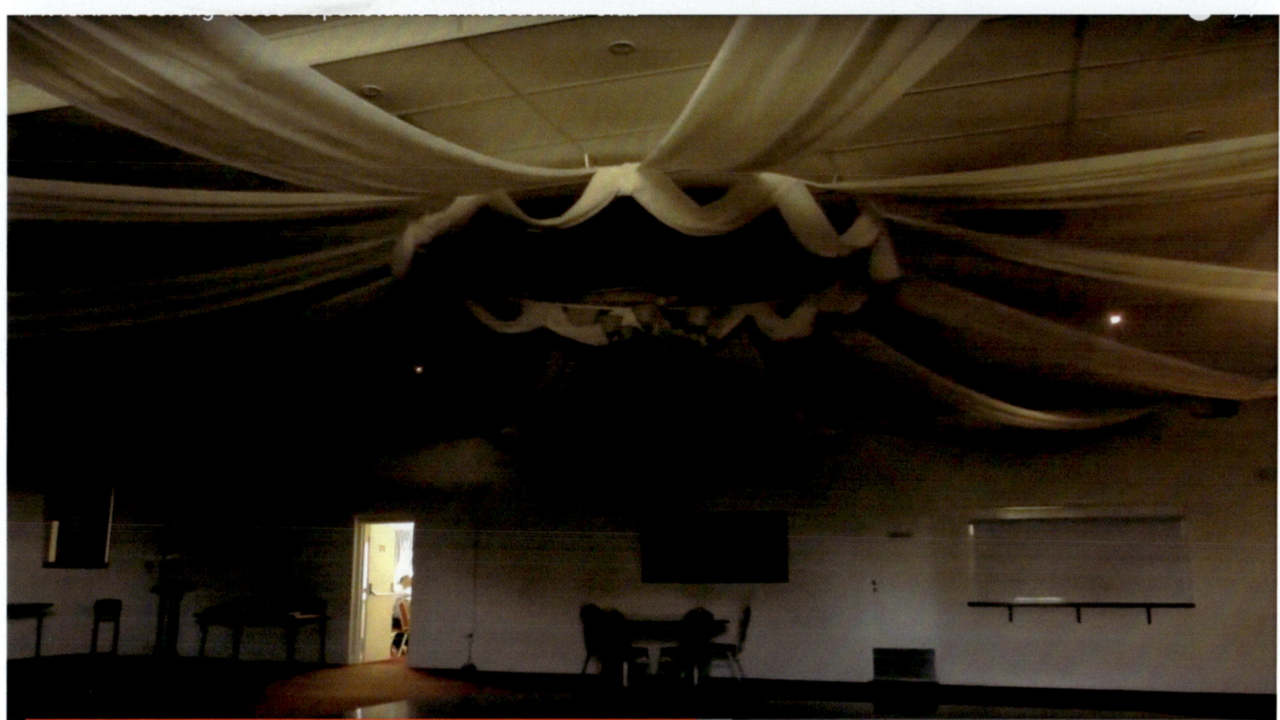

Figure 13.3 Top: Macedonian Orthodox Community Centre ballroom. Bottom: Installation view, Amanda Shone, 2017, VacantGeelong Open Studio, North Geelong.

Figure 13.6 Anne Wilson and Cameron Bishop, *X Marks the Spot*, 2019, performance and film. Anne with children's choir and drone at the VacantGeelong Open Studio in North Geelong. Production still from *X Marks the Spot*.

Figure 14.3 The inviting, permeable facade of Geelong Arts Centre.

CHAPTER 10

LOST LANDSCAPE FEATURES OF COUNTRY: THE WESTERN GULLY IN GEELONG

PAUL SANDERS, MIRJANA LOZANOVSKA AND YOLANDA ESTEBAN

Introduction

The topographical and landscape features that underlie the City of Greater Geelong, established as a town in the mid-nineteenth century based on a settlement grid between the shores of Corio Bay (within Port Phillip Bay) and the Barwon River, have undergone transformative changes, resulting in the loss of significant natural and environmental attributes. These lost landscape features hold importance in comprehending the region's past and recognition of a disconnection with its pre-colonial heritage.

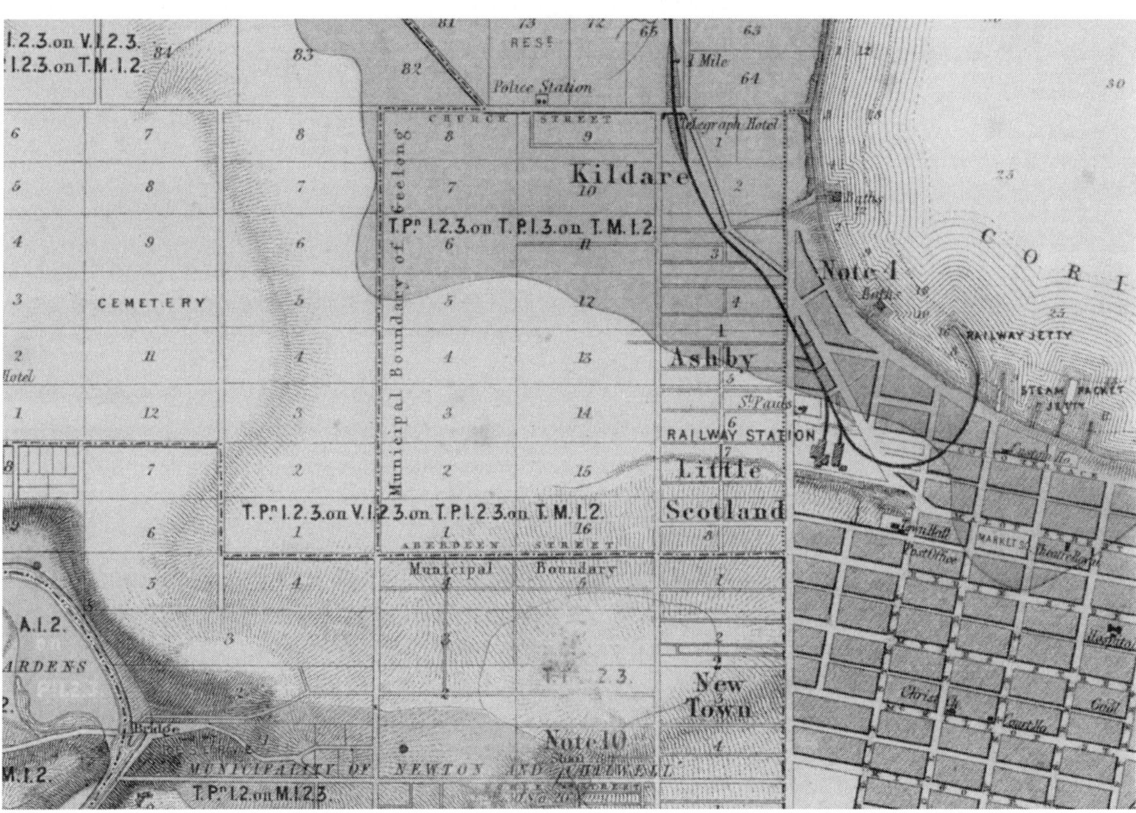

Figure 10.1 Richard Daintree, Geological Survey of Victoria, *Quarter sheet 24 SE. 1:31 680 geological map*, 1863. Map shows the line of the Western Gully draining the valley area extending from Plot 1 at the western end of Aberdeen Street through to Corio Bay.

We commence this discourse by acknowledging the Wadawurrung People, the Traditional Owners of the land upon which Geelong presently stands and pay our respects to their enduring custodianship of Country. Alison Page and Paul Memmott emphasise the importance of understanding that every place is unique and has its own specificity cannot be understated, each site within Country carries cultural significance, the characteristics of which may be coded within stories sung as part of the ceremonies.[1]

The term "Country" represents a profound understanding for Aboriginal and Torres Strait Islander peoples of Australia of the holistic and interconnected relationship between the land, waterways, plants, animals, ancestors, and the communities who continue to inhabit and care for the lands. Its distinction from the Western definition relating to a geographic location relates to the importance of Country as essential to comprehending the spiritual, cultural, and social

---

[1] Alison Page and Paul Memmott, *Design: Building on Country (First Knowledges)*, (Thames & Hudson, 2021), 36.

fabric of Aboriginal and Torres Strait Islander cultures and their enduring connection to the environment. In recent years, there has been an increasing recognition of the importance of Country within broader Australian built environment professions and government agencies. In this context, strategies to identify significant landscape features that were strategically destroyed by the practices of colonial settlement can contribute toward the broader reconciliation process, reconnecting through reparation or memory the connection Aboriginal peoples and Torres Strait Islander peoples have with their ancestral lands. The purpose of this chapter is to identify significant landscape features of Country that have been recorded in archival documents (i.e. maps, photographs, newspapers) that were created as part of a regime of colonising exercises but can be re-examined as evidence of specificities of past environments that preceded colonial settlement. By scrutinising historical records and archival materials, we focus on the case study of the Western Gully in Geelong as an example of a waterway within Wadawurrung Country, highlighting its cultural, ecological and historical value before it disappeared and was subsumed into the urban development of Geelong. According to the local historian Ebenezer Cuzuns[2], the shores of the creek and dam (currently a railway station site and St Pauls Church) were a camping place for around two hundred Aboriginal people:

> The Western Gully was a large natural creek, one of several providing a water source for Wadawurrung people. It drained the area west of the establishment of the town, cutting embankments through the landscape in the course of and flowing into Corio Bay.[3]

The authors recognise that oral histories are a fundamental aspect of indigenous knowledge systems. Ultimately, this chapter seeks to contribute to the ongoing dialogue concerning urban landscapes, and the significance of recognising the past as a complex dimension of contested heritage.[4] New decolonising maps present knowledge of Aboriginal language groups and clans and how these are inscribed onto the land. One example of this are maps of Geelong and its vicinity over which are inscribed the clan names and areas of inhabitation.[5] Wadawurrung Country extended over 7800 square kilometres within which the town of Geelong was established as part of colonial strategies. Clans that have inhabited Greater Geelong include Bengalat balug (Indented Head, including most of the Bellarine Peninsula known as "Beangala"); Watha wurrung balug (Barrabool Hills, known as "Barro-abil", meaning "place of rounded hills"); Neerer balug clan (between Geelong and the You Yangs, the territory known as "Youghon"); and the Yaawangi (You Yangs area).[6]

This research project and its findings are intended to provide evidence in support of the fundamental cultural understandings of place history, contributing to a research base that entwines with oral histories, and contributes to ongoing dialogue concerning urban landscapes, and the significance of recognising the past as a complex dimension of contested heritage. Page and Memmott emphasise that 'while modern design, architecture and landscape architecture can never replace the oral tradition, they can play a vital role in holding the memories of a site'.[7]

Urban morphological approach to contextualise maps and paintings

Urban morphology encompasses the study of a city's physical structure and form, spanning from its initial establishment to subsequent alterations and developments, and provides a rigorous basis in the process of compiling evidence of environmental change through archival maps, photographs and documents.[8] Such accumulated data can attract various points of scrutiny, including new questions that challenge the conventional Western historical narrative that colonial processes of settlement were silent in respect to human and environmental wrongdoing.

In this regard, critical theorist Michel de Certeau offers a critical assessment of maps as more than just objective representations of physical space without an inherent purpose or agenda.[9] They are not neutral in intent, on the contrary, crafted by those in power, maps transmit the control and order of a political ideology and agenda onto the occupants within an existing environment. Not only do maps exert considerable influence on future outcomes, they also exercise

---

[2] Ebenezer Cuzens, "Recollections of early Geelong 1949-56", *Investigator,* Geelong Historical Society, 1998, 142–53.

[3] "Johnstone Park, Wadawurrung country, 24–28 Gheringhap Street, Geelong", City of Greater Geelong, accessed August 2, 2023, https://www.geelongaustralia.com.au/parks/item/johnstone.aspx.

[4] Research and scholarship must confront methods for an open history of place. Publications increasingly include a first chapter on the Indigenous history, and often do not mention Indigeneity beyond, relegating it to a past. In contrast, for example, David Rowe's publication *About Corayo: A Thematic History of Greater Geelong*, 2021, includes a brief section at the start of each theme, each entry presenting a maximum of 10% of the text. David Jones and Phillip Roös editors of *Geelong's Changing Landscape: Ecology, Development and Conservation*, 2019, present one chapter that is written by Wadawurrung Uncle Bryon Powell and Tandop David Tournier and texts written in collaboration with them.

[5] Refer to map in David Rowe, *About Corayo: A Thematic History of Greater Geelong* (Geelong, Victoria: City of Greater Geelong, 2021), 66.

[6] These are the names given in Ian D. Clark, *Scars in the Landscape: A Register of Massacre Sites in Western Victoria 1803–1859*, Australian Institute of Aboriginal and Torres Strait Islander Studies Report Series (Canberra: Aboriginal Studies Press for the Australian Institute of Aboriginal and Torres Strait Islander Studies, 1995), 170–71, quoted in *About Corayo*, 67.

[7] Page and Memmott, *"Design: Building on Country"*, 146.

[8] Karl Kropf, "The Handling Characteristics of Urban Form", *Urban Design* 93 (Winter 2005): 18–19; Anne Vernez Moudon, "Urban Morphology as an Emerging Interdisciplinary Field", *Urban Morphology* 1 (1997): 3–10.

[9] Michel de Certeau, *The Practice of Everyday Life*, trans. Steven Rendall (Los Angeles, CA, USA: University of California Press, 1984).

power in what is omitted, or deliberately withheld. In this manner, what is visible and what is no longer visible provide a distorted understanding of the represented reality, and this serves to further exert control.

The process of colonial surveying of the land served to claim ownership over it. The act of mapping or planning was seen as an envisioning of a future that would be imposed upon the present land, thereby reshaping its physical and socio-cultural characteristics. Through the creation of maps, these speculations materialised and gained a heightened sense of reality, surpassing their original intentions. Consequently, the map anticipated and facilitated the forthcoming changes, alterations, and transformations in relation to then current reality.[10]

In the realm of maps and other artefacts like paintings and photographs, Aboriginal and Torres Strait Islander communities existed alongside the created spaces of early British colonisation of Australia in a manner characterised by de Certeau as "tactics".[11] These tactics involved Aboriginal and Torres Strait Islander people having to navigate and manoeuvre through the newly imposed spatial order of colonising practices and areas altered and controlled by colonial administration and colonial settlers, while also contending with the strategic regulations of laws, boundaries, and structures. The Aboriginal and Torres Strait Islander population's "tactical" coexistence within these systems of place was either absent from official maps or purposely excluded from the mapping process. De Certeau links tactics to the concept of space and contrasts this with strategy that is linked to the concept of place. Tactic and space emphasise the interconnectedness of spatial practices and the coexistences of differentiated spaces within a particular place. From this perspective, tactics can be perceived as being "out of place", underscoring de Certeau's argument that these spatial navigations occur within the framework of a place but operate in ways that deviate from its intended law and use.[12]

Alongside, de Certeau's theorisation about maps as instruments of power, it is important to outline an understanding of the role of visual artists, writers, botanists, anthropologists, and other humanities and cultural professionals as integral to the colonial agenda. Cultural theorist, Edward Said's seminal work on orientalism details the ways the colonial agenda was interdependent with narratives of culture and arts. Said argues that the "Orient" is an idea created by the West, for the West. The "Orient" in relation to the "Occident" is particular but all colonisation is linked to this idea and forms a relationship of power and domination. Literary, artistic and cultural investments made the "colonised" (the orient, the Pacific, the Aboriginal and Torres Strait Islander peoples) a system of knowledge, an accepted grid for filtering realities into Western consciousness. In other words, colonisation becomes "canonical" as colonial imperialism governed entire fields of study, imagination and scholarly institutions.[13]

Figure 10.2 Eugene von Guérard, *View of Geelong*, 1856. Geelong Art Gallery.

View of Geelong (1856) by Eugene von Guérard, a key nineteenth-century landscape artist of Australia, Aotearoa (New Zealand) and colonised lands of the Pacific Ocean, is a most loved painting by Geelong residents and art theorists; it has influenced and resonated with subsequent Australian landscape painters (see Figure 10.2). While von Guérard stated that his interest was to 'illustrate the character of the Australian landscape faithfully and true to nature', art critic John Hook argues, 'there is more than meets the eye in this notion of truth to nature in mid-nineteenth century landscape

[10] Paul Sanders, Mirjana Lozanovska and Lana Van Galen, "Lines of Settlement: Lost Landscapes within Maps for Future Morphologies", *Heritage* 4, no. 3 (2021): 1400–414. https://doi.org/10.3390/heritage4030077.
[11] De Certeau, *The Practice of Everyday Life*.
[12] De Certeau, *The Practice of Everyday Life*.
[13] Edward W. Said, *Orientalism: Western Conceptions of the Orient* (London: Penguin Books, 1978).

painting'.[14] Hook identifies several factors that make this a constructed nature rather than a truth, including the vantage point and von Guérard's ability to identify viewing positions that stage a natural and illuminated landscape drama. Such a position is also related to prospect – a commanding overview of the landscape from a relative height – as discussed in contemporary theories of the picturesque.[15] Eugene von Guérard's extensive sketching expeditions to the southern hemisphere were an imperative of artistic directive to expand beyond the confines of the "Mediterranean", which in the mid 1800s was made possible by the colonial access to the world unknown to Europeans. Eugene von Guérard's comprehensive sketching in Australia linked landscape art to a scientific charter drawn upon by the British colonial administration for its portrayal of geological, botanical and meteorological features.

Intersecting a critical view of colonial survey mapping is a theory that colonisation is not merely about territory, it is about exploration, about the imaginative extension of a familiar reality onto an exotic place. It is structured through vision and fantasy. In this sense, the making of maps are significant techniques and products in the processes of colonisation. Cultural theorist Gayatri Spivak's argument that 'the imperialist project [which] had to assume that the earth that it territorialised was in fact previously uninscribed' is pertinent to the Australian case as the name *Terra Nullius* is embedded in British colonisation and Australia's colonial history.[16]

The potential for understanding the power dynamics that were at play in maps and paintings enables us to engage with the representations of space that contributed to colonial expansion through the formation of new urban centres like Geelong. It suggests a need for a reassessment of value attached to current heritage commodification of colonial history and a reassertion of indigenous presence, inhabitation, histories, knowledge and customs that continue to serve to protect the environment and its unique natural specificities, that were subsumed within a blueprint for colonising strategies.

Topographical landscape features survey

The purpose of surveys conducted to record topographical landscape features was primarily to gain accurate knowledge of all aspects of the terrain under consideration. As a prequel for identifying potential sites for the town planning of new settlements, these surveys provided the basis for the process of British colonial control over the territory. Robert Hoddle, widely recognised for his role in planning and surveying Melbourne, had wide influence on the early establishment of towns in various parts of colonial New South Wales, and in Victoria including the town of Geelong in 1838.[17] Hoddle utilised an identical rectangular grid to that deployed for Melbourne, incorporating characteristics of primary and secondary streets. The thirty-six square configuration of grids was initially set out by Hoddle according to his field notes, and drawn by Smythe.[18] Nevertheless, Hoddle's map presents the erasure of sites of the land in the process of dispossession under the imposition that the land was *terra nullius* (see Figures 10.3 and 10.5).

From a geological perspective, the designated township reserve of Geelong is located on Pleistocene (Newer) volcanic formations and older Pliocene sediments known as Moorabool Viaduct Sands. The volcanic formations span across the area as distinct flows, originating from the west and traversing the central and southern sections of the township reserve. In terms of topography, the central flow manifests as a noticeable east–west ridge, rising to a height of thirty-six metres.[19] The settlement plan took advantage of the location between Corio Bay to the north, and the Barwon River to the south, dissected by an east–west ridge upon which McKillop Street was aligned, being seen as "idea" to colonial settler interests, as illustrated in the early town layouts (see Figures 10.3 and 10.5).

Our approach in seeking multiple and at the least dual interpretations of these records requires a scholarship and research practice of "looking again" as a practice towards dismantling our familiar perceptual tools. Looking at von Guérard's painting alongside William Duke's *Geelong from Mr Hiatts Barrabool Hills* (see Figure 10.4 in the colour plate section), position, vantage point and prospect shift as two Aboriginal (possibly Wadawurrung) people are shown to be looking over the land towards the bay, revealing a view of the open landscape still only very sparsely built. One has their back turned and is standing, the other is in profile and is sitting on a rock, both are draped in Aristotelian white cloths, and command a philosophical, reflective tone. And yet, both hold a spear, a convention for representation of Aboriginal and Torres Strait Islander peoples. They are not interested in the viewers of the painting or indeed the cultural institutions (gallery, archives, heritage) this painting might serve, but are focussed on the lands – their Country – before

---

[14] George Hook, "Brushes with Infidelity: Truth to Nature in Three Composite Landscapes by Eugene von Guérard", *Art History* 40, no. 5 (November 2017): 1027–53; Virginia Ruth Pullin, "Eugene von Guérard and the Science of Landscape Painting" (PhD thesis, University of Melbourne, 2007), 62–137.

[15] See John McCarthur,, *The Picturesque: Architecture, Disgust and Other Irregularities*, (London: Routledge, 2008).

[16] Gayatri Chakravorty Spivak, *The Post-Colonial Critic: Interviews, Strategies, Dialogues*, ed S. Harasym (New York: Routledge, 1990), 1.

[17] Isaac Selby, "Robert Hoddle, and the Planning of Melbourne", *The Victorian Historical Magazine* 13, no. 2 (1928): 53–64; G. Scurfield, *The Hoddle Years Surveying in Victoria 1836–1853* (Canberra: Institute of Surveyors, Australia Inc., 1995); Berres Hoddle Colville, "Robert Hoddle: Pioneer Surveyor, 1794-1881", *Globe* (0311-3930), 57 (2005): 17–26; Brendan Marshall, "Gullies, a Town Grid and a Historical Tip: The Archaeological Site at Harding Park, Geelong", *Australasian Historical Archaeology* 38 (2020): 35–48.

[18] H.W.H. Smythe, Plan of the Town of Geelong, May. Source: VPRS 8168/P5, item FEAT 570: Geelong Town (Public Record Office Victoria, 1838).

[19] Marshall, "Gullies", 35.

them. Indeed, what are they thinking? We may never know, but in that long-distant view perhaps we can sense the trepidation of the future to come – that is an oft interpretation of von Guérard's work as well, according to scholars.[20]

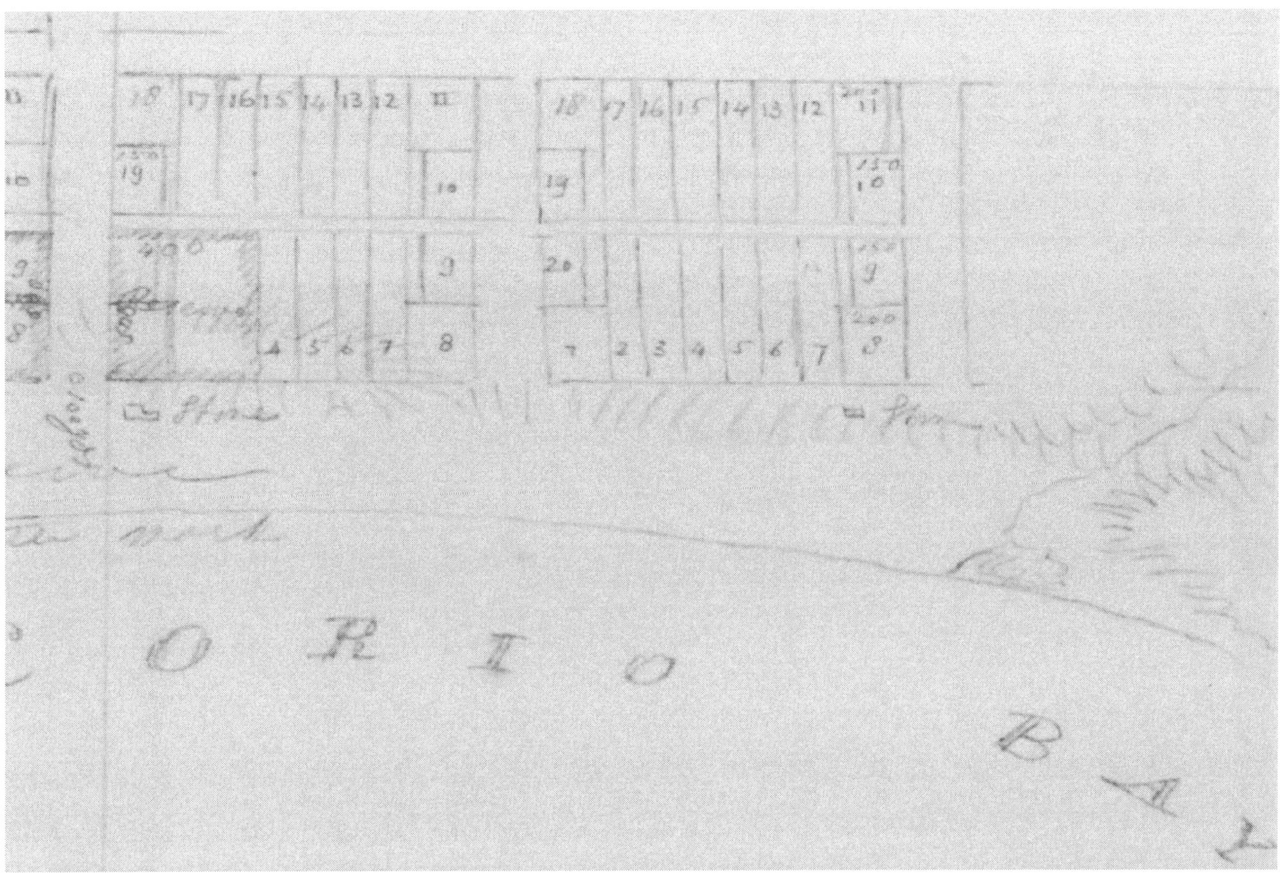

Figure 10.3 Robert Hoddle, *Town of Geelong, Surveyors Field Notes,* 1837. A rough sketch indicating the Western Gully entering Corio Bay through an embankment.

The Barrabool (various spellings, Barrabull) Hills are also noted on an 1835 map with focus on Corio (Carayio) Bay.[21] Pencil lines illustrate the textures and patterns that in later measured and geometric maps are excluded, with additional numerous notes about 'Beautiful meadow', 'very extensive plain', and 'lightly timbered'; to the names – Barrabull Hills and Carayio Bay – are added notes, 'very fine sheep country'.[22] One might interpret that the two Wadawurrung figures viewing this land from the Barrabull Hills were also pondering on it as their Country, and yet seeing the constructions of colonial settlers they may have considered their role as custodians and the foreboding destruction.

The location of von Guérard's painting *Aborigines met on the road to the diggings* (1854) in Wadawurrung Country present Aboriginal people as actively engaging with "others" (British colonial settlers) accentuated especially by the authoritative agency of the Wadawurrung man negotiating a possum skin.[23] Pullin notes that 'the rug may be the one that von Guérard owned, now in the Berlin Ethnological Museum, and the kneeling figure may refer to von Guérard himself'.[24] Pullin elaborates on notes from his diarised observations of constructed shelters, mia-mias made out of tree branches in the form of a large half-open umbrella.[25] The artistic gaze as illustrated in this painting and the context of its production is not outside of colonial transactions as it reveals differential values of artefacts; von Guérard's corporeal "kneeling" implicates that exchange operates as two-way, and that in this moment, could authority be held by Aboriginal members of the Wadawurrung ?

---

[20] Thomas A. Darragh and Virginia Ruth Pullin, "Eugene von Guérard and the Ethnological Museum in Berlin: Correspondence 1878-1880", *Proceedings of the Royal Society of Victoria* 135, no. 2 (2023): 102–26, doi:10.1071/rs23017.

[21] Sketch of Carayio Bay in John Helder Wedge, "Field Book 1835-1836. [Manuscript]", (1835) 163–75, accessed November 4, 2023, http://handle.slv.vic.gov.au/10381/268484.

[22] *Sketch of Carayio Bay* in John Helder Wedge, "Field Book 1835-1836. [Manuscript]".

[23] Eugene von Guérard, *Aborigines met on the road to the diggings,* 1854, oil on canvas, Geelong Gallery, accessed November 4, 2023, https://www.geelonggallery.org.au/collection/explore-the-collection/eugene-von-gu-rard-1803.

[24] Ruth Pullin, "Eugene von Guérard and Colonial Art in Melbourne, 1850-1880", in Christopher Allen (ed), *A Companion to Australian Art* (Chichester, Sussex: John Wiley and Sons, 2021), 141–66; 145.

[25] Ruth Pullin, "Eugene von Guérard and Colonial Art in Melbourne, 1850-1880".

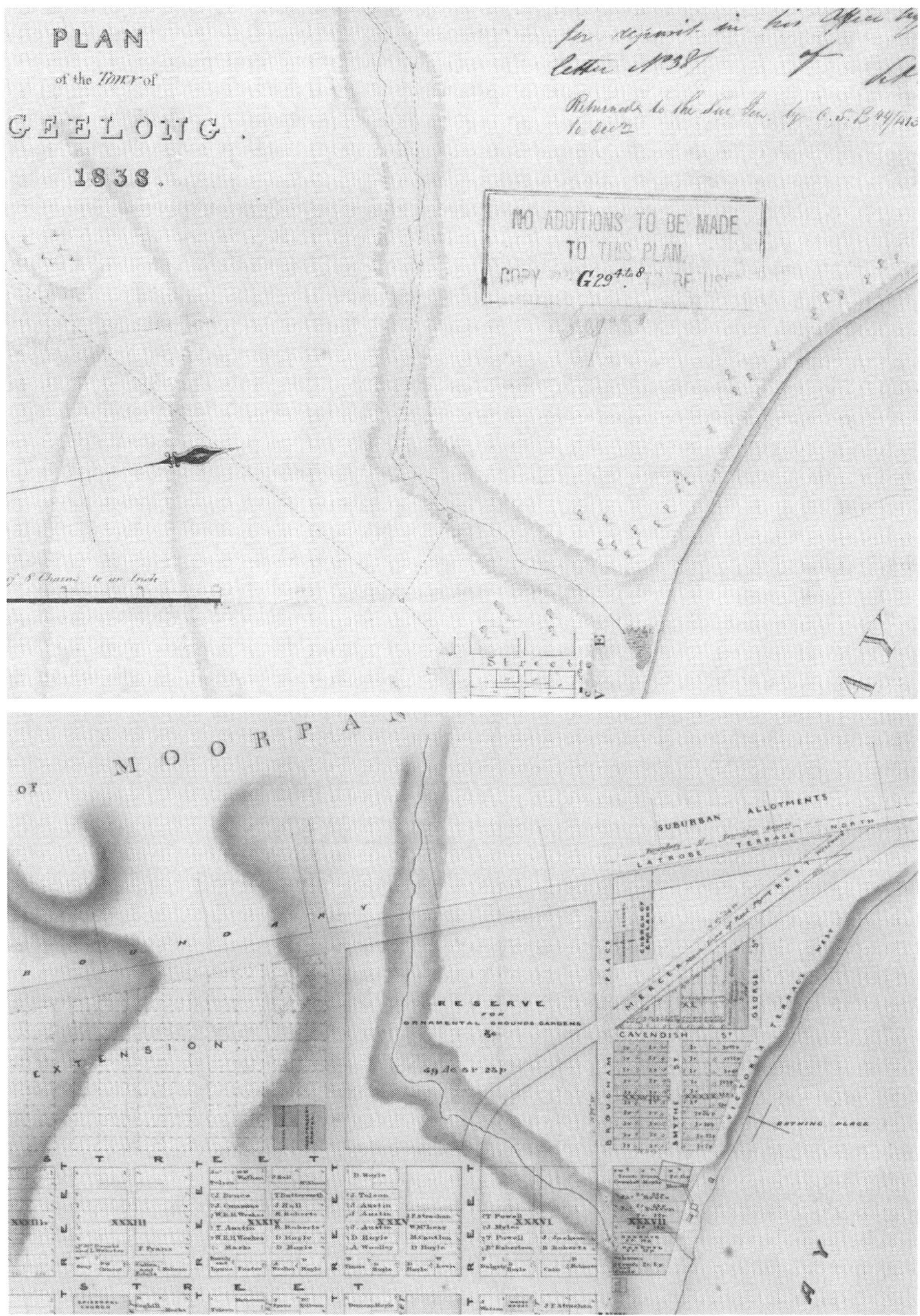

Figure 10.5 Top: H. W. H. Smythe, *Plan of the Town of Geelong,* 1838. A topographical features survey preceding more detailed block and allotment maps that soon followed. The creek of the Western Gully is a major landscape feature that also included ridges, vegetation and waterways.
Bottom: Robert Hoddle, *Town of Geelong,* 1838. Consolidation of Smythe's Map. The Western Gully is charted in its natural course flowing through "Ornamental Grounds Gardens" before discharging into Corio Bay through a smaller reserve allotment, seemingly Hoddle had made allowance for the preservation of the water course in its natural form.

Wadawurrung peoples and Country enter the colonial gaze as a graphic lexicon as seen in the 1804 Map of Port Phillip Bay (copied into a 1902 map).[26] On the top left corner of the map there is an insertion of a typical graphic convention of Aboriginal and Torres Strait Islander people within the lithograph methods.[27] The normative interpretation may be that the local inhabitants are portrayed as welcoming new colonial subjects. A practice of looking again gives rise to alternate interpretations informed by critiques of the colonial gaze.[28] Viewing this from an alternate lens to its colonial agenda of appropriation and exotic ornamentation, the image showing two Aboriginal people, one standing graced by a cloak (a skin?), and holding a spear, the other, sitting with spear, the illustration could be interpreted as a signifier of Aboriginal people's pursuit for the protection to their lands. In addition, the two are standing in front of a graphic sign (as though it is on a rock) stating Port Phillip Bass's Strait. The map illustrates the edge of Port Phillip Bay, which at the site of present Geelong reveals the deep inland incision of the sea, later to be called Carayio Bay. Landscape textures are accompanied by notes and a delicate drawing of the You Yangs, the hills inland from that coastal edge.

The Western Gully

The undulating topography of the volcanic plains prevented the Barwon River from entering Corio Bay, consequently several gullies served as natural drainage for the bayside districts. The initial grid of Geelong, positioned between two gullies known as Harding Park gully and the larger Western Gully are clearly recorded in all early documents.[29] McKillop Street, one of the planned east–west thoroughfares by Hoddle, follows the crest of a prominent ridge, effectively dividing the town reserve into two distinctive drainage catchments. There were five distinct gullies that breached the shallow cliff banks of Corio Bay. Of these, the Western Gully stands out historically due to its extensive reach, hindrance to landward movement, and uncontrolled stormwater flow (see Figure 10.1).[30]

The extent of the gully can be determined through reference to several early maps that chart its line traversing easterly from a point close to West Melbourne Road (now Shannon Avenue) and Aberdeen Street, flowing easterly between numerous allotments and through Johnstone Park before finally flowing northwards and discharging into Corio Bay. The Western Gully posed significant challenges for travellers, particularly during dark and stormy nights, as it was treacherous and intimidating.[31] The formation of the gully consisted of a combination of natural and artificial elements. Certain sections of its embankments served as pathways for traffic to and from Latrobe Terrace.

La Trobe's Dam

A dam was constructed in 1849 within the gully at the junction of Gheringhap Street and Mercer Street as a measure to manage waterflow and mitigate flooding, thereby preventing other parts of the gully from becoming impassable. The dam was 'partly natural and partly artificial in its formation. Portions of its embankment served as traffic ways to and from Latrobe Terrace'.[32] The dam was also intended to provide water for use by horse and bullock teams.[33] However, the embankments were steep and their precarious nature, exacerbated by poor lighting, made the location a hazard, consequently a number of drownings of both humans and animals were reported.[34] The volume of water entering the dam fluctuated and was seasonal '…[it] sometimes reached back to near the Town Hall site but in summer was sometimes nearly empty'.[35] (See Figure 10.6) Furthermore, alterations of levels had affected drainage flow and caused silting of the dam, which by 1886 contained little water and an enormous quantity of mud.

Following the establishment of Geelong as a town, its business and traffic flow had been significantly compromised by the gullies and elevated embankments, necessitating the implementation of construction works to address these challenges. The most formidable difficulties and expenses were encountered during the filling of the Western Gully at Gheringhap Street and the subsequent extension of the street to the bay frontage (see Figure 10.7). In 1871 a determined effort was made to rectify this longstanding issue, and significant progress was achieved which resulted in a more level and cohesive streetscape.[36] Soil from Victoria Terrace, utilised in the construction, played a vital role in these transformational earthworks.[37]

---

[26] Note images of Wadawurrung in top left corner. E. Dossete, *Map of Port Phillip in Bass's Strait*, February 1902, copy of original by J.H. Tuckey, October 1804, State Library of Victoria, quoted in Rowe, *About Corayo*, 71, Figure 2.07.

[27] We see the Aboriginal person with spear almost as graphic symbol again in a map by J.H. Wedge, *Plan of Port Phillip*, 1835, (MS13487 SLV)

[28] Gail Ching-Liang Low, *White Skins/Black Masks: Representation and Colonialism* (Melbourne: Routledge, 1996).

[29] Research project of archaeological focus by Brendan Marshall, 2020.

[30] Marshall, "Gullies", 37.

[31] L.J. Keavy, "Little Scotland (A talk given to the Society on 5/4/67)", *Investigator,* Geelong Historical Society (1968), 18.

[32] W. R. Brownhill, *The History of Geelong and Corio Bay* (Wilke & Co. Melbourne, 1955), 208.

[33] U. Emin, "The Survivors", *Investigator,* Geelong Historical Society (1995), 124.

[34] I. Ward, "In the Beginning", *Investigator,* Geelong Historical Society (1986), 104.

[35] Cuzens, "Recollection", 150.

[36] Brownhill, *The History of Geelong and Corio Bay*, 113.

[37] Rowe, *"About Corayo"*, 680; G. Seaton, "The Ashby Story: A History of Geelong West" (Geelong West City Council, 1978).

Figure 10.6 Samuel Thomas Gill, James Tingle (engraver), *Railway Terminus, St. Paul's Church &c, Geelong*, 1857. The view is looking northwards across the gully with distant views of Corio Bay and the You Yangs range. In the middle ground are the newly constructed St. Pauls Church, Railway Station and former Terminus Hotel.

Figure 10.7 Quarrill & Co, lithographer, from a sketch by Edward Snell Esq., *Geelong and Melbourne Railway Terminus*, 1854. View northward over Corio Bay. In the foreground is the Western Gully flowing through Johnstone Park into La Trobe's Dam on its course towards Corio Bay, passing through a tunnel under Corio Terrace.

Johnstone Park

In 1848, an allocation of 59 acres of land was designated for decorative gardens located between Ryrie Street and Brougham Place, specifically to the east of Latrobe Terrace (see Figure 10.8). It was during this period that plans were conceived and implemented to transform the entire region between Gheringhap Street and Latrobe Terrace on the east and west, and Little Malop Street and Railway Terrace on the south and north, into a public park, eventually to be known as Johnstone Park.[38] At that time there was no thoroughfare along Fenwick Street between Little Malop Street and Railway Terrace, except for a narrow lane or path that crossed a precarious bridge over the Western Gully.[39]

After a few years, the decision was made to widen Railway Terrace. This undertaking, while requiring the alteration of the northern boundary of Johnstone Park, resulted in a beneficial trade-off. The loss of a section of parkland was outweighed by the establishment of a spacious roadway leading to the railway station. This improvement resolved the longstanding issue of a narrow passage that had been a source of frustration for cab drivers and commuters rushing to catch their trains. To facilitate the widening of Railway Terrace, a portion of the northern side of Johnstone Park, situated

---

[38] Rowe, *"About Corayo"*, 665.
[39] Brownhill, *The History of Geelong and Corio Bay*, 208.

between Fenwick and Gheringhap Streets, was utilised. Earth filling, necessary for levelling the area, was sourced from the construction site of the railway subway between Mercer Street and Latrobe Terrace.[40]

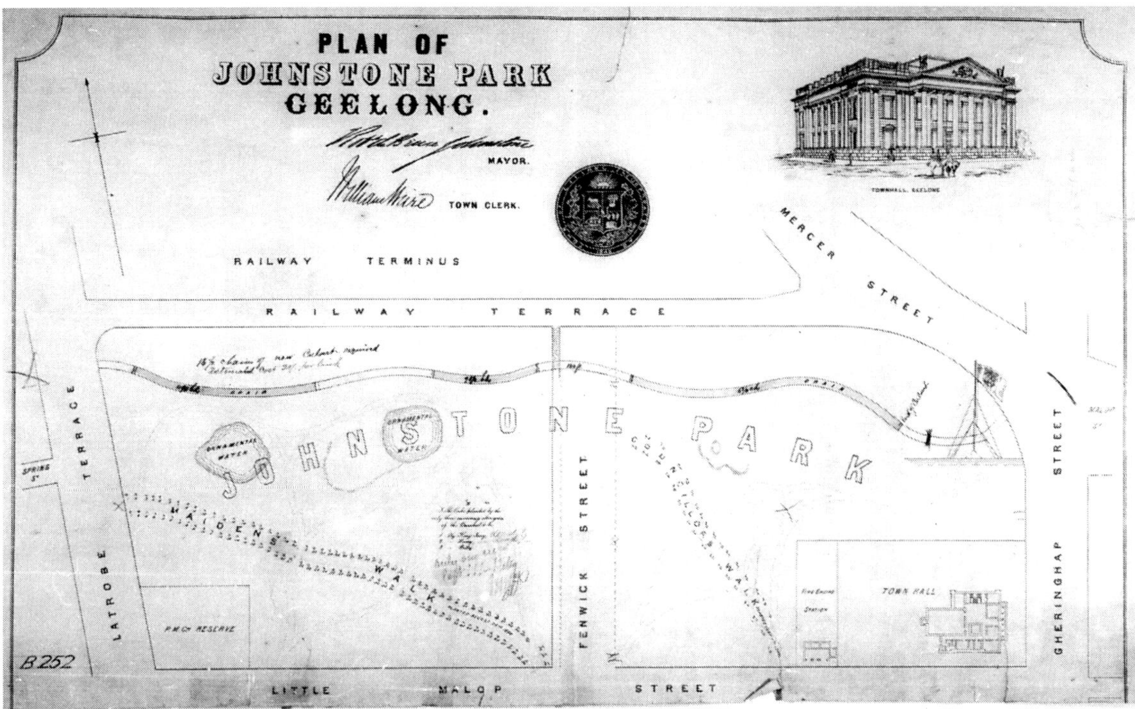

Figure 10.8 Robert Balding, Henry Franks (lithographer), *Plan of Johnstone Park Geelong*, 1867. Showing proposal of a constructed culvert for the Western Gully to flow through Johnstone Park, with a bridge across on the line of the proposed Fenwick Street.

Only a short time had elapsed since the establishment of Johnstone Park when its division into two sections became unavoidable. The primary reason behind this decision was the impending construction of a railway extension from Geelong Station to Colac. The railway project posed a dual threat to the park. Firstly, its implementation would result in the alteration of the park's boundaries, diminishing its original extent. Additionally, there was a need to open Fenwick Street between Little Malop Street and Railway Terrace utilising the earth excavated from the railway cutting and tunnel for filling the gullies in the Fenwick Street area and raising the roadway.[41]

Confinement of the creek: Stormwater management of the Western Gully

Over several phases of construction, the entire length of the Western Gully was 'permanently eliminated' within a stormwater management system of brick culverts and subterranean sewers.[42] Motivation for these engineering works were primarily to improve sanitation and water flow through the creek. In heavy rains, the creek would flood, causing damage to properties positioned too close along its banks. Another factor was that the gully had always presented a physical barrier to movement of people and vehicles westward of the town centre as it was bridged only at one point.[43]

The construction of a stormwater culvert between Johnstone Park and Corio Bay was implemented in 1912 incorporating a drain that was constructed under Cunningham Street past Victoria Terrace, before discharging into Corio Bay (see Figure 10.9).

Due to the Depression, experienced throughout the 1930s, public funds were directed to civil engineering work to provide a much-needed source of employment. One of the more prolonged schemes during this period in Geelong was construction of a brick-lined stormwater barrel drain along the route of the old Western Gully (see Figure 10.10). The scheme was submitted to the Public Works Department in March 1931 and, following approval, construction commenced the following year 'as unemployed relief work, the government providing the labour and the municipalities the cost of materials'.[44]

A final and major phase of confinement of the Western Gully occurred with the construction of a light industrial zone between Latrobe Terrace and Pakington Street in 1964. The council executed a total of eight schemes, with the

[40] Brownhill, *The History of Geelong and Corio Bay*, 114.

[41] Brownhill, *The History of Geelong and Corio Bay*, 211.

[42] Brownhill, *The History of Geelong and Corio Bay*, 113.

[43] Brownhill, *The History of Geelong and Corio Bay*, 113; Seaton, "The Ashby Story", 58.

[44] Seaton, "The Ashby Story", 209.

most substantial one involving Gordon Avenue positioned above the old gully and its drain. This particular project resulted in the creation of fifty-one plots designated for light industry.[45]

Reparation of landscapes and restorative action

.... the large gaps in memory can be restitched together if dormant Country can be reactivated ...[46]

Shaped by distinct historical perspectives, different interpretations of the same document may contradict one another. Survey maps were tools of power, strategically influencing the formation of towns like Geelong, they projected a colonial agenda onto the landscape. Aboriginal and Torres Strait Islander communities dealt with this new order by tactically navigating the spaces between the strategic lines on the map. This tactical approach deployed what de Certeau has called a "turn" of events and thus required a calibrated approach in both time and space. Lines of settlement – grids, fences, roads, ports, boundaries, homesteads, pastoral clearings – separately and in combination became lines of dispossession.[47]

In the process of surveying for British colonial settlement, these early maps unintentionally reveal the original Aboriginal and Torres Strait Islander cultural landscapes that were soon to be threatened. The examination of these historical drawings from the perspective of urban morphology research sheds light on the origins of urban transformation. However, a shift occurs when viewing these maps as representations of a final moment in the physical features and forms of the area. This chapter recognises the cultural heritage significance of the lost landscape features depicted in these maps, such as the Western Gully, a moment in time before their imminent erasure. However, the topographic survey maps also unintentionally reveal the original cultural landscape from which a reference for decolonising practices of reconciliation, truth telling, and urban design can be drawn.

The Wadawurrung comprised twenty-five clans who spoke a related language and were connected through shared spiritual beliefs, cultural interests and marriage ties, as well as trading initiatives. Each was responsible for a distinctive area. In collaboration and through laws with priority to sustain the land and waters as physical and spiritual livelihood, they managed the lands – their clan borders and restrictions of use of resources – and sustained a flourishing and nurturing Country for millennia. By 1835 the rapid and extensive squatter sheep runs irrevocably damaged the land through pastoral and livestock grazing, and sheep trampling grasses and fouling waterways. Hunting in and around Geelong exacerbated this further, altering the lands and the historical trajectory of Wadawurrung Country irreversibly.

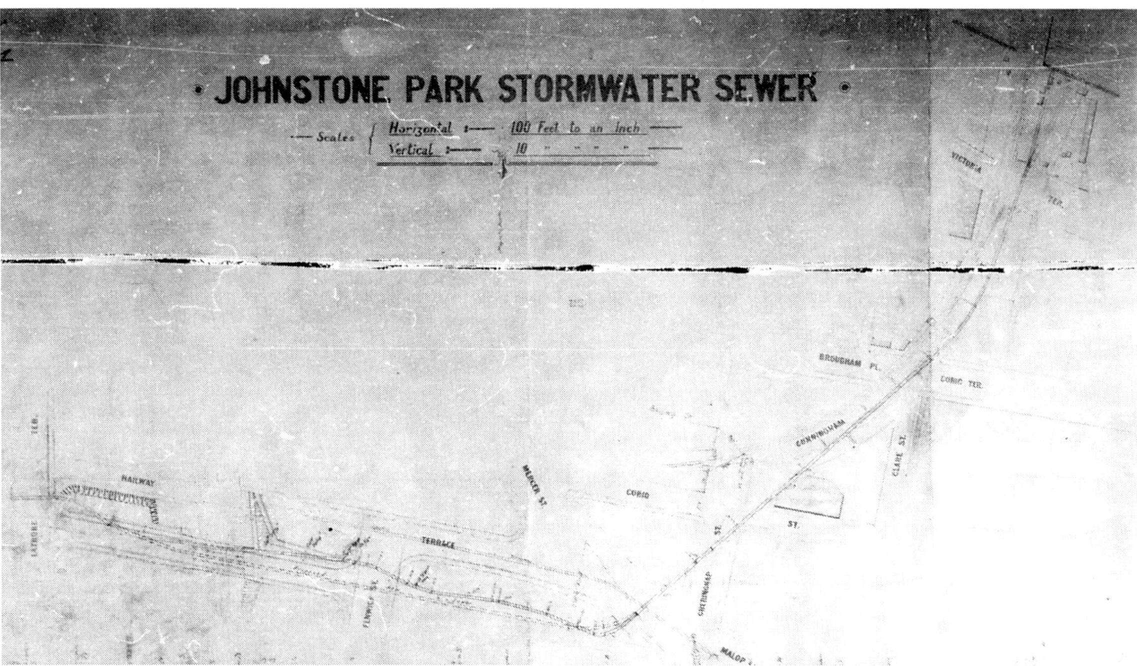

Figure 10.9 *Johnstone Park Stormwater Sewer*, 1912. The realignment of Railway Terrace to form Gordon Avenue between Fenwick Street and Latrobe Terrace is shown to facilitate the construction of an underpass to separate the road and train tracks. This resulted in a major earthwork that disturbed the earlier culvert (see Figure 10.8), requiring redirection with a proposed new line of the "stormwater sewer".

---

[45] R. Hill, "Hodges West End Brewery", *Investigator,* Geelong Historical Society. (2003): 108–11.

[46] Dylan Kombumerri, "Can Lost Memory of Cultural Landscapes be Restored? In Designing with Country", (NSW Government, 2020), accessed August 2, 2023 https://www.aidr.org.au/media/7760/designing-with-country-discussion-paper.pdf

[47] Sanders et. al., "Lines of Settlement".

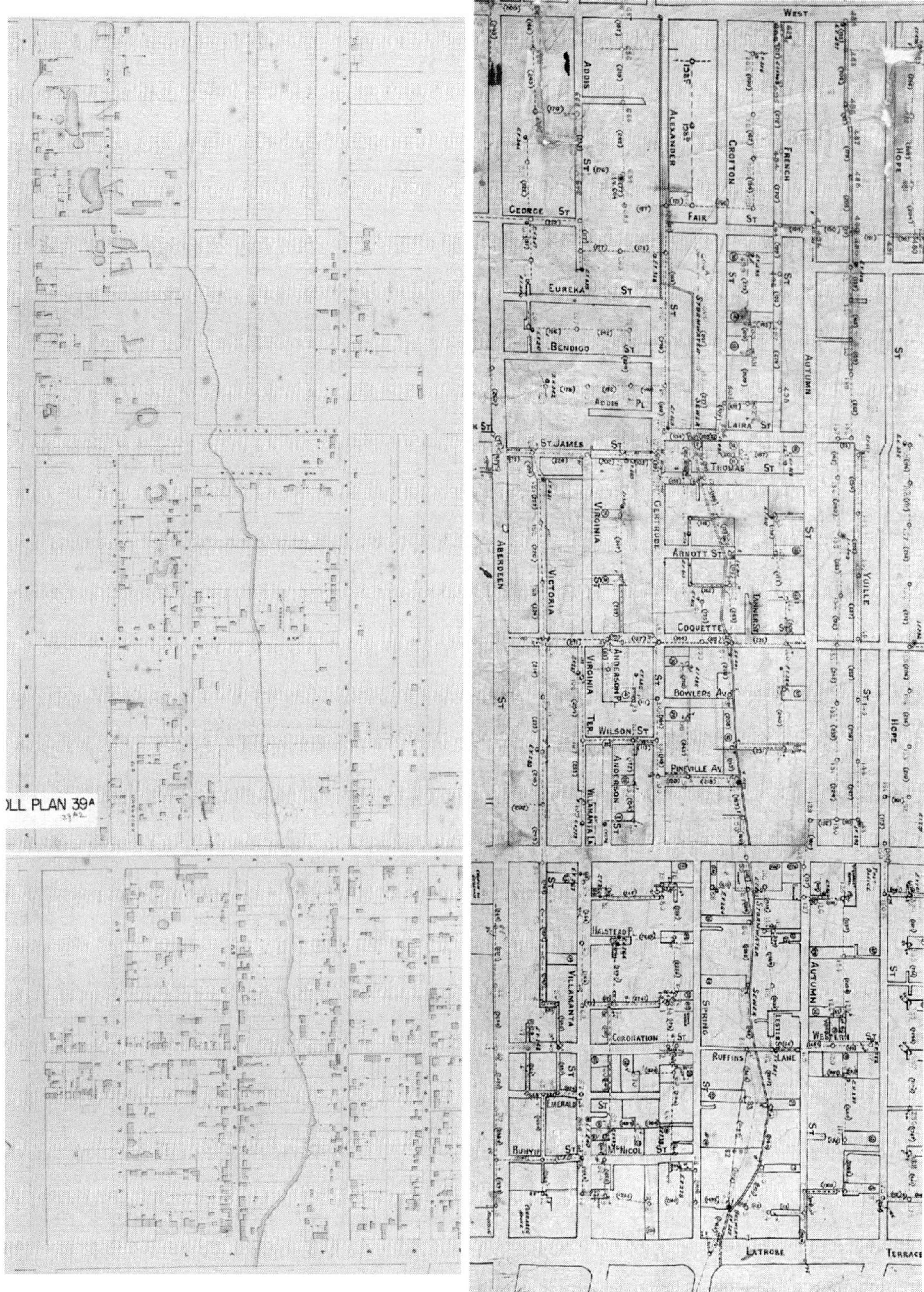

Figure 10.10 Left: J. H. Taylor, *ASHBY KILDARE*, 1854 (above) and J. H. Taylor, *ASHBY LITTLE SCOTLAND KILDARE*, 1854 (below). The course of the Western Gully is charted between Latrobe Terrace westwards to Government Road (later Melbourne Road and Shannon Avenue).
Right: *Geelong Waterworks and Sewerage Trust – Borough of Geelong West*, undated. Depicting the barrel drain following the route of the former gully.

Tactical Aboriginal resistance to this British invasion was evident in the stealing of sheep, as well as through mobility and effort to navigate the colonial law and order of the land. De Certeau is hardly romantic about tactics. Massacres and killings of the Wadawurrung went unreported, and even on the rare occasion when trialled, they were unjustly judged. More realistic is the history that a colonial-settler squatter could only hold onto the stolen land by "slaughtering" the local peoples. This exposed the very real resistance by Aboriginal inhabitants.[48] The Wadawurrung population suffered a massive decline as a result of British colonisation. Introduced diseases, massive killings and massacres, physical displacement to mission stations and protectorates, destruction of traditional food sources and starvation followed invasion.[49] By the 1860s, Wadawurrung numbers had dwindled from thousands to just 100.[50] The British colony proved to be a totalitarian strategy disavowing the space for Aboriginal tactical existence. Page and Memmott clarify that:

> creating new ceremony and ritual, as part of an activation program in cities and towns is an unexplored area with high potential for invigoration of places.[51]

Australia, like other post-settler societies, is grappling with the challenges and consequences of its history. The colonisation of Australia occurred without understanding its environmental context or acknowledging its Aboriginal and Torres Strait Islander inhabitants.[52] Recent efforts towards reconciliation have included political apologies, but the design professions and education sector have been slow to embrace significant change. A revived and continuing active presence of Wadawurrung descendants is evident in both the Wadawurrung Traditional Owners Aboriginal Corporation, and the Wathaurong Aboriginal Co-operative.[53]

Page and Memmott call for the awakening of a new Indigenous architecture in Australia that is based on the fundamental principles of: deep listening, Indigenous led, community specific, shared benefits, respecting Indigenous knowledge.[54] Australia's mainstream design practice is also developing a reparative process within the fields of architecture, urban design, and landscape architecture.[55] New directions for urban and landscape design in Australia are in evidence through projects such as The Australia Garden in Cranbourne Victoria by Taylor Cullity Lethlean and Paul Thompson.[56]

The paintings of von Guérard provide a captivating visual record of the Australian natural environment during the colonial era. His painting of *Tower Hill* portrays a volcanic crater located 200 km west of Geelong in which he meticulously depicts the geological features of the area before the removal of native vegetation by colonial agriculturalists drastically altered the landscape.[57] Over a century later, between 1960 and 1990, local communities have replanted thousands of trees and plant species, following von Guérard's painting as a template to restore as close as possible the original communities of the landscape, that now include returning wildlife.[58] Responding to von Guérard's *View of Geelong*, a creative work by Cameron Bishop and Simon Reis pays tribute to the painting's place in "imaging" the region.[59] By locating Montpellier Park, Highton, Geelong, as the place from which it was painted, Bishop and Reis draw on old technologies – a camera obscura and stereoscope – to set up a viewing device within a ruined fireplace on the hill to disturb our conventional ways of seeing, and to alter our familiar pictures. The stereoscope splits the scene, shifting it from a vast panoramic and commanding view to a "partial, layered and temporal" image.[60] Beauty as it is aligned with von Guérard's landscape painting is also gently shattered. Once seen, to look again at von Guérard's work, the painting itself reveals these partial and temporal layers: the native trees in the foreground are a fragment, a small island of pre-colonial landscape bounded by a "picket" fence and road exposing the effect of intensified British colonial settler pastoral practices on the landscape. Located in the foreground, this earlier landscape fragment is a filter through which the settlement is seen – sparsely settled but definitively an impactful inscription of the processes that altered the landscape.

These are examples of interpretation and critical works and practices in relation to paintings as historical documents that provide the detail and data for reparative measures. Creative strategies and performative events that offer glimpses of lost Country are occurring in Geelong. Mountain to Mouth (or M~M) was conceptualised by Meme McDonald as a way to walk together in the footsteps of Aboriginal ancestors, which in its pilot stage in 2009 went upstream from the mouth of the river to the You Yangs; then altered to go with the natural flow of water, which by 2016 was refined with

---

[48] Clark, *Scars in the Landscape*, 1; 169–75.

[49] Rick Bullers, "Final Report, Western Geelong Growth Area, Batesford, Fyansford, Hamlyn Heights, Moorabool and Bell Post Hill, Victoria: Phase 1 Aboriginal Heritage Assessment", (Ecology and Heritage Partners Pty Ltd. 2016).

[50] See Clark, *Scars in the Landscape*; David S. Jones and Phillip B. Roös (eds), *Geelong's Changing Landscape: Ecology, Development and Conservation* (Collingwood: CSIRO Publishing, 2019), 61.

[51] Page and Memmott, *Design: Building on Country*, 142.

[52] Jefa Greenaway, Janet McGaw and Jillian Walliss, "Designing Australia—Critical Engagement with Indigenous Place Making", in G. Cairns (ed), *Design for a Complex World*, 1st edn (Oxfordshire, UK: Libri Publishing, 2014), 29–54.

[53] See https://www.wadawurrung.org.au/ and https://wathaurong.org.au/.

[54] Page and Memmott, *Design: Building on Country*.

[55] Indigenous architects such as Kevin O'Brien (*Finding Country* Project), Jefa Greenaway (*The Falls* Project/Ngarara Place Project), and Alison Page (*Building on Country*) are provoking new paradigms that engage with Indigenous place-making. Their work aims to uncover hidden landscapes and challenge historical erasure, using maps and creative interventions to initiate new design approaches.

[56] Julian Bollerter, "Postcards from the Edge: A Critical Reading of Representation of the Interior in Australian Landscape Architecture", *Journal of Landscape Architecture* (Winter 2017): 74–85.

[57] Eugene von Guérard, *Tower Hill,* 1855, oil on canvas, Warrnambool Art Gallery, accessed November 5, 2023, https://www.ngv.vic.gov.au/essay/eugene-von-guerard-nature-revealed/3/.

[58] A. Issa, "How we Heal as a Nation: The Replanting and Return of the Forests of Tower Hill", *The Guardian*, Sun April 16, 2023.

[59] Cameron Bishop and Simon Reis, *View of Geelong: Trans Panorama,* accessed November 6, 2023, https://www.publicartcommission.com/project/view-of-geelong-trans-panorama

[60] Bishop and Reis, *View of Geelong: Trans Panorama.*

utmost dedication with the timing falling into place.[61] This annual series of curated walks activated a way of remembering lost views in a changing environment, for example the lost river view at Barwon River depicted in Eugene von Guérard's *View of Geelong* painting.[62] Johnstone Park is now recognised as a place of cultural significance through commemorative events such as the NAIDOC Week trail and Reconciliation Day.[63]

Ideas and recommendations to reveal memories of lost waterways such as the Western Gully in Geelong should be considered within such a context. The potential for symbolic restorative urban landscape projects is clearly evident here. Through opening the buried culvert and re-landscaping Johnstone Park, through remodelling the Geelong Waterfront, and revealing the exit of the culvert into Corio Bay, the presence of the Western Gully Creek could be brought back to life.

---

[61] M~M (Mountain to Mouth). Meme McDonald held several roles prior to her untimely death. In 2007 she was Artistic Director of Connecting Identities and later Artistic Director of Extreme Arts Walk – M~M, appointed by the Arts & Culture Department of the City of Greater Geelong, accessed September 29, 2023, https://www.mountaintomouth.com.au/news/2015/8/7/5-minutes-with-mm-artistic-director-meme-mcdonald.

[62] "Remembering Lost views in a Changing Environment at Barwon River- Songline Station 6", Mountain to Mouth 2016, accessed August 2, 2023, https://www.mountaintomouth.com.au/news/2016/4/6/remembering-lost-views-in-a-changing-environment-at-barwon-river.

[63] David Tournier, Ron Milligan and Brian Hubber, "Johnstone Park Dreaming - an Aboriginal history. / A Reconciliation in the Park", June 2013, podcast, https://www.djillong.net.au/traditions/tandops-stories/dan-dan-nook.html.

PART 3

PROPOSITIONAL GEELONG

CHAPTER 11

RADICAL PEDAGOGIES:
INTIMACIES OF OBSERVATION

AKARI NAKAI KIDD AND MIRJANA LOZANOVSKA

Introduction

The decline of industrial towns is a global phenomenon. Regional cities and towns have been seeking to revitalise their identities to remain viable and have at times appropriated global top-down ideas. There is often a gap between aspiration and reality. Once a prosperous manufacturing town, the city of Geelong, Victoria, is undergoing a process of deindustrialisation, searching to redefine its identity and remain a viable entity in the globalised world. By conceptualising and developing VacantGeelong as a project grounded within the industrial landscape, new teaching and research methodologies have emerged at the crossroads of art and architecture, technology, and visual representation. VacantGeelong works explore creative research and demonstrate a distinct evolution of interdisciplinary pedagogy, especially in the final research thesis subject of the Master of Architecture at Deakin University. Creative research methodology involves creative practice as integral to critical research, rather than as illustrative or representative of critical research. It requires engagement with traditional research as the information platform for the thesis, position, argument, and the creative methods undertaken, but its core work is how creative practices can generate a different perspective on these questions and engender new modes of knowledge and understanding. Initiated in the VacantGeelong project, this pedagogy evolved as a core creative research stream in the curriculum of the Master of Architecture course, bringing about a strong research-teaching nexus. High-achieving students and a collaborative supervision team created a dynamic learning environment and, in the period 2015–2021, produced twenty-four Master's thesis projects and a PhD dissertation. Selected student works were exhibited in *Iconic Industry*, a major exhibition at the National Wool Museum in Geelong (August–October 2017) and in *VacantGeelong* (Gallery Deakin, 2016).[1]

This chapter develops a deeper understanding of creative research as a radical pedagogy through two student projects that address alternate methods of recording, observing, and representing vacancy in, and through, architecture. One centres on the Alcoa manufacturing plant on Point Henry, a thin peninsula that extends into the sea east of Geelong and is visible from almost any point on Corio Bay. In that sense, the industrial site, the silhouette of the plant – the landmark on the sea – is a parallel and visible presence in relation to the urban centre of the town, but its distance diminishes the relationship the town or its people have with it. The nature of the research project is such that it is not an attempt to find a definitive answer to a question, but rather is a process of projections that observes, collects, critiques, combines, disperses and merges each perspective into a textured representation of the embodied observations of a project for vacant industrial sites.

The second project centres on the layers of chronological history of vacant buildings in Geelong's Central Business District (CBD). The work explored here is an alternative response to traditional academic research and to the current top-down corporate or government-led agendas to expedient solutions. The effort was to identify, record, document and draw the many ways to see, observe, perceive, and in fact "get to know" the vacancy in Geelong city centre. These creative labours evolved into what we have called "Intimacies of distant observation" and "Intimacy of layered observation" respectively, and it is these that we examine in this chapter. By focusing on the realm of observation, the chapter proposes a novel lens for research into Geelong's built environment.

Creative research as radical pedagogy

Radical pedagogies in architectural education have often been associated with the experimental projects in the 1960s and 1970s that questioned and shook the foundation of architecture. Often a collaboration between architects, artists, teachers and students, these embodied experimental approaches not only radicalised architectural pedagogy, but also disturbed and transformed architectural discourse and practice. Most recently, scholarship related to architectural pedagogy has documented and reflected on the value of these past experimentations and what they may offer for our contemporary ways of teaching.[2] Research on the history of architectural education has identified innovative curriculum

---

[1] See Mirjana Lozanovska, David Beynon, Cameron Bishop, Diego Fullaondo and Anne Wilson, *Iconic Industry: Exploring the Industrial Built Fabric of Geelong* (Deakin University, 2017).

[2] Beatriz Colomina, Ignacio G. Galan, Evangelos Kotsioris, and Anna-Maria Meister, *Radical Pedagogies: Architectural Education and the British Tradition* (MIT Press, 2022). See also, Jacqui Alexander, Samuele Grassi and George Mellos, "Radical Practices,

concerned with ecology and environmental science in the 1970s.[3] A loose definition of "radical pedagogy" persists in the broader field of education, as in the introductory essay to the journal *Radical Pedagogy*, where the emphasis is on social change as well as new developments in the field of education.[4] In this chapter, we foreground the 1960s and 1970s as a period of immense social change, marked by second wave feminism and the women's movement, decolonising discourse with nation-states emerging from the yoke of colonisation, identity politics and a renewed attention to race and the civil rights movements – areas that the twenty-first century continues to grapple with. While the May 1968 marches in Paris, Belgrade, Melbourne and elsewhere in the world are considered the last gasp of socialism, Marxist and socialist theory continued in tertiary institutions at the height of the Cold War, shaping theory and investigations. The fall of the Eastern bloc and the Soviet Union appears to have opened the gates of the Berlin Wall to a huge influx of scholarship on the former eastern Europe, as well as new theoretical framings of global communism/socialism. New approaches to architectural history and theory have brought attention to historiography with questions of who writes history and how history is written, identifying the marginalisation embedded within conventional history teaching.[5]

At the *2016 Venice Architecture Biennale*, the subject of "radical pedagogy" covered a very large and long wall – a collated series of experiments in architectural education from the 1960s and 1970s – assembled and conceptualised by the theorist, Beatriz Colomina. Colomina's research team later developed this work into a publication, *Radical Pedagogies*, collating 113 accounts of innovative teaching, some familiar like the Venice Architecture school of theorist and historian, Manfredo Tafuri, or Alvin Boyarsky, and the formidable group of students at the Architecture Association – Hadid, Koolhaas, Tschumi and Libeskind – influencing whole movements in architectural practice and generations of students.[6] Other entries of protagonists, dates, techniques and events that are lesser known brought a finer grain to the Venice exhibition.[7] While short-lived, of the moment, and often undocumented, the ideas underpinning these teaching programs and practices were disseminated through conferences, education and professional networks, and presentations.[8] Their influence, while less documented, was nonetheless effective. Students around the world were receptive, even if they were not yet announced as radical pedagogy. In scale and intensity of content, the exhibition illustrated the significance of architectural education, and its role in the discipline of architecture.[9] It is a timely publication, the authors drawing a direct comparison to present day architectural education, critiquing current practices and the state of architectural education. The everyday lives of teachers and academics are submerged within a voracious and expanded bureaucracy, instilling a chain of accountabilities that effectively diminish the possibility of innovation, and possibly even the act of thinking. *Radical pedagogies* argues that innovative teaching is a radical architectural practice, and that the potential for change lies dormant within the 'institutions that swallowed them up'.[10] These ideas resonate with our time and offer an opportunity to re-evaluate our assumptions about content and curricula, the culture of practice and the architectural canon.

In the context of this chapter, there are two interconnected valuable considerations: the importance of research and creative visual approaches. Through movements like Superstudio and Archizoom, creative research and provocative visual representations became the means to express radical and utopian thoughts. In the case of Superstudio, through photo-collage, and for Archizoom, precise line-drawings, where some were coded on a typewriter *(No-stop City/1969 and Gazebo drawings/1966–74)*. The uncanny nature of the collages and drawings introduced theoretical, visual, and creative research as mediators in critiquing then present issues (for example, the crisis of modernism in the 1960s) thus presented alternate future ideas.

VacantGeelong

Our exploration of an alternative pedagogy was prompted by the process of deindustrialisation as it was occurring in the regional city of Geelong and drew upon the pedagogical program developed by Mirjana Lozanovska that linked design teaching with the role of creative processes.[11] On this occasion, it involved linking the Master of Architecture thesis to the VacantGeelong research project. From the School of Architecture and Built Environment campus at Deakin University in Geelong, daily observation of the industrial architecture interfacing the northern coastal edge of Corio Bay

---

Radical Pedagogies: Intercultural Explorations in Language and Meaning", *arq: Architecture Research Quarterly* 26, no. 4 (2022): 315–30.

[3] Stuart King and Ceridwen Own, "A Decade of Radical pedagogy: Barry McNeill and Environmental Design in Tasmania, 1969-79," *Fabrications*, 28, no. 3 (2018): 303–30.

[4] Timothy McGettigan, "An Invitation to All: What is Radical Pedagogy?", *Radical Pedagogy* 1, no. 1 (Spring 1999), http://www.radicalpedagogy.org/radicalpedagogy/An_Invitation_to_All.html.

[5] See Mirjana Lozanovska, *Contemporary Architecture study guide*, Deakin University, 2009.

[6] Alvin Boyarsky, Architecture Association, with students Rem Koolhaas, Zaha Hadid, Bernard Tschumi, Daniel Libeskind.

[7] Beatriz Colomina et al., "Radical Pedagogies in Architectural Education", *Architectural Review*, 28 September 2012, https://www.architectural-review.com/today/radical-pedagogies-in-architectural-education/8636066.article.

[8] Beatriz Colomina et al. (eds), *Radical Pedagogies*, http://radical-pedagogies.com/; See also: Colomina et al. "Radical Pedagogies in Architectural Education".

[9] Mirjana Lozanovska, "The REAL", filmed 13 October 2016 at the Venice Architecture Biennale, REAL Lectures series, 1:26:36, https://www.youtube.com/watch?v=SGP3qWBdQf8.

[10] Colomina et al., "Radical Pedagogies in Architectural Education".

[11] Mirjana Lozanovska and Leilei Xu, "Children and University Architecture Students Working Together: A Pedagogical Model of Children's Participation in Architectural Design", *CoDesign: International Journal of CoCreation in Design and the Arts* (2012): 7.

and the Alcoa smelter at the distant eastern Point Henry inspired the conceptualisation of the VacantGeelong Project (see Chapter 3, "Dialogues Between Space and Time: VacantGeelong's Work on Industrial Vacancy"). VacantGeelong connects architecture with industry and art to provoke thought and action and to go beyond the usual pragmatic utilisation of ex-industrial sites through engagement with the cultural and social memories of vibrant communities embodied in the vacant sites. In 2015, and with funding from the local council, the project embarked on a three-part approach: knowledge generation through student thesis projects, commissioning artists to respond to vacant industrial architecture, and developing community workshops with past industrial workers. This model connected research with teaching and the broader community.

In this chapter, we explore a design thesis pedagogy integral to creative research that focussed student projects to seek, understand and observe place and vacancy, in alternate ways. This is a pedagogy of architecture where students are active and participatory makers, producing multiplicity of readings, observations, notations and mappings. These creative endeavours do not offer answers – but rather aim to acknowledge and engage with the local contextuality of place. Working with students in their final year in the Master of Architecture from Deakin University, our project has developed and explored the interface between existing untold stories, uses, events, activities, and their architectural settings or infrastructure. Such a pedagogical approach was serviced by interlocking teams: the academic research team who worked directly with the artists, and the teaching supervision team who worked directly with the students.[12] In addition, the supervision team – comprising Mirjana Lozanovska, David Beynon, Cameron Bishop, Diego Fullaondo, Anne Wilson, Cristina Garduño Freeman, Robert Fuller, Angela Kreutz, Ciro Márquez, and Akari Nakai Kidd – worked collaboratively with one another, rather than individually with only their own group of students, and thereby provided thesis supervision training for early and mid-career academic staff. Seminars and workshops fostered lively debates and active participation as groups comprising students and staff engaged with the works.[13]

In the first years, two components were the focus of experimentation including the Ford Motor Company complex, especially as it was a significant facility at the height of Geelong's post-war industrial phase but closed its operations in 2016; and identifying levels and meanings of "vacancy".[14] An underlying agenda to find new methods for observation, documentation and data collection developed into alternative modes of mapping as well as alternative modes of visual representation. These works opened up questions about objectivity and scientifically measurable evidence, presenting their limitations and generating debates. Colin van den Brandt drew on real estate records to locate "vacant" facilities, to which was added on-site recording of use or habitation. Facilities officially recorded as vacant were often in use temporarily or illicitly. A more nuanced set of meanings of vacancy challenged conventional modes of data representation and students produced experimental counter-cartographic methods. Drawing on the strict approach of the work of photographers Bernd and Hilla Bercher, who spent their entire careers photographing industrial architecture, Lucas Sánchez Arlt established a set of compositional rules to record the industrial structures of Geelong.[15] The aim was to explore an "aesthetic of indifference" via deadpan photography and to identify how this is connected to Heidegger's term, *Dasein*.[16] Sánchez Artl developed a photographic series of industrial typologies – large sheds, small sheds, wool sheds, chimneys, small chimneys, tanks, elevated water tanks, silos, conveyor belts, large concrete industrial structures, industrial details, and industrial train wagons – comprising the industrial landscape of Geelong, with each presented through six to nine images. The aim was to display their aesthetic qualities objectively without the positive or negative positions influencing visual judgement, to produce a record that forms a substantial evidence base, and yet at the same time, presents "indifference" as a method that allows ontological difference to manifest.

Creative experimentations and projects ranged from those that focused on the image of Geelong by considering its built environment, to observing memory of vacancy through a process of layering. More specifically, one project examined industrial architectural heritage, and the emerging image of contemporary Geelong. By looking into the archival images of twentieth-century Geelong and its contemporary media, such student work traced the changing representation of the city as viewed through the lens of the visual image. It built on the contemporary discourse related to relationships between image, media of architecture, and on visual methodologies in architecture. Considering that Geelong joined the UNESCO Creative Cities Network in 2017 as a City of Design (currently the only such city to receive this designation in Australia, see Chapter 4), which enhanced its visibility both inside and outside of Australia, there is additional emphasis on research into messaging and values communicated through its imagery across media. What follows, creatively and critically explores the work of two students that engage in alternate ways of observing and

---

[12] Deakin University Research Team: Mirjana Lozanovska (lead) – 2016 + David Beynon, Cameron Bishop, Diego Fullaondo; 2017 + Anne Wilson; 2018 + Ciro Márquez, Akari Nakai Kidd. Artists: Bindi Cole Chocka, Sarah Duyshart, Alexander Hamilton, Merinda Kelly, Robert Mihajlovski, Amanda Shone.

[13] Deakin University Thesis supervision team and students (2016–2017): Mirjana Lozanovska, David Beynon, Cameron Bishop, Diego Fullaondo; Anne Wilson, Cristina Garduño Freeman, Robert Fuller, Angela Kreutz, Ciro Márquez, Akari Nakai Kidd. Ciro Márquez also developed a studio brief for the reuse of industrial architecture focusing on crossprogramming. Deakin University Thesis students: Chayakan Siamphukdee, Colin Van den Brandt, Aditya Godbole, Hazirah Hanisah Harun, Jonathan Tan Ern Wei, Arshadl Ibad Mohd Faudzi, Angelina Chan Yee Ching, Megan Jones, Michael Faulks, Evelyn Jing Pan, Daniel Out, Lucas Sánchez Arlt, Mark McKinlay, Bronte French, and Katsuto Ikeda.

[14] Lozanovska et al., *Iconic Industry: Exploring the Industrial Built Fabric of Geelong*

[15] Bernd Becher and Hilla Becker, *Industrial Facades* (Massachusetts: MIT Press, 1995).

[16] Martin Heidegger, "The Origin of the Work of Art," in D. F. Krell (ed), *Basic Writings: Martin Heidegger* (London: Routledge, 1993) 139–212.

visually expressing vacancy: the first, observing the Alcoa Australia smelter in Point Henry in Geelong from afar, and the second, observing accumulated memory of vacancy in Geelong city centre.

Intimacy of distant observation: Alcoa Australia smelter in Point Henry, Geelong

Alcoa's Point Henry aluminium smelter began its operation in 1961 when Alcoa of Australia Limited established a joint venture with Western Mining Group and Aluminium Company of America (ALCOA). The smelter closed down in 2014 due to financial unviability after fifty-one years of operations.[17] The Alcoa landholding at Point Henry spans more than 575 hectares, of that there is around fifty hectares of fenced production area, the rest is variously designated as coastal salt wetland in the headland of Point Henry, salt marsh in the inner Stingaree Bay, and farmland and woodland at the southeast inland. More than seventy per cent of Point Henry is under water or low lying and subject to tidal or seasonal inundation.[18] Point Henry has been a significant part of the growth of Geelong and has been described topographically as an extending welcoming arm into Corio Bay.[19]

Creative methodology

The project on the Alcoa manufacturing plant at Point Henry by Evelyn Jing Pan focussed on alternative ways of observing, experiencing and projecting a new reality for Alcoa, for this site. The creative work examines what it means to observe an architectural subject through two perspectives: seeing and being. The concept of "seeing and being" is borrowed from Taiji Miyasaka's publication, *Seeing and Making in Architecture: Design Exercises*.[20] Based on a similar aspiration, the "seeing" aspect of this project deals with visual observation, the act of a person who sees Alcoa from various locations, distances and visually projects Alcoa's existence at relatively different scales. The visual projection sees the importance of its architectural meaning in contextual, relational, and temporal ways; the project reconstructs the frame of our perception and reference through physical interaction.[21] In contrast, the "being" aspect is relevant to the experience of Alcoa in its current condition. "Being" engaged in a conversation between Alcoa's self-representation of its presence and the space from where observation was conducted. "Being" as a noun implies the characteristic of existence and as a verb describes the progressive changing characters as presented to understand its environment.[22]

What follows presents some of these projections in creative research. The modes of fabrication/making/crafting/projection expand our understanding of seeing and being as embodied in two distances: a "formal-distant" distance, in the layers of accumulation of recorded photographing observed from a distance from Geelong's city centre, and an "intimate" distance through the construction of a drawing machine. The shift of focus from the architectural subject of Alcoa, to viewing it as a field, is not to dismiss the structural, typological, social and cultural thinking. Rather, it reconstructs Alcoa's presence in a much larger context along the driving corridor of Corio Bay (Princes Highway). Importantly, through the experimental creative process of projecting distant observation of intimate encounters, the enquiry explores the potential spatio-temporal nature of the relation between seeing and being. The research was framed and approached from the concept of seeing and being in an experimental manner of investigation through an observation method. The critical reflection was carried out in the format of an architectural photographic study and field study travelled by car. The documentation of such a journey describes the process, motion, views and perceptions, to provoke thinking and understanding.

Observation routes

Point Henry, as the orbiting centre of Corio Bay's drive-through-corridor, offered a 264-degree view towards the bay and vice versa. The two routes of observation were selected for the reason of their respective equivalent viewing scale and relative distance to Point Henry. Various locations were selected along Corio Bay and Point Henry to observe Alcoa from far and near, to study the extent of its visual visibility inland and the range of visual impact it had on the surrounding environment (see Figure 11.1).

By placing the observation points at various locations, Alcoa belongs simultaneously to multiple and interlocking scales, pulled away from the building scale towards a more public scale and as collective reference.[23] Both Journey 1, from Avalon to Clifton Springs, and Journey 2, from Cheetham Road to Point Henry Road, were recorded and photographed. Each of the thirty-six stopping points was selected based on the accessibility to a car and the visibility of Alcoa at each location.

---

[17] Warren Sharp, *Forward, Point Henry Smelter: Our Past, Our People 1963-2014* (Geelong: Alcoa, 2014).

[18] Sharp, *Forward, Point Henry Smelter*.

[19] Danny Lannen, "Alcoa- End of Era, 1961-2014,", *Geelong Advertiser*, February 20, 2014, 20.

[20] Taiji Miyasaka, *Seeing and Making in Architecture: Design Exercises* (New York: Routledge, 2014).

[21] Juhani Pallasmaa, "Newness, Tradition and Identity: Existential Content and Meaning in Architecture", *Architectural Design* 82, no. 6 (2012): 20.

[22] Andrea Simitch and Val Warke, *The Language of Architecture: 26 Principles Every Architect Should Know* (Massachusetts: Rockport Publishers, 2014), 102.

[23] Simitch and Warke, *The Language of Architecture*, 108.

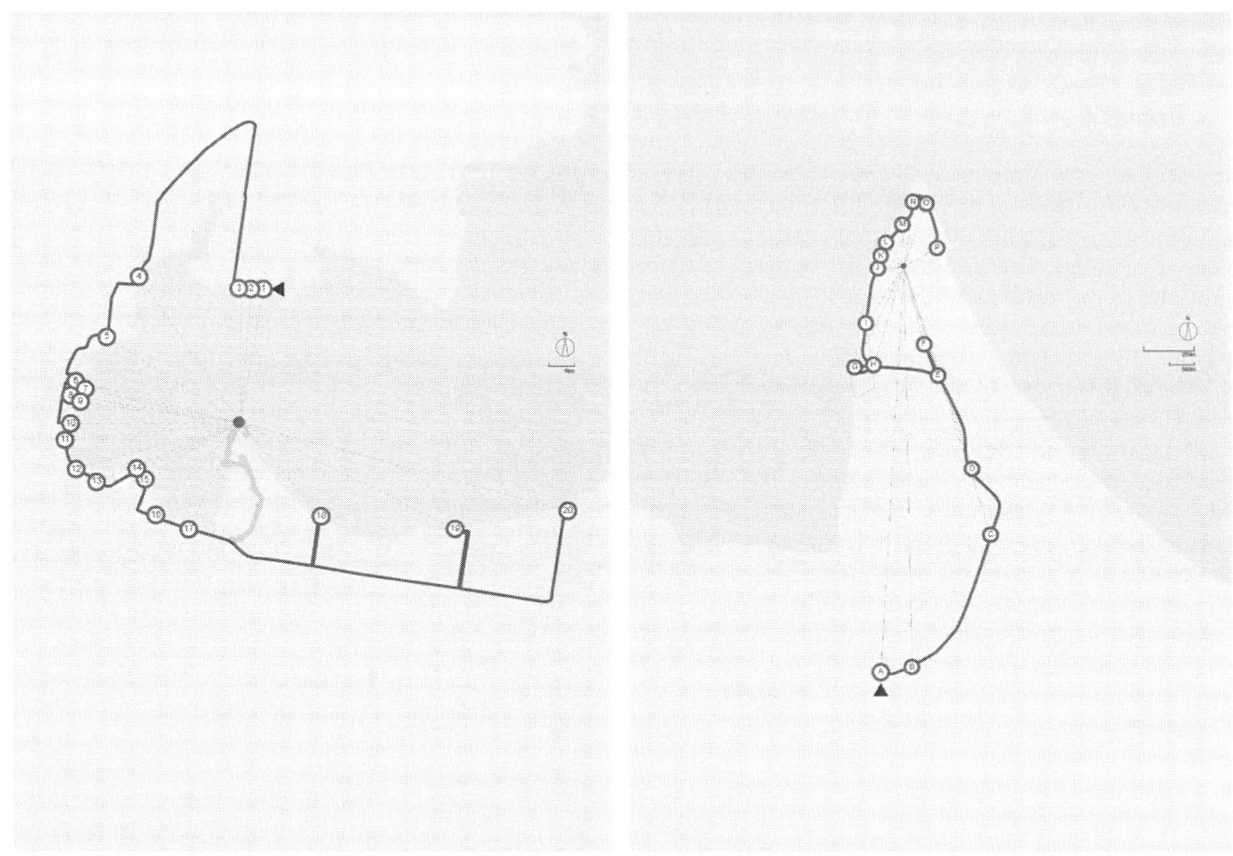

Journey 1 – Observation Route
Total Length: 58.3km
Number of Stops: 20
Begin From Stop 1- Avalon Costal Reserve

Journey 2- Observation Route
Total Length: 6.6km
Number of Stops: 16
Begin From Stop A - Cheetham Rd

Figure 11.1 Left: Observation route map for Journey 1: Avalon Coastal Reserve to Clifton Springs. Right: Observation route map for Journey 2: Cheetham Road to Point Henry Road. Drawing by Evelyn Jing Pan.

Seeing – photography journey: Let your eyes take the lead

Firstly, let us consider seeing through photography and the interpretation of seeing. Architectural photography techniques by Bernd and Hilla Becher, and Charles Negre were studied and explored on the observational seeing journey of Alcoa.[24] As a documentary method, Negre takes three types of photographs: one for architects, one for sculptors, and one for painters.[25] These techniques were applied to the photographic exploration, which focused on depicting the precision of geometric elevation, details of elements and expressive or subjective interpretations by the photographer on Alcoa. The exploration process helped in gaining control of composing comparable visual information in the precision planning of the subsequent photographic journey. A water tower found in Alcoa was used as a consistent reference object and a focal point in Journey 1; a permanent survey mark in Point Henry was used in measuring the direct distance to each observation point in Journey 2 (see Figure 11.2).

Photographs were taken at a static location directly next to the location of the car at each observation point along the two journeys, thus differing from the conventional pedestrian perspective. Although the camera was set at a fixed lens and height, it does not replace reality of the eye, instead it projects a slice of the reality that can be taken away for new discovery. By recognising the visual dominance and reoccurring event or object, the value of Alcoa's existence in each location is prioritised, and the visual implication becomes apparent. Photographs became the method of documentation in this research, providing comparable visual data that was further analysed using Edward R. Tufte's technique on visual

---

[24] James S. Ackerman, "On the Origins of Architectural Photography", in Kester Rattenbury (ed), *This is not Architecture: Media Constructions* (London and New York: Routledge, 2002), 26–35.
[25] Kester Rattenbury, *This is not Architecture: Media Constructions* (London and New York: Routledge, 2002).

Figure 11.2 Seeing and being: photos showing camera set-up and focal reference axis.

explanation (see Figure 11.3).[26] Tufte believed that those 'who discover an explanation are often those who construct its representation.'[27]

Secondly, let us consider the documentation and recording of experience on the same routes where seeing is conducted. A drawing device is designed and assembled to record motion from the moving vehicle, to project the quality of its surrounding environment, human interaction, and time. The investigative framework set out by the concept of seeing and being was realised and synthesised through the experimental drawing device purposely constructed for this research. Inspired by Tim Knowles' apparatus used in the Trans-Alp project, the mock-up version was crafted and used as a drawing tool.[28] This experimental drawing device was made using readily available materials, such as track access wheels, aluminium top mount track, timber, Perspex, pen, and circular aluminium tube in combination with pipe rings as pen holder. While developing a few improvements to reduce damping and impact forces, the 1.0 m × 0.9 m rectangular drawing device was secured at the back of a car, and the pen was designed to slide along the two axial directions when the car was in operation (see Figure 11.4).

---

[26] Edward R Tufte, *Visual Explanations: Images and Quantities, Evidences and Narrative* (Cheshire: Graphics Press, 1997), 19. A constant scale factor is used in this visual table of Alcoa and Point Henry extracted from the twenty locations included in Journey 1. Reading this table in conjunction with location data provides a visual understanding of the distance and its visual representation. This visual representation method has been studied by Edward Tufte and used in the visual table displaying Herbert Matter's Portfolio of photographs of Alberto Giacometti's sculptures.

[27] Tufte, *Visual Explanations: Images and Quantities, Evidences and Narrative.*

[28] Tim Knowles, Vehicle motion drawing (trans-alp), project, 2006. See also, Tim Knowles, "Tree Drawings: The limbs limn", *Cabinet* 28 (Winter 2007-2008), http://www.cabinetmagazine.org.

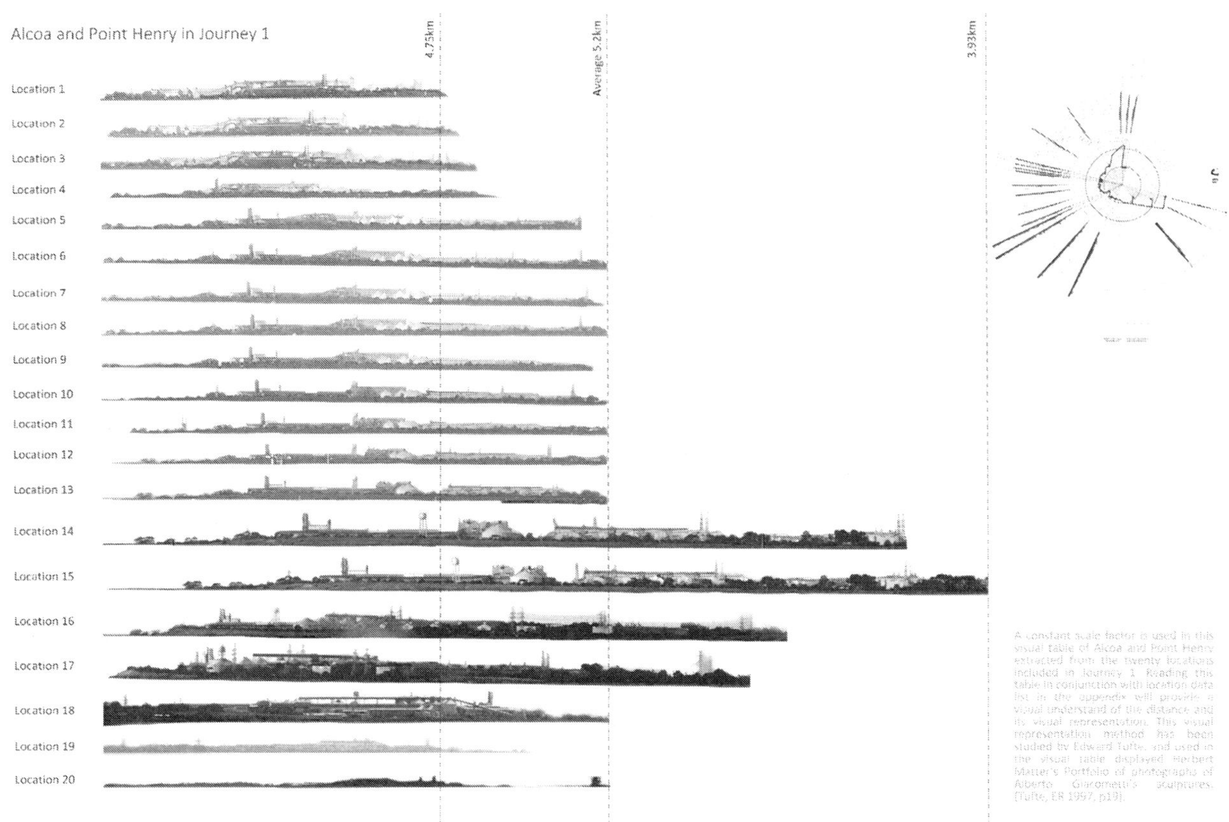

Figure 11.3 Visual table, adapted from Edward Tufte, of Alcoa and Point Henry using a constant scale factor and extracted from the twenty locations included in Journey 1. Drawing composed by Evelyn Jing Pan.

Being – field study, drawing device recording: Let your pen take the lead

The drawings produced are often site dependent and vary with factors such as driving speed, number of stops, road surface condition, and inertia. However, the resemblance of the same directional gesture can still be visible in the same driving routes. The expressive nature of the drawings left room for imaginary inquiries linking experience with visual interpretation (see Figure 11.5). The sensorial topography of the extended distant observation journey travelled by car became visually represented for further elaboration.

Creative reflection

The sensory synchronisation of the seeing and being in this exploratory documentation method allowed a perspectival thinking process to take shape in the visual assembly of photographs and drawings. The seeing is distilled in the photographs, and the being is reflected on the drawings. The photographs taken at a distance diminish the inhuman scale of industrial buildings such as Alcoa (see Figure 11.6 in the colour plate section); the drawings drawn by the drawing device are intimate recordings of the motion from the moving vehicle, yet abstract and distant from the reality seen through our eyes (see Figure 11.7).

As an observer, when the being is visualised and the seeing is experienced, the frame of perception is inverted. The projected reality is "introjected", as in the term Pallasmaa used to describe the simultaneous projection of the self-internalised and the self-projected out in the space.[29] This method offers an alternative way of referencing our point of view in comparison with a conventional site analysis or the presentation of an itinerary map. Seeing and being are often paralleled, as forming the basis of observation. What must be emphasised is that the paired concept reveals the level of intimacy required for extracting distant observations through this experiment. The importance of observation lies in the role of structuring the vivacity of our imaginary perception and the reconstruction of the world we see, understand and experience.[30] Place and movement, view and perception, identity and memory, space and time are never detached as an independent, abstract substance of human culture; instead, these coherent layers of structure rely on interpretation to be pulled away from preconception and to form an alternative perception.

---

[29] Juhani Pallasmaa, "Empathic Imagination: Formal and Experiential Projection", *Architectural Design* 84, no. 5 (2014): 80–85.
[30] Elaine Scarry, *Dreaming by the Book* (Princeton: Princeton University Press, 1999), 9.

Making Of the Drawing Device

Position of the Drawing Device in Car

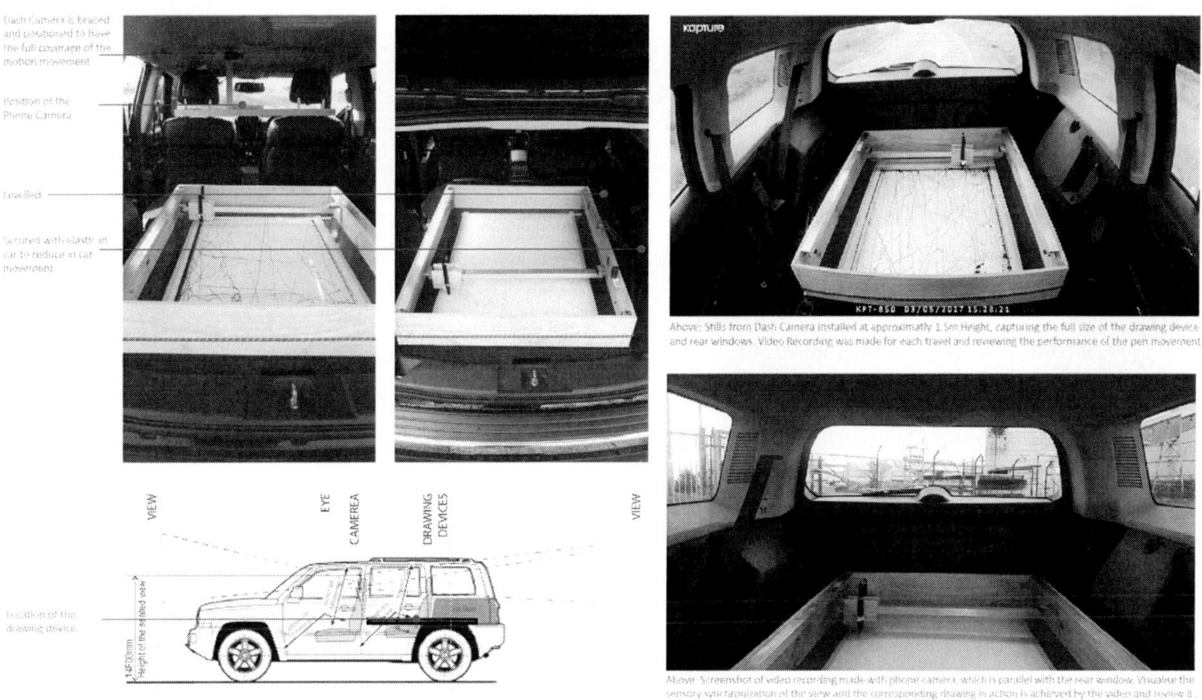

Figure 11.4 Top: Photos showing the construction process of the drawing machine. Bottom: Camera view of the drawing machine secured inside the vehicle. Image composition by Evelyn Jing Pan.

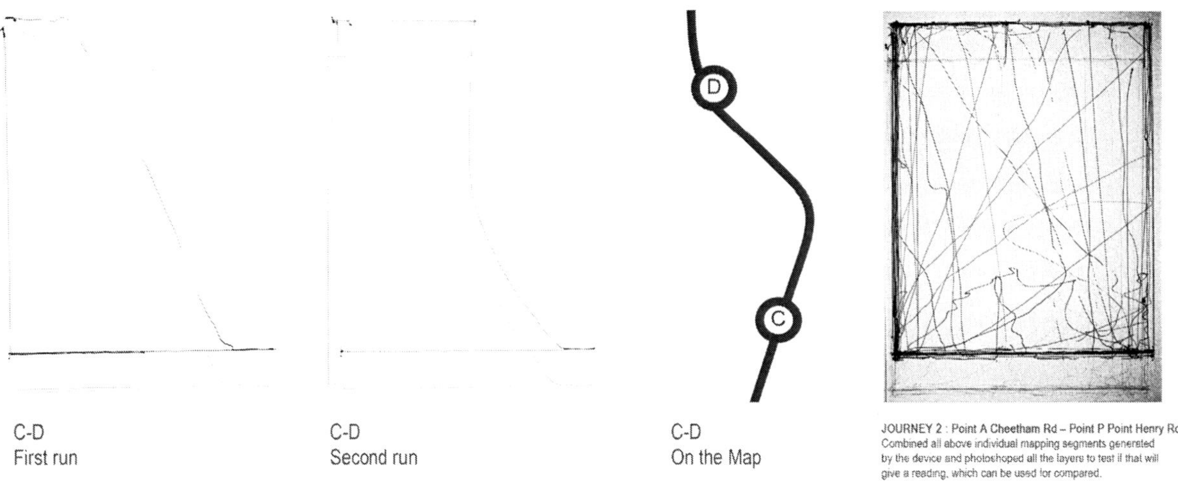

Figure 11.5 Test drawings from the drawing machine finding repetitive behaviour and variance. Drawing composed by Evelyn Jing Pan.

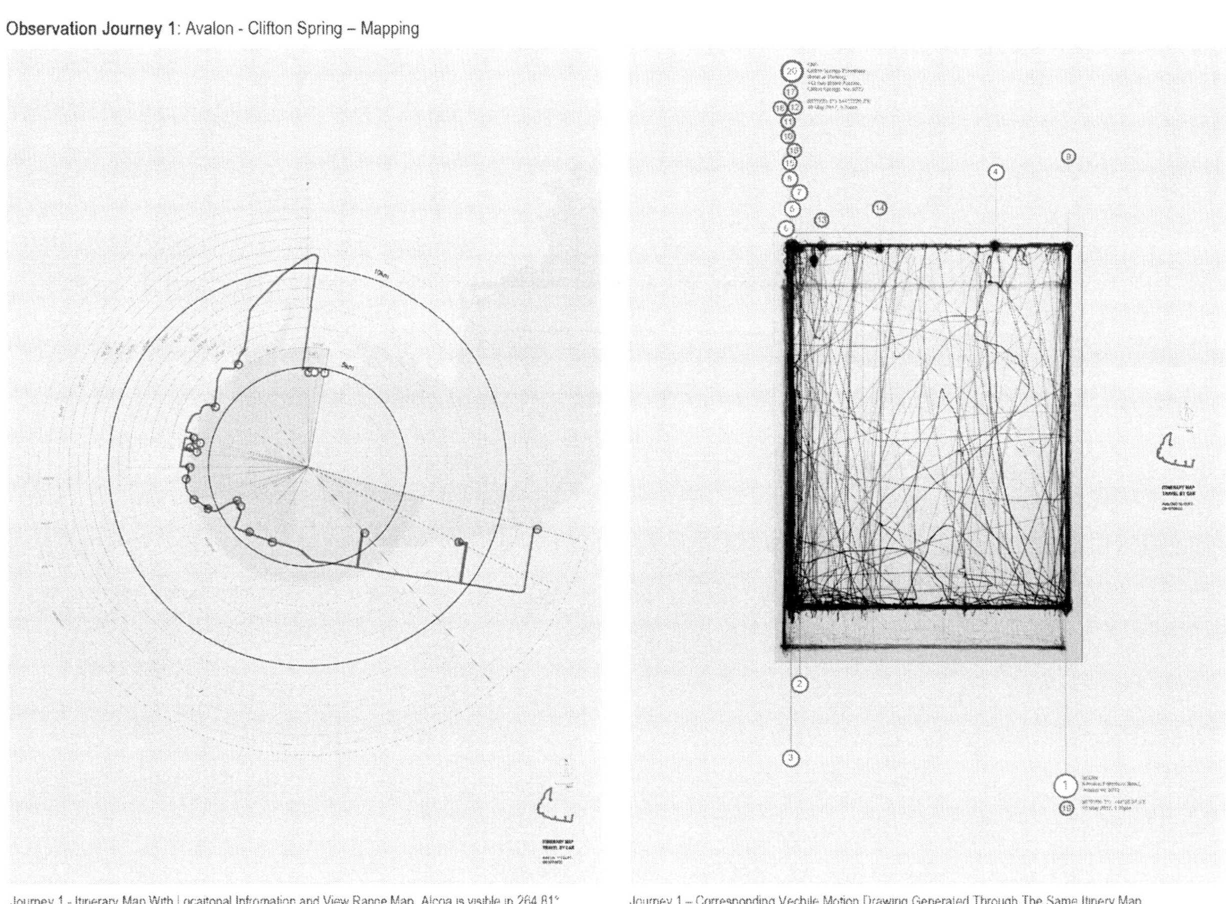

Figure 11.7 Summative mapping and itinerary map of travelled routes of observation Journey 1. Drawing composed by Evelyn Jing Pan.

Intimacy of layered observation: Geelong city centre

The second creative project by Angelina Chan Yee Ching examines vacancy through chronological layers of the history of vacant buildings in Geelong's CBD. In this process, "transparency" becomes a medium through which layering of history and vacant buildings evolves into a visual presence. Specifically in architecture, Colin Rowe and Robert Slutzky write that 'transparency means a simultaneous perception of different spatial locations.'[31] Following Rowe and Slutzky, in this project, transparency means more than a physical overlap, rather it implies more of a spatial characteristic or depth of vacancy that is investigated through mapping – expanding our understanding of memory as embodied in the layers of accumulation of vacant buildings in Geelong's city centre.

The deindustrialisation of Geelong is not only seen at the industrial sites along the shoreline of Corio Bay, but also along the streets of Geelong's city centre. The state of lost identity of Geelong has not only led to negative economic growth, but also to an evident state of absence in the built environment in the CBD. However, this absence could also be seen as an opportunity to seek a new identity for Geelong. Through the operative process of mapping and layering, this creative project investigated how vacancy can be found, gathered and exposed, as well as related, connected and speculated upon, to unfurl the potential of the vacant sites. This potential is a latent dimension of vacancy – it records the present nuanced reality of the vacant site, the past as forgotten history, and the future as a possible (non)vacant site. The focus was not on the precision of scientific mapping and the actual geographical features, instead mapping was used as a creative medium to open reality up to a host of alternate possibilities and reveal the hidden potential of Geelong's vacant sites.

Creative methodology

The creative work adapted and expanded on three mapping techniques following James Corner's work, "The Agency of Mapping: Speculation, Critique and Invention".[32] These mapping techniques included drifting, layering and rhizome.

The first technique of "drift" or "drifting", is described by Corner as a rapid passage through varied ambiances, involving playful constructive behaviours and an awareness of psycho-geographical effects.[33] Exploring vacancy in Geelong through drifting encouraged chance happenings through participation with the environment and was investigated through the spatial experience of the researcher walking through the city centre (see Figure 11.8 in the colour plate section). In this case, drifting precipitated a series of interpretative and participatory acts through the awareness of vacancy and the behaviour of recording the detected vacancy.

The second technique, "layering", drew out and identified data and information gathered in the drifting phase of the mapping process (see Figure 11.9). Here, layering is practiced less as an accumulation or overlay as in traditional maps and prescriptive data, and more as orchestrating the transparency of various layers of vacancy (present vacancy and past vacancy) into a new event (or a "thickened transparency"), where the layering remains open to any number of interpretations, uses and transformations.

The third mapping technique of "rhizome" is described by Corner, referencing Deleuze and Guattari's work, as having 'neither beginning nor end, but always a middle (*milieu*) from which it grows and overspills'.[34] Accordingly, rhizome has a transparent, open ended and indeterminate characteristic. Importantly, rather than limiting the reality of Geelong's vacant buildings and sites, the physical transparency of each mapping process and the resulting crafted drawings, enable the rhizomatic mapping to open reality up to a host of new and alternate possibilities.

Creative reflection

Throughout the creative mapping process, interrelationships between documented and extracted data were isolated from their original states. As Corner states, 'once data is extracted, it may be studied, manipulated, and networked with other figures in the field'.[35] Different field systems will lead to different arrangements of the extracts, revealing alternative patterns and possibilities.[36] The extracted data was manipulated to create new sets of representation (see Figure 11.10 in the colour plate section).

Ultimately, the framework of the suggested mapping process could be used as a guideline in mapping and in manipulating new sets of data to depict completely different outcomes that depend on the methods of identifying vacancies. Although the end products of the mapping process can be looked at as artistic cartography, they depict, through the layers of data, the "absentness" of Geelong. Pickles explains, 'mapping[s] precede the territory they "represent"; they do not simply represent territory but are understood as producing it'.[37] The research undertaken here seeks to demonstrate a creative view of mapping in the context of interrelationships between vacancy in Geelong and its contradictory interface between history and memory.

---

[31] Colin Rowe and Robert Slutzky, *Transparency* (Basel: Birkhauser, 1997), 23.

[32] James Corner, "The Agency of Mapping: Speculation, Critique and Invention", in Denis Cosgrove (ed), *Mappings* (London: Reaktion, 1999), 213–52.

[33] Corner, "The Agency of Mapping".

[34] Corner, "The Agency of Mapping", 244.

[35] Corner, "The Agency of Mapping", 229.

[36] Corner, "The Agency of Mapping", 229.

[37] John Pickles, *A History of Spaces: Cartographic Reason, Mapping and the Geo-Coded World* (London: Routledge, 2004), quoted in Rob Kitchin and Martin Dodge, "Rethinking Maps", *Progress in Human Geography* 31, no. 3 (2007): 334.

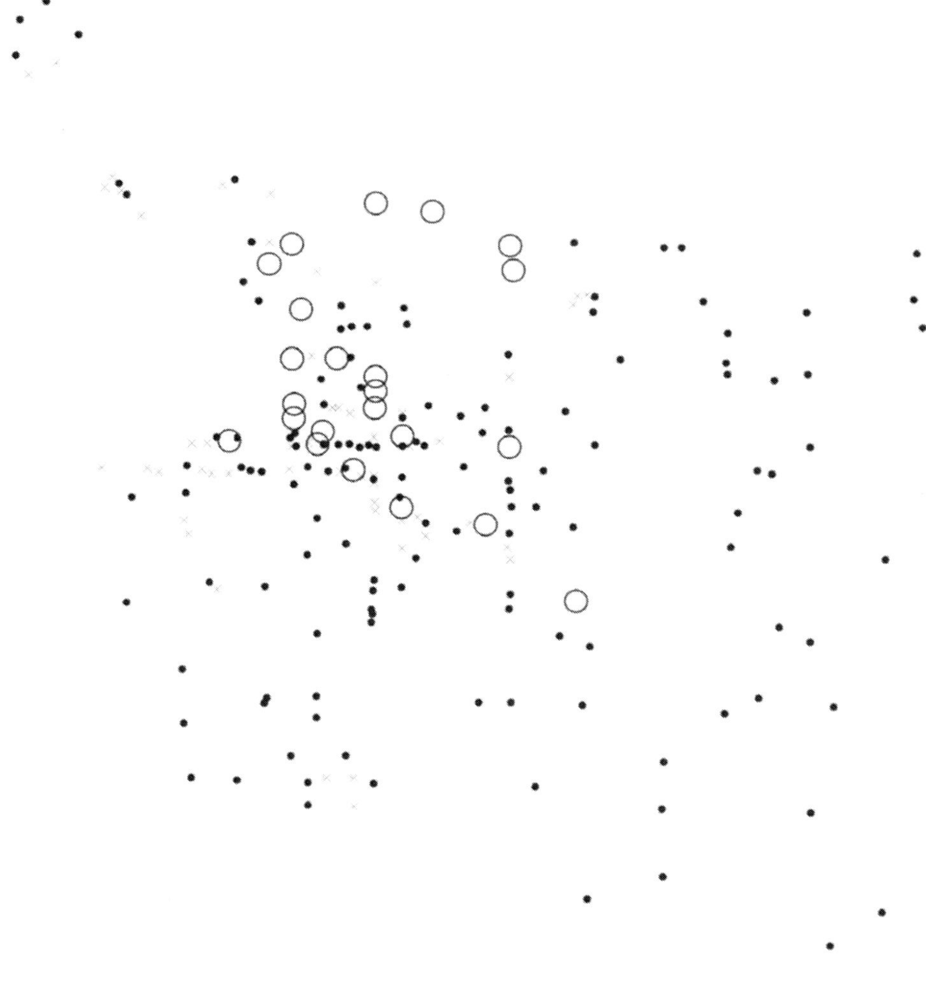

Figure 11.9 Layering: combined vacancy of 2015 and 2016, with overlapped spots marked. Layered drawing by Angelina Chan Yee Ching.

Concluding thoughts: Creative research as basis for radical pedagogy

The VacantGeelong project attracted Master of Architecture students to a new experimental learning program of creative research. Already familiar with the challenges the team of teachers had presented to them in the course, these courageous students embarked on a collaborative educational journey. Diego Fullaondo (Course Director of Master of Architecture) and Mirjana Lozanovska (leader of the pedagogical model) submitted a "creative research" option alongside traditional research as integral to the curriculum. In 2018, creative research became core and has led to a "design research" curriculum focus. A dynamic upper-level student experience empowered learning. This was highlighted by the exhibition of selected student work included in the *VacantGeelong* exhibition (2016) and the *Iconic Industry* major exhibition at National Wool Museum (August–October 2017).

However, inclusion of creative research in the curriculum does not ensure the critical and methodological rigour as demanded by radical pedagogy. Students were often frustrated with what is involved in creative research, and both staff and students were tempted towards a simplistic version of non-traditional research, or a hybrid model, featuring the addition of visual material alongside traditional modes of investigation. The team found they needed to articulate that creative research firstly requires critical and analytical investigation through creative methods – rather than an addition of "creativity" superimposed on the traditional. This is demonstrated in the intensity and rigour of observational recordings, the documentation in the approach of Evelyn Jing Pan, and the precise yet experimental ways of coding, notation, and mapping vacancy by Angelina Chan Yee Ching.

An "intensity of investigation" involves rigour in the methods – whether this be observation, documentation, or data collection. Assumptions are challenged. Rather than maintaining a binary perception between objective and subjective methods (or quantitative and qualitative), the students embarked on a pursuit to bring rigour, discipline and logic into their methods. An interface between objective methods and their dependency on rules, set parameters, limitations, variables, and subjective methods that can challenge paradigms, and bring insight and nuance to results, often evolved.

The teachers played a crucial role in challenging the methods towards more precision and meticulousness. As such, radical pedagogy demands a preparedness to take risk, albeit a measured risk.

Radical pedagogy is also a pedagogy that understands locality and experience in their multiplicities, with often conflicting interpretations and projections. Both projects presented in this chapter – Intimacies of distant observation and Intimacy of layered observation – acknowledge the local contextuality of Point Henry and Geelong city centre respectively and examine the vacancy in these localities through inventive wanderings and journeyings. By encouraging creative research methods through radical pedagogy, students' participation in the momentum and intensity of learning is a courageous interval and pause from the current fast-paced environments and top-down approaches to expedient solutions. The creative and meticulous labours of recording, representing, and expressing vacancy through intimacies of observation, offer an alternative, intriguing and novel lens for new research into Geelong's built environment and beyond.

CHAPTER 12

THE A+B STUDIO:
CONTRIBUTING DRIVERS FOR CHANGE WITH THE CITY
OF GREATER GEELONG 2000–2021

YOLANDA ESTEBAN, JOHN ROLLO AND JAMES DOERFLER

Introduction: Embedding A+B's studio culture within Geelong's CBD

Locating Deakin University's School of Architecture and Building, A+B, (now the School of Architecture and Built Environment) and its ten design studios into Geelong's central business district (CBD) in 1996 provided a step-change in design education within the school. Bringing "town and gown" closer together brought our students in proximity with the arts, business and civic precincts of a city on the verge of experiencing profound growth pressures at a previously unmatched pace of development. With this transition, architectural design education was extended to encompass the urban scale more profoundly than before, with the added opportunity of bringing local and state government-led projects into the studio program as applied design research.

The idea of inspiring Deakin students to engage with significant architecture and urban design projects within the city was first facilitated by Professor Daryl le Grew (head of the school from 1986 to 1994). Le Grew established a national student design competition in 1988, sponsored by the Geelong construction company, Hatwell Builders Pty Ltd. With significant media coverage of the winning entries, the competition became an apolitical vehicle for facilitating greater public awareness and interest in transformational urban change. In this same year, the Geelong Regional Commission (the main body guiding development in the region prior to the 1993 amalgamation of nine local government areas) released three vision documents, which coincided with the development of two major projects in central Geelong. The stage in a sense was set for consolidating a wave of development opportunities and for stimulating urban renewal within the city.

During the mid-to-late 1990s and into the first decade of the 2000s, the City of Greater Geelong established a Major Projects department as resources were being re-deployed from vision making to implementation. Two decades (1975–96) of promoting and refining ideas to enable the city to embrace its north-facing aspect and redevelop the waterfront was to become a reality. A series of adaptive reuse designs led to the expansion of Deakin University into the Dalgety (and later Lascelles) Woolstores. Public support and civic pride grew through the transformation of the waterfront, and new strategic initiatives started to emerge.[1]

In 2002 the Department of Sustainability and Environment (DSE), now the Department of Primary Industries, supported an investigation with the City of Greater Geelong into the revitalisation of the "Western Wedge", a mix of old industrial and residential areas wedged between the rail corridor of Geelong West, Corio Bay and central Geelong. This initiative driven by Rod Duncan, a strategic Planner within DSE, launched the Western Wedge project to key stakeholders and the wider community through A+B's apolitical studio program Urbanheart, which was established in 1999 and had predominantly been working with the City of Port Phillip and the City of Bendigo.[2] The outcome of this initiative was positive. Energy was channelled into consolidating the development of a new suite of urban design guidelines and urban design frameworks.[3] The stage was now set for design studios within A+B to undertake a range of project-based learning outcomes by engaging the students in design briefs in Geelong and regional Victoria, as well as engaging with other stakeholders in programs such as the Prefab 21 (Prefabricated House in the 21st Century) design-build studio, which will be discussed in the second part of the chapter.

---

[1] John Rollo and Yolanda Esteban, "The Promise of Vision-Making a City: A Perpetual Journey", David S. Jones and Phillip B. Roös (eds), *Geelong's Changing Landscape: Ecology, Development and Conservation* (Collingwood: CSIRO Publishing, 2019), 268–92.
[2] John Rollo, "Urbanheart: A Design Research Forum", *Architectural Research Quarterly*, 8, no. 3-4 (2004), 325–31.
[3] Planisphere and Jones & Whitehead Pty Ltd, *Geelong Western Wedge Framework*, (City of Greater Geelong, April 2005, updated September 2005); City of Greater Geelong, *Central Geelong Urban Design Guidelines*, 2008.

Urbanheart – 1999–2021

The pedagogy

Recognising the pressure of United Kingdom government policy 'in the late 1990s to make the final two years of a consecutive five-year course more definitively post graduate', Peter Blundell Jones, Alan Williams and Jo Lintonbon at the School of Architectural Studies, Sheffield University, followed the lead of John Tuomey and Shelley McNamara from University College, Dublin, to incorporate studio teaching with real research on the city and its history.[4] Around the same time that Sheffield began the history studio program, the School of Architecture and Building at Deakin University began developing an integrated design research forum. Referred to as "Urbanheart Surgery", the studio applied an element of rigour to coordinating a pedagogy that facilitated explorative and innovative thinking based on a range of options and permutations to deriving design solutions.[5] This pedagogy was partly inspired by Leslie Martin with his essay "The Grid as Generator".[6]

In his essay, Martin advocated 'a strong theoretical basis for urban design', which provided a fresh perspective on the notion of formal planning and design processes that had previously been challenged by Jane Jacobs with her 1961 work, *The Death and Life of Great American Cities,* and Christopher Alexander's 1966 essay "A City is not a Tree".[7] Methodologically shifting parameters, Martin adapted Frensel's square diagram as an example of how to generate eight "alternatives" regarding the way 'in which buildings [could be] placed on the land'.[8] The diagram (see Figure 12.1) illustrates nine successive annular rings, diminishing in width, yet preserving the same area of its predecessor. Martin's rationale followed that while the different permutations probably wouldn't have been considered through an informal means of designing, they nonetheless 'allow wider scope for decisions and objectives' to be considered and discussed, hence promoting discussion about the complications and implications of each morphological structure.[9]

Involving representatives from the profession, state government and local planning authorities in a conference style method of course delivery, students were provided with a large body of knowledge in the early stages of the program. Students conducted their project work in teams of three, referred to as "design collaboratives". Following a two-week period of preliminary research – involving site/precinct investigation, context analysis and SWOT assessment – tutorial groups generated numerous ideas and "what if?" scenarios within a think tank environment. Working within a set of constructs – such as socio-economic and demographic projections, or public and private space – ideas were pooled across the whole studio and classed within a matrix of permutations (see Figure 12.1). Each design collaborative adopted one of the permutations and resolved their respective strategy into a highly developed proposal.[10]

The studio program

The Urbanheart Surgery program, pioneered in the School of Architecture and Built Environment at Deakin University, has been active in engaging with the city on numerous occasions over the past twenty years (see Figure 12.2). The program was designed with the purpose of allowing local government authorities to bring key projects into the university and to allow students to assist with projecting ideas, exploring both their implications and opportunities, five and ten years into the future. With over 1500 students participating in the studio since 1999, Urbanheart was designed to immerse students within a design research culture that allowed them to engage in critical discourse by working on strategic design projects in three areas critical to the state of Victoria's future development: metropolitan urbanism, urbanism on the periphery and regional urbanism.

The aim of the program was to identify and analyse various factors that make up a precinct's existing conditions, and to develop a range of generic strategies and design proposals that address a set of predetermined issues and parameters. Developed with local planning authorities prior to the commencement of the trimester, these issues often involved the consolidation of suburban sprawl, the resolution of areas of discontinuity, or the development of options for stimulating urban renewal.

---

[4] Peter Blundell Jones, Alan Williams and Jo Lintonbon, "The Sheffield Urban Study Project", *Architect Research Quarterly arq* 3, 3.

[5] John Rollo, "Eco-island: Urban, Heart Surgery :1.002 - Uncharted Territory and Unlimited Horizons", *Architect Victoria* (November 2002).

[6] Leslie Martin, "The Grid as Generator", in Leslie Martin and Lionel March (eds), *Urban Space and Structures* (Cambridge: Cambridge University Press, 1972), 6–27.

[7] Martin, "The Grid as Generator"; Jane Jacobs, *The Death and Life of Great American Cities* (New York City: Random House, 1961); Christopher Alexander, "A City is not a Tree", *Architectural Forum* 122 (1964) 58–61.

[8] John Rollo and Yolanda Esteban, "Urbanheart Surgery - A logic of Design Alternatives", MODSIM, *19th International Congress on Modelling and Simulation, Perth, Australia, 12–16 December 2011,* (2011) http://mssanz.org.au/modsim2011.

[9] Martin, "The Grid as Generator".

[10] Rollo and Esteban, "Urbanheart Surgery - A logic of Design Alternatives".

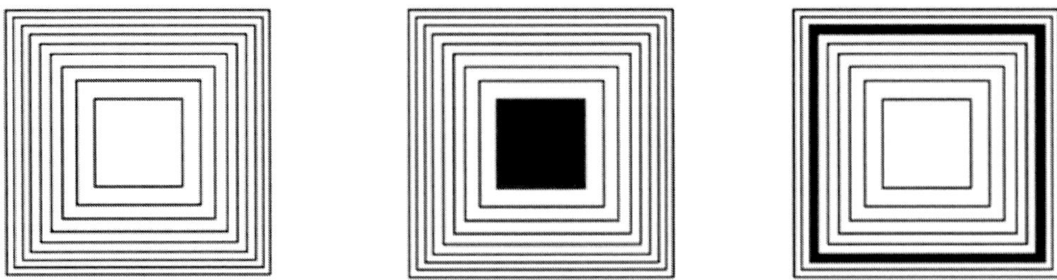

Fresnel's square diagram adapted by Sir Leslie Martin presents nine successive annular rings diminishing in width yet preserving the same area of its predecessor.

Figure 12.1 An example of a design matrix illustrating generic alternatives from a correlation of public and private land use with built form and open space. Although the matrix provides a landscape of hybrid combinations, each combination holds an extensive array of urban design outcomes and architectural visions.

The program introduced seven objectives to the students at the start of a trimester:

- Develop an understanding of the place of architecture within the context of the city.
- Assist local governments in anticipating change and enhancing their brief development processes by presenting the studio as a platform for explorative strategic thinking.
- Engender a sense of social value and receptiveness through the community consultation process.
- Understand the current and future requirements of an integrated urban culture and the significance of a regional city in the state of Victoria.
- Establish a forum that breaks down piecemeal development between neighbouring municipalities and to facilitate a landscape of decision-making that stimulates an integrated approach to design within the urban context.
- Enhance community awareness of the architectural profession.
- Become familiar with the building and construction industries' current action agenda by developing architecture and building through collaborative and interdisciplinary design/development initiatives.

Students were first introduced to urban design as a multi-disciplinary process involving a wide range of stakeholders both within a municipality and across adjacent precincts. They were also made aware that it involves thinking about opportunities and visions at all scales, but in particular, their implications and consequences in the immediate and long term time frame.

By treating study areas with varying levels of objectivity, the purpose of the forum was not to resolve a "finite", "optimum" or "ideal" solution, but to collectively identify a broad range of opportunities. This avoided convergence of ideas within the cohort, which can often leave significant gaps in alternative design solutions. Hence all students became familiar with a more extensive set of outcomes and problem-solving abilities.[11]

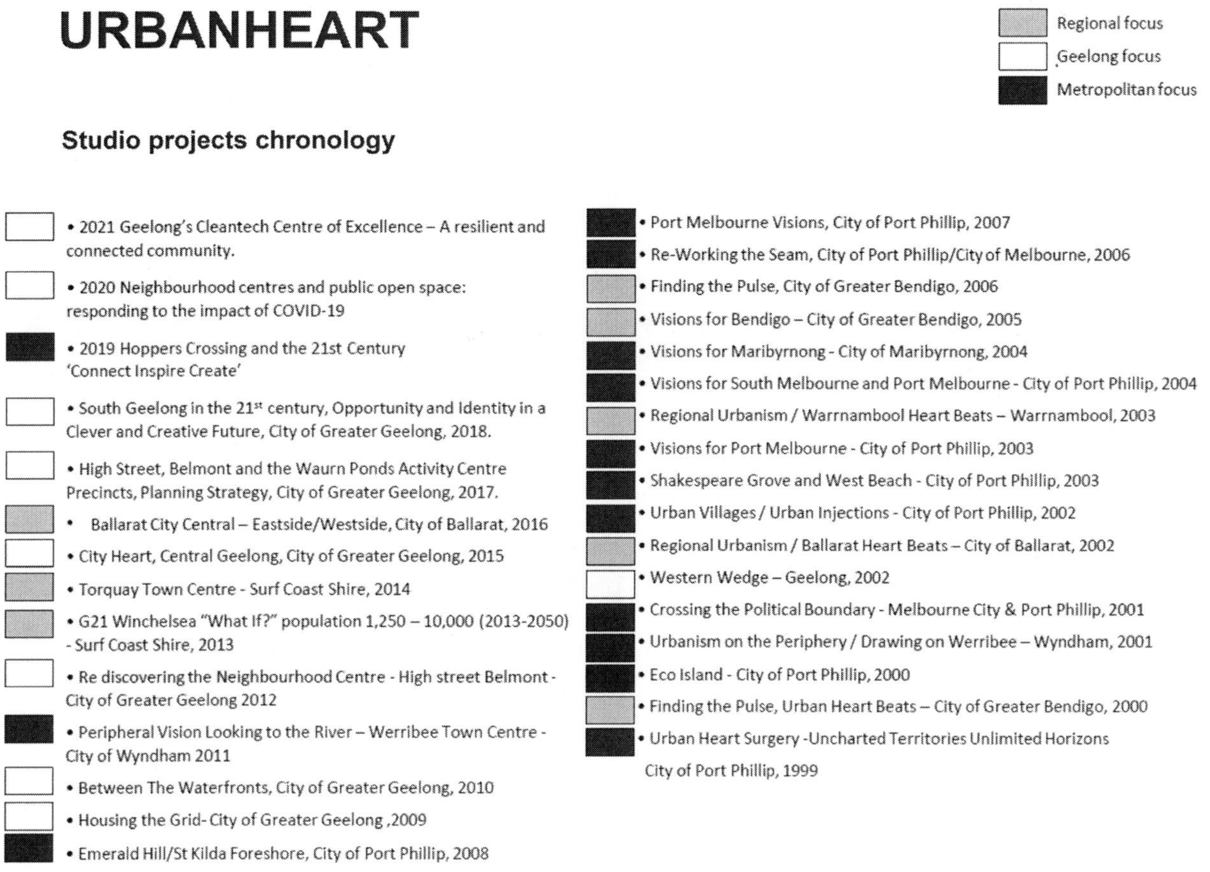

URBANHEART

Figure 12.2 Urbanheart studio programs 1999–2021.

During the 2009 and 2010 workshops, the focus of the Urbanheart Surgery program was centred on two areas: housing provision in the centre of Geelong; and the physical connections between the waterfront, the city centre and the Barwon River. The image in Figure 12.3 presents a series of permutations developed by students exploring the relationships between the Geelong Railway Station precinct, the Arts and Cultural precinct and the Brougham Street spine, including the Deakin University precinct.

A number of CBD-targeted programs saw the development of student visions and ideas for the Western Wedge (2002, see Figure 12.4), inner city student accommodation (2009), the revitalisation of the city's urban morphology through the reinvigoration of streets and laneways (2010), and the development of a city "heart" (2015). Other Urbanheart Surgery programs have focused on areas of Geelong outside the immediate CBD area, such as High Street in Belmont (2012, 2017) and Waurn Ponds Shopping Centre (2017). In 2015, the program collaborated with the City of Greater Geelong on their City Heart strategy whilst they were working on City in a Park, a vision developed by Steven Thorne and Robert Adams.[12] It is important to note that for most of these contributions, the program did not align itself with any official published vision by council, but rather chose to remain as an incubator for generating a range of ideas and design options, which was a key aspect of the studio program.[13]

---

[11] John Rollo and Yolanda Esteban, "Urbanheart Surgery – A Collaborative Interdisciplinary Design Studio" in P. Collins and I. Gibson (eds), *Proceedings of the International Conference on Design and Technology, DesTech 2016* (2017).

[12] Crane, "Geelong Council Announces $90m Green CBD Vision", *Geelong Advertiser*, May 10, 2015.

[13] Rollo and Esteban, "The Promise of Vision-Making a City: A Perpetual Journey".

Urbanheart reflections

Since its introduction in 1999, Urbanheart developed into a successful teaching, research, and public and community relations program. It not only secured an ongoing relationship with various planning authorities, but its core of industrial partnerships expanded to include five regional councils (Bendigo, Ballarat, Geelong, Warrnambool, and Surfcoast Shire), three metropolitan municipalities (Melbourne City, Port Phillip and Wyndham) and close links with various branches of the state government. The ability of local governments to explore strategic planning options is severely limited by time, money and resources. In the process of attempting to help fill this gap, the program became a platform where metropolitan and regional municipalities were, for a brief moment, able to engage in positive apolitical discourse between members of the architectural profession and construction industry, local communities, and both state and local governments. This was executed at two levels, within the studio through interim and final review sessions, and via the installation of a number of public exhibitions. The exhibitions informed the public with regards to the vital role that architects can play in moulding their built environment, and councils are able to utilise the work in testing community response to both the type and degree of change that their community is willing to embrace.[14]

Prefab 21 design-build studio

The A+B studio at Deakin University has a decades long history of engaging with Geelong and regional Victoria. Ongoing studio projects with various stakeholders has exposed the students to working directly with clients to learn about regional concerns and support a culture of community engagement. The projects have been based less on theory and more on providing real world solutions and encouraging social activism.

Among the more significant trends in architectural education in recent decades is the introduction of design-build projects to the curriculum. One of the most prolific and first established design-build programs was the Rural Studio at Auburn University in Alabama, United States. Catering for the needs of an impoverished rural community in Alabama through its design-build activities, Rural Studio lead the way internationally as a university-affiliated architecture program with a social remit.[15] The program at Auburn, developed in 1993, realised built projects in the form of innovative houses for poor people living in Alabama's second-poorest county, by relying largely on donated and salvaged materials.[16]

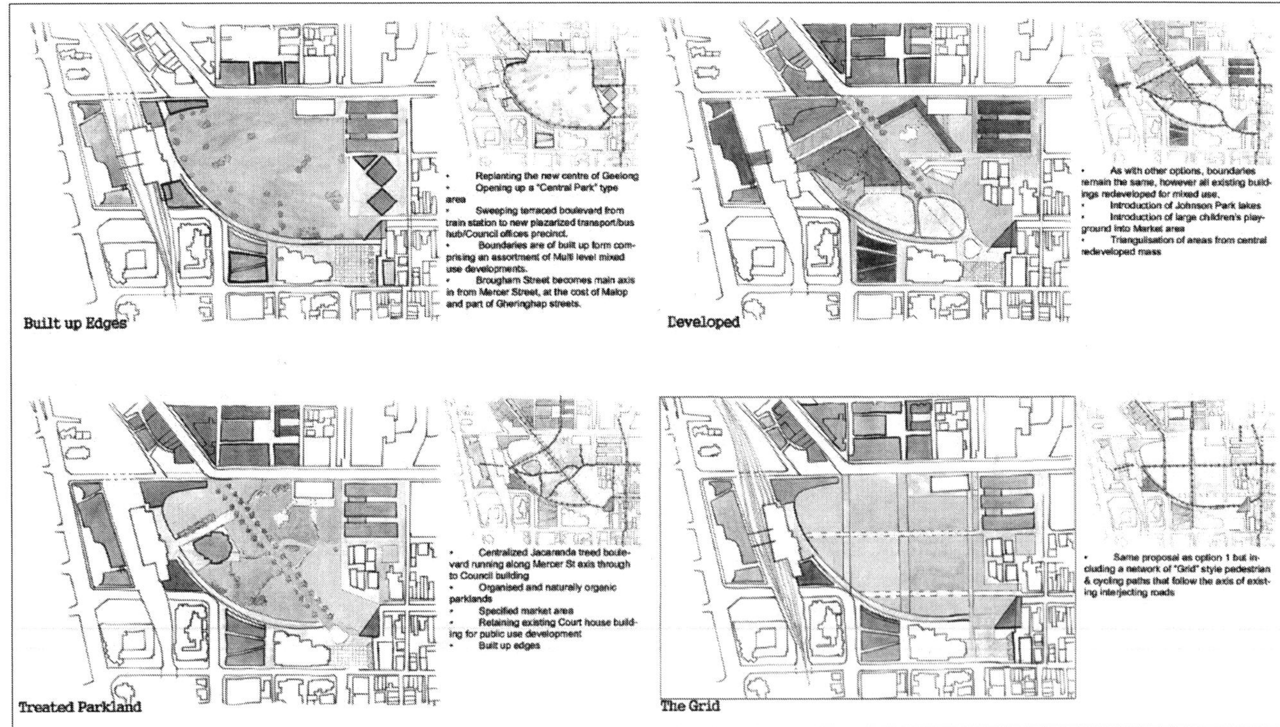

Figure 12.3 City of Greater Geelong, Housing the Grid, 2010. Source: Urbanheart student design team at Deakin University: Jandi Vagg, Tim McErvale, Timothy Fullwood (all plan images are not presented at original scale).

[14] Rollo and Esteban, "Urbanheart Surgery – A Collaborative Interdisciplinary Design Studio".
[15] Michael Ulrich Hensel, "Rural Studio: Incarnations of a Design-and-Build Programme", *Architectural Design* 85, no. 2 (March 2015).
[16] Thorsten Botz-Bornstein, "Cardboard Houses with Wings: The Architecture of Alabama's Rural Studio", *Journal of Aesthetic Education* 44, no. 3 (2010).

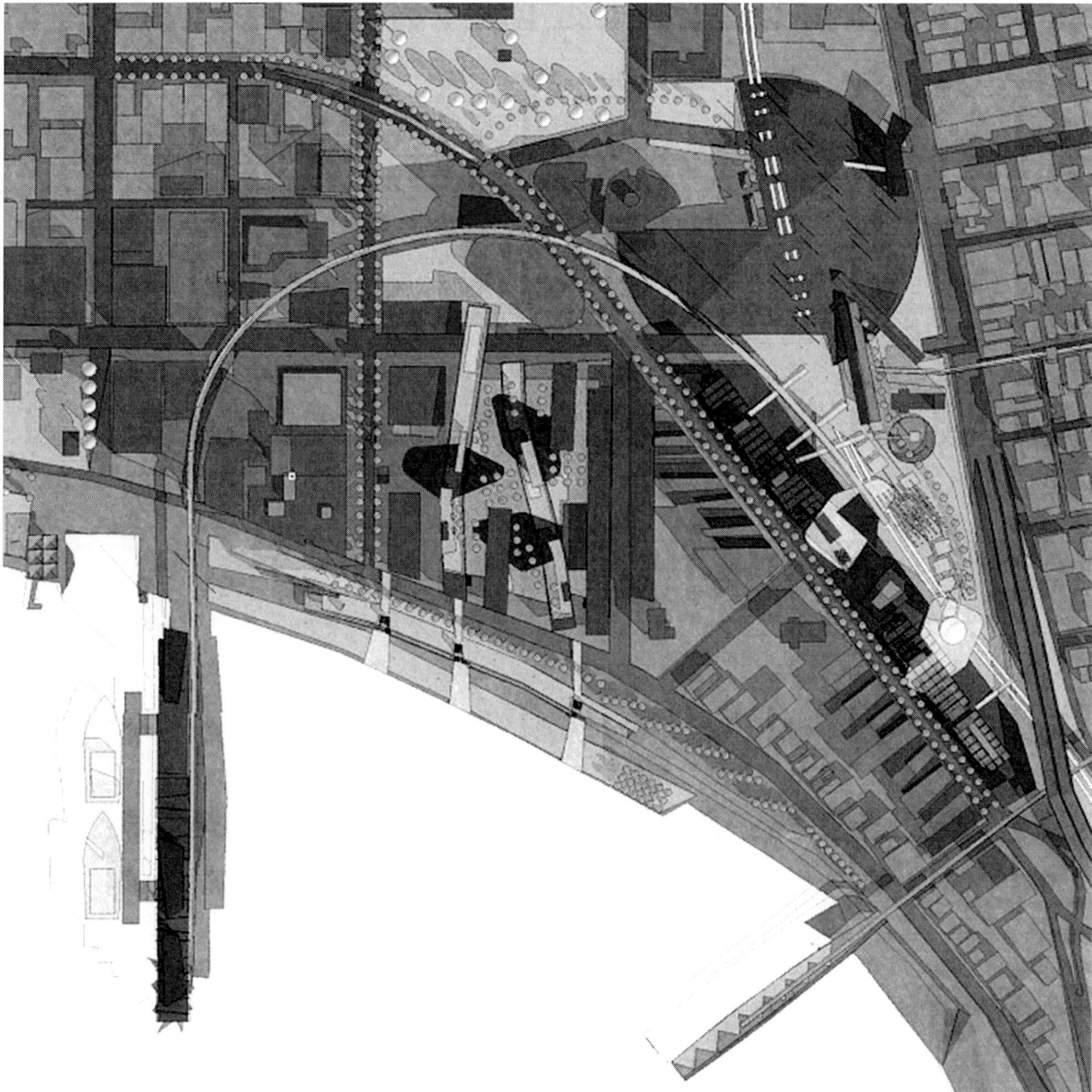

Figure 12.4 Geelong Western Wedge, 2002. Plan drawing by Davin Smith. Urbanheart student design team at Deakin University: Davin Smith, Shem Kelder, Lee-Anne Manski and Jeremy Schulter (all plan images are not presented at original scale).

Like the program at Auburn, Prefab 21 design-build studio engaged with communities and real clients, with students having the opportunity to work at a highly detailed level and gain hands on construction experience. These experiences often involve local community engagement with not-for-profit organisations or local authorities to provide design and build services to improve conditions for the people receiving the services. The aim of this studio was to harness the energy of the students to do interesting design work with a social purpose.

The university has an obligation to provide an education that prepares students for their professions, and to be a partner with the community to create impactful improvements. Community-based design-build studios create the environment for students to have direct contact with the people they are designing for, as well as imparting practical experience for students. The goals of the architecture program at Deakin University are to go beyond the "practice ready" aspect of these projects by exposing the students to alternate models of contemporary practice. This type of "public interest architecture" takes students out of the design studio and identifies local projects, treats the community as an equal partner in the project and creates impactful applied research for the university.

Academically, the design-build structure features the division of the architecture studio into design and construction phases, creating a partnership between the university and not-for-profit organisation or community group and includes efforts to raise funds and secure donations from vendors, manufacturers and government agencies for the materials used in construction. In these projects, the students combine their idealism with direct participation in a community, thus garnering support for the project.

Background of the partnership

FormFlow was founded on a world-first technology to produce sharp bends in corrugated steel, an Australian-made building material icon. Based on this core innovation, they developed new building products, systems and solutions to address housing affordability, accessibility and sustainability. FormFlow develops technologies that are focused on addressing climate change by reducing the carbon footprint of homes, during the build and through the lifetime of a house. Applying new strategies using industry 4.0, lean manufacturing principles and prefabrication, they reduce construction waste and the carbon footprint of materials via modular design for reuse and use recycled/recyclable materials, contributing to a circular economy. FormFlow is pursuing scale-up strategies for their business designed to maximise the social impact of their work and support the ongoing development of new ideas, balancing resource allocation between societal, commercial and research and development activities.

Samaritan House Geelong is a not-for-profit organisation, formed to make a difference to the lives of homeless men in the Geelong region. They exist through the kindness and generosity of the Geelong community – individuals, companies and charitable organisations – both in financial ways and through volunteering. The vision of Samaritan House Geelong is 'to provide a community and a welcoming and safe home for homeless people experiencing crisis, enabling their transition to a better future'.[17] Samaritan House Geelong was formed in 2012 as a community-driven response to the growing problem of homelessness in Geelong.

To combat the need for accommodation of homeless men, the original board with support from the Geelong business community, arranged for the purchase of a dwelling on an acre of land in Moolap, sufficient to meet their future needs. Since 2012, Samaritan House has provided accommodation for more than 600 men. The program has seen over 50% of the participants transitioning to permanent accommodation. In 2015, the expanding need for further accommodation saw the construction of a new nine-bed purpose-designed crisis accommodation facility (See Chapter 6, "Reimagining Geelong Via Systems Thinking").

With transitioning being the focus of the program moving forward, the board determined a need for Independent Living Units (ILU) to facilitate its objectives. ILUs provide homeless men with the opportunity to experience self-sufficiency via affordable rent in supported accommodation for a nominated period, with the aim of transitioning to their own independent public or private housing, thus breaking the homeless cycle. To meet city planning requirements for their site, a project comprising seven single-bedroom units was planned.

The Prefab 21 studio was developed from a new partnership opportunity with FormFlow, and a start-up company that was housed in the Deakin ManuFutures facility, Deakin University's advanced manufacturing hub at Waurn Ponds. FormFlow approached the School of Architecture and Built Environment with the intent of having architects participate in a design-build project using their innovative method of being able to bend corrugated steel. Concurrent with the development of the A+B–FormFlow project, Samaritan House approached FormFlow to develop a housing prototype for their facility. This project developed into an opportunity to bring these three together to create a design-build project designed by Deakin architecture students working collaboratively with FormFlow as builder and Samaritan House as client to produce a prototype prefabricated ILU. This transdisciplinary project was accomplished in design studio and workshop sessions that designed, documented and built an ILU and created the central product for the Geelong Microvillage Project of seven ILUs at Samaritan House (see Figures 12.5 and 12.6).[18] This project is also discussed in Chapter 6, "Reimagining Geelong via Systems Thinking".

Process

The interactive process of developing this new housing type included investigation into sustainability, user experience and social/economic awareness of providing transitional housing for the homeless. This project has ramifications beyond the homeless shelter with the ILU and design of the microvillage allowing for better access to affordable housing, increasing housing equity in the community and allowing a pathway for the homeless to reintegrate into society.[19]

The design team of students began the project with research into historical and contemporary approaches to prefabrication. Working closely with FormFlow, the student team provided a prefabricated system design that is materially innovative and satisfies the client needs. Project goals were determined together by the students, FormFlow and Samaritan House. Students provided design and documentation to meet the goals of a prefabricated system. The three acted together as a collaborative design and construction team, emulating a professional design process, and interacting weekly with builders and clients to realise the project. The functionality, form and sustainability goals that were developed for the project resulted in a unique exterior shape that has passive high performance at its core.

The interactive design process for this project included reviews with several stakeholders and social housing experts HOME, the Deakin University-wide research group with a goal of providing a home for all, and Geelong Sustainability, who contributed significantly to the development of the project. The students visited Samaritan House and interviewed staff and guests to help determine their needs (See Chapter 6, "Reimagining Geelong Via Systems Thinking"). The

---

[17] Samaritan House, accessed November 2023, 'https://samaritanhouse.org.au/about-us/'.

[18] Richard Tucker, Ursula de Jong, Louise Johnson, Nicole Johnston, Adrian Lee, Fabienne Michaux, Elyse Warner and Fiona A. Andrews, *Microvillage Geelong Project: Exploring the Viability of Affordable Compact Homes for People Seeking Sustainable and Socially Integrated Lives* (HOME Research Hub, Deakin University, 2021).

[19] Tucker et al., *Microvillage Geelong Project*.

Figure 12.5 Prefab 21 partnership, ILU project for Samaritan House, 2020. Deakin University students and FormFlow team working on detailed drawings.

Figure 12.6 Prefab 21 partnership, ILU project for Samaritan House, 2021. Seven-unit ILU microvillage installed at Samaritan House.

breadth of first-hand knowledge gave the students an understanding of the functions required for the ILU and contributed to its success. The first ILU prototype was designed and built in 12 weeks. The students provided design drawings, worked closely with the engineers and builders at FormFlow, who translated the design into the Building Information Model (BIM) that determined how the buildings would be constructed.

The ILU prototype became the catalyst for successful grants from both the city and state to build the seven-unit microvillage, ensuring that the Geelong region has the support needed to meet current challenges around homelessness. The impact of this ILU prototype is extensive by providing a new typology for transitional homeless accommodation and jobs in the region.

The Prefab 21 team integrated the project goals of providing shelter and addressing the regions housing affordability crisis, while also providing solutions for reducing the carbon footprint of future homes and reducing waste by implementing alternative modular construction products. The student-designed ILU explores and tests the next generation of design and manufacturing of houses for the twenty-first century, whilst engaging collaboratively with key industry partners. Its application to the challenge of social housing demonstrated that it may be a worthy solution to the urgent need for crisis accommodation in regional centres such as Geelong.

Considerations

This Prefab 21 architecture studio has become a paradigm for industry and university collaboration and research. Prefab 21 projects, in partnership with FormFlow, have since run for three years following this initial project. Participating students have designed and built an emergency shelter for long term post-disaster applications and a fifty-unit microvillage of social housing using new financial models for ownership.[20]

These student-centred applied research opportunities provide a vehicle for questioning and testing new experiments in housing in an effective way. These projects demonstrate that a model for design-build transdisciplinary projects can transform how we teach architecture students, embracing an experimental and experiential-making culture and engaging our communities in a positive way, increasing housing equity and providing access to beautiful and functional sustainable housing.

VITAL SIGNS– Alternative Futures 2017–2100, what if?

Figure 12.7 Yolanda Esteban, *VITAL SIGNS – Alternative Futures* signature image, 2016. Composite image including *View of Geelong* by Eugene von Guérard, 1856, and *5D City Explorer/VR* by Anastasia Globa, 2016.

---

[20] Deakin University, "Future of Emergency Housing on Show at Geelong Design Week", Media release, March 19, 2021, accessed November 2023, https://www.deakin.edu.au/about-deakin/news-and-media-releases/articles/future-of-emergency-housing-on-show-at-geelong-design-week. Tucker et al., *Microvillage Geelong Project.*

Alan Kay, American computer scientist and winner of the 2003 A.M. Turing Award, said that 'The best way to predict the future is to invent it'.[21] *VITAL SIGNS – Alternative Futures* was developed by a team of students and academic staff from the School of Architecture and Built Environment, Deakin University, in collaboration with the City of Greater Geelong, Geelong Library and Heritage Centre, and the Geelong Gallery. Celebrating Geelong's recent designation as a City of Design within the UNESCO Creative Cities Network, *VITAL SIGNS – Alternative Futures* was exhibited as part of the 2019 National Gallery of Victoria (NGV) Design Week in Geelong (a precursor to the annual Geelong Design Week festival), and was shortlisted as a finalist project in four categories of the 2019 Victorian Premier's Design Awards (see Figure 12.7).

Modelling a range of population forecasts over an eighty-year timeframe and anticipating climate change impacts of rising sea levels and increasing average daytime temperatures above pre-industrial levels, concepts and ideas were developed by the project teams as it springboarded into the future from the 2017 community-led thirty-year vision: Greater Geelong: A Clever and Creative Future. The work critically explored the role of Geelong as a twenty-first century city, housing a growing inner-city population from 1600 residents in 2019 to 17,500 by 2050 and a potential 35,000 by 2100, by examining key ecological, social, and economic indicators.

History begins: Time and scale

The inspiration for *VITAL SIGNS – Alternative Futures* initially came from a broadsheet publication of Arthur C. Clarke's "2001 and Beyond the Predictions", published in *The Age* on 13 June 1999.[22] The article printed twenty-five of Clarke's forecasts, beginning with 'Next Millennium and Century begins - 1st January 2000', and extends to 2100 with his final text entry 'History Begins…'. Following a similar style to that of Arthur C. Clarke, Alternative Futures was presented in a "trailer" format, albeit a silent one. This preview strategy is employed in the entertainment industry to tell the story of a film or book in a highly condensed fashion to have maximum appeal. Business journalist and analyst Marich argues that 'The key ambition in trailer-making is to impart an intriguing story that gets film audiences emotionally involved.'[23]

Rather than presenting a complete account, the rolling visual narrative addresses four time periods – 2019, 2026, 2050 and 2100 – and highlights possible milestones described through illustrations, possible data projections, and textual bullet points indicating various policy, technology, environmental, economic, and social changes that the student team envisioned. Hence, rather than presenting a detailed narrative and complete story of the next eighty years, the intention was to provide glimpses and simple triggers for the observer to engage with their own imagination, to somehow question, fill in the gaps with their own thoughts and ask "what if?" from their own first person perspective as they thought about the next eighty years.

The different time periods of the exhibition were presented with a summary of projected data sets, referencing indicators such as suburban tree canopy, water use, and the growth of the creative industries sector, inspired by Geelong's recent designation as the UNESCO City of Design (see Figure 12.8 in the colour plate section).

VITAL SIGNS attained a high level of design excellence by encapsulating three different forms of engagement, each of which was tailored, according to the experiences the students, to create varying representations of alternative design futures. The exhibition comprised an extensive range of mixed media, which was digitally captured and presented on a nine-screen display in the Geelong Library and Heritage Centre, and Geelong Gallery. Three-dimensional printed models of Geelong's central area were also generated and displayed with immersive media (augmented reality/virtual reality) enabling visitors to visually explore new spatial experiences.

The start of a journey …

Five outstanding postgraduate students at Deakin University's School of Architecture and Built Environment – Jarrod Argent, Tom Barker, Jack Hirini, Julie Pham and Blake Sipek – dedicated two weeks of their summer break in January 2019 to explore ideas and "what if" scenarios, leading to the development of the *VITAL SIGNS* exhibition. Alternative Futures was not a curriculum-based project but was developed specifically as an event for 2019 NGV Design Week in Geelong.[24]

The journey begins with recounting the launch of *Greater Geelong: A Clever and Creative Future* in 2017, a published thirty-year vision, which looks forward to 2047 'when Greater Geelong will be internationally recognised as a clever and creative city-region that is forward looking, enterprising and adaptive, and cares for its people and environment'.[25]

This vision introduced thirty-seven baseline measures, heralding the first of the smart city indicators monitoring the vital signs of the city and its people. With the assistance of professional staff from economic development and the smart

---

[21] Alan Kay, "Learning vs. Teaching with Educational Technologies", *EDUCOM Bulletin*, 3/4 (Princeton, New Jersey: Interuniversity Communications Council, 1983).

[22] Arthur C. Clarke, "2001 and Beyond, The Predictions", *The Age* (Melbourne), June 13, 1999, 14.

[23] Robert Marich, "Marketing to Moviegoers: A Handbook of Strategies and Tactics" 3rd edn (Southern Illinois University Press, 2013).

[24] VITAL Signs timeline and flythrough video, https://vimeo.com/360753323/281c049389.

[25] City of Greater Geelong, *A Clever and Creative Future* (Geelong, Victoria, Australia, 2017).

cities units at the City of Greater Geelong, the students confirmed their first data entries on which future projections would be explored: Greater Geelong population 282,000; population (central Geelong) 1600 residents and 21,000 jobs. So began their story moving beyond 2026 to 2050 and 2100.

Geelong 2050

Arthur C. Clarke envisioned that, by the year 2050:

> Neurological research has finally led to an understanding of all the senses, and direct inputs have become possible, bypassing eyes, ears, skin etc. Brain caps are available … Anyone wearing this prosthesis can enter a whole universe of experience, real or imaginary – and even merge in real-time with other minds.[26]

The possible growth scenario of the City of Greater Geelong's population by 2050 is 500,000, with central Geelong accommodating 17,500 residents and supporting between 33,000 and 52,000 jobs. Suburban tree canopy has reached 50%, up from 25% in 2030, and 60% of water use is recycled, 25% of the work force in Geelong is engaged in the creatives industry sector contributing to a thriving innovation economy. The City of Greater Geelong is now rated in the Top 100 of the Global innovation City Index (GICI). Given the success of the Clever and Creative Future vision, the City of Greater Geelong Council engages 30,000 community participants in a 2080 vision making process.

Realising the potential of utilising the roof space as a public domain, three north–south and two east–west autonomous drone hives are established across the commercial sectors of the city. All rooftops are now green and linked by sky bridges. Geelong central reaches 90% tree canopy, with 60% of all roof space being publicly accessible, allowing for between 60–100 autonomous passenger drone flights entering and departing Geelong city airspace daily. Building heights are now capped at fifteen storeys to preserve future city air space. Required setbacks are maintained ensuring daylight penetration along the east–west streets.

The city is now a single mega mixed-use zone with vertical circulation linking both the Moorabool Street and Yarra Street sky parks to the boulevards at ground level. Buildings are wrapped in lungs composed of living green façades providing air filtration and temperature regulation. By 2060, Geelong has become an international leader in the manufacture and distribution of autonomous passenger drones with spin-off business start-ups in dronehive, sky park and breathable green building skins.

Geelong 2100

The possible growth scenario of the City of Greater Geelong's population by 2100 is 1,000,000, with central Geelong accommodating 35,000 residents and supporting between 65,000–105,000 jobs. Suburban tree canopy exceeds 90%, up from 50% in 2050, and 90% of water use is recycled. 40% of the work force in central Geelong is engaged in the creatives industry sector and continues to contribute to a thriving innovation economy. Possible average temperatures are now approaching 4°C above pre-industrial levels. However, this increase is now expected to decline to below pre-industrial levels by 2200 due to carbon extraction from the atmosphere. With the increase in average temperatures, Geelong has become a popular twenty-second century "riviera" lifestyle and vacation destination, with 1000+ autonomous passenger drone flights entering and leaving Geelong city airspace per day.

Rather than trying to hold back an anticipated sea level rise of two metres over the past fifty years, Geelong realised an opportunity to extend the Hoddle grid of the city into Corio Bay. As the sea has progressively risen, so the city has accepted its embrace, with habitats being developed with self-sealing and corrosive-free skins (see Figure 12.9). The benefits provided by the thermal mass of the sea offer a similar relief from extreme temperatures, provided by earth-covered structures and a new perspective on waterfront living.

A new wave of development has pioneered building technologies that allow city blocks to be covered in gigantic parasols spun from spider silk steel, providing a light and radiant-heat sensitive membrane to assist with mitigating extreme temperatures during the summer months. They provide relief in the public realm with urban green spaces and sky parks and assist with mitigating the urban heat island effect.

Projects developed in this scenario included:

- The Ziggurat: The Ziggurat, an ancient building shape, was introduced as a means of extending the city skyline with terraces of urban food production, while still preserving winter and autumn light to penetrate the streetscape below. Offering steps of green active recreational space floating across the city, the Ziggurats provide a 2 km terrace of accommodation and urban farming incubators, linked directly to the health, sport science and nutrition precincts.
- Dom-zats: Dom-zats become a new integrated citadel development. Touching the ground lightly, these amazing high-rise structures can be located in the natural landscape or poised above a city block, preserving 90% of the area of the 2050 sky parks. The Dom-zat has become the twenty-second century's answer to the compact city. The Dom-zat is a carbon neutral, zero-waste neighbourhood. (see Figure 12.10).

---

[26] Clarke, "2001 and Beyond, The Predictions".

Figure 12.9 Geelong 2100. Night view of the City Parasols and Ziggurats providing a 2 km terrace of accommodation and urban farming incubators. SketchUp 3D model: Jarrod Argent, Tom Barker, Jack Hirini, Julie Pham, Blake Sipek. Unity nighttime rendering and animation: Alex Rollo.

Figure 12.10 2100 drone view looking northeast across Geelong's central city area to Corio Bay. Artwork and concept drawing by Jack Hirini.

History from the perspective of the twenty-second century

VITAL SIGNS was presented as an alternative futures journey, structured not by attempting to project a series of significant epochs, but rather proposing a series of future dates defined by the aspirations of a community and its thirty-year goal of shaping a clever and creative future for itself. Assuming that humanity does manage to adapt and make it to 2100, given the challenges that societies and communities around the world have been presented with through the 2021 Intergovernmental Panel on Climate Change (IPCC) publication of *Climate Change 2021*, then how will historians writing in the twenty-second century present the events and innovations that transpired over the previous 100 years?[27]

Will some scholars writing in the twenty-second century engage with the categorisation of transformational change by rediscovering *Technics and Civilisation*, written almost 170 years previously by Lewis Mumford?[28] Or will they extend Patrick Gedde's and Mumford's 'overlapping and interpenetrating three phases of the machine civilisation'?[29] Could a retake on Alvin Toffler's *Future Shock* and the impact of technological change on people's lives, (what Mika Pantzar identified as the 'changing temporal architecture of daily life') gain further reflection and extension when considering present and future events, such as the global and local impact of COVID-19 on the social rhythms of daily life, with the rapid increase and reliance in online communication?[30]

Climate crisis and the dramatic awareness of the impacts of climate change can undoubtedly paint a bleak future. How does this affect a communities' imagination and sense of aspiration if the cup of humanity is presented as less than half full? While the need for creative design to mitigate lifestyle choices is essential, the legacy being revealed nonetheless appears grim and dystopian. The design innovations and responses that *VITAL SIGNS* stimulated provide a collaborative sense of challenge and opportunity. *VITAL SIGNS* flicked thinking toward the hope of inspiring the next generation of young designers to help create positive change for an adaptive future so that communities are better prepared to manage life and living and, if needs be, to accommodate the worst-case scenario.

By 2050, in just thirty years, many of the Deakin University graduates who have just finished their studies, will be at the top of their professional careers in the creative industries sector. They will probably be moulding their environments and innovating in a world quite different from the one in which they had graduated. Their creative output will be a legacy for those coming after them. Their contribution could well be measured by the way challenges have been interpreted, engaged with and addressed.

Conclusion

The work the students have achieved through Urbanheart, Prefab 21 and *VITAL SIGNS* are equally inspiring – within different realities and time frames. The value of pedagogy, of progressively opening up the studios and developing briefs in consultation with the profession, governments and communities has enabled the students to generate truly inspirational work that has purpose. The results have been phenomenal. Helping to drive the conversation around positioning transformational change in Geelong and seeking excellence in quality architecture, was recently encapsulated in the school's contribution to Geelong Design Week 2023, an exhibition showcasing seven different studio projects representing an exciting and diverse range of architectural thinking, imagination and vision-making from second and third year undergraduate students and first year postgraduate Masters students.

The discourse engendered by directly linking studios with key contemporary issues and potentially "live" projects often motivates students with a strong sense of community and the challenge of contributing positive change. Their work is always fresh and stimulating as each generation of students bring forward their shared values and sense of purpose with their work being current and forward thinking. Students inspire hope, their sincerity invites respect, and their ability to imagine is compelling. Welcoming all manner of opinions, they are natural attractors to draw the best out of subject matter experts and to genuinely engage the community. While some might say "it's just students dreaming", for many within the communities they are designing for, the horizon of understanding and the chance to imagine becomes just that little bit more expansive.

Acknowledgements

Supplementary materials: The *VITAL SIGNS* video is available online: https://vimeo.com/360753323/281c049389.
Acknowledgments: The authors gratefully acknowledge the five students – Jarrod Argent, Tom Barker, Jack Hirini, Julie Pham and Blake Sipek – who made *VITAL SIGNS* happen, for without their commitment and positive outlook to address the environmental challenges ahead of all of us, then none of this would have happened.

---

[27] IPCC, *Climate Change 2021: The Physical Science Basis. Contribution of Working Group I to the Sixth Assessment Report of the Intergovernmental Panel on Climate*, In Press, 2021.

[28] Lewis Mumford, *Technics and Civilization* (NY: Harcourt, Brace and Company, 1934).

[29] Mumford, *Technics and Civilization.*

[30] Alvin Toffler, *Future Shock* (Random House press, 1970); Mika Pantzar, "Future Shock – Discussing the Changing Temporal Architecture of Daily Life", *Journal of Future Studies* 14, no. 4 (June 2010): 1–22; Wendy Martin, George Collett, Chris Bell and Amy Prescott, "Ageing, the Digital and Everyday Life During and Since the Covid-19 Pandemic", *Front Psychol.* 14 (September 2023).

The authors also gratefully acknowledge the following partners in providing much appreciated knowledge and technical support: City of Greater Geelong (Matthew Szymczak, Jesse Cardey and Hailey Ince), the Geelong Gallery (Jason Smith, Pip Minney, Alex Rollo), the Geelong Library and Heritage Centre (Gerrard Daniels and Caz Copic), Deakin University (Michael Sharman, Dr Rui Wang and Professor Tuba Kocaturk).

Disclaimer: The *VITAL SIGNS* content of this chapter does not represent the views of Deakin University, the City of Greater Geelong, the Geelong Library and Heritage Centre, or the Geelong Gallery. The work should not be regarded as a forecast or proposal. It is simply a series of loosely based theoretical design concepts and ideas developed through a student project and should only be interpreted as such.

CHAPTER 13

VACANTCITY:
COMMUNITY AND CONNECTION IN A CLEVER AND CREATIVE GEELONG

CAMERON BISHOP AND ANNE WILSON

A bad metaphor for ideologies and hidden infrastructures

In the 1958 film, *The Blob*, a gelatinous alien form descends on a town in the United States and devours all living things.[1] It grows with each organism it consumes to become a giant amorphous shape overtaking the people, the buildings and infrastructures of small-town America. The film as allegory was obvious at the time, as communism sought to re-cast and shackle the relationship between capital and labour; its insidious, creeping ideology threatened the freedoms the West had recently fought for, or so the story went. Cut to 1988 and the remake of *The Blob* landed in a different time, at the end of the Reagan presidency where free market ideology had well and truly traumatised small-town America and its industries.[2] So, the metaphor of the blob, like the form itself, is amorphous and can cut into different eras and places where it can take shape in both benevolent and malevolent ways. It is an image, a metaphor, we use in this chapter to firstly critique the rhetoric that engulfs us when places rebrand themselves – in Geelong's case as "clever and creative" – and further, to intercede in the notion of the march towards the "smart city", with built environments fully operationalised by new technology.

Following Mark Andrejevic's analysis of the "operational city" in his book, *Automated Media*, we are concerned that while policing and commercial sensing systems seem to make life safer and more efficient, at the same time – employing our catch-all metaphor of the blob – the capacity for creative play and politics is being subsumed by the rush to digitise our civic lives.[3] In this chapter we advance an argument for the artist as disruptor, both an irreverent and socialising force, able to engage communities in the politics and the shared histories of a place. We do this through our involvement as curators and artists in the long running research project, VacantGeelong. Initiated by Mirjana Lozanovska at Deakin University in 2015, the project brought together architectural and visual arts researchers to explore the architectures and communities left behind by the city's industrial histories: from wool, textiles, aluminium, and automotive. Several artists were commissioned to make work – across installation, painting, photography, drawing, film, participation, and performance – for the project, to interrogate the developer's dream of start-up hubs, cafes and apartment complexes occupying nineteenth and twentieth century factory buildings. VacantGeelong found creative practitioners an important niche to occupy in the evolution of the city, a pause point between original or adapted use-value, and development.[4]

The research fused and amplified the concerns of architects and artists for the memories that buildings hold; as fulcra for thinking about how built spaces affect us socially, for the particular relations between the body and the machine, and as signposts for the migrant communities that were built up around them (see Chapter 3). Geelong was a city that grew over time and benefited from waves of migrants seeking to prosper through wool, gold, textiles, agriculture and industry. However, the city's multi-cultural layering accelerated greatly after the Second World War, when people from Europe sought a better life, with the promise of jobs in the automotive and other industries. The spaces these people came to

---

[1] *The Blob*, directed by Irvin Yeaworth and Russell Doughten (1958, Criterion, Paramount Pictures).

[2] *The Blob*, directed by Chuck Russell (1988, TriStar Pictures).

[3] Mark Andrejevic, *Automated Media* (New York: Routledge, 2020), 94–112.

[4] VacantGeelong is an ongoing project exploring the industrial architectures, and by extension the communities that evolved with them, of Geelong's recent past. The research team consisted of collaborators from across Deakin University's architecture and creative arts programs, led by Professor Mirjana Lozanovska and including Associate Professor Cameron Bishop, Dr Anne Scott Wilson, Associate Professor David Beynon, Dr Diego Fullaondo, Ciro Marquez and numerous research assistants. Using art as a way to occupy and invigorate these sites, the project researchers – over several artist residencies, exhibitions, symposia, workshops and events - commissioned multiple artists, from across the disciplinary spectrum, to reveal the hidden layers of memory, practice, and community that lie inside the abandoned industrial buildings that were once the beating heart of Geelong. This research project investigates the vacant spaces left behind by the decline of twentieth-century industry, examining their impact on communities and shaping a critical dialogue about their significance. Through artistic interventions and collaboration, the project encourages us to reflect on our relationship with the built environment and the stories it holds. VacantGeelong serves as a model, linked and prompted through the elision of architectural and creative arts researchers, for communities navigating similar transitions, with a view to encouraging them to engage with their past and to reimagine their future before the sometimes-inevitable utopian dens of start-ups, easy-living apartment complexes, and microbreweries move in to these incredibly unique icons of the industrial age.

inhabit and build, from vast factories to modest houses in old abandoned working suburbs, and in new suburbs adjacent to industry, engendered particular kinds of relations between the body, the machine, and other bodies.

VacantGeelong sought to investigate and celebrate these social and labour relations through site-specific studio residencies and exhibitions with artists that foregrounded participation with the communities affected by deindustrialisation, specifically ex-Ford workers from the Macedonian community. This chapter chronicles some of those forays into old spaces with artists and community, while showcasing much of the art that was produced as a result. As the artists' works often investigated the tension(s) between the labouring body and the machine, they prompted a particular series of works that we concentrate on here. In the project, they detail our increasing creative engagement with digital technologies through one key work, *X Marks the Spot* (*XMTS*), 2019. While drawing on the earlier work of commissioned artists in the project, which definitively responded to old industry and their architectures, the effects of deindustrialisation and the maintenance and recuperation of community, the work set out to test our relations with our machines, our digital technologies and artificial intelligence (AI). *XMTS* was future oriented in that regard, building tensions between the body, the storytelling practices that sustain communities, and new technologies. The work used public performance, song, community, video, and pre-programmed drones to re-calibrate the body to an old industrial building in North Geelong, and the industries that built it, and at the same time, to send a warning signal out about our increasing reliance on digital technologies.

Through this chapter we run with two parallel arguments that build a case for both the VacantGeelong project and the artist as ghost in the machine, the glitch in the smooth progression from deindustrialisation into the smooth, frictionless world of the future city. Beginning with a critique of the smart city as a rhetorical device that frames a utopic and elusive view of a future civic life that never arrives, we consider the impacts of deindustrialisation on communities and their sense of connectedness. We interrogate some of the hyperbole around re-skilling in the digital age, and its inevitable tie to deploying new technologies in our working lives by considering some of the language used in the making of a city. At the same time, we contemplate how new ways of working (for example, the gig economy), facilitated by digital technologies, are re-shaping and literally re-mapping (Uber) the city and its built environment, not to mention our labour practices and politics. The theoretical frame draws on a critique of Mark Andrejevic and Franco Berardi to disarm the discourse of the smart city and automated technologies. We then further undermine the premise of the smart city through Hito Steyerl's and additionally through Pangrazio, Bishop and Lee's analyses of how new data collection and sensing mechanisms insinuate themselves into the built environment, and into our working and recreational lives.

Indeed, as we apply some theory and salient examples to the creative work we have done, we pay homage to all the participants, artists and researchers who have worked on the project so far. We acknowledge that without their contribution we could not have arrived at a point where *X Marks the Spot* could have been conceived. Because, just as it draws out the tensions between humans and our technologies, the creative works are inextricably bound to the past and the people of this place, Geelong, that, like other cities of its kind, is on the cusp of great change.

Smart but dumb – cities and bodies shaped

In her 2018 video, *Broken Windows*, artist and theorist Hito Steyerl details the work of a group of engineers and researchers in Cambridge, England, employed by a sound recognition development company, Audio Analytics. Part of their job was to break windows, of varying sizes and thicknesses, and at different distances from the recording equipment. An odd job, to be sure, but some machine learning still requires the human as an intermediary in its education. The team undertook this task, to break and record thousands of windows smashing, for the purpose of training an AI to recognise the sound of breaking glass. This kind of machine learning has obvious applications in protecting commercial and residential properties, and people, while aiding the police in tracking crime. The smart city for new-media theorist Mark Andrejevic, 'envisions the moment when digital enclosure and the space of urban life converge'.[5] Operationalising the city and doubling its events in data capture, storage and interpretation are hallmarks of the urban territories being redefined by digital technologies. What Steyerl picks up on is an interesting phenomenon in our bodily relations to technology, and while humanity's evolution has been entwined with the tools that make life more efficient, safer and entertaining, in the cited case it is the promise of technology that directs the movements of the body. The work begets the question, as proposed by Pangrazio and Bishop in their article "Art as Digital Counterpractice": Is the body merely a ready-made for technology to shape, a step on the way toward the development of artificial intelligence?[6] This is something we look to further challenge and rebut.

Geelong, in company with no lesser a global city than Barcelona, won the International Smart City of the Year award in 2022. The term "smart city" is often attributed to IBM when it used it to describe a part of their smarter planet initiative in the early 2000s. As a generalised notion, we have been using technology – collecting data and deploying it – in cities to improve urban life for centuries by making them more efficient, healthier, safer and governable, in balance with the logic of capital.[7] The *Smart City Strategic Framework*, that ostensibly Geelong won the award for, promises a digital 'ecosystem' that uses a 'network of sensors (Internet of Things)' to 'switch on objects in our physical and natural

---

[5] Andrejevic, *Automated Media*, 94.

[6] Luciana Pangrazio, Cameron Bishop and Fiona Lee, "Old Media, New Gigs: The Discursive Construction of the Gig Economy in Australian News Media", *Work, Employment and Society* 37, no. 3 (2023): 606–24, https://doi.org/10.1177/09500170211034663).

[7] Michel Foucault, *Security, Territory, Population: Lectures at the College de France, 1977–1978*, Michael Senellart (ed), trans. Graham Burchell (London: Palgrave Macmillan, 2007).

environment so they can draw valuable information'.[8] This sounds exciting, and benign enough - a built environment wired with sensors, fully automated, constantly calibrating its elemental interventions to safely and productively guide us through the urban environment.

What is missing in the *Smart City Strategic Framework* is any kind of critical view of what the smart city promises, where all of our movements, interactions, and social and financial transactions capture us in what Andrejevic calls the "automated subject": 'the consumer whose needs are met before they arise, the citizen whose actions are shaped by the nudges of "libertarian paternalism", the criminal whose actions are pre-empted before they can take shape'.[9] The slavish embrace of the rhetoric of the smart city ushers in technologies integrated into our urban environments without contest, at the expense of politics, protest or any form of collective desire. Rather, desire – in the smart city – is "disaggregated" to the individual, an isolated and self-enclosed subject whose every whim and bias is fed back to them in an unending loop of self-perpetuation and aggrandisement. Calling on urban studies academic, Kafui Attoh, Mark Andrejevic warns of the drift into the 'idiocy of urban life' and the dissolution 'of a robust civic and public life'.[10] The city might become smart, but at the expense of the citizen and their relationship to other citizens. We argue here that to stave off the dumb revery of automated solipsism, creative arts practice offers an antidote, evident in the ongoing project, VacantGeelong.

One hundred years ago, Geelong was on the cusp of rapid change when Ford established itself in the city in 1925. There is a famous aerial photograph that looks down on the new factory, an imported saw-tooth architecture with a snow loading of six feet that was replicated across the world, plonked in a paddock with no infrastructure or housing around it (see Figure 3.2). Already a powerhouse of the wool and textile industry, Geelong's shift into the automotive and similar industries brought with it a boom in population, particularly after the Second World War, with a wave of European refugees and migrants creating new lives for themselves. Overlaying a more positive networked image of the blob, the city's suburbs rapidly expanded, bringing into being a vibrant, genuinely multi-cultural city, built on a complexity of languages, practices and traditions. These practices and traditions, drawn from across Europe, evolved from connections to varied countries of origin, and they added readily identifiable dimensions to, among other things, Australian culture through art, architecture and cuisine.[11]

The city has been through its share of tribulations and, from the early 2000s, many of the migrant workers, who had built houses and communities in Geelong, have been made redundant. A number of iconic industries synonymous with the city now face the effects of deindustrialisation, including the closure of the Alcoa aluminium refinery (2014), the cutting of the Qantas maintenance fleet at Avalon (2013), and the large reduction of staff at the Boral Cement plant (2013).[12] This precipitous onset of deindustrialisation, catalysed by Ford's decision to end their ninety-year manufacturing operations in Geelong (2016), was a provocation for researchers at Deakin University to explore the vacant spaces and still vibrant communities left behind by the disappearing industries. As the rhetoric around the smart city was ramping up, and while industries were laying off staff and vacating their industrial homes, a group of architects, artists and curators sought a pause point, within which to intervene, to ask important questions about the memories the built environment (i.e. workplace, city and home) prompted for migrant workers, many of whom were recently made redundant or had retired. The VacantGeelong project was thus built around the themes of migration, labour, memory, community and the built environment.

The first major commissioning phase of the project in 2017 saw six artists invited to make work inspired by place. A mix of emerging and established artists working across a variety of media – Merinda Kelly, Alexander Hamilton, Bindi Cole Chocka, Amanda Shone, Robert Mihajlovski and Sarah Duyshart – undertook extensive, archival, ethnographic and collaborative enquiry with researchers and community groups.

VacantGeelong took over an old factory warehouse space in North Geelong, which we coined the Open Studio, a space that was once a Ford car parts distributor. The name designated an openness of enquiry, of community connection and of practice, signifying for the artists, over the six months they were asked to make work there, that they were open to respond to the built environment of Geelong's northern industrial precinct, as well as the communities that sprang from it. This included a prolonged and repeated engagement with the Macedonian community, many of whom worked for Ford and/or Alcoa. Researchers and artists worked closely with the community of Macedonian ex-Ford workers, their partners and children, using formal and informal ethnographic methods including interviews, workshops, and feedback sessions. We also sang, danced and ate with the participants, which gave us a deeper insight into the rich connections they shared with the place and each other.

Numerous works sprang from the Open Studio (detailed in Figures 13.1 and 13.3 in the colour plate section and Figures 13.2 and 13.4). They included an exhibition of sculptural interventions, installations, films, paintings, and sound works in the space where hundreds of people – from the communities we worked with, to architecture and visual arts students – gathered to share dialogue about the work, and by extension their stories about labour, migration and place, in a space built as a result of Geelong's twentieth century industrial bloom, prompted by Ford. We could criticise and critique the industries for leaving, as well as the spaces they left behind, for their toxic spread into the atmosphere and surrounding ecosystems to find correlatives in colonisation and territorialisation. Once cared-for Wadawurrung

---

[8] City of Greater Geelong, *Geelong Smart City Strategic Framework* (2017), https://www.geelongaustralia.com.au/smartcity/documents/item/8d8eea93d413524.aspx.
[9] Andrejevic, *Automated Media*, 133.
[10] Andrejevic, *Automated Media*, 100.
[11] Mirjana Lozanovska, *Migrant Housing: Architecture, Dwelling, Migration* (Abingdon, Oxon: Routledge, 2020).
[12] Pangrazio, Bishop and Lee, "Old Media, New Gigs".

foreshore, wetlands and Country are now irrevocably damaged. We could use concepts from new-materialist philosophy, such as entanglement, to redeem, recuperate and equalise the schism in the relation between the non-human and human elements in the environment. For the purposes of this chapter though, we acknowledge the original custodians of the land on which this project took place and recognise their ongoing care for Country. Our attention is centred on the human relationships, facilitated by a diversity of artists, and other participants, material and creative practices, that the built environment and associated labour practices have engendered in the city of Geelong. We do this, as stated earlier, to perhaps claim the term "smart city" for the creative arts, to at least intervene in the rhetoric that serves its interests, while materially, speculating on what the AI-enhanced smart city actually does to notions of cleverness, creativity and community.

Far from undertaking a historical materialist view of Geelong's emergence as a manufacturing powerhouse, and the society it created, we suggest that the work in the twentieth century factory, and by extension in creative practice and projects like VacantGeelong, are constitutive of community. Clearly, work and money attracted many of the Macedonians in the 1950s–1960s to come and earn a salary at Ford in Geelong, and to forge and foster communities on the other side of the world that challenge the emergent, fragmented and automated subject of the smart city described above. Pangrazio, Bishop and Lee, in their 2021 article, "Old Media, New Gigs: The Discursive Construction of the Gig Economy in Australian News Media", suggest that the "Uberisation" of the workforce in the "gig economy" undermines the solidarity of workers, and that the "platformisation" of our social and working lives in the digital sphere make-up the new infrastructural core of society.[13] In the switch to the rhetoric of the smart city, Pangrazio, Bishop and Lee discovered a media complex all too willing to run with the narrative that the transition, for vast swathes of the labour force, from secure (and shift) work in manufacturing to insecure casual labour in the gig economy would be smooth and comparable in terms of worker protections and remuneration. Plainly, it is not.

Figure 13.2 Sarah Duyshart, *Oil Arch*, 2017. Sump oil, sound, projection. VacantGeelong Open Studio.

The VacantGeelong project sought to demonstrate how creative and labour practices can mirror one another in ways that are productive of community, rather than alienating, for both the solo artist in the studio, and for the Uber driver navigating the streets of the smart city. This is where research methods across disciplines elide to turn participants into active agents. While the project took its leave from Clifford Geertz's style of ethnography and the thick description process, in the many interactions with the Macedonian community that the researchers and artists had, coupled with the Open Studio model, the final outputs for artists might be described as co-productive rather than as products of the solitary artist.[14] Claire Bishop flagged in her controversial 2006 essay, "The Social Turn", the trend for contemporary art practice to put an emphasis on 'the intersubjective space' and the ethical processes artists employed in engaging with communities to make 'socially collaborative art'.[15] It was not the imperative of the project to dilute the artist's role in responding to

---

[13] Pangrazio, Bishop and Lee, "Old Media, New Gigs"; Josie Van Dijck, Thomas Poell and Martijn de Waal, *The Platform Society* (Oxford: Oxford University Press, 2019).

[14] Clifford Geertz, *The Interpretation of Culture* (New York: Basic Books, 1973), 311.

[15] Claire Bishop, "The Social Turn: Collaboration and its Discontents", *ARTFORUM* (February 2006), https://www.artforum.com/features/the-social-turn-collaboration-and-its-discontents-173361/.

the changing nature of Geelong, but we, as a group of researchers used the Open Studio model to encourage a dialogic and collaborative approach to the generation of ideas with community. The artists and researchers, over numerous formal and informal meetings with the Macedonian community, built up a sense of trust and reciprocity that extended into the production of the final works.

A case in point is the body of works that Amanda Shone produced over her six-month residency. Her light box photographs, film, and architectural interventions into the Open Studio space (see Figure 13.3 in the colour plate section and Figure 13.4) in North Geelong exemplify the close conversations, and immersion in the social atmosphere of the Macedonian Orthodox Community Centre (MOCC) on the outskirts of Geelong. The artist, whose mother migrated from Latvia to Melbourne in the 1950s and whose father sold Ford car parts, toured the centre and spoke to numerous ex-Ford workers and their families. Captured in one of the two documentary videos made for the project, Shone asked a group of people at the MOCC about the evident loyalty they had for Ford and asked if this was, in part, the result of company organised social events. The response was effusive, as they recalled that Ford brought together their workers for regular family days, particularly around Christmas and Easter. Families from across the globe (mainly Europe) would come together several times each year, a social circumstance brought about by the exigencies of war, migration and work. If we imagine the Uber workforce in Geelong now, criss-crossing the city, it conjures a stark contrast as, often migrants (more recent or ex-twentieth century industry workers) atomised, without the capacity to organise, let alone socialise with their fellow workers.

In deft homage to the overlapping and affective dimensions of place, Shone spliced together two distinct spaces, the social sphere of the MOCC, and the labouring, utilitarian atmosphere of the Open Studio (the old car parts distributor). The participants took her into the ballroom at the MOCC, where for over sixty years people have gathered for all kinds of celebrations, and while in the room, Shone noticed the ceiling drapery, with intricate twists of fabric emanating from the centre of the room, above the dance floor, out into the dining area. At the Open Studio she had noticed small tears in the insulation in the ceiling, signs of dilapidation and perhaps metaphors for deindustrialisation and community. In these fissures the artist saw something else, well springs for reimagining the industrial space as a social one. Shone created a large ceiling work (see Figure 13.3 in the colour plate section) mimicking the form of the ceiling adornment at the MOCC, and during an open day event held at the Open Studio – where hundreds of people came to see and talk to artists about their work in progress – they did so under Shone's monumental transposition of form.

In his book, *Seeing Power*, Nato Thomson talks about 'sites of becoming'.[16] Borrowing from Deleuze and Guattari, he uses the term "becoming" in relation to both the subject and the spatial frameworks within which identity is framed, arguing that neither is stable and always in a process of change.[17] For Thomson, 'sustained engagement' with spaces like the MOCC and the Open Studio, produce political communities because of their 'inherent refutation of the dominant logic of capital'. He lists sites that demonstrate 'new models for being in the world', where free exchange takes precedence over the transactional logic that we bring to many of the encounters we have in our everyday lives. In spaces like 'free-schools, churches, union halls, collectively run music venues, social centres … community gardens etc…' we find the possibility for a kind of social production that operates outside of the systems that would only look to capture us in quantifiable information to police us, place us or sell ourselves back to us.[18]

Figures 13.4 Left: Amanda Shone, *Spare Parts*, 2017, architectural intervention in the VacantGeelong Open Studio. Right: Open Studio Open Day with artists Bindi Cole Chocka, Sarah Duyshart, Robert Mihajlovski, Merinda Kelly and Alexander Hamilton, with researchers and community, 2017. Amanda Shone's work is emerging from the ceiling.

Of course, the Open Studio was once a productive space in the twentieth century sense of "productive", with a workforce on the clock, under the watchful eye of a boss. However, Shone, alongside the researchers and other artists, saw something else in it, a site brimming with possibility, a place for aesthetic experimentation and social exchange. This was evident during the Open Studio Open Day where we brought together a diverse range of people – from emerging and established creatives, academics from multiple disciplines, the Wadawurrung community, and ex-Ford workers from the Macedonian and other migrant communities – to share conversation, experience the artists' works across film, sculpture, architectural intervention, painting and sound, and to immerse themselves in an 'atmosphere of

---

[16] Nato Thomson, *Seeing Power* (Brooklyn: Melville House), 131–33.

[17] Thomson, *Seeing Power*.

[18] Thomson, *Seeing Power*.

mutual respect, curiosity and analysis'.[19] We hope that even if it was for a short time only, in this atmosphere of free and open exchange, in a space under radical transition, that mimicked the accelerated change in the city outside of it, that the hundreds of people who came through the Open Studio recognised themselves as a part of something bigger: a temporary community galvanised by creativity, shared stories and place.

The blob becomes slime mould becomes urban planner

Shone's splayed ceiling drapes are a fitting visual metaphor for the way VacantGeelong spread throughout the city in creative and critical exchanges of various kinds, where researchers not only learnt from the people we engaged with at various sites and the artists' responses to them, but came to understand that the project had its own expansionary logic to it, one that was not contained by the academy, technology, bureaucracy or geography. The project developed a kind of organic and situational quality, one produced by a variety of forces, not always under the researchers' control where local context and community, specific to site and event, became an over-arching prompt for our responses. The project we highlight in the next section helps us to set up a tension between the creative arts as a readily deployed agent in the city's imaginary, and the smooth, apolitical safe space of the smart city. For that, we need to go back to the blob, or "slime mould" to be exact.

Demonstrating how we learn from other intelligences, without knowing why a human being can do what it does, author, artist and technologist James Bridle relates the anecdote of Japanese engineers, aiming to design the fastest public transport routes in a large city, given the many obstacles present in the built environment (see Figure 13.5). Scientists observed single-cell beings, slime mould, and noted their facility to navigate complex, albeit microscopic landscapes. Whilst not understanding how they enacted this facility, they made use of just knowing that a specific idiosyncratic intelligence, not shared with humans or computers, could be utilised for the design of transport routes.[20] The scientists constructed an experiment where they tested some slime mould on a glass surface, with pieces of food positioned at locations that stood for major stations in the network. As stand-ins for impassable mountains and rivers they regulated that topography with lights at different strengths. The slime mould was remarkable for its ability to find the most efficient train routes from the centre, Tokyo, out to the hubs over twenty-six hours. It found paths that had taken city planners 200 years to evolve. He posits that the slime mould's cleverness may be something we cannot understand.

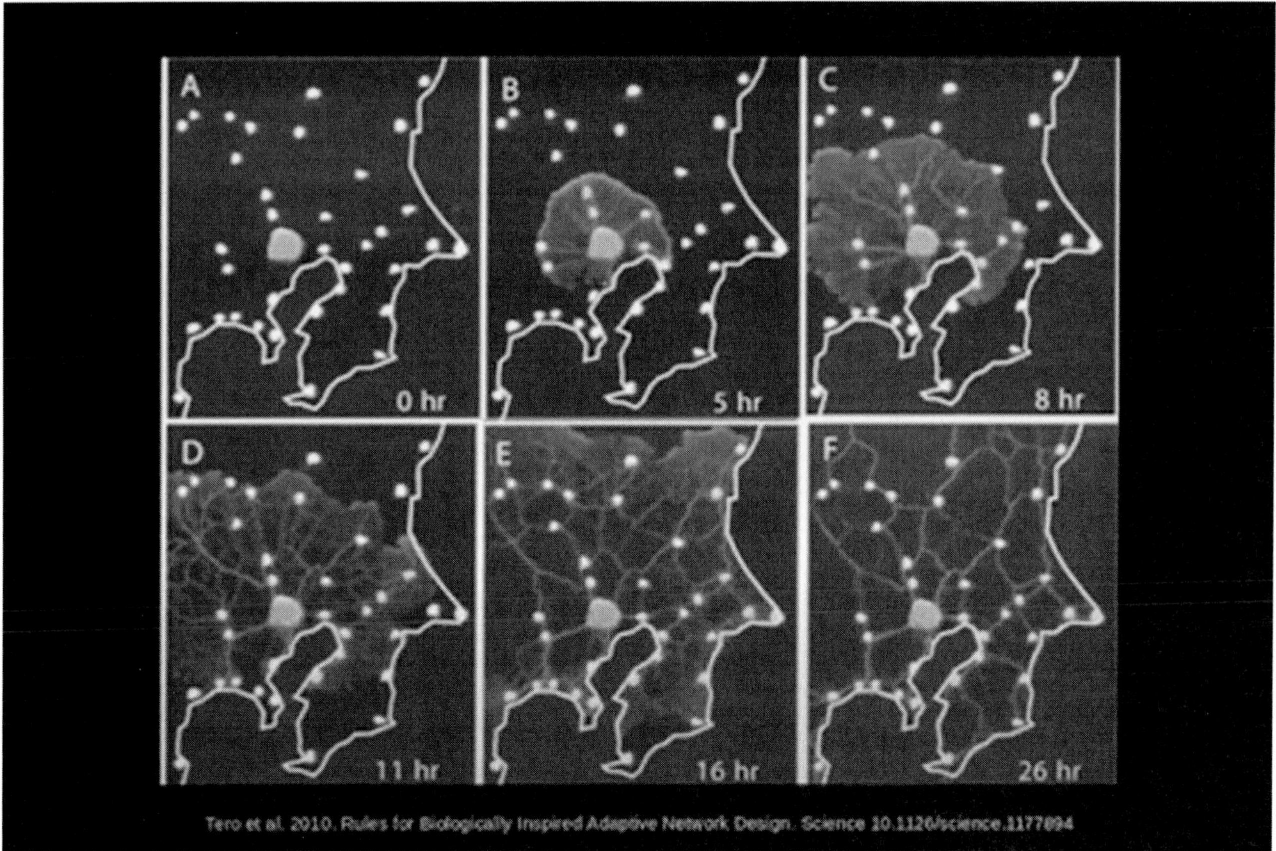

Figure 13.5 Image from slime mould lecture, "Ways of Seeing, Ways of Being", by James Bridle.

---

[19] Thomson, *Seeing Power*, 135.
[20] James Bridle, "Ways of Seeing, Ways of Being", filmed 2021 at Tokyo University of the Global Arts, special lecture, 1:32:50, https://www.youtube.com/watch?v=VB_JryFndPQ.

In Geelong, the auto industry gave rise to cultures and peoples coming together from around the world, building houses and forming intimate connections, forging diverse and empowering lifestyles around what was once a factory in a paddock. When the industry declined, these cultures and communities were deemed dispensable. As far as the logic of the market was concerned, and in turning towards re-gearing the city as smart, we uncovered a desire that rationalises down the vital contribution of community into a stronger desire for entrepreneurialism and what amounts to a kind of automated solipsism and alienated forms of labour found in the gig economy.

The hidden city

As more and more people are forced into insecure labour, often diving into the vicissitudes of the gig economy to pay the rent and sustain themselves, cities like Geelong are in danger of losing the practices and architectures that bind us. Increasingly, the workforce is atomised, even in post-pandemic academia, and this is no more evident than in the empty halls and seminar rooms of university campuses. Many international students studying in Geelong support themselves by working in the gig economy, criss-crossing the city in their Uber or conveying food for one of the many food delivery platforms. Algorithms capture their paths, as workers, collecting information at every data point from who is driving to who is ordering, and rating a service experience to maximise efficiencies and profit.

If we could imagine the intersecting lines of these journeys, accruing over time, the data-field and sensing city mapping movements, opinions and emotions, feeding back into a closed loop of captured subjects, we could again conjure the image of the blob devouring everything in its path, but wholly terrestrial, and created by humans. This entity controls the virtual and real space of the city, and the beings inside that space.[21] The same could have been said of the factory floor and the way bodies were controlled in relation to machines, but in this instance the factory floor precedes the territory, where like the blob, it is everywhere, in our workspaces, our play and public spaces, our homes and our hands.

The Italian philosopher, Franco "Bifo" Berardi, laments that the recent breakthroughs in AI and generative modelling put us on a slippery downhill slope in our relations to each other. He makes the point that human intelligence is in danger of being usurped in favour of algorithmic efficiency, creating a world where human creativity and unpredictability are side-lined for predictable, machine-driven outcomes. AI generative models are syntactically driven, recombining signifying units from a suspect corpus of data, where 'the interpretation of signs does not have the character of experience in an ambiguous', or unfamiliar, 'context', such that confronts human bodies all the time.[22] It is where the immediacy of our senses gets mixed up with our emotions, our thoughts, our moods and our affective relations with space and others around it. These senses, and extra-sensory sense of context, is not something an AI has, but as it proliferates and expands into the everyday aspects of our lives, Berardi worries that it will lead to a 'full subsumption' implying a 'pacification of the human, a complete acquiescence, an order' and 'harmony, albeit totalitarian'.[23] Concomitantly, we end up back at the bad metaphor, the blob.

Artists are well schooled in dealing with metaphor, and in 2019, after numerous iterations in and around Geelong with a diverse collection of artists and community groups, the VacantGeelong project revisited the Open Studio in North Geelong. Slime mould intuits its path through physical interaction. In contrast, the smart city connected by AI channels of networked instructions and programming necessitating human interpretation, as well as the language it uses, forms new social contexts. While providing efficient non-physical functions, the networked city also denies physicality, and our project, *X Marks the Spot*, sought to engage the physical – the audience, artistic mediums and the built environment – connecting people, like slime mould, through an intuited conversation of performance, video and singing (see Figure 13.6 in the colour plate section and Figure 13.7).

X Marks the Spot additionally utilised a fully automated pre-programmed drone camera, designed to respond to human movement via sensors on the bodies of a children's choir. *XMTS* brought together this local choir in a post-industrial disused storage space location, covered with red soil. The choir of children, dressed in white sang *Donna Nobis Pacem,* meaning "Give us Peace", a Latin song performed in harmonies as they moved either away from or towards the flying camera, which was left to its own devices during the shoot. Over time, the children's white clothes became covered in red soil, signifying a perception of AI and human relationships in a "smart" city. The children's sensors on their bodies "communicated" with the drone camera, programmed to respond to patterns of movement initiated by the singers in a kind of inverted video game where the eye of the (non-human) camera replaces the "user". Our performers were encouraged to hold their ground, to sing, and to band together *en masse*, to demonstrate solidarity – like old time Ford workers. Designed to contest relations between the subject and the automated machine, *XMTS* challenges the premise that human beings are being overwhelmed or subsumed by AI, while at the same time engaging with it.

The project performs ideas proposed in this chapter. While the interplay between AI and humans initially creates a sense of adventure and play, it devolves into a game of control. Regardless of how our participants played, the children, as a group, needed to leave the locked dead eye of the drone to escape it, rather than engaging in an interchange where skill, intention, strategy and spatial sensibility are challenged (as in sport).

---

[21] Andrejevic, *Automated Media*, 94–112.
[22] Franco Berardi, "The Completion", *e-flux Journal*, 137 (2023), https://www.e-flux.com/journal/137/544269/the-completion/.
[23] Berardi, "The Completion".

Figure 13.7 VacantGeelong, production still from *X Marks the Spot* (*XMTS*), 2019.

The artists and curators in the VacantGeelong project worked with intergenerational communities, physically engaging in conversation as a starting point. Each project emphasises what sentient beings and living forms contribute towards an evolution of community and values, while the forces of "smartness" are by comparison restrictive and restricting. The threat of life being trained by AI, rather than life training AI, is real, and art, community, physical engagement and "in real life" communication are foundational to the future of humanity.

Conclusion

In imagining the future of Geelong, and other deindustrialising regional cities of its type, we return to the metaphor of the blob to capture the perils of an AI-driven, fully automated urban environment where citizens are remembered only for their consumer, behavioural, or dissenting potentials. The VacantGeelong project, a rich collaboration in architectural and creative arts, gives us a crucial counter-narrative, as it privileges the human experience – solidarity and creativity – to emerge, even in spaces originally designed to wed the body to a production line. Like Nato Thomson, the project advocates for participants to reflect on their old work spaces and the communities that evolved with them, to envisage them as "sites of becoming": dynamic, human-centric spaces that defy the predictability and control inherent in the smart city paradigm.[24] These are not just spaces, but crucibles of human interaction, where politics, play, social, and labour practices unfold in ways that cannot be known in advance, nor can they be captured, or commodified. The project embodies a vision where the digital solipsism Andrejevic warns us of is resisted in favour of a deeply engaged citizen, living collectively and cooperatively with others and their environment, contributing to the organic evolution of the city.[25] For this reason, against the metaphor of the blob, we declare an analogous solidarity with James Bridles' slime mould, a cleverness and intelligence not wrapped up in the individual's entanglement with digital technologies but separate from it. Just as we cannot understand the intelligence of the slime mould, AI cannot understand the cleverness of humans and can, at best, only simulate it.

This is not to say that Geelong will evolve without digital infrastructures, and that they do not have their place in helping us navigate through the undeniable scars on the environment left behind by industry. However, we do look to at least introduce a level of scepticism about the city's fast embrace of new technologies and their deployment, asking questions like: Will they foster genuine community connection or merely offer an illusion of it? The VacantGeelong project, through its artist residencies and community engagements, has demonstrated a commitment to retaining human narratives in the life of the city, driven by reflection, analysis and creative interpretation. It underscores the importance of remembering and celebrating the physical histories, labour practices, and communal memories embedded in Geelong's industrial architectural forms. By intertwining art and technology, the final project, *XMTS*, suggests a future where AI is not a dominating force, but a companion on the journey; one to be wary of and one to work with in tension,

---

[24] Thomson, *Seeing Power.*
[25] Andrejevic, *Automated Media*, 164.

perhaps even using it to help preserve and enhance the human elements that make a place and its people unique. This future vision for Geelong is not about the city adapting to us, but rather us adapting, evolving, and thriving alongside our creations, in spaces that foster unpredictability, affective engagement, and human solidarity.

CHAPTER 14

CO-DESIGNING A NEW KIND OF ARTS CENTRE

JOEL MCGUINNESS

Introduction

In order to remain relevant, arts presenters and producers must radically re-conceptualize the relationships between their programs and their spaces in order to reach younger and more diverse audiences.[1]

Theatres and cultural institutions currently create barriers for theatre goers, with styles of presentation in these institutions promulgating a perception for many that "the arts are not for me". Geelong has recently completed a $180 million capital redevelopment project to build and expand new performance spaces at the Geelong Arts Centre (the Centre). The Geelong Arts Centre, now the largest regional arts centre in Australia, is connected to diverse communities and much loved by First Nations communities. Aboriginal people living in the region have been a major part of the project's development journey – "dreaming" this project to life. They have been meaningfully engaged through "deep listening" and collaborating from the inception of the project through to design development. Gunditjmara Keerray Woorrong artist Tarryn Love reflects:

> It's deeply meaningful to see my culture and heritage embraced and celebrated at Geelong Arts Centre. This opportunity not only allows me to share my artistic vision but also serves as a powerful statement of recognition for my art and its significance in contemporary society. Seeing my work finished and displayed at scale, and knowing that it will inspire and resonate with the community and visitors for generations to come, is really special.[2]

Coming together as co-designers – Ashton Raggatt McDougall Architecture (ARM), and Wadawurrung Traditional Owners Aboriginal Corporation and the wider First Nations community – have woven traditional stories of the land, language, water and sky, the colours and textures of Moonah trees, ochre, and granite stone throughout the layers of the building. Amplifying the voices of the local First Nations community, ARM Architecture and Geelong Arts Centre have worked closely with Wadawurrung artist Kait James and local First Nations artists Tarryn Love, Gerard Black and Mick Ryan to showcase First Nations stories through the Centre and present their works in new and fascinating ways. An integral part of the Geelong Arts Centre Little Malop Street Redevelopment has been building a meaningful connection to Country and the wider Geelong community through its design. Christine Couzens MP notes:

> These creations not only celebrate the rich cultural heritage of our community but also symbolise the profound impact they will have on inspiring future generations of visitors and performers alike. Having these works embedded in the brand-new Geelong Arts Centre will strengthen the bonds within our community, leaving a lasting legacy of unity and creativity for years to come.[3]

Radical change for cultural institutions: Thinking about arts centres differently

Prioritising the inclusion of First Peoples of Australia's voices, stories and art is not only about reconciliation and celebrating more than 60,000 years of sharing culture, dance, language and song, but it is also an opportunity to think about arts centres differently. This project has challenged traditional notions of black box theatres that turn their back on the world and has instead created spaces that are connected to place, are open and full of meaning.

ARM founding director, Ian McDougall, led the architectural design of this building. He worked collaboratively to bring the vision to life, ensuring that First Nations narratives complemented and fused meaningfully with the project brief. McDougall says: 'How come we haven't been doing more of this? I want to get better at doing this. I want to be able to work with other people on a wider range of projects, from the lessons that we've learned here'.[4] Echoing

---

[1] Alan Brown, "All the World's a Stage: Venues and Settings, and the Role they Play in Shaping Patterns of Arts Participation", *Grantmakers in the Arts Journal* 23, no. 2 (Summer 2012): 1–8, 10.2307/j.ctv36xvtc6.9.

[2] Geelong Arts Centre, "Gunditjmara Keerray Woorrong artist, Tarryn Love", Media release, 2023, https://geelongartscentre.org.au/about-us/media-centre/media-releases/extraordinary-first-nations-artworks/.

[3] Geelong Arts Centre, "Christine Couzens MP, Member for Geelong and Parliamentary Secretary for First Peoples", Media release, 2023, https://geelongartscentre.org.au/about-us/media-centre/media-releases/extraordinary-first-nations-artworks/).

[4] Ian McDougall, Video interview, https://geelongartscentre.org.au/about-us/little-malop-street-redevelopment/.

McDougall's sentiment, this project and organisational transformation have been a culmination of many years of professional enquiry by the author. A seminal paper titled, "All the World's a Stage", written by San Francisco-based arts leader Alan Brown in 2011, started this journey of reflection, that has led to the author ardently advocating for "radical change" for cultural institutions.[5] Alan Brown's work argues that:

> … entirely new types of facilities are needed to breathe new life into the art forms. Arts presenters who learn how to carefully match setting with artistic content, both live and digital, including the use of unusual or dispersed performance locations, will earn the patronage of a new audience.[6]

Important and relevant questions currently relate to the idea of place and connecting to culture differently.

As CEO and Creative Director of the Geelong Arts Centre, the author challenges Dove's idea that 'theatres are the best way to keep people from the arts'.[7] The Centre has been reinvented to respond to global challenges in the sector and industry, and through co-design to connect to Aboriginal Australian's story and wisdom. Like many other arts centres, the average age of subscribers at the Centre is over sixty years and the total number of subscribers has halved over the last ten years.[8] In considering who the audiences of the future might be, the Centre explores global practice for inspiration, and invests in artistic programs that resonate with local communities. The recent redevelopment project provided an opportunity to learn from the Wadawurrung Traditional Owners and many other Aboriginal community members living in this region. In leading a state government funded cultural institution, "magical powers" to foresee a future are needed, as well as partnerships to authentically engage with audiences and creatives in the region and state. Becoming a cultural leader and arts presenter (presenting arts performances in a professional capacity) has involved learning how to create culturally safe spaces and hold that space actively. The Geelong Arts Centre redevelopment project has had a deep impact on the way the author works with the Indigenous wisdom shared by Aboriginal colleagues (now friends). This journey has profoundly shifted practice and changed the organisation for the better.

Brown's work initiated an enquiry into the cultural building or edifice taking on an almost revered place within a community, and a shared concern about the problems with venues and institutions as they are set up in Western culture. Regional Australian centres, with ageing patrons and subscriber base, provide first-hand evidence of the phenomenon where an institution 'assumes the character of its art as much as an old pair of shoes assumes the personality of its wearer'.[9] The Geelong Arts Centre can also testify to deep and engrained patterns of behaviour in audience attendance trends among Geelong (and the Geelong Region Alliance – G21) citizens, who choose to never step foot inside a formal theatre setting.[10] This low attendance is further exacerbated by the local population increasing at nearly double the rate of the rest of Victoria, which is not translating to a corresponding increase in theatre attendance, despite changes in programming, marketing and engagement techniques.[11] This trend is not unique to Geelong, as Lindelof observes:

> … audience development epitomises current dilemmas in theatres, concert halls and museums across the world: as the audience seems to increase in age and decrease in number, the role of art institutions is debated … .[12]

Choose your own adventure

As an antidote to this apparent apathy, where whole sections of the community stay away from theatres, the strategy is to weave together successful elements of immersive theatre experiences with First Nations wisdom, and to deliver concepts and attributes in our programming and facilities found within self-determination theory (SDT), described by Stephen Conway (and others) as 'underlining human motivation'.[13] The primary STD attributes are autonomy, competence, and relevance or relatedness (see Table 14.1).

The success of new kinds of cultural experiences and institutional design need to be linked to such attributes to provide us with insights to developing new audiences, ensuring all people feel included, and in offering opportunities for cultural institutions to remain relevant. At the Geelong Arts Centre, Conway's self-determination theory has been translated into practice. Distilled down, consideration of the mantra "choose your own adventure" has been introduced

---

[5] Brown, "All the World's a Stage".

[6] Brown, "All the World's a Stage".

[7] Simon Dove, Utrecht Festival, Dance USA Forum (January 2011), quoted in Brown, "All the World's a Stage", 1. At the time of writing (2023) the author was CEO of The Centre. He is now (2024) Director of Experience at the State Library of Victoria, Australia.

[8] Geelong Arts Centre, *GPACT Annual Reports 2008–2018* (2020), www.gpac.org.au.

[9] Brown, "All the World's a Stage", 4.

[10] Geelong Region Alliance (G21) is the formal alliance of government, business and community organisations working together to improve the lives of people within the Geelong region across five municipalities – Colac Otway, Golden Plains, Greater Geelong, Queenscliffe and Surf Coast.

[11] H. Tippet, "High Population Growth Breaks Region Milestone", *Geelong Advertiser*, March 30, 2019, https://www.geelongadvertiser.com.au/news/geelong/high-population-growth-breaks-region-milestone/news-story/8321106ce4163aaab490969c9a5bf043.

[12] Anja Mølle Lindelof "Audience Development and its Blind Spot: A Quest for Pleasure and Play in the Discussion of Performing Arts Institutions", *International Journal of Cultural Policy* 21, no. 2 (2015): 200–18; 201.

[13] Stephen Conway, "Zombification: Gamification, Motivation and the User", *Journal of Gaming & Virtual Worlds* 6 no. 2 (2014): 129–41.

Autonomy	is defined on 'a phenomenological level [...] reflected in the experience of integrity, volition, and vitality that accompanies self-regulated action'[*]. Anything that takes away one's sense of control and choice is demotivational.
Competence	is the ability one has to succeed in meeting the goals of an activity; it is thus always relational, based upon the capacities of the actant within her environment as outlined within ecological psychology[†]
Relatedness	is defined as the feeling of connection to others: trust, love and care are all signifiers of a deep sense of relatedness (we may extend this to feeling connected to the goals and practices of an organisation).

Table 14.1 The three key concepts of self-determination theory[‡]. These concepts inform much of the author's work as CEO and Creative Director of the Geelong Arts Centre.

[*] Richard M. Ryan and Edward L Deci, "Self-Determination Theory and the Facilitation of Intrinsic Motivation, Social Development, and Well-Being", *American Psychologist* 55, no. 1 (2000): 68–78.

[†] Jonas Linderoth, "Why Gamers Don't Learn More: An Ecological Approach to Games as Learning Environments", *Journal of Gaming and Virtual Worlds*, 4, no. 1 (2012): 45–62.

[‡] Stephen Conway, "Zombification: Gamification, Motivation and the User", *Journal of Gaming & Virtual Worlds* 6 no. 2 (2014): 129–41.

when considering visitor experiences. This mantra was part of the Geelong Arts Centre's architectural design process and informs much of the Centre's organisational programming and planning.

In his 2010 TED talk, "The True Power of the Performing Arts", Ben Cameron, program director for the arts at the Doris Duke Charitable Foundation, acknowledged that many purpose-built arts venues 'were designed to ossify the ideal relationship between artist and audience most appropriate to the nineteenth century'.[14] This rigidity of building and form within our cultural centres resonates with the lived experience in Geelong. Almost in protest to this outdated "ossification", the Geelong Arts Centre sought to connect with international practice and combine this with a greater shared understanding of First Nations people's deep connection to place and culture which challenges this constructed separateness.

Brown argues that, where institutions often cling to the conventions of attending a theatrical production, practitioners in arts presentation (as well as those working across the broader cultural sector) need to understand that 'while multipurpose venues can expand access to the arts, important connections between art and setting have been lost'.[15] Confronted with so much cultural stimulation, choice, and ability to self-curate a cultural experience in ones' home through gaming, streaming and social media, the cultural sector needs to face facts: cultural consumers now have 'expectations of personalisation and customisation that the live performing arts that have set curtain times, set venues, attended inconveniences of travel, parking and the like, simply cannot meet'.[16]

For example, why do shows start at 8 pm "sharp"? Why do ushers rove up and down the aisles stopping people from using mobile phones during performances? Why if we leave to get a drink or go to the bathroom, may we not be allowed back into the auditorium? The notion of "institution" must surely include those seemingly inducted into how one should act when attending "the theatre", behaviours that perpetuate exclusion, between those who know all the rules and dictate to others how they must enjoy the performance with strict codes that seem immutable to the uninitiated. A young, non-theatre goer in a focus group for Alan Brown's research echoed what many have surely thought as some point: 'sitting in a dark room for two hours and not being able to talk to my girlfriend is not my idea of an enjoyable evening'.[17] There is much research demonstrating that experiences must be curated to give autonomy back to the consumer, to deliver what Brown describes as "audience sovereignty", in which the audience members have choices in how they experience, consume and take part of the action.[18]

Researcher and author Winifred Gallagher explores the relationships and influence that "place" has on our experiences and asserts that 'people feel best in settings that, like parks and cars, foster a sense of control, impose few constraints, and offer multiple choices'.[19] Over the past decade the cultural sector has been building empirical evidence that this ability for people to self-determine their experience can be highly successful. New ways of staging performances in response to audiences' needs include multi-modal ways of engagement and self-determination.

Wadawurrung narratives and the Geelong Arts Centre design development

The Geelong Arts Centre community felt deeply that changing the way the arts centre is designed could completely disrupt how we think arts centres "should" be. The Geelong Arts Centre is deeply grateful to Wadawurrung woman and Traditional Owner Corinna Eccles (and many others) for walking alongside those involved in the project, as an ancient

---

[14] Ben Cameron, "The True Power of the Performing Arts", TED Talks, filmed 2010 at TEDxYYC, video, 12:44, https://youtu.be/pbIas5MAQn0?si=ZGv6Vzpp1WLb4ygt.

[15] Brown, "All the World's a Stage", 2.

[16] Cameron, "The True Power of the Performing Arts".

[17] Brown, "All the World's a Stage", 2.

[18] Brown, "All the World's a Stage", 4.; Winifred Gallagher, *The Power of Place: How Our Surroundings Shape our Thoughts, Emotions and Actions* (New York: Random House; Ragsdale, 1993).

[19] Gallagher, *The Power of Place*, 74.

connection to storytelling was explored. Through the gifts of a narrative framework wrapped around the building, the Centre has been able to connect and respond to these stories to inspire fresh ways to gather and celebrate culture. Eccles notes that:

> Dance, song and story has been happening on these lands for over 60,000 years … and where this building is actually located in this vicinity, is actually where Wadawurrung people were coming together for dance, song and story … you get to feel what we feel and deeply listen to the stories that we share.[20]

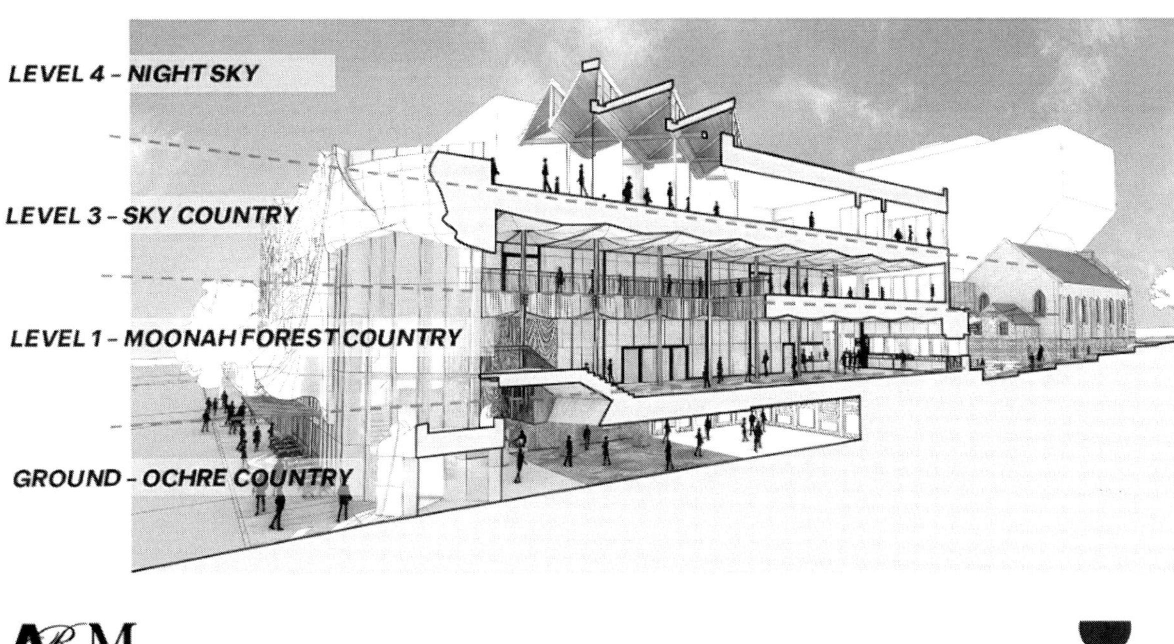

Figure 14.1 Wadawurrung narratives, developed as part of the Geelong Arts Centre design development by ARM and Wadawurrung Traditional Owners Aboriginal Corporation.

By grounding the Geelong Arts Centre's design in First Nations stories (see Figure 14.1), people feel connected to something unique and timeless, yet fresh and open to new possibilities. The Centre has set out to embrace all cultures and invites people to engage in whatever way feels right for them and to find their own connections. Over a number of years, Ian McDougall and the team at ARM worked closely on the co-design process with First Nations artists to bring about a cohesive design aligned with the Geelong Arts Centre's mission and connection to the community:

> The brief and the ambition for Geelong Arts Centre was to make it a welcoming space and to express the diversity, cultural difference, demographic difference that is the community of Geelong … the idea of it being welcoming is that there isn't one theme. All worlds are possible. It's an expression of the diversity and also of richness and joy.[21]

The Geelong Arts Centre has been overwhelmed by the response from nearly 100,000 people coming through the centre in the first four months of opening (August to December 2023). The Centre is thrilled that people seem to intuitively understand that 'When people are standing here, they are part of the stories that belong to this land and Country', thus embracing ideas that were intended through the design development.[22]

The generosity and genuine connection through First Nations co-design is encapsulated by the concept of "Koling Wada Ngal". Eccles says, 'We use a word a lot, Koling Wada Ngal, let us walk together'.[23] This walking together is both welcoming and familiar. With the bold ambitious architecture and bright interiors of ARM Architects, combined

---

[20] Traditional Owner Corrina Eccles, interviewed as part of the re-opening of Geelong Arts Centre. Corinna Eccles, Video interview, https://geelongartscentre.org.au/about-us/little-malop-street-redevelopment/.

[21] Ian McDougall, Video interview, https://geelongartscentre.org.au/about-us/little-malop-street-redevelopment/.

[22] Corinna Eccles, Video interview, https://geelongartscentre.org.au/about-us/little-malop-street-redevelopment/.

[23] Corinna Eccles, Video interview.

with the extraordinary, commissioned artworks, the space feels like you are invited into a party, to a place where belonging and choosing your own adventure is par for the course (see Figure 14.2)!

Figure 14.2 The Moonah Forest Country narrative incorporated into the carpets in the foyer, dynamic lighting and references of the Night Sky Country narrative.

Regeneration of the Geelong Arts Centre through self-determination and play theory

At the Geelong Arts Centre, motivational design, gamification and play appear as fundamental to weaving together experiences that allow for self-determination, enjoyment, feeling connected and "walking together". The author argues that the design of the Centre subscribes to Sebastian Deterding's notions of "gamification", '(as) an umbrella term for the use of video game elements (rather than fully-fledged games) to improve user experience and user engagement in non-game services and applications'.[24] Deterding explores how game design elements have been incorporated into many non-game contexts such as sales, education and design where researchers and commercial users have tried to identify design patterns that might afford 'joy of use' under the moniker 'funology', explicitly drawing inspiration from game design and encouraging heuristic learning, understanding and positive experience journeys.[25] The team at the Geelong Arts Centre set out to renew the organisation itself, as well as the buildings, in ways to create spaces of joy and fun. This has been fused with the depth and richness of First Nations narratives to create spaces that allow for people to gather, create and collaborate, 'encourage[ing] a sense of play that is play as an intrinsically rewarding activity'.[26] This results in a hybrid cultural experience that resonates with audiences on a deep and joyful level with vital outcomes for health, well-being and community connectedness. As Hayes describes:

> …freedom, separateness in time and space, rules, uncertainty about the outcome, non-productiveness, and make believe…these qualities help to spur on the culture created by play and games.[27]

Connected to these elements of self-determination and joy are themes of creativity, curiosity, possibility and freedom found in technological play theory (TPT). Introduced in Byker's "I Play I Learn", it emerged in 1960s grounded theory from comparative and international field studies about the meanings and uses for computer technology among

---

[24] Sebastian Deterding, "Gamification: Using Game Design Elements" (workshop presentation, Non-Gaming Contexts, Hans-Bredow Institute at the University of Hamburg, 2011), 1–4.

[25] Deterding, "Gamification".

[26] Conway, "Zombification: Gamification, Motivation and the User", 131.

[27] A. Hayes (2019).

elementary school teachers and students.[28] These concepts have been used within the design of the Geelong Arts Centre, where they have been subtly applied to provide a loose framework for how a cultural institution can incorporate and utilise gamification elements, and harness the innate curiosity, learning and playfulness explored in these theoretical frameworks.

By way of example, the newly completed Little Malop Street façade is designed as a literal curtain, drawn back around the entire frontage of the Geelong Arts Centre (see Figure 14.3 in the colour plate section). The façade is visually permeable, open, and inviting. The design signals that these spaces are creative and have the potential for fun. In practice, the Centre has almost created a new kind of live game, whereas 'games used to be that we were spoon-fed goals and rules first, now with video and digital games, the motivation is the feedback loop, the possibilities and discovering what is possible'.[29] The Centre invites visitors into a newly created world based on self-determination. It invites people to play as they explore. Applying Byker's "I play I learn" framework (see Figure 14.4) creates a highly curated world of possibility at the Geelong Arts Centre, and to almost all great cultural experiences, to provide an enhanced, playful and meaningful user journey.

Deep connection to place is made through First Nations co-design, through Wadawurrung language outside, through circles and ochre colours in paving, piquing curiosity of the stories of place; once inside the space, the visitor or patron is drawn to explore the venue further. First Nations stories are embedded into carpets, walls, murals and soundscapes that unfold around every corner. These are juxtaposed with LED lighting that can be programmed and changed through projection and sound. Comfortable furniture encourages people to linger, to stay and dwell in places that they feel welcomed even when not attending a performance.

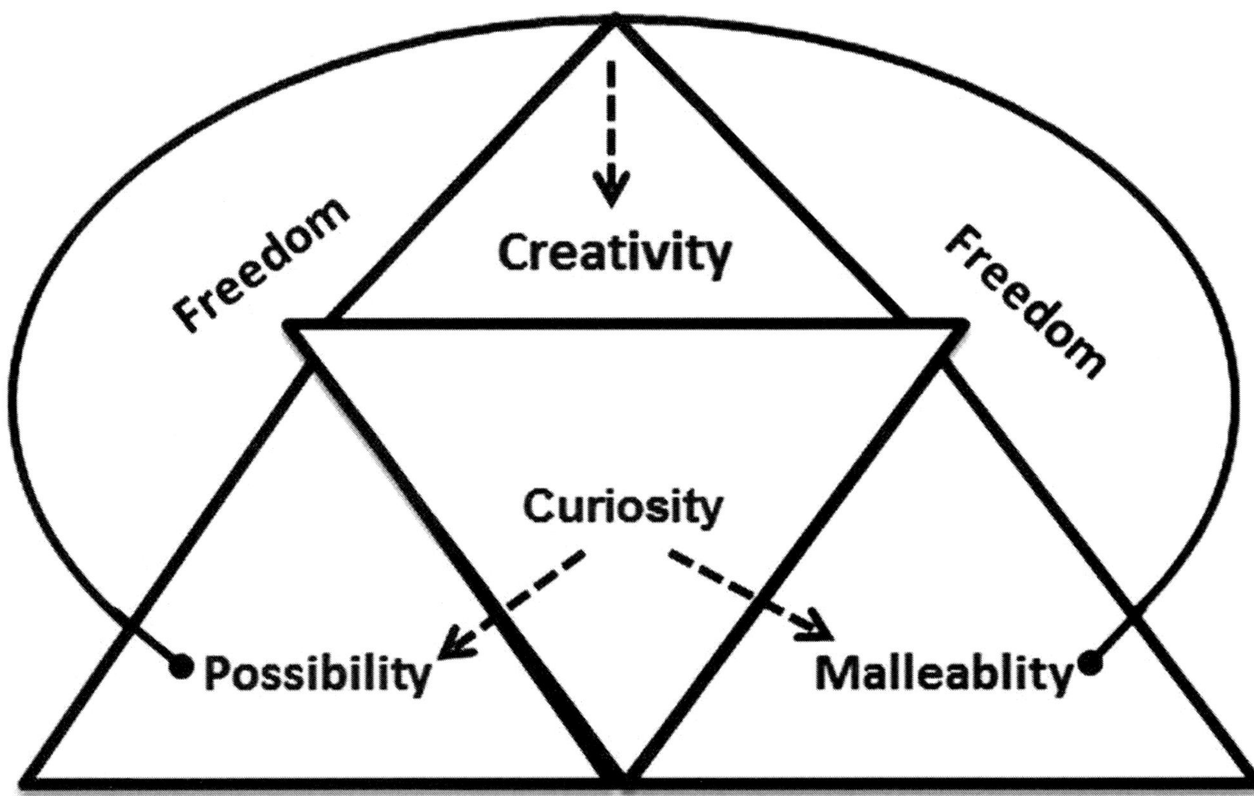

Figure 14.4 The model for technological play theory from Erik J. Byker, "I Play I Learn: Introducing Technological Play Theory".

Figure 14.4 shows technological play theory centred in curiosity and bounded by freedom. Technological play is facilitated when users have the freedom to be curious about computer hardware or digital devices. When curiosity is encouraged, technological play often flourishes. Here at the Geelong Arts Centre that possibility has been encouraged. Creativity comes first. As experiences are built for users, they always start with the artist, the creative. These elements not only guide the cultural experiences, but all the thinking for programming and staging events. Byker's theory is illustrated in practice at the Geelong Arts Centre. The "creativity" is evident in the striking and bold nature of the façade as well as in the First Nations narratives, inviting "curiosity" and "possibility". All are given "freedom" to explore and engage with this purposeful built public space created for the sharing of live performances.

---

[28] Erik J. Byker, "I Play I Learn: Introducing Technological Play Theory", in Drew Polly and Christie Martin (eds), *Handbook of Research on Teacher Education and Professional Development* (IGI Global, 2016), 296–306; Barney G. Glaser and Anselm L. Strauss, *The Discovery of Grounded Theory: Strategies for Qualitative Research* (Aldine Transaction, 1967).

[29] Jane McGonigal, *Reality is Broken* (New York: The Penguin Press, 2011), 27.

Figure 14.5 Blue-lit tunnel showing an engaging and fun "portal" between parts of the campus of buildings

The Centre offers the "possibility" of choice in numerous spaces: a digital immersion white box foyer with projections, a blue lit tunnel that is reminiscent of a portal between worlds (see Figure 14.5), are all engaging experiences. "Malleability" 'shares similarities [with] possibility but has a more active and social quality to it'.[30] This is where the Geelong Arts Centre team and the artists are critical to the experience, as they enhance and guide "users" on a journey, encouraging "freedom" of exploration and discovery within a bounded safe world. At the Geelong Arts Centre, people are invited to momentarily suspend belief, to be fully present in the spaces and connect to something different and far removed from the business of daily life. At the Centre there has been 'value in applying game design features within non-game context(s)' as it was 'aligned with a constructivist, user-centred design, sensitive to the sociocultural situation'.[31]

The spaces in action

The team at the Geelong Arts Centre will now need to encourage people to play, to explore and to invest in this world they have voluntarily stepped into. The Centre rewards their curiosity with possibility, freedom and curatorial (malleability) through shows, events, food, music, dance and gathering in a setting that has been designed for its audience (see Figure 14.6). The depth of experience is further enhanced through a palpable connection to First Nations stories. The feedback from tens of thousands of visitors to these spaces in the first few months of opening confirms that people are responding in beautiful ways, both expected and unexpected. As the spaces come to life with people, the design of the Centre all starts to flow and to make sense. As Jane McGonigal argues in relation to video games 'if the goal is truly compelling, and if the feedback is motivating enough, we will keep wrestling with the game's limitations – creatively, sincerely, and enthusiastically…'.[32]

The Geelong Arts Centre's organisational vision is to be 'a leader, connector and creator of extraordinary cultural experiences for local and global communities'.[33] The master plan brief states that:

> … our spaces and performance venues need to allow audiences to immerse themselves in new worlds, demand a sense of occasion and ensure that we can create exceptional and extraordinary experiences.[34]

---

[30] Byker, "I Play I Learn", 298.

[31] Conway, "Zombification: Gamification, Motivation and the User", 132.

[32] Jane McGonigal, *Reality is Broken.*

[33] Geelong Arts Centre, *GAC 2022–25 Strategic Plan.*

[34] Geelong Arts Centre, *Geelong Performing Arts Centre – Masterplan Brief.*

Figure 14.6 The spaces in action, with First Nations art by Gerard Black incorporated into café and foyer.

The Geelong Arts Centre aspires to a bold future in the region and the state. Through this once-in-a-generation physical capital redevelopment transformation, there must also be an organisational transformation that evolves with and capitalises on the physical change, mirroring the innovations demonstrated through co-design. As the only state government owned cultural institution outside of Melbourne, it is essential that the Centre becomes a "testing ground" for new work and an incubator of talent, which in turn, is shared in other regional or capital city centres and exported to the world.

Conclusion

Since 2018, the Geelong Arts Centre has set out to embrace change and to be bold in its leadership role as a state government institution in a regional setting. Through consultation, collaboration and investigation, the Geelong Arts Centre team has uncovered a deep connection to First Nations stories, history and wisdom, which is incredibly rich and beautifully humbling in its ability to hold space for all creativity. All at the Geelong Arts Centre are deeply grateful for the opportunity to embed this into the very fabric of the architecture. As CEO and Creative Director of the Geelong Arts Centre, the author hopes for a legacy of thinking differently about what creativity means for community institutions and for the application of the genuine transformative qualities of self-determination, play and true collaboration.

The purpose of the Geelong Arts Centre is 'to nurture creative expression, lead artistic collaborations and inspire audiences, reaching out to all parts of our community'.[35] Surely buildings can be more than inanimate containers. Programs and people bring them to life. Through this redevelopment, and the accompanying organisational transformation, the Geelong Arts Centre is on the right path and looks forward to the next chapter unfolding, as it activates, creates and celebrates the power of creativity in all it undertakes!

---

[35] Geelong Arts Centre, *GAC 2022–25 Strategic Plan*.

CONTRIBUTORS

Editors

Mirjana Lozanovska

Dr Mirjana Lozanovska is Professor in Architecture and Director of the Architecture Vacancy Lab at Deakin University. Her work investigates the creative ways that architecture mediates human dignity and identity through multidisciplinary theories of space. Her books include *Migrant Housing: Architecture, Dwelling, Migration* (2019), *Ethno-Architecture and the Politics of Migration* (2016), and *Iconic Industry* (2017). Her research is published in journals focussing on architectural history and theory, and beyond these to spatial and cultural disciplines. In the Architecture Vacancy Lab, Mirjana works in collaboration with a team of scholars, practitioners and research students. Mirjana was editor of the architectural history journal, *Fabrications* 2018–2021; and is currently in a multi-institutional team investigating industry, architecture and immigrant contribution to nation-building (Australia Research Council Discovery Project).

Ursula de Jong

Dr Ursula de Jong is Honorary Associate Professor at Deakin University. She is an architectural historian and researcher of place and widely published in both fields. She is a scholar, heritage advocate and environmental activist. Ursula is Research Associate of HOME, a Deakin University Strategic Research and Innovation Centre and an Honorary Fellow in Deakin's School of Architecture and Built Environment, Architecture Vacancy Lab. Ursula is full member of the Heritage Council of Victoria; full international member ICOMOS; founding member of SAHANZ; President of the Nepean Conservation Group Inc.; and 2023 Honorary Member of the National Trust of Australia (Victoria).

Authors

David Beynon

David Beynon (PhD) is an Associate Professor in Architecture at the University of Tasmania. His research involves investigating the social, cultural and compositional dimensions of architecture, and adaptations of architectural content and meaning in relation to migration and cultural change. His current work includes investigations into the diasporic and postcolonial manifestations of contemporary urban environments and the creative possibilities for post-industrial architecture in Australia and Asia.

Cameron Bishop

Cameron Bishop (PhD) is an Associate Professor in Art and Performance at Deakin University. As a curator, artist and writer working in the public realm he has been acknowledged for his community-focused approach to public art in the numerous grants, awards and commissions he has received, and in the large-scale projects he has devised, working with leading curators (mostly David Cross) and many of Australia's leading artists. All of the work he does explores the shifting nature of the term "public", alongside ideas around place-making, and the body's appearance and experience as a political, private, and social entity in the digital age.

James Doerfler

Professor James Doerfler has international experience leading administrative, teaching and research initiatives in academia and practice. He designed new curricula for architecture programs in the United States and Australia. He led research projects in facade design and technology, and prefabricated building systems. Collaborating with faculty, students and industry partners, James has launched new programs, guided accreditation and advanced the missions of colleges of architecture, design and construction that prepare students for their professions. James was interim head of the department at Cal Poly San Luis Obispo, Director of Architecture Programs at Thomas Jefferson University and Chair in Architecture at Deakin University.

Yolanda Esteban

Dr Yolanda Esteban is a Senior Lecturer in Architecture at Deakin University's School of Architecture and Built Environment. Yolanda has developed an extensive teaching expertise across design disciplines, both in architecture and urban design, engaging with local government and immersing her students in real-world design projects. Her research has focused on the changing profile of urban places, with specific expertise on the development of built form scenarios based on demographic modelling, and the nexus between vision-making and policy implementation. Yolanda has developed strong links between her teaching and research, building a portfolio of traditional and non-traditional research outputs.

Diego Fullaondo

Dr Diego Fullaondo is an architect and educator, based in Madrid, Spain. With over twenty-five years of experience combining practice with academic positions, Diego has worked extensively in Spain and Australia. He founded his architectural office, Estudio Fullaondo, in 1992, which is dedicated to professional work and design research. He held an academic position and was Director for Master of Architecture at Deakin University in Geelong, Australia. From 2015 to 2017, he was part of the VacantGeelong project where he actively contributed as a researcher and supervising staff.

Deanne Gilson

Dr Deanne Gilson is a proud Wadawurrung woman residing in Ballarat, Victoria, Australia. With an award-winning multi-disciplinary art practice spanning forty years, Gilson uses different mediums, including ochre pigments sourced from her ancestral Country. Her art practice draws on history and oral story-telling that includes her Creation Story and depicts artefacts and Wadawurrung objects found in museums and in private collections. She has reclaimed traditional marks found on artefacts, mixing them with new contemporary marks, highlighting the lived experiences of her family and ancestors. The many plants and birds of the Australian bush feature in her artworks and align with her deep connection to Country. Her art has been collected by many public and private collections throughout Australia and worldwide, including the National Gallery of Victoria.

Louise Johnson

Dr Louise Johnson is an Honorary Professor at Deakin University and Honorary (Professorial Fellow) at the University of Melbourne. A human geographer, she has studied Geelong's textile industry, displaced car industry workers, the creative economy and, most recently, the city's economic resilience. A co-founder of the Deakin HOME Strategic Research and Innovation Centre, she has also done work on affordable housing and apartment design. She co-chairs Northern Futures in Geelong, working to assist the long-term unemployed into training and jobs. Publishing over 130 articles and chapters, in 2011 she received the Institute of Australian Geographers Australia and International Medal in recognition of her contribution to urban, social and cultural geography.

Russell Kennedy

Dr Russell Kennedy is an academic and practitioner of communication design and filmmaking at Deakin University. Kennedy's research is in the fields of cultural identity and design advocacy. His PhD, titled "Designing with Indigenous Knowledge", led to the co-authorship of the multi-award-winning Australian and International Indigenous Design Charters. Kennedy served as President (2009–2011) of the International Council of Design (ICoD), which included a UNESCO Creative Cities Network (UCCN) advisory role. In 2017 he initiated the City of Greater Geelong's venture to join the UCCN as a designated City of Design and was a member of the successful application committee.

Chin Koi Khoo

Dr Chin Koi Khoo is a Lecturer in Architecture (Digital Design) at Deakin University with a focus in areas of architectural design and communication. His current position is to undertake research, teach and publish in the fields of digital design in architecture, digital fabrication, digital heritage, virtual and augmented reality (VR/AR), human–building interaction (HBI), material computation, and responsive environments.

Tuba Kocaturk

Tuba Kocaturk is Professor of Circular Cities and Deputy Head at Deakin University's School of Architecture and Built Environment, as well as founding director of MInD Research Lab, which advances the intelligent and sustainable transition of the built environment and urban ecosystems. She is a registered architect in Turkey, with a PhD degree from Delft University of Technology in the Netherlands. Globally, she has held notable academic positions and is on the advisory committee of the Seoul Design Awards for sustainable daily life. Tuba is currently collaborating with the City of Greater Geelong for the development of the city's future agenda as a UNESCO City of Design.

Igor Martek

Dr Igor Martek earned his PhD from the University of Melbourne. He also has an MBA from the Australian Graduate School of Management, University of NSW, and an MA in International Relations from the Australian National University, Canberra. His first degree is a Bachelor of Architecture (Honours) from the University of Melbourne. Igor has worked extensively in industry; evaluating, generating, managing, and turning around large capital projects in various locations around the world. He has worked in Europe, including Eastern Europe, the Middle East, China, Korea and Singapore. Igor is currently an academic at Deakin University, Australia.

Joel McGuinness

Joel McGuinness is an executive administrator, creative director, entrepreneur, and industry leader who is passionate about communities and the vital role of creativity in changing culture. In 2023 Joel was Chief Executive Officer and Creative Director at Geelong Arts Centre, successfully delivering more than $200m in transformational projects since 2018 as part of Creative Victoria; including a major capital redevelopment (now the largest regional arts centre in Australia), designing and implementing a ten-year strategic and creative vision for the organisation, and launching Geelong Arts Centre and "Creative Engine" into a new era that positions the organisation at the forefront of both audience and sector development. In 2024 Joel McGuinness was appointed Director, Experience, Executive Team, State Library Victoria, slv.vic.gov.au

Akari Nakai Kidd

Dr Akari Nakai Kidd's work through research and pedagogy aims to construct a creative and critical dialogue between the socio-ethical responsibility of architecture practice, processes and interactions, and present-day society concerns through the lens of affect and intersectionality. She currently leads a cross-disciplinary team at Deakin investigating the relation between social housing design and the physical and mental wellbeing of its diverse occupants through co-design. She has published in international journals and conference proceedings, and is the author of *Affect, Architecture and Practice: Toward a disruptive temporality of practice*, published by Routledge (2021).

Md Mizanur Rashid

Dr Md Mizanur Rashid is a Senior Lecturer of Architecture and the Deputy Director of AV Research Lab at the School of Architecture and Built Environment at Deakin University. He is an architect–academic specialising in historical narrative, digital design, and 4D cultural heritage preservation through virtual and augmented reality tools. Dr Mizanur's expertise is in South Asian and Islamic architectural history, and he uniquely explores architecture within the context of multiple historical narratives. His work enriches digital heritage documentation, making historic buildings accessible to a broader audience, and unravelling their connection to geographical, social and cultural domains.

Sanja Rodeš

Dr Sanja Rodeš is a Lecturer in Architecture at Deakin University in Geelong, Australia. She teaches design and architectural history, theory, and criticism of the late twentieth- and twenty-first centuries. Rodeš is the author of the monograph, *Architecture and the Image at the Turn of the 21st Century* (Routledge, 2024), and an external editor and contributor (Serbia) for Lori A. Brown and Karen Burns (eds), *The Bloomsbury Global Encyclopaedia of Women in Architecture 1960-2015* (forthcoming, 2024). She has published on the relationships between contemporary architecture, media and image.

John Rollo

Dr John Rollo is senior lecturer with the School of Architecture and Built Environment at Deakin University, Geelong. With a focus on urban design and the perception of the built environment, he has provided public-sector based architecture and urban design research throughout his academic career. He is an honours graduate of the Deakin School of Architecture, and holds qualifications at both Masters and Doctorate levels from UCLA and Cambridge University. John developed and coordinated "Urbanheart Surgery", a graduate studio that facilitated twenty-five student-led design forums within nine municipalities in regional Victoria and Greater Melbourne.

Paul Sanders

Paul Sanders is the Professor and Chair of Architecture at the School of Architecture and Built Environment at Deakin University. Paul has experienced three career phases in architecture, in both academia and practice, that has been rooted in urban architecture upon an underpinning of how architecture affects and is affected by its urban context. Paul's PhD in Urban Morphology developed strategies to apply research in the field as a tool to guide the form for appropriate urban architecture. Paul is currently active in research into new environments for intergenerational living, as well as integrated scholarship towards Design for Circular Cities.

Chayakan Siamphukdee

Dr Chayakan Siamphukdee's PhD examined the heritage history of industrial architecture. He is a Research Assistant at Deakin University and a member of the Architecture Vacancy Lab. From 2014 to 2017, he participated as a Master of Architecture student in the VacantGeelong research team. In 2021 he completed his PhD, titled "Conceptualising Sensitive Patterns in the Adaptive Reuse of Industrial Architecture". His works were exhibited at the *Iconic Industry* exhibition (National Wool Museum, Geelong, 2017) and the Architecture Vacancy Lab exhibition (2023). His research interests include adaptive reuse, architectural conservation, historic preservation, industrial regeneration and architectural documentation.

Heather Threadgold

Dr Threadgold is an anthropologist, historian, heritage advisor, strategic planner and expert advisor in urban design and architectural projects across Australia. She has lectured in Master of Architecture Indigenous Narratives and Protocols for six years at Deakin University, where she studied. Heather grew up living in Wilsons Promontory, a remote coastal place in Victoria, and living in this extraordinary environment has enriched her process of academic research, creativity, and deep understanding of place and people. For over twenty years, Dr Threadgold has developed cultural mapping methodologies to understand and interpret Aboriginal and post-colonial manipulated landscapes, waterways and living spaces throughout Victoria by listening, learning and conducting extensive research and fieldwork. Heather works with Traditional Owners and landowners across Victoria to protect cultural heritage, and this experience along with her knowledge of 1790–1880s colonial Victoria aids in her anthropological and historical works. Dr Threadgold has recently been appointed Director and Treasurer of Indigenous Architecture Design Australia (IADA).

Richard Tucker

Professor Richard Tucker (PhD) has published well over 130 outputs on sustainable and universal design, urban design, accessibility, and inclusivity in built environment design. He is a director of the HOME Strategic Innovation and Research Centre – an interdisciplinary group of thirty researchers that works with communities to co-design solutions to complex problems of affordable housing, homelessness, and social inclusion. His work is founded on the efficacy of interdisciplinary-disciplinary teamwork. He has formed research teams with colleagues from seven academic institutions, and numerous industry and governmental partners. His research is focused on trans-disciplinary approaches at the intersection of systems thinking and design thinking.

Anne Wilson

Anne Scott Wilson is a Senior Lecturer in Art and Design at Deakin University. She has received grants and residencies from government funding bodies, and philanthropic and private organisations. Her PhD, received from Monash University in 2009, is titled "Memory, Motion and imagination: an investigation into the subjective experience of studio practice". Her work is held in public and private collections in Australia and internationally. Her solo, collective and curatorial practices draw attention to that which cannot be measured, to both celebrate and explore the depths and dimensionality of experience within the human condition.

Joshua Zeunert

Dr Joshua Zeunert is a Scientia Associate Professor at the University of New South Wales and an AILA Registered Landscape Architect. Motivated by a deep care for the more-than-human world, he is fascinated by Earth's dynamics connected to human activities and landscape-scale change over time. His research utilises visual and multimedia landscape depictions, exploring spatial-scales, temporality, impact and agency. Josh has published three multi-award-winning books and has taught in thirteen academic programs at five universities, encompassing fifty unique courses. Josh has won a range of awards, grants and fellowships in professional practice and academia.

INDEX